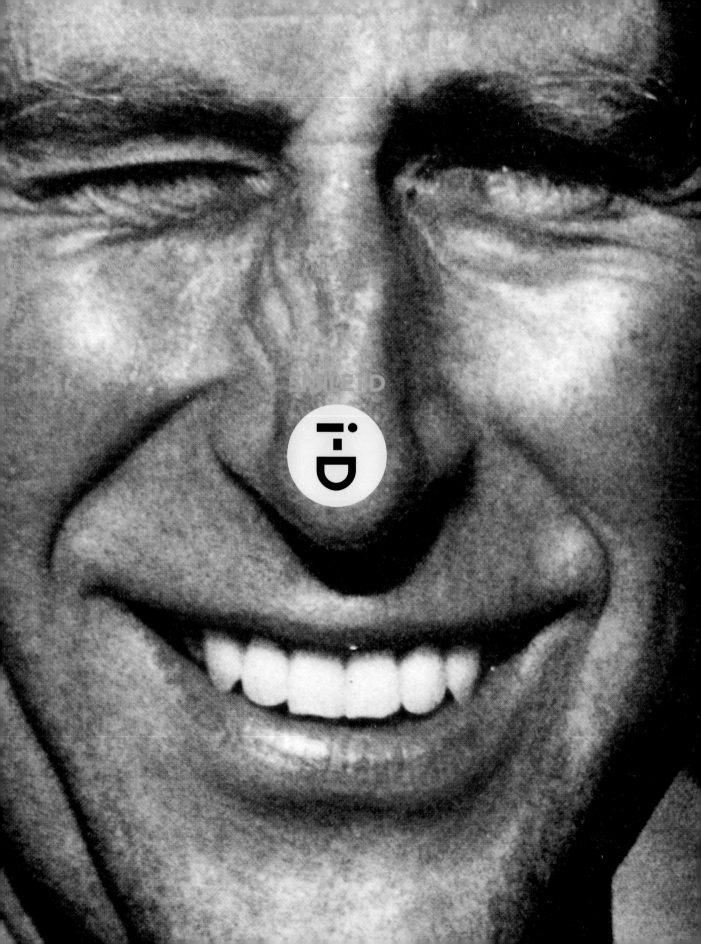

Over the past 20 years, so many people have been a part of i-D. I know the list of credits will never be complete but my family have to be highest on the list for all their patience and support. Particularly Tricia, my personal trainer, with her energy and inspiration, who has smoothed the way so often! Against the odds, we have survived as an independent voice; we've stayed true to our original concept with the long and solid support of our partner Tony Elliott, financial director Kevin Ellis and Angelo Careddu, our Italian agent. My thanks to every editor, photographer, writer, stylist, assistant and all the people who have been so hands-on for the last 20 years, particularly Avril Mair and Edward Enninful for their sheer longevity and wonderful loyalty to the magazine. All that energy has no price and thanks can never be enough. I just feel extremely privileged to be a guardian of that energy and to have entered in spirit the conscience of the fickle world of fashion. Our aim has always been to get under the skin of fashion and to be a testament to creative free enterprise. We are now a young but adult magazine which will continue to communicate and inspire future generations and we hope that this book of fragments will give a chronology to our foundation and an understanding of our roots. TERRY JONES

**Fiorucci**
Special thanks to Elio Fiorucci for continued enthusiasm and support

# SMILE i-D

**TASCHEN**

KÖLN  LONDON  MADRID  NEW YORK  PARIS  TOKYO

FASHION
AND STYLE:
THE BEST
FROM
20 YEARS
OF i-D

Edited by Terry Jones

## A Wink's As Good As A Nod by Dylan Jones

It started, naturally enough, with a wink, which is often the way with relationships, particularly ones that last. A wink, a smile and the promise of a great new tomorrow.

The original idea was a simple one, something i-D's major-domo Terry Jones hatched while still Art Director of British *Vogue*. Terry was at *Vogue* from 1972 to 1977, only leaving when it became evident that his colleagues didn't share his enthusiasm for the fresh and exciting new direction in streetstyle that exploded in tandem with punk. So he left the magazine, eventually starting i-D in the summer of 1980. Initially looking like little but a punk fanzine, i-D was essentially an exercise in social documentation; a catalogue of photographs of 'real' people wearing 'real' clothes, what Terry liked to call 'straight-ups'. People on the street. In bars. In nightclubs. At home. And all of them on parade. And although in the 20 years since, the magazine has developed into an internationally renowned style magazine, full of fancy photographers and the very fanciest models, this 'straight-up' element has never been lost. Above all else, i-D has always been about people.

When it launched, i-D didn't look like any other magazine on the shelves, and in many respects still doesn't. Turned on its side, the i-D logo resembles a wink and a smile, and every cover since the first issue has featured a winking, smiling face; a theme that has given the magazine an iconic identity as strong as that developed by *Playboy* in the 1950s (which always included a bunny silhouette somewhere on its cover). I can still remember where I was when I saw the first issue, in September 1980. I saw it on a friend's desk in the first-floor second-year graphics department of St Martins School of Art in Covent Garden, where I was a student. Having long been an avid reader of domestic style magazines (*New Style, Viz, Midnight, Boulevard*), as well as their American counterparts (*Interview, Punk etc*) – all of which focused on tightly-knit groups of micro-celebrities – it was refreshing to find something which plugged right in to British subculture, a heat-seeking style-sheet which found room for every fledgling youth cult in the country – from punks, soul boys and new romantics to psychobillies, rockers and penny-ante trustafarians. Along with *The Face*, which had launched just a few months previously, i-D was suddenly the voice of a generation: a generation with no name.

Terry Jones felt that the best way to reflect the creativity he admired in streetstyle was through 'immediacy', through visual imagery rather than just straight text, and so the magazine used typewriter-face print, ticker tape headlines and wild, often perverse graphics. And although this was a style born of necessity as much as any ideology, it gave the magazine an identity which it preserves to this day.

The magazine has always been A4 in size (slightly thinner than most glossies), though in the early days it was landscape as opposed to portrait and opened – somewhat annoyingly – longways. The first issue was just 40 pages, stuck together with three rickety staples, and cost 50p. A bargain. "Fashion magazine No.1" it said on the cover, and that was all you really needed to know. Inside were several dozen 'straight-ups' of various upwardly and downwardly mobile exhibitionists: Cerith Wyn Evans, a St Martins student, some fairly dodgy looking Blitz kids, a rockabilly or two, a goth and some teddy boys from Brighton. A girl called

Pennie, interviewed about what she was wearing, had this to say about her jumper: "I got it from some shop in Oxford Street. I can't remember the name. I get so mesmerised when I shop along Oxford Street I never notice the names." (For the first few issues Terry only allowed photographers to shoot two frames per person, so the contact sheets became works of art in themselves, a sort of sartorial police file.) There were also a few fashion ads from Fiorucci, Robot and Swanky Modes. It even had a manifesto of sorts: " i-D is a Fashion/Style Magazine. Style isn't what but how you wear clothes. Fashion is the way you walk, talk, dance and prance. Through i-D ideas travel fast and free of the mainstream – so join us on the run!"

To print the magazine, Terry turned to Better Badges, a London-based company largely responsible for producing most of the fanzines in the capital. He told them he wanted to produce the world's first fashion fanzine, and they agreed to print 2,000 copies on the condition that Terry himself bought the entire print run. The launch was rather troubled as newsagents complained about the staples: people were piercing their fingers and getting blood over other magazines on the stands. This proved to be such a problem that there were only two newsagents who agreed to stock the second and third issues. Then Virgin stepped in, guaranteeing nationwide distribution, enabling the magazine to increase its print run exponentially. "It just grew from there," says Terry.

Terry was keen to reflect the fact that streetstyle was a democratic, amorphous process. And i-D isn't, if truth be told, anything like a barometer of style. Even though the magazine originally branded itself 'The Worldwide Manual of Style', it was never – has rarely been – prescriptive. Sensibly, Terry has always believed that it's important to like the bad stuff too. "I wanted to get the concept over that we don't lay down the rules about what you wear, the idea of 'in-out' fashion," he said at the time. He's never been particularly keen on drive-by journalism, not interested in ring-fencing people in arbitrary social groups. For the quintessential style magazine this is ironic, seeing that the 'style' magazines and newspaper lifestyle sections that came in its wake seemed devoted to the reductive. i-D has been many things – irritating, infuriating, wilfully obscure, over-extravagant and often impossible to read – but it has rarely been without substance.

In a world now awash with style magazines aimed at every different type of demographic, it is easy to forget that 20 years ago magazines like i-D just didn't exist. i-D was the first street fashion magazine, a pick'n'mix grab-bag of punk fashion and DIY style, a pop-cultural sponge soaking up everything around it with inelegant haste. During a decade when the safety net of society was gradually folded away, i-D catalogued a culture of self-sufficiency, even if that culture was at times only sartorial. Sure, the Eighties was the decade when "designer" became not just a prefix but also an adjective, but it was also the decade of unreconstructed, and often rabid individualism.

The Eighties had a lot to live up to. If the Sixties had been a decade of confrontational happiness, and the post-punk Seventies full of agents of social change, the Eighties were crowded with a generation devoted to self-empowerment and self-improvement. It was a decade which couldn't wait to get ahead of itself. Reinvention became almost a prerequisite for success as soap stars became pop stars, pop stars became politicians and politicians became indistinguishable from their *Spitting Image* puppets. Everyone was a party catalyst, everyone a star. When Andy Warhol said that in the future everyone would be famous for 15 minutes, he wasn't talking about New York in 1973; he was unwittingly describing London in 1985. A vortex of entrepreneurial hedonism, London hadn't swung so much since 1966.

And i-D got jiggy before anyone else, being the first magazine to hold a mirror up to what it saw, exploiting the boom in youth culture and London's burgeoning reputation as a crucible of transient young talent. In a way the magazine made a genuine – if not always coherent – attempt to return control of the fashion world to those who actually inhabited it.

Enjoying the freedom of a magazine that was bound by no constraints, Terry could often be perverse in his art direction and design. Contrary. Bloody-minded. If a picture suggested that it be used full frame, full bleed, then Terry's inclination would be to crop it in half and print it upside down with a 30% cyan tint running through it. The best picture from a session would be used small while the worst one would be used across a spread. When asked why he did it, he'd cut back with, "Why do it like everyone else?" And usually he was right. Video grabs and TV stills were used to provide a sense of speed and the unexpected. Body copy and headlines were unflinchingly distorted while computer type became one of the magazine's defining characteristics a decade before it arrived in publications such as *Wired* and *Dazed & Confused*. Terry likes to describe his graphic discipline as "instant design", a saturated "mash" of photography and graphics, of colour and type. But although the result often looks as though it were arrived at randomly, this belies the rigour of its execution. "I don't like the concept of perfection," Terry once said, "because it implies finality. I like the end product to look easy and that takes a lot of effort. Instant design is [actually] a lie: it is never instant."

If you left anything lying around the office for long enough, it would probably end up in the magazine. Passports, address books, taxi receipts, Terry would find a use for them all. I once made the mistake of showing Terry some old family snapshots, only to come back from holiday and find they were in the magazine. Heigh ho. If you couldn't get an original copy of a particular photograph then why not just photocopy the book you found it in? It was unlikely anyone was ever going to notice. It was a very democratic place to work, too, where a receptionist could be fired one day and hired the next as a features writer. That particular receptionist is now the television critic of *The Observer*. Which is just as well because she was a lousy receptionist.

Because i-D was a vehicle for art direction as much as journalism, the magazine found itself being haphazard, irrational and wildly pretentious. The readers understood this and somehow went along with it. Some of them, anyway. In the fifth anniversary issue – which also contained Nick Knight's unforgettable studies of 100 of the most influential personalities ever to appear in i-D (a bizarre enough group including household names like Patsy Kensit, Morrissey and John Peel as well as some of the least tightly-wrapped people you could ever meet) – various readers were asked how they'd sum up the magazine. "You discover all the secret talents and mad scientists," wrote Michael Odimitrakis from Kostas, while J Dominic from Deptford compared the magazine to Marks & Spencer's Continental Biscuit Assortment (a rare accolade indeed). My favourite comment, and one that I'd forgotten until I looked through the issue recently, was sent anonymously and is nothing if not succinct: "You are a stupid lot of wanking ignorant trendies." Charmed, I'm sure.

For a journalist, Terry's often total disregard for the printed word was, on occasions, supremely painful. I remember the first time I was victim to his vagaries. As a club reporter on the magazine, I had just returned from an assignment – no doubt interviewing some equally artless fashion designer, club runner or nascent pop star – to find Terry laying out the next issue. As I glanced at the layout of one of my articles, I saw Terry cutting the bottom three inches off the galley, so my piece ended inelegantly, slap-bang in the middle of a sentence. Sensing my apprehension, he turned to me and smiled: "Well, it won't fit."

It was to be the first of many such arguments, most of which Terry won. I was there from the end of 1983 to the end of 1987, four years in which we tried – relentlessly, religiously and, I must say, with a modicum of success – to reinvent our own particular wheel. Using guerrilla graphics, cutting-edge fashion photography and tongue-in-cheek text ("Why did God make homosexuals?" asked one gay fashion editor in a particularly flippant editorial. "To take fat girls to discos"), Terry Jones's i-D quickly gained a reputation as the complete Situationist tip sheet and street fashion bible. Terry not only gave me a career, he gave careers to hundreds of other teenage and twenty-something wannabes. From Nick Knight and Juergen Teller to Caryn Franklin and Alix Sharkey, from Corinne Day and Robin Derrick to Simon Foxton and Ray Petri, from Judy Blame and Mark Lebon to Richard Burbridge and Donald Christie, from Craig McDean and Edward Enninful to Kathryn Flett, Beth Summers and Georgina Goodman. To name only the few.

The real stars of the magazine weren't the contributors, they were the subjects, whether it be Leigh Bowery cavorting about in the depths of Taboo, a Japanese cycle boy in an Eisenhower jacket or some UK garage DJ whose name no-one can ever remember. Or Sade, Madonna, Björk, Kate Moss or L'il Kim, all winking as though their careers depended on it (often they did). Any fashion designer, photographer, stylist, hairdresser, film-maker, actor, model, style journalist, make-up artist, club-runner, DJ or pop star who has contributed anything to what is laughingly called the zeitgeist in the last 20 years has, at some time or another, appeared in i-D. "How much do I spend on clothes?" Frankie Goes To Hollywood's Paul Rutherford tells us in i-D in 1984. "Is Jean Paul Gaultier a rich man? Does Yohji Yamamoto fly first class?" The i-D story is the story of pop culture in the last 20 years of the 20th century; a roll-call of the great, the good and the unseemly, a litany of bad behaviour and unhealthy diets. While *The Face* could claim to be no less influential, no magazine has produced such a rogue's gallery of achievement as i-D.

I have dozens of favourite i-D covers – Kirsten Owen by Paolo Roversi from May 1998, Leigh Bowery by Johnny Rozsa from May 1987, Kate Moss by David Sims from February 1996 and Scary Spice by Terry Richardson from November 1997 for starters – though ironically, the two I like best bookend my time at the magazine. The first is Nick Knight's photograph of Sade, which was produced at the tail end of 1983, not just because it was the first issue I worked on, but also because in one small wink it said more about the Eighties than a thousand editorials ever could. Striking a defiant pose and offering an immaculate statement of intent, Sade looked as though she was about to conquer the world. (And 18 months later she did.) The other cover I love is the last one I worked on, the "smiley" cover from December 1987, which incorporated the i-D wink as well as heralding the advent of acid house. It's one of the best magazine covers of the Eighties.

Since that issue Terry Jones has produced over 150 editions of i-D, and his passion for the magazine is still all-consuming. Terry has always had an unerring sense of what constitutes good "content" and is not often swayed by the faux or the flighty. He doesn't suffer fools gladly and has become adept at giving people the fish-eye. When you say something a little too expected or maybe even a bit dumb (as people sometimes do when in the presence of one of the best art directors in the world), he can cock his head slightly and look at you out of the corner of his eye. If you're lucky, he'll break into a smile; if you're not, he'll just nod slowly and probably never speak to you again.

Two decades since its launch, there should be little doubt that i-D is one of the most influential magazines in the world. Of course it always claimed to be (the arrogance of youth!), but now it is surely irrefutable.

Terry couldn't have done it alone, and apart from the people I've already mentioned, there are others – Terry's lovely long-suffering wife Tricia, their daughter Kayt and son Matt, Tony Elliott (co-owner of the magazine since 1984), Perry Haines, Al McDowell, Steve Dixon, Steve Johnston, Mark Lebon, Moira Bogue, Nick Knight, Edward Enninful, Avril Mair, John Godfrey, Matthew Collin, David Swindells, Craig McDean, Jane How, Pat McGrath, Stephen Male, Karl Plewka, Eugene Souleiman, Kevin Ellis, Suzanne Doyle, Rick Waterlow – who I know have all played enormous roles in the magazine's continued success.

In a way, these people have all helped institutionalise i-D. The last 20 years have seen the fashion industry become as powerful, as all-consuming and as ubiquitous as any branch of celebrity culture, yet through it all i-D has managed to somehow stay one spotlight away from the main stage. While it now looks more like a cat-killing phone directory than a fashion fanzine, it still sits resolutely on the cutting edge; still a bastion of individuality and a champion of the avant garde, the ridiculous and the outrageous. From Steve Strange to Craig David, what a long strange trip it's been.

My advice is to keep on winking. You never know where it might get you.

**Dylan Jones is the editor of *GQ* magazine.**

**Modelling i-D T-shirts on the sausage stall at Camden Market, 1980**

"My ambition is to be married with two kids and a washing machine"

**Jackie, model, no12**

Au début des années 90, plusieurs des photographes travaillant pour i-D acquirent une certaine notoriété, comme cela s'était passé pour les modèles à la fin des années 80. i-D n'était pas une question d'argent et on rechignait à traiter certains collaborateurs comme des mini-célébrités, refusant de tenir compte de leur standing en dehors du magazine. Heureusement, le génie de i-D a prévalu et chacun a continué à se comporter comme le membre d'une équipe, en particulier en échange de pages supplémentaires. Alors que je préparais le livre « Catching The Moment » (Saisir l'instant), j'ai été frappé par le fait que ce qui a sous-tendu mon activité, au cours de ces trente dernières années, c'est ce sens du travail d'équipe. Comme dans une trame, il n'y a aucun ordre chronologique à ma carrière, plutôt une série de coïncidences et de relations créatives avec un grand nombre de personnes douées.

Sur le plan commercial, i-D est aujourd'hui sur un pied d'égalité avec les grands organes de presse. J'ai pris cette décision quand nous sommes entrés dans notre dix-huitième année. En faisant « Catching The Moment », je me suis rendu compte qu'il était ridicule de faire tellement de travail de prospection et de refuser de considérer i-D comme une entreprise commerciale. Aujourd'hui, nous consacrons le maximum d'espace possible aux pages de mode. Le mélange créatif de chaque numéro, c'est comme un film ou un roman visuel, sans ligne continue, rien qu'un thème central. Pour souligner le langage photographique, les graphismes sont réduits au minimum. La photographie est le médium le plus rapide alors que les mots entravent le contact total.

Au cours des deux dernières décennies, le magazine a mûri, du point de vue organique : l'œil ouvert sur le théâtre qu'est la rue, celui du changement quotidien, celui de la mode. Nous n'avons pas été fabriqués selon une idée de marketing, ou un créneau spécifique. Aujourd'hui, le style i-D, on le suit, on l'interprète, on le copie sans vergogne. Nous avons été accueillis sur le Net avec un retentissement international, nous sommes devenus les grands maîtres dans ce monde de la diffusion visuelle. Un flot d'ex-rédacteurs continue de travailler pour le magazine. Nous avons vu des concurrents mourir sur le bord de la route ou se faire avaler par des sociétés gloutonnes. Je n'aurais jamais cru qu'on pourrait survivre et si longtemps. Choisir un unique témoignage de chaque numéro a été une exercice éprouvant, frôlant parfois l'impossible. Les images qui suivent ont souvent été choisies sur un coup de tête, ou comme indication d'un modèle graphique dont nous avons pu alors nous divertir. Smile i-D doit se voir comme la marque d'une époque.

Je suis un rêveur qui rêve d'un seul jour à la fois. Je veux juste prouver qu'il existe aussi d'autres rêveurs.

**Naturellement, Terry Jones est le directeur artistique et le rédacteur en chef de i-D.**

You might wonder why these six pages of archive Fiorucci images appear at the end of this book. Well, to explain the connection, it started before i-D was born. I was introduced to Elio Fiorucci by Oliviero Toscani sometime in the mid-1970's. During the early Eighties, I worked as his creative director for several years, travelling a week each month to Milan. At that point of i-D's early life, Fiorucci secured the magazine's survival during a critical third year, purchasing and distributing i-D globally in his shops and outlets. In 1986, I was invited by Fiorucci to take part in a Tokyo exhibition called 'Italian Rising Stars'. I was the only adopted Italian and got my first trip to the East, which was a great eye opener and a lesson for life. The exhibition also helped inspire my first book on design, *A Manual Of Instant Graphic Techniques*, published around 1990. Fiorucci's world was a world of fantasy and I learnt through working with Elio how he empowered creative people to be free – thinking with a passion for life. He passed any problem on with a simple "whatever you want to do do... you decide..." Like in the movie *Being There* with Peter Sellers, I always thought Elio could have been the president by doing or saying little. His success was not about creating a global fashion corporation. What the name Fiorucci has become in the dictionary of fashion is a spirit that has survived over time and continues to inspire, from the piazze of Milan to Broadway in New York. For this reason it made total sense to ask for his support with this project before anyone else – luckily he said yes! Big thanks, Elio.

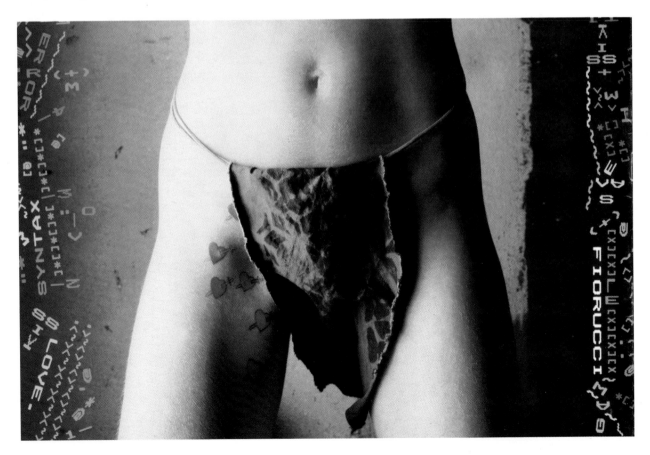

for spring'n summer 1986

fi●rucci
**1st**
album
of style

**August 1980. The i-D One Issue no1.**
**Creative direction by Terry Jones**
Straight-up style on London's Kings Road photographed by Steve Johnston/ backstabbing: art on the backs of jackets/ T-shirt fashion story styled by Caroline Baker/ Brighton rockabillies

**November 1980. The Star Issue no2.**
**Creative direction by Terry Jones**
Straight-up style on London's Kings Road photographed by Steve Johnston/ how to make it big/ rent a dress/ milliner Stephen Jones interviewed/ teddyboys/ i-D's club night/ karate

**January 1981. The i-Deye Issue no3.**
**Creative direction by Terry Jones**
Fad Gadget/ the great wall of London W1/ street straight-ups/ tomorrow revisited/ The Okonwo Twins fight back/ New York report/ portable club/ The Comic Strip/ The membranes/ Madness

**April 1981. The Dance & Stance Issue no4.**
**Creative direction by Terry Jones**
i-Dance: a history of funk/ body wrap fashion/ interview with a parrot/ Ted Polhemus/ Classix Nouveaux/ biker straight-ups/ the aliens have landed/ lowriders/ fashion photography by James Palmer, Simon Brown, Thomas Degen

**July 1981. The Do It Yourself Issue no5.**
**Graphics Malcolm Garrett, Creative direction by Terry Jones**
Adam Ant interviewed/ Glastonbury/ watersports/ Brighton beach/ Paul King/ Edwardian style/ Paris and New York straight-ups/ fashion photography by Simon Brown, Peter Anderson, Steve Dixon, Hugh Johnson, James Palmer

**August 1981. The Sweat Is Best Issue no6.**
**Photography by Thomas Degen, Terry Jones**
Tokyo/ eyes on Simon Forbes/ Princess Julia/ Kahn & Bell/ Dennis Morris/ a guide to posing/ Martin Dagville/ tipi dwelling/ Japanese straight-ups/ fashion photography by James Palmer, Steve Dixon, Mike Owen, Simon Brown

**September 1982. The In Future Issue no7.**
**Photography by James Palmer**
James Brown interviewed/ Steven Berkoff/ Issey Miyake's Spring Summer '82 collection/ Judy Blame/ martial arts/ reports from Berlin, Leeds, Belfast/ fashion photography by James Palmer, Mike Muschamp

**October 1982. The Head To Toe Issue no8.**
**Photography by Thomas Degen, Terry Jones**
Vivienne Westwood's Autumn Winter '82 collection/ Boy George/ Marilyn/ Edinburgh i-D parade/ round the clock in Amsterdam/ Animal Nightlife/ yoga

**November 1982. The Wuli Dancing Issue no9.**
**Creative direction by Terry Jones**
The new jazz/ Blancmange interviewed/ Martin Degville/ Thomas Dolby/ club organiser Chris Sullivan/ a short history of the T-shirt/ Brighton/ alternative fashion from Central St Martins/ Milan straight-ups/ fashion photography by James Palmer, Steve Johnston, Steve Dixon

**December 1982. The Out Already Issue no10.**
**Cover star: Moira Bogue. Photography by Steve Johnston**
Haysi Fantayzee interviewed/ skinhead style/ Dennis Morris/ dancing down the Dirtbox/ Pam Hogg/ a guide to astrology/ Everything But The Girl/ how to become an astronaut/ Antenna hair extensions/ a letter from Japan/ fashion photography by James Palmer, Steve Johnston

**January 1983. The Health & Herpes Issue no11.**
**Cover star: Fiona Skinner. Photography by Steve Johnston**
The Smiths interviewed/ John Peel/ pirate radio guide by Nick Knight/ sexual selection/ Kathryn Hamnett/ survival tips/ Swedish straight-ups/ Animal Nightlife/ Manchester designers/ Tommy Roberts/ fashion photography by James Palmer, Steve Johnston

**February 1983. The Love & Romance Issue no12.**
**Cover star: Sophie. Photography by James Palmer**
Bodypoppers and cybernetic soul/ Gene Loves Jezebel/ holiday in Brixton/ how to survive in Leeds/ the language of fans/ street couture/ drugs guide/ romance in Munich and New York/ fashion photography by Nick Knight, Steve Johnston, James Palmer, Max Vadukul

**March 1983. The Wet 'n' Wild Issue no13.**
**Cover star: LA. Photography by Steve Johnston**
Are you a true trendy? i-D's survival quiz/ Simon Foxton interviewed/ King's dress codes/ Shellagh Sisters/ Eddie & Sunshine/ alternative nightlife/ Gary Crowley/ Robbie Vincent/ Kensington Market/ fashion photography by Steve Johnston, James Palmer

**April 1983. The All Star Issue no14.**
**Cover star: Sade. Photography by Nick Knight**
"I want stardom!" Madonna exclusively interviewed/ Joseph Beuys/ Marilyn/ sportswear fashion/ Frank Bruno/ crazy make-up/ Chris Sullivan/ Paris and London straight-ups/ Gary Crowley's top ten/ Barry Island Butlins/ fashion photography by Mark Lebon, James Palmer

**May 1984. The SexSense Issue no15.**
**Cover star: Madonna. Photography by Mark Lebon**
Madonna's first ever cover/ Frankie Goes To Hollywood/ Billy Bragg/ are your desires normal?/ Stephen Jones/ Andrew Logan/ sex sense/ Prefab Sprout/ leather fashion/ Sisters Of Mercy/ Cerith Wyn Evans/ Fiorucci/ Greenham Common straight-ups/ fashion photography by Nick Knight, Mark Lebon, Oliviero Toscani, Robert Carra, James Palmer

**June 1984. The E=mc² Issue no16.**
**Cover star: Sophie Hicks. Photography by David Bailey**
St Martin, patron saint of fashion/ Kate Garner/ how to swing/ Steve Strange/ Nottingham clubs/ men in make-up/ Jools Holland/ Blancmange/ Matt Bianco/ illustrator Ralph Steadman/ casuals/ a history of socks/ Propaganda/ fashion photography by Cameron McVey, Jamie Morgan, Mark Lebon, Nick Knight

**July/Aug 1984. The Language Issue no17.**
**Cover star: Jo Kelly. Photography by Mark Lebon, styling by Mitzi Lorenz**
Why video is the language of now/ BodyMap/ Paul Morley/ synchronised swimming/ Crolla/ street hockey/ Barcelona/ Demob/ Nick Kamen and Ray Petri/ John Maybury/ Manchester/ wet straight-ups/ Dallas/ fashion photography by Mark Lebon

**September 1984. The Money Issue no18.**
**Cover star: Sherron. Photography by Nick Knight**
Peter York and Divine on improving your status/ jewellery designer Tom Binns/ student fashion special/ Maria Cornejo/ Leigh Bowery/ John Richmond/ cycling/ the history of denim/ fashion photography by Jamie Morgan, Nick Knight

**October 1984. The Inside Out Issue no19.**
**Cover star: Anna Pigalle. Photography by Nick Knight**
Ken Livingstone interviewed/ Leigh Bowery and Trojan at home/ Marco Pirroni/ Brighton/ Tommy Roberts/ William Orbit/ design commentator Stephen Bayley/ Keith LeBlanc/ performance art/ Tom Dixon's creative salvage/ a celebration of nudism/ The Blow Monkeys/ fashion photography by Mark Lebon, Andrew Macpherson

**November 1984. The Fun & Games Issue no20.**
**Cover star: Jane Khan. Photography by Monica Curtain**
Phillip Salon/ Judy Blame/ Alice Rycroft/ Iain Webb/ June Montana/ Then Jericho/ Clare Grogan

**Dec/Jan 1985. The Body & Soul Issue no21.**
**Cover star: Mary Emma. Photography by Mario Testino**
John Galliano interviewed/ Bodymap/ evangelists/ David LaChapelle and New York clubbing/ i-D's survival guide to religion/ psychedelic mods/ the new ruralists/ Neville Brody/ seaside straight-ups/ Sheffield/ Cabaret Voltaire/ homeopathy/ classic cars/ Greece/ fashion photography by Nick Knight, Roger Charity

**February 1985. The Gourmet Issue no22.**
**Cover stars: Helen and friend. Photography by Nick Knight, Eamonn McCabe**
"The most tastefully dressed person is a naked one!" Franco Moschino interviewed/ Scott Crolla and Georgina Godley/ John Richmond and Maria Cornejo/ Bernstock & Spiers/ the i-D guide to manners and etiquette/ Dianne Brill/ Roald Dahl interviewed/ plastic surgery/ Venice carnival/ Dublin/ Patsy Kensit and Eighth Wonder/ fashion photography by Mark Lebon, Nick Knight

**March 1985. The i-Spy Issue no23.**
**Cover star: Carol Thompson. Photography by Eamonn McCabe, styling by Carol Thompson**
Jean-Paul Gaultier interviewed/ James Bond, Man From UNCLE and suave spies/ Richard Ingrams/ a guide to body language/ Rachel Auburn/ Berlin club straight-ups/ Pam Hogg/ breakdancing/ English Eccentrics/ i-D's first club night/ fashion photography by Eamonn McCabe

**April 1985. The Flesh & Blood Issue no24.**
**Cover star: Katie Westbrook. Photography by Nick Knight, styling by Helen Campbell**
"We're not into fashion, we stick to Adidas!" Run DMC interviewed/ Fay Weldon/ Julien Temple on Absolute Beginners/ the incestuous directory of happy families/ Leigh Bowery and the Taboo tribe/ Mary Quant/ team sports/ Manhattan clubs/ Belouis Some/ fashion photography by Nick Knight, Mark Lebon, Robert Erdmann

**May 1985. The Red-Hot Issue no25.**
**Cover star: Patsy Kensit. Photography by Mark Lebon, styling by Caroline Baker**
Why Stephen Sprouse is the new Halston/ directional New Yorker Marc Jacobs/ furniture designer Ettore Sottsass/ fashion and fetish/ Allen Jones/ Sky TV launches/ Yello/ Propaganda/ introducing Bristol's Wild Bunch/ curator Maureen Paley/ Toronto guide/ fashion photography by Nick Knight, Johnny Rozsa, Mark Lebon

**June 1985. The Laid Back Issue no26.**
**Cover star: EK. Photography by Martin Brading, styling by Caroline Baker**
Young, gifted and black: Andre Walker interviewed/ is minimalism an excuse for laziness?/ the fear of clothes/ Curiosity Killed The Cat/ Doug Thompkins of Esprit/ skateboarding style/ The Woodentops/ Leeds, Bristol and Bath clubs/ Princess Julia/ fashion photography by Nick Knight, Mark Lebon, Kate Garner

**July 1985. The Love-In Issue no27.**
**Cover star: Kathy Kanada. Photography by Robert Erdmann**
English Eccentrics and London's young textile designers/ Barbara Cartland interviewed/ John Barry/ Jamie Morgan and Cameron McVey/ a guide to wigs/ Birmingham clubs/ Washington DC music report/ cross dressing couples/ Simply Red/ fashion photography by Robert Erdmann

**August 1985. The Art Issue no28.**
**Cover star: Lizzy Tear. Photography by Nick Knight**
The state of art/ London's new art cults/ Britain's best graduate designers/ scrap metal jewellery/ Ron Arad/ John Flett/ bikers/ Kenny Scharf/ a guide to gallery gatecrashing/ Hipsway/ Paris/ Maxi Priest/ Nile Rogers/ fashion photography by Mark Lebon

**September 1985. The Health & Efficiency Issue no29.**
**Cover star: Caryl Dolores. Photography by Nick Knight, styling by Paul Frecker**
Marie Helvin on beauty/ Sigue Sigue Sputnik interviewed/ Michael Nyman/ girls who ride motorbikes/ introducing the Pet Shop Boys/ baggy shorts/ Long Beach straight-ups/ i-D's survival guide to drugs/ women designing menswear/ tough sports

**October 1985. The Grown Up Issue no30.**
**Cover star: Jenny Howarth. Photography by Mark Lebon**
Special fifth birthday issue featuring 100 portraits by Nick Knight: Paul Weller, Gary Kemp, Leigh Bowery, Tom Dixon, Katharine Hamnett, Dick Bradsell, Adam Ant, Lynne Franks, Nick Logan, Stephen Jones, Cerith Wyn Evans, John Peel, Genesis P Orridge, Michael Clark, Marc Almond, Tony Wilson, Ray Petri, John Galliano, Martin Fry, Morrisey, Everything But The Girl, Patsy Kensit, Neville Brody/ why Old Street is cool/ Peter Stringfellow/ John Maybury

**November 1985. The Spectator Issue no31.**
**Cover star: Blair Booth. Photography by Eamonn McCabe**
Leigh Bowery and Taboo/ Frank Clarke on Letter To Brezhnev/ Norma Kamali interviewed/ fashion exhibitionists/ Propaganda/ Belouis Some/ the future for TV/ commentator Harry Carpenter/ Australia/ Swing Out Sister/ Hong Kong straight-ups/ fashion photography by Eamonn McCabe

**Dec/Jan 1986. The Jet Set Issue no32.**
**Cover star: Kate. Photography by Nick Knight, styling by Simon Foxton**
Martin Amis interviewed/ Bryan Ferry/ Antwerp star Dirk Bikkembergs/ Red Hot Chilli Peppers/ the survival guide to sexual diseases/ the strange life of Howard Hughes/ what you should know about photography/ i-D's top 100 records of '86/ Spring Summer '97 London catwalk report/ Tony Blackburn/ fashion photography by Nick Knight, Robert Erdmann, Mark Lebon

**February 1986. The Cool Issue no33.**
**Cover star: Corinne Drewery. Photography by Nick Knight, styling by Helen Campbell**
Soho café society/ Paul Rutherford interviewed/ Jon Savage/ Vivienne Westwood ten years on/ furniture designer Fred Baier/ Nick Coleman/ how to make it in the fashion industry/ Joseph Heller/ the A-Z of uncool/ Fat Tony/ fashion photography by Ellen von Unwerth, Eamonn McCabe, Robert Erdmann, Mark Lebon

**March 1986. The Madness Issue no34.**
**Cover star: Scarlett. Photography by Mark Lebon, styling by Judy Blame**
John Lydon interviewed/ Jean Paul Gaultier/ Nitzer Ebb/ George Melly/ mad fashion moments/ The Beastie Boys/ Quentin Crisp/ conceptual artist Jason Bratby/ Judy Blame's subversive jewellery/ Ryuchi Sakamoto/ Madrid clubs/ the i-D guide to heavy metal/ Pete Shelley/ fashion photography by Robert Erdmann, Eamonn McCabe, Jenny Howarth, Michel Momy, Martin Brading

**April 1986. The Dance Issue no35.**
**Cover star: Akure. Photography by Robert Erdmann, styling by Caroline Baker**
From breakdance to trashdance: dancing in the '80s/ Sigue Sigue Sputnik/ Michael Clark interviewed/ safe sex/ Absolute Beginners/ Jean Paul Gaultier/ Janet Jackson/ Godley & Crème/ Tokyo goes pop/ Loose Tubes/ Joe Casely-Hayford/ Moscow/ fashion photography by Ellen von Unwerth, Mark Lebon, Robert Erdmann

**May 1986. The Magic Issue no36.**
**Cover star: Alice Temple. Photography by Nick Knight, styling by Simon Foxton**
Jon Moss interviewed/ Duran Duran's John Taylor/ Style Council and the suburban soul boys/ Doris Stokes/ New Age music/ Fay Presto/ Peter Gatien and London's Limelight club/ the A-Z of the supernatural/ London's new couturists/ Joe Casely-Hayford/ Tornoto/ Brighton club guide/ fashion photography by Mark Lebon, Nick Knight, Robert Erdmann

**June 1986. The Conservation Issue no37.**
**Cover star: June Montana. Photography by Robert Erdmann, styling by Caroline Baker**
George Clinton interviewed/ where next for British fashion?/ Autumn Winter '97 catwalk report/ Nik Cohn/ CND, Friends Of The Earth and ten organisations that will save the world/ Karen Finley/ the rebirth of country music/ Manchester club guide/ soul weekenders/ young, gifted and proud parents/ Artists Against Apartheid/ The Green Party/ fashion photography by Martin Brading, Robert Erdmann, Mark Lebon, Nick Knight, Eamonn McCabe

**July 1986. The Photographic Issue no38.**
**Cover star: Ann Scott. Photography by Robert Erdmann, styling by Simon Foxton**
Oliviero Toscani interviewed/ Klaus Kinski/ Alex Cox on Sid & Nancy/ guide to horse racing/ Larry Fuente/ The Communards/ Liverpool report/ New York's bike messangers/ Then Jericho/ the A-Z of postmodernism/ Brian Griffin/ New York's art-club connection/ Steve Arrington/ fashion photography by Kate Garner, Mark Lebon, Robert Erdmann, Eamonn McCabe, Jonathan Root

**August 1986. The Dramatic Issue no39.**
**Cover star: Naomi. Photography by Nick Knight, styling by Caryn Franklin**
Naomi Campbell's first fashion story/ Neil Jordan and Cathy Tyson/ Harry Enfield/ why Jonathan Ross should be on TV/ Gilberto Gil/ P-Funk/ 30 years of youth culture photographed by Nick Knight/ method acting/ Lisa Stansfield/ who are the paninari?/ Richmond Cornejo/ Tokyo/ Edinburgh Festival/ Brighton clubbing/ fashion photography by John Hicks, John Stoddart, Sam Brown, Eamonn McCabe, Sandro Hyams

**September 1986. The Education Issue no40.**
**Cover star: Amanda King. Photography by Nick Knight, styling by Simon Foxton**
Introducing Chicago house: record company hype or genuine dancefloor explosion?/ why ignorance is bliss/ Frankie Goes To Hollywood/ Barcelona clubbing/ The Christians/ Roger Dack/ menswear fashion special/ Naples funk/ Art Pop/ Heaven 17/ Workers For Freedom/ sun bed kids/ fashion photography by Robert Erdmann, Nick Knight, Adrian Peacock

**October 1986. The Media Issue no41.**
**Cover star: Muriel Gray. Photography by Nick Knight, styling by Simon Foxton**
Tom Waits interviewed/ Janet Street Porter/ how much media do we need?/ Jim Jarmusch/ Muriel Gray/ Georgina Godley/ Christopher Nemeth and the House Of Beauty And Culture/ London's media brats/ Anthony Hopkins/ Jean-Jacques Beineix/ Meatloaf/ Anita Baker/ indie scene report/ fashion photography by Graeme Richardson, Jamie Long

**November 1986. The Beauty Issue no42.**
**Cover star: Angie Hill. Photography by Nick Knight, assisted by Charlotte & Andy**
Are our perceptions of beauty changing?/ Iggy Pop interviewed/ Julian Schnabel/ Oliver Stone/ Nile Rogers/ Norman Foster on shop design/ Was Not Was/ Fred & Judy Vermorel/ Britain's best make-up artists/ Marina Warner/ fashion photography by Geoff Stern, Nick Knight, Mark Lebon, John Stoddart

**Dec/Jan 1987. The Comic Issue no43.**
**Cover star: Mickey. Photography by Robert Erdmann, styling by Caroline Baker**
Big Audio Dynamite/ comic book special/ Alan Moore/ Frank Miller/ Daryl Hall/ AIDS update

**February 1987. The Flirt Issue no44.**
**Cover star: Paula Thomas. Photography by Jamie Long, styling by Robert Leach**
Katherine Hamnett interviewed/ Terence Trent D'Arby/ trash porno flik king Russ Meyer/ consumer kitsch and pop art/ menswear special/ The Shamen/ Welsh language cinema/ continental cursing/ flirting/ guide to condoms/ underwear/ fashion photography by Robert Erdmann, Mark Lebon, Jamie Long

**March 1987. The Metropolitan Issue no45.**
**Cover star: Isabella Rossellini. Photography by Fabrizio Ferri**
The move-makers of '87: Naomi Campbell, Gavin Rossdale, Terence Trent D'Arby, Jonathan Ross, Joe Corré/ Vivienne Westwood interviewed/ the new entrepreneurs come of age/ computer games/ Randy Travis/ Spike Lee/ the changing face of London/ haute coiffures/ Milan/ fashion photography by Sandro Hyams, Eamonn McCabe, Mark Lebon, Robert Erdmann

**April 1987. The Pop Issue no46.**
**Cover star: Grace Jones. Photography by Nick Knight, styling by Andy Knight**
Paninari, cuties, metalists, west-enders, goths, brash pack: six subcults for '87/ Malcolm McLaren interviewed/ Grace Jones/ AIDS update/ Rupert Everett/ Mad Professor/ a dictionary of pop music/ Richard Butler and the Psychedelic Furs/ the heavy metal underground/ shoe special/ fashion photography by Jamie Long, Sandro Hyams, Nick Knight

**May 1987. The Good Sport Issue no47.**
**Cover star: Tess. Photography by Nick Knight, styling by Simon Foxton**
Sinead O'Connor interviewed/ the Lonsdale story/ Latin hip hop/ Britain's new sports/ Salman Rushdie/ Sly & Robbie/ Yohji Yamamoto by Nick Knight/ Latin hip hop/ Stetsasonic/ Renagade Soundwave/ Autumn Winter '87 London catwalk report/ modern classical music/ The Proclaimers/ fashion photography by Jamie Long, Jonathan Root, Simon Fleury

**June 1987. The Plain English Issue no48.**
**Cover star: Leigh Bowery. Photography by Johnny Rozsa, styling by Clive Ross**
"You'll believe anything's beautiful eventually!" Leigh Bowery interviewed/ Boy George goes solo/ Boys Wonder/ Stephen Sprouse/ Autumn Winter '87 catwalk report/ Nashville's New Country/ Cuba/ Black Market Records/ Trouble Funk/ the vintage denim boom/ fashion photography by Simon Fleury, Michael Nafziger

**July 1987. The Film Issue no49.**
**Cover star: Elizabeth Westwood. Photography by Nick Knight**
"We never go over the top": U2 interviewed/ David Bowie in Amsterdam/ Robbie Coltrane/ Gilbert and George/ Nell Campbell/ why there's now no business but showbusiness/ Nic Roeg/ Aria/ T-shirt special/ Emma 'Wild Child' Ridley/ Japanese heavy metal/ DJ Code Money and Schooly D/ fashion photography by Nick Knight

**August 1987. The Holiday Issue no50.**
**Cover star: Sarah Stockbridge. Photography by Nick Knight, styling by Simon Foxton**
Fiftieth issue extravaganza: highlights from the last seven years/ Paul Oakenfold/ new reggae stars/ Chicago/ cyberpunks and the new wave of hardcore sci-fi/ Tom Waits/ Robert Cray/ Swatch/ Vivienne Westwood styling/ London straight-up style/ the Hacienda's fifth birthday party

**September 1987. The Boy's Own Issue no51.**
**Cover star: Rachel Weisz. Photography by Kevin Davies, styling by Caryn Franklin**
Celebrating 20 years of Fiorucci/ Curtis Mayfield interviewed/ Kevin Atherton/ Dave Dorrell/ The Duffer of St George/ Mike Pickering and the Hacienda/ Riccione, the rave riviera/ essential menswear items by Terrence Trent D'Arby/ how Super-8 will redefine film/ fashion photography by Mike Owen

**October 1987. The New Brit Issue no52.**
**Cover star: Alice Walpole. Photography by Mark Lebon**
Morrissey interviewed/ Larry Blackmon and Cameo/ odd Manchester haircuts/ Oliver Peyton and the year's hot talent/ Antwerp designers report/ couch potatoes/ Howard Jacobson/ Bhundu Boys/ Slim Barrett/ the changing face of British fashion/ interiors special/ fashion photography by Mark Lebon

**November 1987. The Fear Issue no53.**
**Cover star: Mariko. Photography by Kevin Davies, styling by Caryn Franklin**
Zodiac Mindwarp/ Hunter S Thompson interviewed/ the guide to good and evil/ J G Ballard/ Viennese fashion/ brash brats/ Steven Sprouse

**Dec/Jan 1988. The Happy Issue no54.**
**Creative direction by Terry Jones**
Eight for '88 from Dylan Jones, Martine Sitbon, Peter Saville, Simon Foxton, Nick Knight, Caryn Franklin, Jean Paul Gaultier and Leigh Bowery/ Clive James/ Sly Stone/ Mark Thomas, Jo Brand and the new British comedy/ Fat Tony/ blaxploitation/ Norman Jay's rare grooves/ Coldcut/ the return of funky fashion/ bootlegged status symbols/ Michael Clark/ radical chic

**February 1988. The Worldwide Issue no55.**
**Cover star: Lucy. Photography by Terry Jones**
"The '90s will be a very dull decade": Tom Wolfe interviewed/ Soul II Soul/ karaoke/ A-ha and Norwegian pop/ DJ Cash Money/ Graeme Park/ why we're living in theme park UK/ Alasdair Gray/ the end of the Yappies and good karma capitalism/ sixties meets eighties fashion/ Tokyo designers/ fashion photography by Sean Cunningham, Noli

**March 1988. The Tribal Issue no56.**
**Cover star: Silvia Ross. Photography by Willy Biondani, styling by Lica**
Paddy McAloon and Prefab Sprout/ British DJs/ i-D's dance directory/ Red Hot Chilli Peppers interviewed/ hat special/ tribal fashion

**April 1988. The Surreal Issue no57.**
**Creative direction by Judy Blame**
Kevin Rowland/ Joyce Sims/ Detroit house/ Chicago's new acid tracks/ Ziggy Marley/ Afrika Bambaataa/ Leigh Bowery's surrealist fashion/ Judge Dredd/ film-maker Frank Clarke/ Georgina Godley interviewed/ London's new funk bands/ Manchester's new youth cult, the Baldricks/ the jazz funk revival/ swimwear/ fashion photography by Mark Lebon

**May 1988. The Revolution Issue no58.**
**Cover star: Wendy James. Photography by Wayne Stambler**
Public Enemy and radical rap/ West Berlin clubbing/ Wendy James/ Mica Paris/ Gwen Guthrie/ Walter van Beirendonck/ Situationism/ Smith and Mighty/ Penelope Spheeris and slam dance cinema/ British comedy/ history of revolution/ London Fashion Week report/ Japanese bootlegging/ club uniforms/ fashion photography by Eddie Monsoon

**June 1988. The Body Issue no59.**
**Cover star: Karen. Photography by Wayne Stambler, styling by Malcom Beckford**
Acid housemaster Timothy Leary/ Simon Costin's exotic jewellery/ James Brown/ Cutmaster Swift/ Ibiza and the real smiley culture/ football injuries/ bhangra/ football sponsorship/ Lycra fashion/ designer cycling chic/ AR Kane/ Matt Bianco/ fashion photography by Norman Watson, Paula Bullwinkel, Kevin Davies

**July 1988. The Graduation Issue no60.**
**Photography by Terry Jones**
Helmut Lang, Austria's finest designer/ 5 Star/ the year's best graduates/ Acid Jazz/ Mike Dunn/ John Waters interviewed/ pool/ young French designers/ Tokyo clubbing/ Living Colour/ Martin Millar/ the diary of a perpetual student/ Saturday night ravers/ black soul style/ fashion photography by Eddie Monsoon

**August 1988. The Adventure Issue no61.**
**Cover star: Cleopatra Jones. Photography by Norman Watson**
Skateboarders redefine surfing/ do the world: the best international travel itinerary/ i-D's survival guide/ London street soul/ Martin Stephenson & The Daintees/ art on jackets/ Austrian Alpine couture/ The Raincoats/ A Man Called Adam/ Stephen Sprouse/ fashion photography by Gubther Parth, Daniel Kohlbacher, Christian Thompson

**September 1988. The Party Party Issue no62.**
**Cover star: Jade. Photography by Mark Lebon**
Latino reports from New York, Madrid and Rio/ the ska scene and the new skinheads/ Belgian New Beat/ Eric B and Rakim/ Liz Torres/ Frazier Chorus/ a guide to religious accessories/ dinner party dressing/ Balearic beats/ Lisa Stansfield/ fashion photography by Mark Lebon

**October 1988. The Heroes & Sheroes Issue no63.**
**Cover star: Shero**
Beetlemania/ P-Funk lives on/ the death of the superhero and the birth of the shero/ dubious pop iconography/ Eartha Kitt interviewed/ women bodybuilders/ Pam Hogg/ Jungle Brothers/ Nicky Holloway/ Antwerp Academy focus/ Shinehead/ Kym Mazelle/ fashion photography by Kevin Davies

**November 1988. The Trash Issue no64.**
**Cover star: Camilla. Photography by Guido Hildebrand, styling by Camilla Thulin**
European special featuring the cities challenging London club culture: Paris, Stockholm, Amsterdam, Frankfurt, Hamburg/ Rick Astley/ Nitzer Ebb, Front 242 and electronic bodymusic/ bad taste in football/ face-painting/ the rise of the fanzine/ Monie Love/ bad journalism/ the new heavy metal/ Bootsy Collins/ Katie Puckrick/ fashion photography by Nigel Law, Richard Weeden

**December 1988. The Love Issue no65.**
**Cover star: Claudia. Photography by Eddie Monsoon**
The new breed of '80s hippies/ Tokyo love hotels/ Paris club fashion/ Spring Summer '89 catwalk reports from Paris and London/ Copenhagen clubs/ lovesexy fashion/ car boot parties/ Mutoid Waste Company/ S'Xpress/ Jamie Hewlett, Grant Morrison and the future of British comics/ De La Soul/ Dee-lite

**Jan/Feb 1989. The Earth Issue no66.**
**Cover star: Lisa Stansfield. Photography by Phil Inkelberghe**
Paganism/ the A-Z of earth magic/ tattoos/ the Green Indian movement/ Coldcut singer Lisa Stansfield/ Camden's recycling artists/ the Soul II Soul sound system/ clubbing in New York and Amsterdam/ The Sundays/ high street chic/ Electribe 101/ the birth of Asian Rap/ Ten City and deep house/ fashion photography by Simon Pearce, Kevin Davies, Vikki Jackman, Tess Hallman

**March 1989. The Secrets Issue no67.**
**Cover star: Kathleen. Photography by Philip Sinden, styling by Beth Summers**
Martine Sitbon interviewed/ Christine Keeler and Scandal/ provocative dressing/ ninja warriors/ the modern soul scene/ clubbing in Iceland, Madrid and Dublin/ hip house/ freestyle/ Miami Bass/ 808 State

**April 1989. The Power Issue no68.**
**Cover star: Charlotte. Photography by Nick Knight**
Black Muslims in British rap/ Japanese designer b-boys/ Tony Wilson/ Asian street gangs/ Paris fashion/ Speaker's Corner/ heavy metal disco/ religious cranks

**May 1989. The Rich Issue no69.**
**Cover star: Dominique. Photography by Eddie Monsoon, styling by Nikos**
Young British talent special including Nellee Hooper, Normski and Caron Wheeler/ KRS-One and the future of rap/ Franco Moschino interviewed/ shop assistant straight-ups/ Frankie Knuckles/ remixing/ Happy Mondays/ how to avoid the credit trap/ hip hop dancing/ clubbing in Hamburg, Athens and Barcelona/ Judge Jules/ fashion photography by Eddie Monsoon, Simon Pearce

**June 1989. The Loud Issue no70.**
**Cover star: Drena. Photography by Eddie Monsoon**
Walter van Beirendonck interviewed/ ska fashion/ porn and violence in computer games/ African hi-tech music/ the martial art which is a registered religion/ new names in Belgian fashion/ audience participation chat shows/ clubbing in Australia and Vienna/ ABC/ House Of Love/ fashion photography by Nina Schultz, Kate Garner, Mark Lebon, Tim Loftus

**July 1989. The Pure Issue no71.**
**Cover star: Kayla. Photography by Angus Ross, styling by Jane How**
Exclusive Shawn Stussy interview/ Maria Cornejo/ straight edgers: the hardcore punks who don't drink, drug or have sex/ MC Merlin/ haircuts from clubland/ Timberland, the year's leisurewear label/ the house sound of Milton Keynes/ Texas/ young evangelists/ Todd Haynes/ Stereo MCs/ what is swingbeat?/ Bruce Withnail And I Robinson/ Buenos Aires/ Frankfurt clubs/ fashion photography by Eddie Monsoon, Nina Schultz

**August 1989. The Raw Issue no72.**
**Cover star: Pam Hogg. Photography by Kevin Davies**
Spike Lee interviewed/ raw fashion talent Pam Hogg/ London's S&M fetish scene/ horror movies and special FX/ Heavy D & The Boyz/ the health food boom/ Patrick Forge/ A Certain Ratio/ Minneapolis nightlife/ Dr Robert/ Dublin clubs/ The Chimes/ fashion photography by Kate Garner, Richard Varden

**September 1989. The Energy Issue no73.**
**Cover star: Diana Brown. Photography by Normski**
Summer of Love '89: why it's all gone a bit mental/ santeria/ Margi Clarke/ Diana Brown and Barrie K Sharpe/ the reincarnation of heavy metal/ Ian Banks interviewed/ the power of dreams/ Dutch fashion/ New York dancehall reggae/ Glasgow/ the sport-fashion crossover/ club door staff/ Paul Anderson/ L'il Louis/ Italian disco/ fashion photography by Simon Pearce

**October 1989. The Politics Issue no74.**
**Cover star: Liza Minelli. Photography by Mark Lebon**
Britain's art school crisis/ student fashion special/ how the Green Party can succeed/ pirate radio tears up the airwaves/ designer tracksuits/ MC Buzz B/ A Tribe Called Quest interviewed/ Digital Underground/ Fresh Four

**November 1989. The Fantasy Issue no75.**
**Cover star: Judith. Photography by Kevin Davies, styling by Caryn Franklin**
Selling the New Age/ John Galliano interviewed/ Sarah Stockbridge/ Peter Greenaway/ people who believe they are Elvis, Marilyn and Michael Jackson/ French movie icon Isabelle Pasco/ Leeds clubbing/ Giles Peterson and the Acid Jazz mods/ A Guy Called Gerald/ Spring Summer '90 Paris menswear report/ The Beloved/ D-Mob/ Kym Mazelle/ fashion photography by Mark Lebon, Donna Trope, Simon Pearce

**December 1989. The Into The Future Issue no76.**
**Cover star: Queen B**
Winner of the D&D magazine design award! Natural highs/ Soul II Soul/ John Richmond/ street jeans report/ cyberspace/ Jim Jarmusch/ Belfast/ Lisa Stansfield/ Frankie Bones

**Jan/Feb 1990. The Good Health Issue no77.**
**Cover star: Billie. Photography by Mark Lebon, styling by Anne Witchard**
Freaky dancing and scally fashion/ Electribe 101/ sex and the spiritual orgasm/ how health clubs are turning into amusement arcades/ designer food that alters your mind and body/ Spring Summer '91 catwalk report/ what is suckerball?/ the new fashion entrepreneurs/ Pedro Almodovar interviewed/ Paul Oakenfold/ Joe Smooth/ Billy Boy/ Goldie's customised teeth/ Madrid clubbing/ fashion photography by Kate Garner

**March 1990. The High Spirits Issue no78.**
**Cover star: Victoria Wilson James. Photography by Mark Lebon**
Hanif Kureishi interviewed/ healing and psychic warfare/ brain machines/ fashion outsiders: Martin Margiela, The House Of Beauty And Culture, Abyss Studio, Michiko Koshino/ Victoria Wilson-James and Soul II Soul/ Boy George finds God/ Richard O'Brian/ KLF/ David Hare/ Kiss FM go legal/ Northside/ Fabio and Grooverider/ Lloyd Cole/ fashion photography by Simon Pearce

**April 1990. The Chaos Issue no79.**
**Photography by Nick Knight, Craig McDean and Mark Mann**
Is this the end for Acid House already?/ The Beloved/ Nick Coleman/ Kenneth Anger/ the new jazz-hip hop fusion/ Inspiral Carpets/ Chaos Theory explained/ should female boxing be allowed?/ the Freedom To Party protest/ old school tracksuit style/ is Alfredo the DJ of the decade?/ Beats International/ The Farm/ The Charlatans/ fashion photography by Nick Knight

**May 1990. The Dangerous Issue no80.**
**Cover star: Marni. Photography by Jean-Baptiste Mondino, styling by Judy Blame**
Julien Clary interviewed/ Toxic Avenger Lloyd Kaufman/ Viking Combat, Britain's new martial art/ how safe is water to drink?/ poisonous fashion/ Monie Love/ The Kray Twins and the Kemp brothers/ hip hop suits/ Blaze/ San Francisco poets/ Carlton/ Carl Cox/ Rebel MC/ fashion photography by Jean-Baptiste Mondino, David Sims

**June 1990. The Life & Soul Issue no81.**
**Cover star: Jas. Photography by Brett Dee**
Candy Flip, 808 State and Manchester's club scene/ why drugs are in the news again/ Vic Reeves interviewed/ Dolph Lundgren/ Massive Attack, Coldcut, Caron Wheeler and Adrian Sherwood on reggae/ African football/ St Etienne/ fashion fabrics and textile technology/ Primal Scream/ Professor Griff/ Robert Owens/ New Order and the England squad/ fashion photography by Mark Lebon, Brett Dee

**July 1990. The Anarchy Issue no82.**
**Cover star: Kersten Sheffield. Photography by Paolo Roversi**
The house sound of Sheffield/ Inspiral Carpets/ anarchists and the poll tax/ DIY fashion/ social anarchy in Prague/ Kinky Gerlinky's Vogue Ball/ World Of Twist/ E-Zee Possee/ ballet kite-flying/ how last year's ravers are turning into this year's hippies/ a guide to office sabotage/ Adamski/ fashion photography by Brett Dee, Paolo Roversi

**August 1990. The Paradise Issue no83.**
**Cover star: Christy Turlington. Photography by Andrew Macpherson**
Forget Ibiza, forget Goa: welcome to Thailand, party paradise/ Happy Mondays interviewed/ the new mods/ why some people believe we can now live to 150/ positively pregnant fashion/ Richard Stanley/ LFO/ Larry Heard/ eco-sabateurs/ new black comedy/ fashion photography by Glen Luchford, Juergen Teller

**September 1990. The Birthday Issue no84.**
**Cover stars: Tasmin and Kerry. Photography by Nick Knight**
Mega 10th Birthday issue! Includes i-D forums exploring the future of music, fashion, design, books and film featuring Tony Wilson, Boy George, Norman Cook, Peter Saville, Nigel Coates, Dave Dorell, John Richmond, Michael Bracewell and more/ global street fashion special including photographs by Nick Knight, Andrew Macpherson, Anton Corbijn, Craig McDean, David Sims, Mark Lebon, Nigel Shafran, Normski, Simon Foxton, Travis

**October 1990. The Get Smart Issue no85.**
**Cover star: Lady Miss Keir. Photography by Nick Knight, Craig McDean**
Groovy! Deee-Lite interviewed/ neurospace: the mind revolution/ sport psychology/ The Duffer Of St George interviewed/ who are the Church of The SubGenius?/ puck off: ice hockey/ Tackhead/ Barcelona clubbing/ New York beadology/ fashion photography by Nick Knight, Craig McDean, Travis, Simon Foxton

**November 1990. The Born Again Issue no86.**
**Cover star: Mica Paris. Photography by Craig McDean, styling by Zoe Bedeaux**
Robert De Niro and Martin Scorsese interviewed/ Mica Paris/ neo-mod fashion/ why religious cults are on the up/ Nigel Benn's clothing range/ William Gibson and Bruce Sterling interviewed/ how permaculture could change the world/ the shift in trainer style/ Sydney clubs/ A Man Called Adam/ Jah Wobble/ Rocky & Diesel/ fashion photography by Donald Christie, Nick Knight, Juergen Teller

**December 1990. The Action Issue no87.**
**Cover star: Aure Attika. Photography by Nigel Shafran, styling by Melanie Ward**
Genius or madman? Adamski/ surveillance and bugging/ action fashion/ Britain's new gay activism/ knitwear/ sex toys/ Omar/ straight-up fashion special/ Spring Summer '91 catwalk report/ Lush/ The Beautiful South/ Inner City/ Danny Rampling/ Scottish clubbing/ fashion photography by Mark Lebon, Trevor Key

**January 1991. The Pioneer Issue no88.**
**Cover star: Sophie Okonedo. Photography by Xavier Guardans, styling by Camilla Nickerson**
The Farm and terrace fashion/ black British film-makers/ how new media technology will change TV/ dance music bootlegging/ teenage precinct fashion/ Christopher Nemeth: fashion without frontiers/ Wigan's club art/ Galliano/ female arm-wrestling/ Frazier Chorus/ Manchester fashion post-flares/ Italian clubbing/ fashion photography by Nigel Shafran, Craig McDean

**February 1991. The Communication Issue no89.**
**Cover star: Michelle Le Gare. Photography by Mark Lebon**
Dream Warriors and the jazz rap collision/ sound systems and anarchist house culture/ biker fashion/ fax art and pranks/ black TV in the USA/ what models really look like/ how Ziggi Golding changed the face of beauty/ alternative therapy/ Amsterdam clubbing/ Shabba Ranks/ Dirk Bikkembergs/ PM Dawn/ Throwing Muses/ baggies with attitude/ MC Kinky/ fashion photography by Norbert Schoerner

**March 1991. The Love Life Issue no90.**
**Cover star: Kylie Minogue. Photography by Robert Erdmann**
Oh, you are naughty! Kylie uncovers a new look/ fetish holidays/ dating agencies/ why S&M will soon be a crime/ Gary Clail/ the new wave of Liverpool bands/ customising fashion/ feminist pornography/ industrial workwear/ New York drag clubs/ Iain Sinclair interviewed/ Lover's Rock fashion/ Ride

**April 1991. The News Issue no91.**
**Cover star: Moni. Photography by Derek Ridgers**
Is Seal the '90s first real pop star?/ ravers take over motorway service stations/ does the news put business before truth?/ fashion for party people/ new wave of British film-makers/ 808 State/ indie dance clubs/ James Kelman interviewed/ Shut Up And Dance/ Sasha/ Yugoslavia's crisis culture/ Gulf War opinions/ Thailand: Paradise Lost?/ Chapterhouse/ fashion photography by Travis, Derek Ridgers

**May 1991. The Visionary Issue no92.**
**Cover star: Sister Souljah. Photography by Renee Valerie Cox**
Why Goa is having a summer of love/ Public Enemy's Sister Souljah/ conspiracy theories/ how to predict the future/ De La Soul interviewed/ do women have the right to kill men?/ London Fashion Week special: Vivienne Westwood, Phillip Treacy, Joe Casely-Hayford/ S'Xpress/ women only clubs/ Caroline Aherne/ The Wonder Stuff/ fashion photography by Juergen Teller

**June 1991. The Travel Issue no93.**
**Cover star: Adeva. Photography by Andrew Macpherson**
A guide to alternative tourism/ Jean Paul Gaultier's Paris extravaganza/ Christopher Walken interviewed/ Berlin's booming house scene/ circus raves/ a guide to global clubbing/ Flowered Up/ walking boots/ fashion adventures on the road across the USA

**July 1991. The High Summer Issue no94.**
**Cover star: Lorraine Pascale. Photography by Hugh Stewart**
Primal Scream/ drug testing/ Definition Of Sound/ New York's art terrorists/ Primal Scream interviewed/ urine testing comes to the UK/ scary film-maker John McNaughton/ summer fashion special: hanging out in LA and Sydney/ surfwear in San Francisco/ get ready for a fourth summer of house/ New York clubs/ radical ramblers/ Kraftwerk/ Finitribe/ fashion photography by Travis, Shawn Mortensen, Angela Hill

**August 1991. The One World Issue no95.**
**Cover star: Elaine. Photography by Mark Lebon**
How can we save the world? Eco-faz forum/ pop pranksters The KLF/ cyberpunk circus/ what is the New World Order?/ Hollywood goes green/ slashed black street fashion/ Tim Burton/ Frankie Knuckles/ artist Richard Long interviewed/ golf fashion/ Balaeric networking/ Young Disciples/ Joey Beltram/ fashion photography by Mark Lebon

**September 1991. The Fundamental Issue no96.**
**Cover star: Michelle. Photography by Eddie Monsoon, styling by Judy Blame**
Are you ready for Ladchester? London's new club bands/ genetic engineering/ Moby interviewed/ Rimini/ football in crisis/ instant customising/ Belgian clubs/ Bella Freud/ student fashion/ independent film special: Ice T, Margi Clarke, Todd Haynes, Hal Hartley/ designers do denim/ Teenage Fanclub/ Nightmares On Wax/ fashion photography by Eddie Monsoon

**October 1991. The Identity Issue no97.**
**Cover star: Rozalla. Photography by Hugh Stewart**
The power of love: disco diva Rozalla/ PM Dawn/ Leningrad's youth culture underground/ who are the psychedelic skinheads?/ street fashion in Japan/ political prostitutes/ the men's movement/ cosmetic surgery/ Roddy Doyle/ i-D Japan launches/ why the long skirt is back/ JG Ballard interviewed/ VW Beetle raves/ Tokyo clubbing/ Orbital/ fashion photography by Hugh Stewart

**November 1991. The Hyper Real Issue no98.**
**Cover star: Sandra Bernhard. Photography by Michel Comte**
Real wild woman: Sandra Bernhard bites back/ Jungle Brothers/ Shawn Stussy interviewed/ Cuba/ Liverpool's club scene reinvents itself/ supernatural weirdness/ electric cars/ Bizarre Inc/ what Japan has planned for the future of computer games/ technicolor fashion/ movie pioneer John Sayles/ Vic Reeves/ Darren Emerson/ fashion photography by Nick Knight

**December 1991. The International Issue no99.**
**Photography by Terry Jones**
Techno, the new sound of Europe/ Dario Argento and Italian horror/ Zoe/ beach bummed: Surfers Against Sewage/ rude boy fashion/ Malcolm X's daughters/ European fashion special: Sybilla, Romeo Gigli, Helmut Lang, Andre Walker, Jean Colonna, Veronique Leroy, Martin Margiela/ Shamanism/ Maria Carey/ Japan's young Otaku/ My Bloody Valentine/ fashion photography by Peter Anderson

**January 1992. The Positive Issue no100.**
**Cover star: Neneh Cherry. Photography by Jenny Howarth and Mark Lebon**
Think positive! 100th issue AIDS special: Neneh Cherry interviewed/ 100 quotes about your generation/ global guide to AIDS policies/ euthanasia/ AIDS activism/ can sex still be fun?/ condoms/ The Orb/ Apache Indian/ Underground Resistance/ positive portfolio photographed by Simon Foxton, Peter Anderson, Mark Lebon, Juergen Teller, Wolfgang Tillmans, Anette Aurell, Takashi Homma

**February 1992. The Performance Issue no101.**
**Cover star: Christie. Photography by Simon Martin, styling by Edward Enninful**
Minimalism rules! Spring Summer '92 London and Paris catwalk report/ the art of chilling/ Altern 8/ shock choreography/ Argentina/ live hip hop bands/ Gus Van Sant interviewed/ rave dancing/ American and Mexican wrestling/ cyberperformer Stelarc/ Verve/ Sounds Of Blackness/ M-People/ Cypress Hill/ Alison Limerick/ fashion photography by Simon Martin, Diane Cashman

**March 1992. The Technology Issue no102.**
**Cover stars: Lorella and Tatiana. Photography by Takashi Homma, styling by Gili**
Inner City and Detroit techno report/ David Cronenberg interviewed/ Eurofashion special featuring Martin Margiela, Veronique Leroy, Jean Colonna, Dirk Bikkembergs, Christopher Nemeth, Romeo Gigli, Bella Freud, Joe Casely-Hayford, Duffer Of St George/ techno art/ i-D Now: live fashion in Florence/ Verve/ hackers, cyberpunks and the new digital freedom fighters/ Space Time and holographic fashion/ James/ live ambient house/ Ragga Twins

**April 1992. The Activism Issue no103.**
**Cover star: N'Dea Davenport. Photography by Nick Knight, styling by Zoe Bedeaux**
Brand New Heavies interviewed/ America's new black cinema/ the government clampdown on squatting/ Gio Goi: Manchester streetwear with real attitude/ anti-fascist activism/ Scotland's fight for independence/ customisation/ One Dove/ Nervous Records/ Chic/ Aphex Twin/ fashion photography by Pierre Rutschi, Adam Howe

**May 1992. The Glamour Issue no104.**
**Cover star: Helena Christensen. Photography by Henrik Bülow**
What is glamour?/ Rei Kawakubo of Comme des Garçons interviewed/ Bernard Sumner, Johnny Marr and Electronic/ disco divas/ Wim Wenders/ new Brit actors/ Bunty Matthias and the changing face of dance/ Paris flea market chic/ the science of beauty/ XULY.Bet/ Chaka Khan/ Leftfield/ Jessica Ogden/ classic cars/ glam clubbing/ Roger Sanchez/ Wayne's World/ fashion photography by Eddie Monsoon, Anette Aurell

**June 1992. The Olympic Issue no105.**
**Cover star: Kathy Read. Photography by Craig McDean, styling by Edward Enninful**
Barcelona Olympic special: what happened to sport for sport's sake?/ sport on drugs/ Athens club report/ The Shamen interviewed/ adrenaline sports/ endurance athletics/ Autumn Winter '92 catwalk report/ SL2/ Arrested Development/ Italian menswear/ Omar/ Future Sound of London/ club holidays/ fashion photography by Craig McDean, Peter Anderson

**July 1992. The Destination Issue no106.**
**Cover star: Sarah Wietzel. Photography by Nick Knight, styling by Edward Enninful**
San Franciscos's acid revival/ Shut Up And Dance, German techno fashion/ Yardie and inner city Black Britain/ abortion in Ireland/ Loleatta Holloway/ Deee-Lite/ Rimini clubbing/ Tony Humphries/ Suede/ free festivals/ denim directory photographed by Simon Foxton, Peter Robathan, Juergen Teller, Donald Christie, Corrine Day, Wolfgang Tillmans, Craig McDean, David Sims, Mark Lebon, Adam Howe

**August 1992. The Artist Issue no107.**
**Cover star: Beatrice Dalle. Photography by Craig McDean**
Who are the twentynothings?/ Richard Linklater, Douglas Coupland and Gen X culture/ rewriting art history: young black artists/ Public Enemy interviewed/ DIY art/ Britain's graffiti underground/ Beatrice Dalle/ Terence McKenna/ The Orb/ The Sugarcubes/ Masters At Work/ Carl Cox/ Spiritualized/ American DJs in the UK/ fashion photography by Mark Lebon, Peter Robathan, David Sims

**September 1992. The Parade Issue no108.**
**Cover star: Nora Kryst. Photography by Eddie Monsoon**
Visionaries and idealists: the Parade portfolio including Walter Mosley, Wiz, Disposable Heroes Of Hiphoprisy, Jamiroquai, Philip Glass, Dennis Cooper, Blake Baxter, Brian Eno, The Big Issue, Steve Hillage/ DJs as remixers: Paul Oakenfold, Sasha, Leftfield, Andrew Wetherall and Darren Emerson/ The Prodigy/ Berlin Love Parade/ Patrick Cox/ Anna Sui/ London Gay Pride

**October 1992. The New Season Issue no109.**
**Cover star: Cecilia Chancellor. Photography by Simon Fleury, styling by Edward Enninful**
Special Fashion Issue: how we'll dress in '93/ terrace boys and casual fashion/ Hispanic gang culture in LA/ Paul Weller interviewed/ funk rock fashion/ Icelandic club culture/ L'il Louis/ House Of Pain/ Black Dog/ why English football is rubbish/ new technology guide/ fashion photography by Craig McDean, Juergen Teller

**November 1992. The Sexuality Issue no110.**
**Cover star: Holly Davis. Photography by Simon Fleury, styling by Edward Enninful**
Let's talk about sex! i-D's sexuality special/ the Wolfgang Tillmans story that got i-D banned/ Salt 'n' Pepa interviewed/ the A-Z of safe sex/ fetish fashion/ the new pornography/ 808 State/ General Levy/ Genesis P-Oridge/ Queercore/ do the bogle: ragga dancing/ Aphex Twin and the future sound of Britain/ club tours/ the war against women/ sexual images by Nick Knight, Anette Aurell, Eddie Monsoon, Nigel Shafran, Matthew R Lewis, Craig McDean, Nina Schultz

**December 1992. The Strength Issue no111.**
**Cover star: Michaela Straccen. Photography by Sivan Lewin**
Rebel music: the year of ragga/ Jamaica's rising stars/ Joe Casey-Hayford writes on black pop culture/ Shabba Ranks/ Native Americans fight for their culture/ L7, Babes In Toyland and America's grunge girls/ Coldcut/ Tanith and Berlin clubbing/ gay Manchester/ Tim Westwood, the Boogie Bunch and London's underground rap scene/ ragga Barbie fashion/ Dogs Of Heaven/ fashion photography by Anette Aurell, Nigel Shafran

**January 1993. The Screen Issue no112.**
**Cover star: Sonic The Hedgehog. Illustration by Sega**
Spike Lee on the making of Malcolm X/ Jesus Jones/ i-D's computer games forum/ pepsi cola kids: kitsch fashion/ Ministry and industrial rock/ grunge couture/ chill-out videos/ new British film-makers/ Sasha/ Gregg Aracki, Todd Haynes and New Queer Cinema/ youth TV's identity crisis/ Gina Bellman/ Cologne clubs/ fashion photography by Norbert Schoerner, Corrine Day

**February 1993. The Survival Issue no113.**
**Cover star: Monie Love. Photography by Simon Fleury**
Crisis! How to survive the '90s/ Monie Love interviewed/ why snowboarding is the fastest growing winter sport/ the A-Z of surviving the apocalypse/ pirate radio/ John Galliano/ roots dub music/ the blag economy/ Cornershop/ Azzedine Alaia/ Emily Woof/ Rage Against The Machine/ the new suits/ student poverty/ the rise and rise of techno/ George Clinton/ sex and deconstruction and rock'n'roll: Spring Summer '93 Paris catwalk report/ fashion photography by Craig McDean

**March 1993. The Comedy Issue no114.**
**Cover star: Jane Horrocks. Photography by Matthew R Lewis**
Vic Reeves and Bob Mortimer interviewed/ the rise and rise of British comedy/ Ren and Stimpy/ skatewear/ Ice-T, rebel with a cause/ performance theatre/ Frank Black/ Britain's best new DJs/ Giant Steps and New York's jazz-rap funk-jam/ Sunscreem/ Living Colour/ Jane Horrocks/ fashion photography by Craig McDean, David Sims, Richard Ellis

**April 1993. The Sound Issue no115.**
**Cover star: Sarah Cracknell. Photography by Matthew R Lewis**
Keanu Reeves on Buddhism/ i-D's dance music forum with Terry Farley, 808 State and East 17/ Apache Indian and bhangramuffin/ survivalist fashion/ St Etienne/ Riot Girls and the new 'Girl Positive' activists/ ambient clubbing/ the first interview with Suede/ James Lavelle/ where now for Manchester?/ why acid house is the sound of '93/ the fiftieth anniversary of LSD/ street fashion confusion/ San Francisco fashion

**May 1993. The Europe Issue no116.**
**Cover star: Björk. Photography by Matthew R Lewis**
"I think my head is about to explode..." Björk goes solo/ Europe's immigration problem/ creativity in Russia/ Jamiroquai interviewed/ the A-Z of European football/ Eastern European models/ Anne Parillaud/ Spiral Tribe/ Laurent Garnier/ European rap/ Ann Demeulemester interviewed/ Gang Starr/ Costume National/ clubwear designers Sabotage/ Rotterdam techno scene/ fashion photography by Matthew R Lewis, Jenny Howarth

**June 1993. The Beauty Issue no117.**
**Cover star: Kristen McMenamy. Photography by Juergen Teller, styling by Edward Enninful**
Supermodel or super ugly? Kristen McMenamy and the new beauty/ ambient special: The Orb and Aphex Twin interviewed/ introducing the male supermodels/ undercover with the new animal liberation army/ Riot Girls/ Jungle Brothers/ Orbital interviewed/ Sheffield clubs/ Autumn Winter '93 catwalk report/ fashion photography by Anette Aurell, Mark Lebon

**July 1993. The Open Air Issue no118.**
**Cover star: Karen Ferrail. Photography by Juergen Teller, styling by Venetia Scott**
U2 on Zooropa/ whatever happened to the peace movement?/ Britain's new eco warriors and the battle for Twyford Down/ camouflage fashion by Wolfgang Tillmans/ sex in cyberspace/ Michael Stipe's American travelogue/ David Morales/ swingbeat fashion/ denim special photographed by Juergen Teller, Simon Foxton, Jenny Howarth, James Fry, Simon Martin, Matthew R Lewis, Angela Hill

**August 1993. The Festival Issue no119.**
**Cover star: Gillian Gilbert. Photography by Donald Christie, styling by Grant Boston**
Summer of love or hate? The government vs travellers and sound systems/ New Order on the price of fame/ Moby photographed by Wolfgang Tillmans/ Eddie Izzard/ Buju Banton and ragga on trial/ Jude Law, Sadie Forst and new Brit cinema/ Mario van Peebles/ Iceland/ Smashing Pumpkins interviewed/ Juan Atkins/ Steve Reich/ fashion photography by Jason Evans, Craig McDean

**September 1993. The Boys & Girls Issue no120.**
**Cover star: Naomi Campbell. Photography by Jenny Howarth, styling by Edward Enninful**
"I don't really want to be a rock star!" Naomi Campbell interviewed/ cannabis special: is it time for legalisation?/ Stereo MC's conquer America/ Cypress Hill interviewed/ Gilbert and George explain themselves/ can English football get any worse?/ Scotland's club clampdown/ M-People/ functional sportswear/ Credit to the Nation/ the skateboarding revival/ fashion photography by Juergen Teller, David Sims, Peter Anderson, Jenny Howarth, Mark Lebon

**October 1993. The New Look Issue no121.**
**Cover star: Tania Court. Photography by Stefan Ruiz, styling by Edward Enninful**
Young Brit fashion special featuring the first Alexander McQueen interview plus Copperwheat Blundell, John Rocha, Abe Hamilton/ Depeche Mode/ female football fashion/ William Burroughs meets Disposable Heroes Of Hip Hoprisy/ Brian Eno/ Ken Loach/ Gabrielle/ William Gibson/ John Woo/ Paul Smith/ Shaun Ryder/ are big name DJs killing clubs?/ the multimedia revolution/ Derrick May/ Beavis & Butt-head

i-D, im Grunde ein Fanzine, das eine Mini-Fragebogen-Struktur mit O-Tönen von der Straße verquickte, ging mit einem journalistischen Ansatz an Mode heran und bediente sich experimentellster Produktionstechniken. Die jeweils dreimonatige Reifezeit zwischen den ersten Ausgaben erzeugte eine einmalige Layout-Landschaft; Fotocollagen wurden auf Pappkarton geklebt, dieses Blatt wurde dann durch die Kamera gerastert, hiervon wurden Kontaktabzüge gemacht, um Druckvorlagen anzufertigen, die bei Better Badges reproduziert wurden. Von Beginn an war i-D-Merchandising von zentraler Bedeutung. Wir ließen Badges mit der Aufschrift „As seen in i-D" herstellen, um sie an die Leute zu verteilen, die auf der Straße fotografiert wurden. T-Shirts waren eine weitere Maßnahme, um das Magazin zu bewerben und Geld aufzutreiben. Trotzdem verlief die Finanzierung des Magazins so, als würde man das Sparschwein plündern. Die meisten Hefte wurden über Plattenläden, Modeboutiquen und den einen oder anderen Zeitschriftenstand verkauft.

Meine nächtliche Arbeit an i-D wurde noch belastender, als Better Badges das Handtuch warf, während unsere Ausgabe Nr. 3 noch unbezahlt und Nr. 4 mit dem Gold-Cover gerade druckreif war. Die Arbeit, mit der ich meinen Lebensunterhalt bestritt, brachte es mit sich, dass ich wochen- und monatelang nicht in London war, sondern zum Beispiel als Artdirector Fiorucci-Kampagnen in Mailand leitete oder beratend in Frankfurt und Düsseldorf tätig war. Mein Frau Tricia unterrichtete, um unsere Familie mit zwei kleinen Kindern durchzubringen, und dieses Zeitschriftenhobby verschlang die knappe Freizeit, die uns noch blieb. Bei unserer selbstausbeuterischen Nachtarbeit schlossen sich uns Max Vadukul, James Palmer, Ronnie Randall und Thomas Degen an. Meine Kinder Matthew und Kayt lernten lauter seltsame Leute kennen, die bei uns zu Hause in den obersten Stock stiegen, wo das Heft produziert wurde. Als Moira Bogue, die kam, um ihre Dissertation über Fanzines zu schreiben, schließlich bei uns blieb und auch den Journalisten Alix Sharkey mit an Bord brachte, war klar, dass die Leute hellhörig wurden. Wie ein Magnet zog i-D die unterschiedlichsten kreativen Kräfte an.

Jede einzelne Seite wurde wie ein Kunstwerk behandelt, und im dritten Erscheinungsjahr wurde die Gestaltung von i-D ausgefeilter. Die Kugelkopfschreibmaschine, die wir für die Texte benutzten, gab den Geist auf, und ich benötigte einen Computer für die von mir angestrebte Optik. Als die Kosten für die Sorgfalt, die wir so überreich in die Zeitschrift investierten, und die Verkaufszahlen schließlich in keinem Verhältnis mehr zueinander standen, rettete Fiorucci i-D. Da ich sein Creative Director für Europa war, dachte er sich für mich ein Projekt aus; ich sollte für Pannini 100 Sticker-Designs entwerfen. Das Budget erlaubte es mir, meinen ersten Computer zu kaufen, einen Apple IIE mit Grafiktablett. Obwohl das erst 18 Jahre her ist, ging dieses Werkzeug weit über unseren technischen Horizont. Über Kontakte am St Martins erfuhr ich von Robin Derrick. Er wußte, wie man damit arbeitete, und brachte uns mit Marion Moisy zusammen, die dann ebenfalls einstieg. Die i-D-Belegschaft wuchs: Caryn Franklin, eine Grafikstudentin, kam auf Arbeitssuche zu uns. Wenn sie nicht auf der Straße oder in Clubs castete, arbeitete sie für Fiorucci. „Frankie", wie ihre Freunde sie nennen, zog für uns Steve Male an Land, später kam noch die Empfangsdame und spätere Kolumnistin Kate Flett dazu. Für ein Jahr war unsere Auflage gesichert und ging zum internationalen Vertrieb direkt an Fiorucci.

Obwohl wir auch weiter an unserem Fanzine-Ethos festhielten, brauchten wir Anzeigenkunden, aber das A4-Querformat und giftige Neonfarben vertrugen sich nicht mit deren kommerziellen Erwägungen. Als der Fiorucci-Vertrag auslief, standen wir noch immer vor einem nicht unbeträchtlichen Schuldenberg, und es sah so aus, als müssten wir nach einem neuen Partner suchen. Ich wandte mich an Tony Elliott, den Herausgeber von *Time Out*. Er hatte ein wohlwollendes Interesse an der Underground-Zeitschriftenkultur, vielleicht wegen seiner Beziehung zu den Machern von *Oz*. Vor die Wahl zwischen einer Beteiligung bei i-D oder *Blitz* gestellt, kaufte er sich schließlich mit 51 Prozent bei uns ein und übernahm alle Schulden. Von Heft 5 an nahmen wir fast nur noch Gesichter auf den Titel und griffen dabei das Zwinkern aus unserem Logo auf, das eine so zentrale Bedeutung für die Identität der Zeitschrift hatte. Mit Nr. 14 gingen wir vom Querformat zum Hochformat über, um es WHSmith, unserem neuen Grossisten, recht zu machen.

Die Rolle von i-D als Imagemacher übertraf die eher bescheidenen Umstände seiner Produktion bei weitem, und unsere Titelporträts gaben einigen der größten Stars der damaligen Zeit einen entscheidenden

Karriereschub. Das Sade-Cover vom Januar 1984 erschien ein Jahr vor ihrem ersten Plattenvertrag. Mark Lebon hatte ein Studio gebucht, um eine Anzeige für Fiorucci zu schießen, als wir erfuhren, dass Madonna, die gerade ihr erstes Album herausbrachte, an diesem Tag in London sein würde und für ein Porträt vorbeischauen könnte. Ob sie auch einmal zwinkern könnte? Nach sechs Aufnahmen wurde ihr rechtes Auge – die Seite, die wir normalerweise nehmen – müde, aber mit dem linken klappte es besser. Seht euch die Nr. 15 einmal genau an, und ihr werdet feststellen, dass ihr berühmtes Muttermal auf der falschen Seite ist. Die meisten Londoner glaubten, das Wesen auf dem Cover sei Marilyn, Boy Georges damaliger Freund, der sich seine Haare bei Antenna machen ließ, wo Michael Forbes die eingeflochtenen weißen Dreadlocks zur Mode des Tages machte. Das Heft mit dem Madonna-Foto unter dem Titel „The SexSense Issue" missfiel WHSmith. Der neonrosa Hintergrund biss sich mit ihrem neu designten Look, und die Verwendung der anstößigen Vokabel „Sex" ging ihnen ebenfalls gegen den Strich. Bitte, danke! In der Geschäftswelt schrieben wir immer noch 1984, das dunkle Zeitalter, in dem Männer, die Kilts oder Make-up trugen, mit verrückten, drogensüchtigen Perversen gleichgesetzt wurden. Zeitschriften, die solche Typen porträtierten, wurden ins oberste Verkaufsregal verbannt. Der Versuch von WHSmith, i-D ins Abseits zu drängen, hatte auf Leute, die dem Mediengeschmack ihrer Zeit voraus waren, den gegenteiligen Effekt. Fans von i-D fanden auch weiterhin den Weg in die Sherriff Road, um uns ihre kreativen Dienste anzubieten.

Die kreativen Impulse durch i-D machten sich während der 80er auf vielen Gebieten bemerkbar. Das Magazin blieb respektlos und widerstand allen Kommerzialisierungsversuchen, wurde aber unverkennbar zur Inspirationsquelle für den Mainstream der Mode- und der Kulturindustrie. Wir produzierten Videos, die Einfluss nahmen auf die grafische Gestaltung im Fernsehen und in der Clublandschaft. Mit unserer i-D-Tour zogen wir überall hin, wo man uns haben wollte. Von New York bis Amsterdam, von Sydney bis Reykjavik benutzten wir Mode als gigantisches interaktives Spiel, um auszudrücken, wer wir waren, was uns gefiel und wo wir hin wollten.

Die einzelnen Ausgaben entstanden weiterhin um besondere Themenschwerpunkte herum, oft abstrakte und häufig frivole. Der Inhalt spiegelte die Vorlieben und Wünsche der Mitarbeiter wieder, seine Originalität bestärkte alle Beteiligten in ihrer bedingungslosen Loyalität. Wir ließen uns eher mitreißen, als dass wir nüchtern-kritisch in unseren Anschauungen waren. Sobald ich das Gefühl hatte, dass Leute, über die berichtet wurde, als die Dummen dastanden, oder ein Editorial zu borniert geraten war, wurde es verworfen, weil es sich nicht mit der Idee vertrug, die zum Entstehen von i-D geführt hatte. Nick Knight kam in mein Studio, als er noch Student war. Er hatte *Not Another Punk Book* gesehen und dachte, ich wüsste vielleicht, wie und wo er sein Buch über Skinheads veröffentlichen könnte. Die Skinhead-Thematik hatte mich schon immer interessiert, daher schlug ich ihm vor, Fotos für i-D zu machen. Und das tat er dann während der gesamten 80er Jahre. Ich arbeitete damals als europäischer Creative Director für Esprit, dessen Direktor, Doug Thompkins, von mir erwartete, dass ich meine gesamte Zeit für die Koordination zwischen Mailand, Düsseldorf, Paris, London und San Francisco einsetzte. Daher bat ich Nick, als geschäftsführender Bildredakteur mit Steve Male zusammenzuarbeiten, der Artdirector wurde, nachdem Moira Bogue zurück ans Royal College of Art gegangen war.

Steve und ich verständigten uns auf nahezu telepathische Weise. Seine unbekümmerte Einstellung zu Layoutfragen und sein gutes Auge für Illustration in Kombination mit Neil Edwards' trash-inspirierter Typografie und Nicks künstlerischem Feingefühl und Genie waren das Erfolgsrezept. Die redaktionelle Oberaufsicht ging vom Herausgeber auf den Assistenten über. In einer Periode in den späten 80 Jahren, als Mode nicht so interessierte, verlagerte John Godfrey den inhaltlichen Schwerpunkt der Zeitschrift auf Umweltpolitik und gesellschaftliche Themen.

In dieser Hinsicht entwickelte das kreative Zusammenspiel bei i-D ein Eigenleben. Ich vergleiche die i-D-Redaktion oft mit einer Küche. Zuerst schaffen wir einen Rahmen beziehungsweise „Topf", den wir mit kreativen Ideen füllen. Die Zutaten ändern sich von Ausgabe zu Ausgabe, und in den einzelnen Ausgaben beziehungsweise „Menüs" dominiert unter Umständen ein spezielles Thema. Die Autoren und Fotografen arbeiteten auf der Basis gegenseitigen Vertrauens. Sie wussten, dass sie Teil eines Experiments waren.

Steve Johnston beantwortete Anrufe in der Redaktion in seinem breiten schottischen Dialekt mit dem Satz: „i-D-Magazin, handgearbeitet von Metzgern." Es stimmt schon, die Autoren waren regelmäßig verzweifelt, wenn ihre Texte einfach passend gekürzt oder unleserlich gedruckt oder mit farbigem Marker hervorgehobene Stellen unkorrigiert gelassen wurden. Mitte der 80er hatten wir eine Phase, in der wir uns damit brüsteten „die Kunst der Unleserlichkeit perfektioniert" zu haben, und unseren Headlines Untertitel zufügten. Das Layout entstand häufig aus praktischem Experimentieren. Caryn wurde dann in den nächsten Copyshop geschickt, um Schriften und Bilder drei- oder viermal auf dem Kopierer zu vergrößern, was oft Fehler verursachte. Geldnot brachte zahllose Ideen hervor; beide Seiten des Papiers wurden benutzt und oft zweimal durch die Druckerpresse geschickt.

Zu Beginn der 90er wuchs das Prestige vieler der Fotografen aus i-D, so wie es Ende der 80er mit den Models gewesen war. Aber bei i-D ging es niemals um Geld, und wir waren nicht bereit, bestimmte Mitarbeiter als Mini-Berühmtheiten zu behandeln, egal welches Ansehen sie außerhalb des Magazins genossen. Glücklicherweise überwog das i-D-Ethos, und alle bewahrten weiterhin Teamgeist, besonders im Tausch gegen zusätzliche Seiten. Während der Arbeit an dem Buch *Catching The Moment* fiel mir auf, dass genau dieser Sinn für Teamarbeit sich wie ein roter Faden durch all meine Tätigkeiten der letzten 30 Jahre zieht. In meiner Laufbahn gibt es keine chronologische Abfolge, sie ist eher eine Serie parallel verlaufender kreativer Beziehungen mit einer Vielzahl talentierter Menschen.

Kommerziell nimmt i-D es heute mit dem Mainstream auf. Ich traf diese Entscheidung, als wir ins 18. Jahr gingen. Bei der Arbeit an *Catching The Moment* begriff ich, wie lächerlich es war, derart viele externe kommerzielle Jobs zu übernehmen, i-D aber weiterhin als nicht-kommerzielles Unternehmen zu behandeln. Heute widmen wir den Modeseiten so viel Platz im Heft wie möglich. Die kreative Mischung jeder einzelnen Nummer ist wie ein Spielfilm oder Fotoroman, der keine Handlung hat, nur ein zentrales Thema. Um die fotografische Aussagekraft hervorzuheben, ist das Layout noch weiter zurückgenommen. Fotografie teilt sich schneller mit, Worte stehen der globalen Kontaktaufnahme nur im Weg.

Während der letzten zwei Jahrzehnte ist das Magazin ganz natürlich gereift – mit einem offenen Auge für das Straßentheater der täglich wechselnden Mode. Wir haben unsere Zeitschrift nicht konzipiert, um Marketingplänen gerecht zu werden oder eine bestimmte Marktlücke zu füllen. Der Stil von i-D wird heute zum Vorbild genommen, weiterentwickelt oder einfach kopiert. Wir sind jetzt mit Talenten aus aller Welt vernetzt und wir sind heute Großmeister in der Welt visueller Befruchtung. Ein Strom ehemaliger Mitarbeiter arbeitet weiterhin für das Magazin. Wir haben zusehen können, wie Konkurrenten auf der Strecke blieben oder durch feindliche Übernahmen geschluckt wurden. Ich hätte nie gedacht, dass wir so lange überleben würden. Es war eine Qual, aus jeder Heftnummer nur eine Doppelseite auszuwählen, und oft war es fast unmöglich. Die Bilder, die nun folgen, sind oft ganz impulsiv ausgewählt oder als Hinweis auf einen speziellen Stil, mit dem wir damals vielleicht gerade experimentierten. Smile i-D sollte man als Wegmarke in der Zeit betrachten.

Ich bin ein Tagträumer, der immer nur einen Tag weit träumt. Ich will lediglich zeigen, dass es noch andere Tagträumer gibt.

**Terry Jones ist (falls es jemand noch nicht bemerkt hat) Creative Director und Chefredakteur von i-D.**

**Jusqu'ici, tout va bien** par Terry Jones

L'an 2000, sortie du n°200 et vingt années de i-D de plus. Regard en arrière, puis droit devant. La mise au clair des deux dernières décennies de i-D a généré bien plus qu'un livre d'histoire. Croisement entre le menu et le journal intime, Smile i-D retrace le parcours du magazine au-delà du vernis de la mode ordinaire. Dans ce livre, j'ai voulu présenter, au moins une fois, chacun des nos collaborateurs, faire une espèce de « Qui-est-qui ? » et « Que fait-il-maintenant ? ». Ceux dont nous avons perdu la trace reprendront contact, espérons-le, quand ils auront lu ces lignes. A revoir les 200 premiers numéros, je me souviens de ma réponse à la question « Pourquoi faire i-D ? ». J'avais alors répondu que « ça m'obligeait à garder les yeux ouverts ». i-D n'est pas le premier magazine pour lequel j'ai travaillé, ni même le premier que j'ai lancé. En 1980, à la sortie du premier numéro, je travaillais déjà pour des revues de mode depuis dix ans, et surtout j'avais passé de longues années (1972–77) à *Vogue* Londres, comme directeur artistique. Bien qu'ayant de bons amis dans cette industrie, vers 1976, je me suis senti fatigué de cet aspect répétitif de la mode. De plus, je trouvais les clubs de musique et la culture de la rue bien plus inspirants que les défilés de mannequins.

A cette époque, j'essayais de trouver de l'argent pour un projet de magazine nommé *Picture Wallpaper*. Je pensais naïvement pouvoir persuader *Vogue* de s'y intéresser. Le photographe Steve Johnston – qui venait de sortir des Beaux-Arts – est venu chez Vogue me montrer son press-book. Je lui ai dit que j'aimerais un reportage sur ce qui se passait à Kings Road. Trois mois plus tard, il m'a appelé et m'a dit qu'il avait des choses à me montrer, surtout des « portraits prise unique », pour limiter les coûts. Inspirées d'Irving Penn et d'August Sander, il s'agissait de représentations en pied, contre un mur blanchi à la chaux. Visiblement, ses images étaient influencées par la mode Punk. Mais Steve lui-même s'était transformé : il revenait chez *Vogue* avec les cheveux teints et une veste déchirée, retenue par des épingles de sûreté et enfilée par-dessus une chemise couverte de graffitis. Quand Beatrix Miller, la rédactrice de *Vogue*, est entrée, elle a vu ce qu'il y avait à voir et elle a oublié ce qu'elle était venue me demander. Ensuite, nous avons eu une chaude discussion sur les rapports entre Punks et mode. Mais on était en 1976 et les réactions de la Grande-Bretagne au mouvement Punk étaient fortement influencées par les articles débiles du *News Of The World*.

Chez Aurum Press, les éditeurs des « Maîtres de la photographie érotique », dont j'étais le directeur artistique, souhaitaient rencontrer Oliviero Toscani, avec qui j'avais étroitement collaboré chez *Vogue*. Au Portobello Hotel, nous avons été rejoints par Francis Grill, l'agent d'Oliviero, et ils m'ont persuadé de prendre la direction de leur premier livre. Ils avaient demandé à Caroline Baker, l'ex-styliste de *Nova*, de travailler sur une nouvelle campagne publicitaire pour Benetton. Nous étions tous un peu désabusés par les revues de mode et bien que Caroline l'ait été plus que nous tous, elle avait besoin de payer son emprunt immobilier. A part quelques articles pour *Vogue*, elle aidait son amie Vivienne Westwood à creuser des idées sur mode et bondage. Nous avons discuté de l'idée de faire grève pendant six mois, puis de revenir aux revues de mode commerciales, avec un espèce de manifeste.

En 1977, j'ai envoyé à *Vogue* mon préavis de départ, qui était officiellement d'un an. En juillet, je faisais face à un avenir incertain. J'avais signé un contrat avec Aurum Press pour la publication d'un livre en collaboration avec Steve Johnson. Le projet devait s'intituler « What The Fuck's Punk ? » (C'est quoi, ces putains de Punk ?), réponse aux innombrables questions posées lors de visites chez les imprimeurs italiens ou au magazine allemand *Sportswear*, auquel je participais. Comme je m'y attendais un peu, Aurum s'est lassé du projet. Ils avaient des difficultés à trouver un partenaire prêt à payer 10 000 pages de couverture revêtues de soie rose fluo. De mon côté, je souhaitais reproduire la peinture d'Al McDowell's, « Dumb Readers Eat Shit » (Les crétins lisent de la merde) et je savais que la distribution ne serait pas facile. Après une période difficile, j'ai accepté que le livre paraisse sous le titre « Not Another Punk Book » (Quoi ! encore un livre Punk ?), en 1978, deux ans avant le premier numéro de i-D.

L'année suivante, j'ai beaucoup voyagé comme conseiller du *Vogue* allemand et de Jesus Jeans à Paris, comme directeur artistique de Fiorucci Europe et pour travailler sur les premiers numéros du magazine *Donna* en Italie. Convaincu que la rue était un environnement bien plus créatif que les boutiques de mode, j'ai demandé à Steve Johnston des portraits en pied dans Kings Road, à paraître dans *Donna*. Mais Flavio Lucini, le rédacteur en chef, était peu réceptif à la notion de style de la rue et il doutait fortement de sa réussite commerciale. Il m'a conseillé d'attendre que *Donna*, ainsi que *Mondo U'Omo*, soient suffisamment sur rails, pour pouvoir concurrencer *Vogue Italia* et *L'Uomo Vogue*.

Après six mois chez *Donna*, j'ai rencontré Jolly, un ami de Caroline Baker, dont la société Better Badges imprimait des fanzines punks et j'ai voulu tenter mon idée de magazine « style de la rue ». J'avais déjà en tête le logo « i-D ». Il avait pris forme dans les différents griffonnages destinés à Informat Design, la société que j'avais fondée tout en étant chez *Vogue*. Jolly était prêt à imprimer 2 000 exemplaires à ses propres frais, et je lui en achèterais autant que je pourrais en vendre. Le format devait être en A4, à cause de sa machine à feuillet unique. J'ai insisté pour qu'il soit agrafé sur le petit côté, de sorte que la double page s'étale bien à plat, symbole et illustration du « street fashion ». Toutefois, ce format s'est avéré problématique, car les marchands de journaux refusaient de le stocker et se plaignaient des agrafes.

Tout en travaillant sur « Not Another Punk Book », je m'étais lié d'amitié avec Al McDowell, qui allait devenir un des principaux collaborateurs aux premiers numéros. Au début, i-D avait ses bureaux à la fois chez moi et dans son studio de Berwick Street, le Rockin' Russian, nom inspiré par une lettre se plaignant du T-shirt de Vivienne Westwood imprimé au dos du livre Punk. Le studio d'Al était essentiellement consacré à la musique. Son premier client était Rich Kids, figure de proue de cette mode de club, en pleine émergence, à Londres, avec Glen Mattlock, Midge Ure et Rusty Egan.

Perry Haines fut le premier rédacteur en chef/ciseleur de mots de i-D. Al et moi, nous nous occupions des clients et, très vite, on a senti qu'il nous fallait un « mondain » capable d'interpréter la scène contemporaine. Perry était arrivé à i-D, alors qu'on finissait le premier numéro. Son sens de l'entreprise en fit très vite le porte-parole du magazine. Gosse du Blitz et de Folkstone, Perry étudiait le journalisme de mode à St Martins. C'est lui qui avait inventé le terme New Romantics qui allait s'appliquer à des groupes comme Spandau Ballet et Duran Duran. Perry a investi toute son énergie à distribuer i-D, à partir du coffre de la Cadillac de Malcolm Garrett, sans parler des nuits blanches i-D à Londres, dans Meard Street, à s'occuper du look d'Adam Ant, ou des soirées avec Chris Sullivan, son associé au club, à fraterniser avec des habitués du Wag and Blitz tels Steve Strange, Rusty Egan et Boy George. A l'époque de la parution des premiers numéros, tout le réseau des Brit-styles, de Rocker à Rockabilly, de Psycho à Psychobilly, Punk, Goth ou Hippy, reçut un écho international.

Fanzine pour l'essentiel, centré autour d'un mini-questionnaire mêlé de vox-pop, i-D a adopté un style journalistique et utilisé les techniques de production les plus expérimentales. La période de gestation de trois mois entre chacun des premiers numéros a généré un paysage artistique sans précédent. Des photocollages ont été appliqués sur planches et imprimés en similigravure afin d'être reproduits chez Better Badges. Ces produits dérivés ont été, dés les débuts, essentiels. Nous avons créé des badges « Vu dans i-D » à distribuer aux gens photographiés dans la rue. Les T-shirts ont été une autre façon de promouvoir le magazine et d'améliorer nos revenus.

Même avec ces méthodes, le magazine était comme un puits sans fond où nous fonctionnions à perte. On vendait surtout dans les magasins de disques, les boutiques de mode et quelques kiosques à journaux. Mon travail de nuit, la production de i-D, est devenu encore plus aléatoire quand Better Badges a mis la clé sous la porte alors que la publication du n°3 n'était toujours pas financée et que la fabrication du n°4, avec sa couverture dorée, allait débuter. Mon travail salarié signifiait des semaines et des mois passés hors de Londres, à diriger les campagnes de Fiorucci à Milan ou à partir comme consultant à Francfort ou à Düsseldorf. Tricia, ma femme donnait des cours pour entretenir notre famille de deux jeunes enfants, et mon hobby pour ce magazine absorbait le peu de temps qui nous restait. Travaillant sans relâche jusqu'à l'aube, et gratuitement, nous avons été rejoints par des collaborateurs comme Max Vadukul, James Palmer, Ronnie Randall ou Thomas Degen. Mes enfants, Matthew et Kayt, ont fini par connaître toutes ces personnes étranges qui traversaient notre maison pour aller au grenier, où le magazine était conçu. Quand Moira Bogue, venue écrire sa thèse sur les fanzines, a fini par rester avec nous, faisant monter à bord le journaliste Alix Sharkey, il fut clair que la nouvelle s'était répandue. Tel un aimant, i-D, attirait les esprits créatifs et diversifiés.

Chaque page était comme une œuvre d'art et, dans sa troisième année, l'élaboration artistique de i-D se raffina à l'extrême. La machine à écrire à boule que nous utilisions commençait à se fatiguer et moi, j'avais besoin d'un ordinateur pour atteindre le look espéré. Au moment où le coût de cette réalisation s'avéra sans commune mesure avec le nombre limité de lecteurs, i-D put être sauvé par Fiorucci. En tant que directeur créateur européen de sa société, Fiorucci a conçu un projet pour Pannini et moi, qui consistait à concevoir cent autocollants. Grâce à ce budget, j'ai pu m'offrir mon premier ordinateur, un Apple IIE, avec manette de dessin. Même si cela se passait il y a dix-huit ans à peine, ce matériel dépassait nos compétences techniques. Par St Martins, j'ai entendu parler de Robin Derrick. Il savait s'en servir et nous a mis en contact avec Marion Moisy, qui est venue travailler avec nous. Le personnel de i-D s'agrandissait : Caryn Franklin, étudiant en graphisme, est venu y chercher du travail. Quand elle n'explorait pas les rues ou les clubs, elle travaillait pour Fiorucci. « Frankie » pour ses amis, elle nous a amené Steve Male. Puis on a vu arriver Kate Flett, notre réceptionniste-éditorialiste. Pendant une année, notre impression a été garantie, avec transmission directe à Fiorucci pour la distribution internationale.

Bien que toujours dans la mouvance fanzine, nous avions besoin de publicité, même si le format A4 et les couleurs fluo continuaient de choquer l'esprit des commerciaux. Tandis que le contrat Fiorucci touchait à sa fin, on avait toujours une grosse dette sur le dos, ce qui menaçait de nous faire fermer boutique. Je contactai Tony Elliott, l'éditeur du magazine *Time Out*. Peut-être à cause de ses relations avec les producteurs de *Oz* magazine, il était ouvert à l'idée des revues underground. Faisant un choix entre i-D et *Blitz* il a acheté 51 pour cent de nos parts et payé nos dettes. A partir du n°5, nous avons essentiellement utilisé des visages pour nos couvertures, et incorporé le clin d'œil du logo i-D, support identitaire de notre magazine. Pour le n°14, nous sommes passés du format paysage au portrait, afin d'attirer WHSmith, qui devenait notre principal diffuseur.

Le rôle de i-D, en tant que créateur d'images, dépassait de loin les conditions peu recommandables de sa fabrication, et nos portraits de couverture ont donné de l'impulsion à certaines des plus grandes vedettes de l'époque. La couverture avec Sade, en janvier 1984, a paru un an avant qu'elle n'obtienne son premier contrat de disque. Mark Lebon avait loué un studio pour tourner une pub Fiorucci quand on apprit que Madonna, qui lançait son premier album, passerait par Londres ce jour-là et pouvait s'arrêter pour se faire prendre le portrait. Savait-elle faire un clin d'œil ? En l'occurrence, son œil droit – celui que nous choisissions le plus souvent – se fatigua au bout de six clichés. Son œil gauche se révéla meilleur. Regardez bien le n°15 et vous verrez que le célèbre grain de beauté est à l'inverse. La plupart des Londoniens ont cru que le portrait était celui de Marilyn, le petit ami d'alors de Boy George, qui se faisait coiffer chez Antenna, où Michael Forbes, imposa ces dreadlocks blanches comme la mode du jour. Avec pour titre « The SexSense Issue », cette couverture montrant Madonna choqua WHSmiths. Son fond rose fluo détonnait avec leur nouveau design et ils protestèrent contre l'utilisation salace du mot « sex ». Sorry ! Dans le monde du commerce, on était toujours en 1984, à l'âge des ténèbres, où les hommes portant des kilts ou maquillés étaient mis au rang d'inquiétants pervers drogués. Les magazines montrant de tels individus étaient relégués en haut des étagères. Les tentatives menées par WHSmith pour marginaliser i-D ont eu l'effet inverse sur les dispensateurs de goût dans les médias. Les fans de i-D ont continué de se diriger vers les bureaux de Sherriff Road, afin d'offrir leur aide et leur créativité.

Au cours des années 80, les idées créatrices de i-D se sont répandues dans bien des sphères. Le magazine restait irrévérencieux et hostile au corporatisme, mais il devenait visiblement une source d'inspiration pour les industries de la mode et de la culture grand public. Nous avons créé des vidéos qui ont inspiré des graphismes pour la télévision et les clubs. Nous avons emporté i-D autour du monde, partout où nous avons été invités. De New York à Amsterdam, de Sydney à Reykjavik, nous nous sommes servi de la mode comme d'un immense jeu de communication pour exprimer ce que nous étions, qui nous aimions et où nous allions.

Les numéros continuaient de s'organiser autour d'un thème souvent abstrait, fréquemment frivole. Le contenu reflétait le goût et les fantasmes des participants, inspirant par son originalité une formidable loyauté chez tous ceux qui y étaient impliqués. Dans nos objectifs, nous nous sommes davantage livrés à la célébration qu'à la critique. Chaque fois que j'avais le sentiment que les gens étaient montrés comme des victimes ou que l'édito était trop provocateur, je le refusais pour rester non conforme à mes motivations quand j'avais lancé i-D. Nick Knight était venu dans mon studio quand il était encore étudiant. En voyant mon livre « Not Another Punk Book », il a pensé que je pourrais l'aider à publier son ouvrage sur les Skinheads. Les opinions politiques des Skins m'avaient toujours tracassé et je lui ai donc proposé de prendre des photos pour i-D. Il a poursuivi tout au long des années 80. En 1989, j'étais employé comme directeur artistique européen pour Esprit, et le directeur, Doug Thompkins, m'avait demandé de consacrer tout mon temps à la coordination entre Milan, Düsseldorf, Paris, Londres et San Francisco. J'ai alors proposé à Nick de prendre le poste de rédacteur photo tandis que Steve Male devenait directeur artistique, succédant à Moira Bogue qui retournait au Royal College of Art.

Steve et moi, nous communiquions de façon quasi télépathique. Son approche irrévérencieuse de l'illustration, dans sa conception et sa visualisation, alliée à la typographie « trash » de Neil Edwards, et à la sensibilité et la vision esthétiques de Nick, c'était ça notre formule gagnante. La responsabilité éditoriale passa du rédacteur en chef au sous-directeur. Vers la fin des années 80, quand la mode est devenue moins intéressante, John Godfrey a tourné le magazine vers les questions écologiques et sociales.

A ce moment-là, la dynamique créative de i-D s'est envolée de ses propres ailes. Je compare souvent le studio de i-D à une cuisine. Au début, on construit un cadre, le « pot », dans lequel la créativité va se touiller. A chaque numéro, les ingrédients varient, et le numéro, ou « menu », peut être influencé par tel ou tel thème.

Les créateurs de mots et d'images collaboraient sur la base de la confiance. Ils ont toujours su qu'ils faisaient partie d'une aventure. Steve Johnston répondait au téléphone du studio avec ce message cryptique, énoncé avec un fort accent écossais : « i-D magazine, fabriqué à la main par des bouchers. » Bien sûr, les auteurs se désespéraient quand leur texte était coupé, imprimé de façon illisible ou quand des excès de couleur étaient laissés non corrigés. Vers 1985, nous avons traversé une période où on se plaisait à affirmer qu'on avait « perfectionné l'art de l'illisibilité », et on imprimait les sous-titres avec nos titres. Souvent, les graphismes étaient conçus par expérimentation. Caryn était envoyé à la boutique de photocopie d'à côté pour agrandir de trois à quatre fois les textes et les images, ce qui suscitait pas mal d'erreurs: Le budget restreint générait toujours un foisonnement d'idées. Les deux faces du papier étaient utilisées et passaient souvent deux fois à l'impression.

**November 1993. The Hard Issue no122.**
**Cover star: Linda Evangelista. Photography by Juergen Teller, styling by Camilla Nickerson**
Why Will Smith is the rapper your parents would approve of/ PJ Harvey interviewed/ Right Said Fred/ Ultra Hard Females: shaved, pierced, tattooed/ Carleen Anderson/ Stella Tennant on Agnès B/ why this year's fashion will be hardcore/ Future Sound Of London/ the scooter revival/ fashion photography from Mark Alesky, Matthew R Lewis, Donald Milne and James Fry

**December 1993. The Smart Issue no123.**
**Cover star: Kate Moss. Photography by Corinne Day**
"I used to be desperate for tits!" This year's modelling sensation Kate Moss tells all/ rising star Helmut Lang interviewed/ Snoop Doggy Dogg introduced/ Malcolm McLaren/ Pulp's Oxfam glam/ Tim Roth/ the return of the suit/ six new American novelists/ electronic rock'n'roll/ Spring Summer '94 catwalk report

**January 1994. The Urgent Issue no124.**
**Cover star: Veronica Webb. Photography by Steven Klein, styling by Anna Cockburn**
Special Anti-Racist issue: includes Apache Indian, Credit To The Nation, Joe Casely-Hayford, Veronica Webb, Fun-Da-Mental/ despatches from the frontline: East End Asian youth get radical/ Tricky/ Underworld/ DJ Shadow/ Mr C/ Jodeci/ Joe Casely-Hayford on racism in fashion/ new black designers/ fashion photography by Juergen Teller, Peter Anderson

**February 1994. The Talent Issue no125.**
**Cover star: Justine Frischman. Photography by Juergen Teller**
Meet the rising stars of '94: Ewan McGregor, Elastica, Hussein Chalayan, Portishead, Gavin Turk, Irvine Welsh, Andy Cole, Jessica Ogden, James Lavelle, Underdog/ Ice Cube/ George Clinton/ Manic Street Preachers/ tacky glamour/ Prozac/ men in skirts/ José Padilla and the Café Del Mar/ Charlie Chuck/ fashion photography by Juergen Teller, Corrine Day

**March 1994. The Network Issue no126.**
**Cover star: Amber Valetta. Photography by Craig McDean, styling by Isbelle Peyrut**
The Beastie Boys interviewed/ Orbital in San Francisco/ why the internet is the future of communication/ '90s communes/ fresh fashion from Paris/ London's punk revival/ Richard Linklater interviewed/ new Dutch designers/ Gang Starr/ stilettos, minis and fashion's obsession with bad taste/ Goa/ fashion photography by Stefan Ruiz, Laurence Passera

**April 1994. The Sex Issue no127.**
**Cover star: Courtney Love. Photography by Juergen Teller**
The first Oasis interview/ what our generation really think about sex/ the A-Z of smut/ Courtney Love interviewed/ Jean Colonna's fashion sextravaganza/ rap's gender wars/ Manchester street style/ why everything you know about AIDS may be wrong/ Carl Craig/ Rachel Weisz/ fashion photography by Craig McDean

**May 1994. The Drugs Issue no128.**
**Cover star: Christy Turlington. Photography by Juergen Teller, styling by Camilla Nickerson**
Drugs special: the facts, the future, the forum/ Irvine Welsh meets Primal Scream/ Christy Turlington interviewed/ jungle: the last dance underground photographed by Wolfgang Tillmans/ sexy sportswear/ Junior Vasquez/ street basketball/ Felix Da Housekatt/ Spiral Tribe/ Wu-Tang Clan/ Glasgow under surveillance/ fashion photography by Mark Borthwick, Steven Klein

**June 1994. The Rock 'n' Roll Issue no129.**
**Cover star: Sonya Aurora Maden. Photography by Craig McDean**
Get your rocks off! Rock'n'roll special featuring Sonic Youth, Soundgarden, Underworld, Echobelly/ Costume Nationale/ Prague's rock underground/ how technology will kill the music business/ jazz greats unite against AIDS/ Kurt Cobain remembered/ Brussels and Frankfurt club reports/ World Cup fever/ fashion photography by David Sims, Anette Aurell, Mark Alesky

**July 1994. The Fun Issue no130.**
**Cover star: Kylie Minogue. Photography by Ellen von Unwerth, styling by Cathy Kasterine**
Kylie turns dance diva/ Erasure photographed by Wolfgang Tillmans/ Pedro Almodovar interviewed/ why the anti-roads protests just keep on growing/ Fuct/ L7/ ambient clubs/ Dave Clarke/ Gravediggaz/ summer denim special photographed by David Sims, Craig McDean, Anette Aurell, Mark Alesky, Mark Lebon, Stefan Ruiz, Juergen Teller

**August 1994. The US Issue no131.**
**Cover star: Kate Moss. Photography by Steven Klein, styling by Edward Enninful**
City heat: New York fashion special photographed by Steven Klein/ Timothy Leary interview/ hedonistic glamour from Marc Jacobs/ Broadway street style photographed by Christian Witkin/ Rage Against the Machine/ Nine Inch Nails/ Grateful Deadheads/ Nick Knight/ Joie Lee/ Laurie Anderson/ ambient California/ The Prodigy/ rollerblading/ Pavement

**September 1994. The Street Issue no132.**
**Photography by Ellen von Unwerth**
International street fashion special photographed by Wolfgang Tillmans, Juergen Teller, Shawn Mortensen, Steven Klein, Kayt Jones/ a night on the town with Björk/ the return of Public Enemy/ Russell Simmons on Phat Farm/ The Drum Club/ the future for football/ Massive Attack are back/ ethical shoplifting/ Rebel MC, paranoia in cyberspace/ David Sims first retrospective/ fashion photography by Mark Lebon

**October 1994. The Visionary Issue no133.**
**Cover stars: Brett Anderson and Stella Tennant. Photography by Jean-Baptiste Mondino, styling by Zoe Bedeaux**
Heart of darkness: Quentin Tarantino on Pulp Fiction/ Suede/ girls kick ass: Kim Gordon and America's new skatewear designers/ Luscious Jackson/ Liza Bruce/ Steve Albini/ hip hop heroine The Lady Of Rage/ branding/ street fashion forum/ the new mods/ Britain's art terrorists/ fashion photography by Craig McDean, Donald Christie, Phill Knott

**November 1994. The Underground Issue no134.**
**Cover star: Bridget Hall. Photography by Steven Klein, styling by Edward Enninful**
Sound of the underground music special: Mixmaster Morris, Richie Hawtin, Goldie/ why stylists are the most important people in fashion/ Hollywood outsider Gus Van Sant photographed by Wolfgang Tillmans/ Larry Clark/ Irene Jacob/ death and drugs in Scottish raves/ the BMX is back/ Franco Moschino remembered/ Autechre/ Danny Tenaglia/ Jeff Noon/ fashion photography by Mark Borthwick, Donald Milne

**December 1994. The Saturday Night Issue no135.**
**Cover star: Heather Small. Photography by Christian Witkin, styling by Christine Fortune**
Best of British: M People, Blur, The Prodigy/ Tricky, Roni Size and the new Bristol sound/ Linda Evangelista interviewed/ Dennis Cooper/ Bill Drummond and Zodiac Mindwarp/ British club fashion portfolio/ techno prodigy Daniel Pemberton/ lowrider bikes/ fashion photography by Mark Borthwick, Dana Lixemberg

**January 1995. The Future Issue no136.**
**Cover star: Kiara. Photography by Craig McDean, styling by Edward Enninful**
First-ever Supergrass interview/ film-makers Danny Boyle and Andrew McDonald/ Michael Young/ life in cyberspace special: The Black Dog, policing the internet, techno subversives, cyberfeminism/ A Guy Called Gerald/ Throwing Muses, Jon Pleased Wimmin/ what the future of music will sound like/ why you can't watch Natural Born Killers/ Todd Terry/ Spring Summer 1995 catwalk report/ fashion photography by Craig McDean, Jamil GS

**February 1995. The New Faces Issue no137.**
**Creative direction by Terry Jones**
The class of '95: talent special featuring Kate Winslet, Mary J Blige, Portishead, Daryl K, Arman van Helden, Tracey Feith, Chemical Brothers, Spiritualized, Menswear, Alex Szaszy, Mel and Sue, Alan Warner, Howie B, Blue Source, Pat McGrath, Kitty Boots, Moving Shadow, Dave Clarke, Shop, Michael Boadi

**March 1995. The Pin Ups Issue no138.**
**Cover star: Drew Barrymore. Photography by Ellen von Unwerth, styling by Joe McKenna**
Teen screams and wet dreams: Ant and Dec on the boy band phenomenon/ pretty on the inside: Drew Barrymore interviewed/ schoolgirl R&B superstar Aaliyah/ the A-Z of cybersex/ LTJ Bukem/ Deep Dish/ animal rights fights/ fashion photography by Terry Richardson, Donald Christie

**April 1995. The Tough Issue no139.**
**Cover star: Nicki Umberti. Photography by Terry Richardson, styling by Patti Wilson**
Irvine Welsh/ techno legend Carl Craig photographed by Wolfgang Tillmans/ Boy George takes it like a man/ The Orb/ screen star Julie Delphy/ Masters At Work/ Farley Jackmaster Funk, Cajmere, Felix Da Housekatt, Chez Damier and Chicago's house renaissance/ Toronto's jungle scene/ Money Mark/ fashion photography by Jamil GS, Terry Richardson, Platon

**May 1995. The Sharp Issue no140.**
**Cover star: Tank Girl. Illustration by Jamie Hewlett**
Tanked up: the cartoon goddess hits Hollywood/ The Shamen interviewed/ Happy Hardcore raves on/ why Sean 'Puffy' Combs is the face of future hip hop/ Barbara Tucker/ film-maker Kevin Smith/ graffiti legend Futura/ a backstage view of Milan fashion by Juergen Teller/ Roger Sanchez/ Bronx homegirl chic photographed by Jamil GS

**June 1995. The Subversive Issue no141.**
**Cover star: Shalom. Photography by Craig McDean, styling by Edward Enninful**
Supergrass, Menswear and indie's new boy babes/ are supermodels out of fashion?/ Ian Hart/ film-maker Mario van Peebles revives the Black Panthers/ introducing Britain's most exciting young DJs/ why The Verve are the best band in the world/ how aliens are taking over the world/ DJ Rap/ Derrick Carter/ fashion photography by Terry Richardson

**July 1995. The Boy's Own Issue no142.**
**Cover star: Nadja Auermann. Photography by Craig McDean, styling by Edward Enninful**
Nadja Auermann's blonde ambition/ on the blag with Shaun Ryder interviewed/ software crime and Britain's new hi-tech underworld/ jean genius: definitive denim directory/ Billie Ray Martin/ anti-car anarchy with Reclaim The Streets/ graffiti legend Eric Haze/ Roy Davis/ David Holmes/ breakdancing/ the Zapatista revolution in Mexico/ fashion photography by Craig McDean, Anette Aurell

**August 1995. The Most Wanted Issue no143.**
**Cover star: Greta. Photography by Ellen von Unwerth, styling by Patti Wilson**
New kid on the block: Chloé Sevigny interviewed/ how eco warriors kicked Shell's ass/ Bernard Butler/ how Camden became the new Seattle/ Cast/ battling Big Mac/ the indie boy model brigade/ L'il Louis/ literary terrorist Hakim Bey/ fashion photography by Donald Christie, Ellen von Unwerth

**September 1995. The Fun & Games Issue no144.**
**Cover star: PJ Harvey. Photography by Craig McDean, styling by Edward Enninful**
Wonder Woman! Polly Harvey pulls it off/ the Wu-Tang Clan interviewed/ computer hacker culture/ all-star football forum/ jungle hits Japan/ Wolfgang Tillmans shoots Gay Pride/ Kruder & Dorfmeister/ American rave scene report/ fashion photography by Donald Christie, Liz Johnson-Artur, Steven Klein

**October 1995. The Fifteenth Birthday Issue no145.**
**Creative direction by Terry Jones**
Celebrating 15 years of youth culture with a little help from our friends: Blur, Robbie Williams, Kate Moss, Jarvis Cocker, John Galliano, Supergrass, Elastica, Paul Weller, Damien Hirst, Anna Friel, Phil Daniels, Steve Coogan, Aphex Twin, Massive Attack, Leftfield, The Charlatans, Patrick Cox, The Prodigy, Bernard Sumner, Prince Naseem, Wolfgang Tillmans, Nick Knight, Alexander McQueen, Jake and Dinos Chapman, Jenny Saville, Oliver Peyton, Juergen Teller

**November 1995. The Real Issue no146.**
**Cover star: Emma Balfour. Photography by Craig McDean, styling by Edward Enninful**
Alexander McQueen, Clements Ribiero, Hussein Chalayan, Antonio Berardi, Jessica Ogden/ Brit fashion's brightest bite back/ is Goa Trance the new Acid House?/ why heroin is hip again/ Harmony Korine interviewed/ Menswear photographed by Craig McDean/ Ione Sky/ St Etienne/ PPQ/ Neal Stephenson/ the Criminal Justice clampdown/ new boy bands/ fashion photography by Terry Richardson

**December 1995. The Performance Issue no147.**
**Cover star: Stella Tennant. Photography by Craig McDean, styling by Edward Enninful**
New Art Riot: who are British art's next superstars? Marc Quinn, Chris Offili, Tracey Emin, Gillian Wearing, Sarah Lucas and Abigail Lane photographed by Wolfgang Tillmans/ The Charlatans/ Human League/ dance music radio/ New York clubscene update/ electronic tagging/ Ann Demeulemeester/ she's electric: future perfect make-up by Pat McGrath/ Vanessa Dauo/ fashion photography by Francesca Sorrenti, Donald Christie, Derrick Santini

**January 1996. The Wonderland Issue no148.**
**Cover star: Carolyn Murphy. Photography by Terry Richardson, styling by Edward Enninful**
Patsy Kensit, Andrew Macdonald and Brit cinema's new stars/ the Stone Roses on their thorny year/ maximum rock'n'roll: why American punk's not dead/ Coolio/ Green Day/ raving in Russia/ an anti-nuclear protestor's diary/ Nicolette/ Craig McDean, Terry Richardson and Mark Borthwick behind the scenes at the Spring Summer 1996 catwalk shows

**February 1996. The Survival Issue no149.**
**Cover star: Kate Moss. Photography by David Sims, styling by Anna Cockburn**
Irvine Welsh, Ewan McGregor and Jarvis Cocker on Trainspotting/ the artist known as Prince Naseem/ death warms up: Nick Cave interviewed/ Lou Reed/ LL Cool J/ Faith Evans/ looks can kill: dangerous beauty portfolio by David Sims, Ellen von Unwerth, Mario Sorrenti, Craig McDean, Terry Richardson, Paolo Roversi, Juergen Teller, Jeremy Murch, Mark Borthwick, Kent Baker

**March 1996. The Alternative Issue no150.**
**Cover star: Kristen McMenamy. Photography by Juergen Teller, styling by Edward Enninful**
The future of dance music forum: Orbital, Carl Cox, James Lavelle, Roger Sanchez, Mr C and DJ Rap/ The Prodigy go snowboarding/ The Pharcyde interviewed/ pagan protest/ Howie B/ Catatonia/ Bis/ Goa report/ the ultimate guide to trainersfashion photography by Christian Witkin, Kent Baker

**April 1996. The Fresh Issue no151.**
**Cover star: Lorraine Pascale. Photography by Craig McDean, styling by Edward Enninful**
Malcolm McLaren interviewed/ Ash, Northern Uproar and the new Britpop boys/ Faithless/ Father Ted/ DJ Hype/ raving In Bosnia with Desert Storm/ the UK's sonic youth/ drug-free clubs/ tribute bands/ the acid revival/ fashion photography by Anette Aurell, Carter Smith

**May 1996. The Sound Issue no152.**
**Cover star: Guinevere van Seenus. Photography by Mark Bothwick, styling by Jane How**
Larry Clark, Harmony Korine, Chloé Sevigny and Kids/ beer, beats and brothers in rhythm: Orbital, Leftfield, Underworld and the Chemical Brothers interviewed/ Everything But The Girl/ casualities of the chemical underground/ techno toys and the future of music making/ Photek/ Basement Jaxx/ Kula Shaker/ fashion photography by Jamil GS, Marl Borthwick, Derrick Santini

**June 1996. The Supernova Issue no153.**
**Cover star: Shirley Manson. Photography by Ellen von Unwerth, styling by Patti Wilson**
Who you callin' trash? Garbage interviewed/ Irvine Welsh on Ecstasy/ clubland's new pulp fiction/ Johnny Lee Miller and Brit cinema's new stars/ the real score with Scotland the Rave/ Dana Bryant/ Carl Cox/ Roni Size/ Gregg Aracki/ Busta Rhymes/ Jeff Mills/ fashion photography by Lorenzo Agius, Anette Aurell

**July 1996. The Love Life Issue no154.**
**Cover stars: Björk and Goldie. Photography by Lorenzo Agius**
Love bites: Björk and Goldie interviewed/ Shampoo/ Edinburgh life after Trainspotting/ John Galliano interviewed/ Britain's best new DJs/ Underworld/ Reclaim The Streets, London's eco terrorists/ summer menswear special/ video directors focus/ sunglasses

**August 1996. The High Summer Issue no155.**
**Cover star: Naomi Campbell. Photography by Paolo Roversi, styling by Paul Sinclaire**
Sex, success and supermodel excess: Naomi stripped bare/ The Fugees interviewed/ Julien MacDonald/ Tommy Hilfiger/ new Brit house/ Beth Orton/ Alex Reece/ the Northern Soul revival/ Neneh Cherry/ Brighton scene report/ Timothy Leary remembered/ definitive denim directory photographed by Elaine Constantine, Kevin Davies, Terry Richardson, Juergen Teller, Carter Smith, Steven Klein, Lorenzo Agius, Matt Jones, Kayt Jones, Mark Borthwick

**September 1996. The Pioneer Issue no156.**
**Cover star: Brett Anderson. Photography by Nick Knight**
"I'd like to dress the Queen Mother!" John Galliano interviewed/ Suede/ Eva Herzigova uncovered/ a clubber's guide to Berlin/ David Baddiel/ the new casual's kit/ Josh Wink/ Wolfgang Tillmans shoots Berlin Love Parade/ introducing Air and the French new wave/ fashion photography by Paolo Roversi, Ellen von Unwerth, Lorenzo Agius, Francesca Sorrenti

**October 1996. The Capital Issue no157.**
**Cover star: Iris Palmer. Photography by Max Vadukul**
London's fashion faces photographed by Max Vadukal/ Emily Watson/ Skunk Anansie/ Kula Shaker/ the K Foundation's art attack/ Terence McKenna interviewed/ DJ Shadow/ Robert Mapplethorpe retrospective/ direct action: how to take the law into your own hands/ London club portfolio/ jungle's new dark side

**November 1996. The Energised Issue no158.**
**Cover star: Angela Lindvall. Photography by Juergen Teller**
Juergen Teller's flash photography/ Chloé Sevigny/ Vincent Gallo/ Ocean Colour Scene/ head rush: sport's new hard line/ the legacy of Tupac/ bombing the bass in Bosnia/ Evan Dando on Oasis/ introducing New York's new cool/ A Guy Called Gerald/ fashion photography by Frederike Helwig, Max Vadukal, Kent Baker

**December 1996. The Undressed Issue no159.**
**Cover star: Jamie Rishar. Photography by Matt Jones, styling by John Scher**
Unzip! Kylie gets her kit off/ Wolfgang Tillman's candid camera/ Ellen von Unwerth gets down to it/ the backstage view at Gucci/ the final word on fashion and sex/ sexy photography portfolio/ real sex on the internet/ introducing the New Celibacy/ Basement Jaxx, Steve Coogan/ fashion photography by Steen Sunderland, Juergen Teller

**January 1997. The Escape Issue no160.**
**Cover star: Kelli. Photography by Stephane Sednaoui, styling by William Baker and Neil Rodgers**
The ultimate guide for escapists: snowboard special/ JG Ballard and David Cronenberg interviewed/ the A-Z of moral panics/ eco tourism/ Daft Punk/ London's Acid underground/ Sneaker Pimps/ would you die to save some trees?/ Douglas Coupland on life after Gen X/ Massimo Osti's new womenswear/ fashion photography by Carter Smith, Ellen Nolan

**February 1997. The Next Generation Issue no161.**
**Cover star: Annie Morton. Photography by Terry Richardson**
Who's looking good for '97? Special talent issue starring Travis, Emily Watson, Annie Morton, Antonio Berardi, The Propellerheads, Alek Wek, Peter Gray, Seraph, Cerys Mathews, Joelynian, Deep End, Hardy Blechman, James Jarvis, Naomi Filmer, Roland Mouret and a host of fresh faces who look likely for tomorrow

**March 1997. The New Beauty Issue no162.**
**Cover star: Sharleen Spiteri. Photography by Craig McDean, styling by Edward Enninful**
Pleasures of the flesh: Sophie Dahl by Nick Knight/ Miuccia Prada unzipped/ Sharleen Spiteri makes the year's best comeback/ No Doubt's Gwen Stefani interviewed/ Luscious Jackson/ Prince Naseem and the marketing of sportswear/ is our generation caught in the grip of pre-millennium tension?/ Jimi Tenor/ fashion photography by Terry Richardson, Jamil GS, Donald Christie, Julie Sleaford

**April 1997. The Outlook Issue no163.**
**Cover star: Courtney Love. Photography by Ellen von Unwerth, styling by Wendy Schecter**
Sex! Success! All-American excess! Courtney Love comes clean/ San Francisco hip hop special/ how did we become the chemical generation?/ Davide Sorrenti remembered/ Martin Margiela, Junya Watanabe and Hussein Chalayan/ the A-Z of politics/ snowboarding/ Michael Hutchence kicks off/ Finley Quaye/ Helmut Lang updates designer denim/ fashion photography by Donald Christie, Matt Jones

**May 1997. The Desirable Issue no164.**
**Cover star: Gaz Coombes. Photography by Lorenzo Agius, styling by Greg Faye and Justin Laurie**
"You could find me in a loony bin in a couple of years": Leonardo DiCaprio interviewed/ still young and free, it's Supergrass/ Erykah Badu/ Claire Danes/ cloning/ streaking/ Tracy Emin/ Notorious BIG remembered/ Shelly Fox/ men in make-up/ Autumn Winter London catwalk report/ fashion photography by Orion Best, Jo Lalli, Julie Sleaford, Terry Richardson, Wolfgang Tillmans

**June 1997. The Hot Issue no165.**
**Cover star: Susan Carmen. Photography by Craig McDean, styling by Edward Enninful**
The Wu-Tang Clan interviewed/ is cannabis good for your health?/ what Kate Winslet did next/ Paris is burning: French music and club scene special/ the essential guide to sportswear/ John Squire/ Sukia/ Brit boxing hopeful Ryan Rhodes/ Brand New Heavies/ fashion photography by Andrew Williams, Christian Witkin, Frederike Helwig, Bob Richardson

**July 1997. The Clean & Fresh Issue no166.**
**Cover star: Raina. Photography by Matt Jones, styling by Karl Plewka**
Martin Margiela exclusively interviewed/ Talvin Singh and the rise of the Asian underground/ The Prodigy and The Chemical Brothers take on America/ are you taking too many drugs?/ sexy furniture/ Seraph/ Cath Coffey/ clean and serene summer style photographed by Matt Jones, Michel Momy, Steven Klein, Julie Sleaford, Donna Francesca

**August 1997. The Obsession Issue no167.**
**Cover star: Kate Moss. Photography by Terry Richardson**
Why the Beastie Boys are fighting for Tibet's rights/ the new skin trade: make-up science/ the A-Z of obsession/ Pat McGrath on the barogua girls of Spanish Harlem/ all together now: collective culture/ Bobby Gillespie/ the pop/ art crossover/ introducing Tuff Jam and London's new garage sound/ fashion photography by Carter Smith, Chayo Mata, sixsixfour, Mark Mattock, Darryl Turner

**September 1997. The Next Issue no168.**
**Cover star: Kylie Minogue. Photography by Mark Mattock, styling by Fiona Dallenegra**
Burn the negatives, bury the tapes, banish the rumours: Miss Minogue seeks a fresh start/ marvel at the madness of U2's PopMart concept/ nasty girls: L'il Kim and Foxy Brown interviewed/ Mark Whitaker/ the world's top cults/ Attica Blues/ Brighton Love Parade/ Mike Myers/ fashion photography by Roberto D'Este, Julie Sleaford, Mark Borthwick, Orion Best, Ellen von Unwerth

**October 1997. The Killer Issue no169.**
**Cover star: Audrey. Photography by Juergen Teller, styling by Venetia Scott**
The first All Saints interview/ girl power: boxer Jane Couch/ British film's hottest line-up/ happy happy, joy joy: the truth about Prozac/ the A-Z of body manipulation/ Ryan Giggs interviewed/ Deborah Anderson/ Photek/ curator Aaron Rose/ fashion photography by Mark Mattock, Terry Richardson, Jeremy Murch, Francois Rotger

**November 1997. The Influential Issue no170.**
**Cover star: Mel B. Photography by Terry Richardson, styling by Patti Wilson**
Fifty Of The Most Influential Faces In British Fashion: Alexander McQueen, Alek Wek, Antonio Berardi, Ashley Heath, Beverley Streeter, Brian Dowling, Charlie Speed, Chris Bailey, Craig McDean, David Sims, Edward Enninful, Eugene Soulieman, Glen Lutchford, Goldie, Guido Paolo, Hussein Chanlayan, Isabella Blow, Jane How, Joan Bernstein, Jo McKenna, John Galliano, Joseph, Judy Blame, Juergen Teller, Karen Elson, Kate Monkton, Kate Moss, Katy Barker, Kim Sion, Lynette White, Mark Hare, Melanie Ward, Michael Coppelman, Naomi Campbell, Nick Knight, Nick Logan, Pat McGrath, Patrick Cox, Paul Sunman, Paul Smith, Phil Biker, Philip Treacy, Rankin, Richard Ashcroft, Robin Derrick, Simon Foxton, Sophie Dahl, Stella Tennant, Stephen Jones, Suzy Menkes, Terry Jones, Wendy Dagworthy

**December 1997. The Outrage Issue no171.**
**Cover star: Laura Foster. Photography by David Sims, styling by Edward Enninful**
Artrageous! Why out-grossing everybody else is the surest way to artworld success/ sour times: Portishead interviewed/ Johnny Depp's fear and loathing/ all-American hero Bruce Weber/ the A-Z of enviromental outrage/ Hussein Chalayan/ Spring Summer 1998 London catwalk report/ fashion photography by Donald Christie, Josh Jordan, Kayt Jones

**Jan/Feb 1998. The Active Issue no172.**
**Cover star: Naomi Campbell. Photography by Elfie Semotan, styling by Edward Enninful**
i-D's adrenaline special explores the pure pleasure of extreme sport/ Naomi Campbell's fabulous physique/ Stephen Sprouse and the art of hip pop/ Richard Linklater, Gregg Araki, Kevin Smith, Harmony Korine and new US cinema/ Beastie B Mike D gets instant karma/ Spring Summer 1998 Paris catwalk report/ fashion photography by Jeremy Murch, Anette Aurell, Eddie Monsoon, Matt Jones, Armin Linke

**March 1998. The Ego Issue no173.**
**Cover star: La Vera Chapel. Photography by Donald Graham**
Banish the stylists, the hairdressers, the make-up artists: the world's most beautiful women face the camera alone/ is our generation going through an identity crisis?/ Anna Friel interviewed/ dancehall queens: why the fashion world is waking up to the gold-plated glamour of London's garage girls/ Jake and Dinos Chapman/ fashion photography by Sarah Moon, Mario Sorrenti, Jason Evans, Jami GS

**April 1998. The World Class Issue no174.**
**Cover star: Alec Wek. Photography by Mark Mattock**
Meet the future! A talent special featuring Helmut Lang, Martin Margiela, Erin O'Conner, Dai Rees, Tristan Webber, Karen Elson, Andrew Groves, Rhys Ifans, Jeremy Scott, Shelly Fox, Campag Velocet, Fridge, Beth Winslet, Raf Simons, Boudicca, Sharon Dowsett, Aaron Rose, Self Service, Bless, Veronique Branquinho, Simon Costin, Kostas Murkidis, Eric Halley, 6876, Babylon Design, Amy Wesson, Stuart Shave

**May 1998. The Supernatural Issue no175.**
**Cover star: Kirsten Owen. Photography by Paolo Roversi, styling by Edward Enninful**
Heaven-sent: All Saints come clean/ Milan style special/ the adult entertainment industry uncovered/ Finley Quaye/ Anita Pallenberg and Marianne Faithful interviewed/ London Fashion Week report: after the hype and headlines have gone, is Britannia still making waves?/ Lo-Fi Allstars/ The Beta Band/ fashion photography by Juergen Teller, Paolo Roversi, Marcus Tomlinson

**June 1998. The Urban Issue no176.**
**Cover star: Maggie Rizer. Photography by Craig McDean, styling by Edward Enninful**
It's a mad, mad world: Tricky interviewed/ Juergen Teller and Terry Richardson's first photographic retrospectives/ skateboard special/ Henry Bond/ watch this space: inner city living/ the new comedy/ Ian McCulloch/ Les Rhythmes Digitales/ Arab Strap/ fashion photography by Craig McDean, Francois Rotger, Kayt Jones, Frederike Helwig, Terry Richardson

**July 1998. The Global Issue no177.**
**Cover star: Naomi Campbell. Photography by Jamil GS, styling by Jason Farrer**
Storm from the East: Tokyo style takes over the West/ disco 2000: the millennium countdown starts here/ Welsh dragon Cerys Mathews/ A Tribe Called Quest/ Jenny Saville and Glen Lutchford's contorted art/ has tourism gone too far?/ fashion photography by Mario Sorrenti, Kate Garner, Liz Johnson-Artur, Dana Lixemberg, Eddie Monsoon, Jeremy Murch, Pete Drinkell

**August 1998. The Very Blue Issue no178.**
**Cover star: Erin O'Connor. Photography by Juergen Teller**
Sado-masochism, crucified monkeys and dwarves... and they call this art? Photography's new ability to shock/ Chloé Sevigny interviewed/ Spiritualized/ Faithless/ Mix Master Mike/ Mr C/ fashion special: denim directory photographed by Carter Smith, Tesh, Eddie Monsoon, Stefan Ruiz, James Dimmock, Julie Sleaford, Mark Mattock, Jason Evans, Elfie Semotan, Jamil GS, Paul Wetherall, Francesca Sorrenti, Matt Jones, Orion Best, Marcus Tomlinson, Steen Sundland, Mario Sorrenti, Pete Drinkell, Kayt Jones, Craig McDean, Jeremy Murch, Michel Momy, Andres Serrano

**September 1998. The Adult Issue no179.**
**Cover star: Devon Aoki. Photography by Ellen von Unwerth, styling by Edward Enninful**
All grown up: Kate Moss, Alexander McQueen and James Lavelle interviewed/ stealing beauty: why fashion's new faces are all under age/ why sex on drugs is the new rock'n'roll/ highlights from 18 years of i-D/ glamour queen Donatella Versace interviewed/ Jarvis Cocker/ Canibus/ Placebo/ fashion photography by Ellen von Unwerth, Kayt Jones, Koto Bolofo, Jami GS

**October 1998. The Forward Issue no180.**
**Cover star: Shalom. Photography by Carter Smith, styling by Jane How**
Does the devil have the best tunes? Marilyn Manson interviewed/ special creative thinkers portfolio/ why photography has become the definitive art of the decade/ Jonathan Rhys Meyers/ Hollywood's new indie kids/ Issey Miyake interviewed/ why intelligence is the new black/ fashion and film fast-forward to the future/ David Bowie/ Bob Sinclair/ fashion photography by Carter Smith, Sophie Delaporte, Donald Christie, Bettina Komenda, Elfie Semotan

**November 1998. The Extravagant Issue no181.**
**Cover star: Alissa. Photography by Kayt Jones, styling by Merryn Leslie**
Jean Paul Gaultier gives a kick to couture/ Paris is revolting: young designers get ugly/ Johnny Depp and Terry Gilliam interviewed/ today's trash is tomorrow's collectors item: youth culture obsesives/ what luxury means to Paul Smith, Naomi Campbell, Air, Helmut Lang and Manolo Blahnik/ speed queen Donna Dee/ fashion photography by Duc Liao, Mark Lebon, Kayt Jones, Thelma Vilas Boas

**December 1998. The Cheeky Issue no182.**
**Cover star: Gisele. Photography by David Sims, styling by Anna Cockburn**
Gisele's first photos/ last of the famous international playboys: Adam Clayton interviewed/ Faith Evans/ self-abuse with Simon Costin/ is Spike Jonze the coolest film-maker in the whole galaxy?/ oh, you lot are naughty: provocative photographic portfolio/ Jeremy Scott's live bed show/ fashion photography by Matt Jones and Takay

**Jan/Feb 1999. The Emergency Issue no183.**
**Cover star: Mel C. Photography by Donald Christie, styling by Merryn Leslie**
Sporty Spice put through her paces/ there's more to Switzerland than skiing/ Glasgow, city of architecture/ dangerous sport/ kung fu monks/ Tom Sachs/ Spring Summer 1999 catwalk report/ why the future's not so bright for London Fashion Week/ Irvine Welsh interviewed/ fashion photography by Donald Milne, Tesh, Kayt Jones and Dmon Prunner

**March 1999. The Kinetic Issue no184.**
**Cover star: Amber Valetta. Photography by Richard Burbridge, styling by Edward Enninful**
Grand master flash: Yohji Yamamoto interviewed/ how far can Dutch designers push fashion?/ Softroom's designs for future times/ choreographer Pina Bausch/ Ian Brown/ DJ Spooky/ The Roots/ the A-Z of millennium movements/ why craft is making a fashion comeback/ fashion photography by Mario Sorrenti, Duc Liao, David LaChapelle, Eddie Monsoon, Elfie Semotan, Julie Sleaford, Takay, Mark Mattock

**April 1999. The Serious Fashion Issue no185.**
**Cover star: Colette. Photography by Richard Burbridge, styling by Edward Enninful**
Designers' secret weapons: the fashion muse/ there's more to Brazil than Gisele, you know/ brilliant Belgians, Veronique Branquinho and Raf Simons interviewed/ beauty conceptualism by Pat McGrath/ the future of textiles/ New Order's Bernard Sumner/ fashion photography by Richard Burbridge, Sophie Delaporte, Mark Lebon, Pete Drinkell, Dmon Prunner, Kayt Jones, Sølve Sundsbø and Juergen Teller

**May 1999. The Skin & Soul Issue no186.**
**Cover star: Heidi Klum. Photography by Max Vadukul, styling by Debbi Mason**
Size does matter: Sharleen Spiteri of Texas interviewed/ basketball on the Arizona Apache reservations/ the art world shows its wild side/ let there be flesh: special body portfolio/ Salman Rushdie on U2/ Gilbert and George/ catwalk soundtrack specialists The Two Freds/ Andrea Parker/ fashion photography by Richard Prince, Matt Jones, Max Vadukul, Duc Liao

**June 1999. The Intrepid Issue no187.**
**Cover star: Lisa Ratcliffe. Photography by Paolo Roversi, styling by Edward Enninful**
Karl Lagerfeld exclusively interviewed/ St Petersburg's young art elite lead Russia's cultural revolution/ no sex, drugs or rock'n'roll – how much fun can you have in Iran?/ how utility sportswear is shaping the future of fashion/ the return to fur/ make-up goes green/ Chemical Brothers/ fashion photography by Orion Best, Markus Jans, Hidemi Ogata, Frederike Helwig, Paolo Roversi, Kayt Jones

**July 1999. The Romance Issue no188.**
**Cover star: Bridget Hall. Photography by David Sims, styling by Anna Cockburn**
Scary monsters and super freaks: Chris Cunningham interviewed/ meet Natalie Portman, Darth Vader's wife/ prince of darkness Olivier Theyskens/ what's love got to do with it: couples who work together/ Moby comes out to play/ Vexed Generation and the bag that ate the world/ Gaz from Supergrass/ fashion photography by Mark Lebon, David Sims, Amber Rowlands, Matt Jones, Ellen Nolan, Paolo Roversi, Donald Christie

**August 1999. The Audible Issue no189.**
**Cover star: Oluchi. Photography by Richard Burbridge, styling by Edward Enninful**
Hedi Slimane interviewed/ why Shanghai will soon be the world's most exciting city/ why base jumping is the world's most dangerous sport/ the ghetto fabulous Hype Williams/ Autumn Winter catwalk report/ on the frontlines in Kosovo/ Pet Shop Boy Chris Lowe/ soul saviour MJ Cole/ fashion photography by Carmen Freudenthal, Jan-Willem Dikkers, Giasco Bertoli, Anette Aurell, Julie Sleaford and Larry Dunstan

**September 1999. The 1.9.99 Issue no190.**
**Cover star: Christy Turlington. Photography by Richard Burbridge, styling by Edward Enninful**
Putting the chic in rock chick: Ann Demeulemeester interviewed/ Air get psychedelic/ Tom Ford on Rush/ the new Berlin underground/ eccentric individualist and Tricky's twisted sister Zoe Bedeaux/ American graffiti/ Prince Naseem hits out/ space is the place: virtual communication/ fashion photography by Sølve Sundsbø, Takay, Tesh, Koto Bolofo, John Spinks, Larry Dunstan, Duc Liao, Paolo Roversi, Takashi Kumagai, Matteo Ferrari, Kent Baker and Matt Jones

**October 1999. The Elevator Issue no191.**
**Cover star: Guinevere. Photography by Craig McDean, styling by Edward Enninful**
Fashion's movers and shakers photographed in elevators: a special portfolio including Karl Lagerfeld, Vivienne Westwood, Puff Daddy, Marc Jacobs, Naomi Campbell, Manolo Blahnik, Stella McCartney, Hedi Slimane, Kylie, Helmut Lang, Trent Reznor, Raf Simons, Erin O'Connor, Alexander McQueen, Veronique Branquinho, Tricky, Harmony Korine, Nick Knight, Vanessa Beecroft, Hussein Chalayan, Jeremy Scott, Boudicca, Maison Martin Margiela, Bryan Ferry, Rhys Ifans, Neneh Cherry, Nick Knight, Peter Saville/ fashion photography by Duc Liao, Kayt Jones and Ellen von Unwerth

**November 1999. The Ideas Issue no192.**
**Cover star: Naomi Campbell. Photography by David LaChapelle, styling by Patti Wilson**
"I am so much smaller than I look on TV": Kylie interviews herself/ Viktor & Rolf/ Spike Lee/ Nick Knight and Peter Saville/ mad dogs and Englishmen: celebrating the eccentric/ who owns ideas?/ Future Systems/ the weird and wonderful world of David LaChapelle/ Damon Albarn comes of age/ Juergen Teller on his model life/ fashion photography by Anushka Blommers and Niels Schumm, Collier Schorr, Juergen Teller, Eddie Monsoon and Mario Sorrenti

**December 1999. The Wisdom Issue no193.**
**Cover star: Milla Jovovich. Photography by Matt Jones, styling by Cathy Dixon**
The Age of Reason: Buzz Aldrin, Patti Smith, John Lee Hooker, Louise Bourgeois and Quentin Crisp interviewed/ does wisdom come with age?/ Tibetan Lamas spread the word/ speed garage: sound of the underground special/ Nan Goldin documents a dark existence/ Milla Jovovich, martyred saint/ Barry White/ The Artful Dodger/ fashion photography by Takay, Bianca Pilet, Michel Momy, John Spinks, JB and Duc Liao

**Jan/Feb 2000. The Dynamic Issue no194.**
**Cover star: Chloé Sevigny**
Chloé Sevigny and Harmony Korine interviewed/ Hollywood and beyond: new Asian cinema/ women artists in New York/ the future's orange: menswear brightens up/ extreme sports portfolio from the X Games by photographer Craig McDean/ William Orbit/ clubbing in Cairo/ fashion photography by Willy Vanderperre, Davide Cernushi, Mark Mattock, Orion Best, Marcus Tomlinson, Kent Baker, Elfie Semotan and Matt Jones

**March 2000. The Drenched Issue no195.**
**Cover star: Gisele. Photography by Steven Klein, styling by Patti Wilson**
The gospel according to St Marc: Marc Jacobs interviewed/ Junya Watanabe, the shyest man in fashion/ tortured teen Fiona Apple/ Miguel Adrover/ Bernhard Wilhelm/ Roland Mouret/ anti-corporate protest in Seattle/ artful dodger Maurizio Cattelan/ Spring Summer 2000 catwalk report/ why bourgeois is no longer a dirty word/ Norman Cook/ Mike Leigh/ fashion photography by Sølve Sundsbø, David Slijper, Donald Christie, Michel Momy, Takay, Kayt Jones and Thomas Schenk

**April 2000. The Hotel Issue no196.**
**Cover star: L'il Kim. Photography by Steven Klein, styling by Patti Wilson**
"I just can't believe I'm a fashion icon!" Up close and personal with L'il Kim/ Giorgio Armani interviewed/ hotel, motel: fashion moments captured within four walls and featuring Larry Clark, Bijou Phillips, Clements Ribeiro, David LaChapelle, Visionaire, Badly Drawn Boy/ Alexander McQueen versus PETA/ how Ian Schrager invented the world's leading luxury brand/ Moloko return/ the Wu-Tang Clan's RZA/ fashion photography by Donald Milne, Duc Liao and David LaChapelle

**May 2000. The Aesthetic Issue no197.**
**Cover star: May Anderson. Photography by Richard Burbridge, styling by Edward Enninful**
How Stella McCartney gave Chloé back its cool/ Hussein Chalayan interviewed/ is Beirut the new Brixton?/ Brit Art's next generation/ show me the money, honey: introducing the New Baroque/ why Gilbert and George don't have good taste/ Body & Soul's Joe Claussell/ Noel Gallagher interviewed/ hip hop twisted sister Rah Digga/ fashion photography by Carmen Freudenthal and Ellen Verhagen, Jason Evans, Michel Momy, Christoph Sillem, John Spinks and Matt Jones

**June 2000. The Cruising Issue no198.**
**Cover star: Marlene. Photography by Matt Jones, styling by Jeremy Scott**
Scott of the anarchic: Jeremy Scott interviewed/ is Marc Newson the Tom Ford of furniture?/ make-up madness in Japan/ how Vanessa Beecroft makes art with several hundred sailors/ hell for leather with Mexico's urban cowboys/ Sophia Coppola/ David Gray/ fashion photography by Duc Liao, Matthias Vriens, David Slijper, Collier Schorr, Donald Christie and Murillo Meirelles

**July 2000. The Heartbeat Issue no199.**
**Cover star: Alek Wek. Photography by Richard Burbridge, styling by Edward Enninful**
"To you and me, sensationalism is not how other people see it": Alexander McQueen in conversation with Nick Knight/ John Galliano interviewed/ prints Charming with Eley Kishimoto/ why the AIDS story still isn't over/ from Creation to revelation with Alan McGee/ Badly Drawn Boy/ Jeremy Healy/ fashion photography by Richard Burbridge, Jason Evans, Marcus Mam, Takay, Thierry Le Gouès, David Lasnett and Terry Richardson

**August 2000. The 200 For 2000 Issue no200.**
**Creative direction by Terry Jones**
Celebrating our 200th issue by incorporating the best of the past with a wink towards the future, i-D asked 200 people who have contributed to its success and survival to nominate a young talent who will help inspire readers for the next twenty years. This issue showed you their choices. Contributors include Wolfgang Tillmans, Marc Jacobs, Raf Simons, Issey Miyake, Nick Knight, Paul Smith, Ron Arad, Hussein Chalayan, Judy Blame, Robin Derrick, Basement Jaxx, Ann Demeulemeester, Vanessa Beecroft, Veronique Branquinho, Neville Brody, James Lavelle, Dylan Jones, Ian Brown, Sharleen Spiteri, Alan McGee

If you have been a part of i-D's history and are not mentioned in these pages, please understand that this has been, and continues to be, a work in progress. The contents of this book will develop and expand through our website www.i-dmagazine.com and we would love you to be involved. Contact us at art@i-dmagazine.co.uk to let us know where you are and what you're doing now.

**So Far So Good** by Terry Jones

Year 2000, No. 200 and twenty i-D years on. Looking back and looking forward. Sorting through the last two decades of i-D has produced more than a history book. A cross between a menu and a diary, Smile i-D maps the magazine's journey beyond the veneer of regular fashion. In creating this book, I wanted to represent as many of our contributors as I could at least once: a sort of 'Who-was-who-and-what-are-they-doing-now'. Those we have lost track of will hopefully make contact when they read this. Retracing the first 200 issues, I recall my response to the question 'why do i-D?'. I replied that 'it forces me to keep my eyes open'.

i-D wasn't the first magazine I worked on, or even the first one I initiated. When it was first published in 1980, I had been working on fashion magazines for ten years, spending the longest time as Art Director of British *Vogue* from 1972-77. Although I had good friends who worked in the industry, by 1976 I had grown tired of fashion's repetitive nature and found music, clubs and street culture more inspiring than catwalk shows.

Around this time, I was trying to raise money for what would ostensibly be a magazine project called *Picture Wallpaper,* naively thinking I could persuade *Vogue* to take an interest. The photographer Steve Johnston came to *Vogue* House to show me his portfolio, having just left art school. I said that he should try to document what was happening on the Kings Road and he called me three months later, saying he had some pictures; mainly 'one-click-per-person' to keep costs down. Inspired by Irving Penn and August Sander, Steve's portraits were full-length, posed against a whitewashed wall. Not only were his images visibly influenced by punk, Steve himself was transformed, re-entering *Vogue's* offices with dyed hair and a ripped jacket, held together with safety pins, worn over a graffitied shirt. Beatrix Miller, *Vogue's* Editor, walked into my room, took one look and forgot what she was going to ask me. We later had a heated debate about punk's relevance to fashion, but this was 1976 and Britain's perception of punk was heavily reliant upon dumbed-down reports in the *News Of The World*.

Aurum Press, the publishers of the *Masters of Erotic Photography* book I was art directing, wanted to meet Oliviero Toscani, whom I had worked closely with at *Vogue*. Sitting down at the Portobello Hotel, we were joined by his agent, Francis Grill, and I was persuaded to put their first book together. They had asked the ex-*Nova* stylist Caroline Baker to work on a new advertising campaign for Benetton. We had all become disenchanted with the world of fashion magazines and though Caroline was seen as extreme, she needed work to pay her mortgage. Apart from a few editorial pages for *Vogue*, she was helping her friend Vivienne Westwood develop ideas about fashion and bondage. We discussed the idea of going on strike for six months then returning to the commercial fashion magazines with some kind of manifesto.

In 1977, I worked out my notice at *Vogue*, which formally took a year. That July, I faced an uncertain future. I had struck a deal with Aurum Press that they would publish a book collaboration with Steve Johnston. The project was initially entitled *What The Fuck's Punk?*, in response to countless questions on trips to the printers in Italy or to work on *Sportswear* magazine in Germany. Perhaps unsurprisingly, Aurum became disillusioned with the project. They had trouble finding a global partner for the cost of producing 10,000 fluorescent pink, silk-screened covers. My own desire to reproduce Al McDowell's painting *Dumb Readers Eat Shit* was also making distribution look unpromising. After a period of stalemate, I compromised and the book was published as *Not Another Punk Book* in 1978, two years before the first issue of i-D.

Within a year, I was travelling regularly as a consultant to German *Vogue*, to Jesus Jeans in Paris, as European Art Director of Fiorucci and working on the first issues of *Donna* magazine in Italy. I commissioned Steve Johnston to shoot head-to-toe portraits on the Kings Road for *Donna*, believing the street to be a vastly more creative environment than fashion stores. However the Editor, Flavio Lucini, was unreceptive to the notion of streetstyle and was sure it would never be commercially successful. He advised me to wait until he had established *Donna* and *Mondo U'Omo* so they could compete with Italian *Vogue* and *L'Uomo Vogue*.

After six months at *Donna*, I met a friend of Caroline Baker's called Jolly, whose company Better Badges printed punk fanzines; I wanted to finally try out my idea for a streetstyle magazine. 'i-D' was always in my mind as a logo; it originated out of doodles for Informat Design, the company I started while at *Vogue*. Jolly would print 2,000 copies at his own cost and I bought what I thought I could sell. The page format had to be A4 to fit his single sheet machine. I wanted the staples on the narrow edge, so that the double page opened out wide to symbolise the diversity of street fashion. This landscape shape proved to be problematic, however, as newsagents would refuse to stock this format and objected to the staples.

While working on *Not Another Punk Book*, I had become friends with Al McDowell, who became one of the main contributors to the first issues. i-D's early production was balanced between my own house and his Berwick Street studio called Rockin' Russian, the name inspired by a complaint letter about the Vivienne Westwood T-shirt that was printed on the back of the punk book. Al's own studio work was mainly for the music business. His first client was Rich Kids, featuring key figures of the emerging London club culture: Glen Mattlock, Midge Ure and Rusty Egan.

Perry Haines was the first Editor of i-D. Al and I had commercial clients as our day jobs and felt we needed a 'man about town' to interpret the contemporary scene. Perry joined i-D as we were completing the first issue and his entrepreneurial approach swiftly made him the mouthpiece of the magazine. An ex-Blitz kid from Folkstone, Perry was studying fashion journalism at St Martins and had been responsible for coining the 'New Romantic' title which would categorise bands like Spandau Ballet and Duran Duran. Perry invested 100% of his energy into distributing i-D from the boot of Malcolm Garrett's cadillac, not to mention hosting i-D nights in London's Meard Street, styling Adam Ant or socialising with fellow club host Chris Sullivan and Blitz club regulars Steve Strange, Rusty Egan and Boy George. At the time of the first few issues, the mesh of Brit-styles – rocker to rockabilly, psycho to psychobilly, punk, goth or hippy – went global.

Essentially a fanzine using a mini-questionnaire structure mixed with vox pop, i-D adopted a journalistic approach to style and embraced the most experimental production techniques. The three-month gestation period between each of the early issues of i-D created a unique landscape of artwork; photocollages were stuck onto boards and contact-printed through a halftone screen to make prints to be reproduced at Better Badges. i-D merchandise was central to the enterprise from the magazine's inception. We made 'As seen in i-D' badges to be given to people photographed on the street, and T-shirts were another method of promoting the magazine and raising revenue. Even so, paying for the magazine was like raiding the piggy bank. Most copies were sold through record stores, fashion shops and occasional newstands.

My night job producing i-D became more of a liability when Better Badges went out of business during issue 3, which was, as yet, unpaid for, with the gold-covered issue 4 about to go into production. My paid work meant weeks and months spent out of London, art directing Fiorucci campaigns in Milan or doing consultancies in Frankfurt or Düsseldorf. My wife Tricia was teaching to support our family of two small children, plus this magazine hobby that absorbed what little time we had left. Regularly working into the small hours for no fee, we were joined by contributors Max Vadukul, James Palmer, Ronnie Randall and Thomas Degen. My children, Matthew and Kayt, got to know all the weird people that passed through our house to the top floor, where the magazine was produced. When Moira Bogue came to write her thesis on fanzines and ended up staying, bringing journalist Alix Sharkey on board, it was clear the word was out. i-D, like a magnet, was attracting a diverse, creative force.

Each page was treated as an art piece and into its third year, i-D's artwork became more elaborate. The golfball typewriter we used for text was wearing out and I needed a computer to achieve the look we wanted. When the cost of the attention lavished on the magazine and the number of punters who bought it simply didn't add up, Fiorucci saved i-D. As I was his European Creative Director, he devised a project for me with Pannini to create 100 sticker designs. The budget meant that I could buy my first computer, an Apple IIE, with a drawing pad. Although this was just 18 years ago, this device was beyond our technical expertise. Through connections at St Martins, I learnt about Robin Derrick. He knew how to work it and put us in touch with Marion Moisy, who soon came to work with us. i-D's staff was expanding: Caryn Franklin, a graphics student, came seeking work. When she wasn't casting on the street or in clubs, she worked for Fiorucci. 'Frankie' to her friends, she roped in Steve Male to work for i-D and, later still, we were joined by receptionist-come-columnist Kate Flett. For a year, our print run was guaranteed, passing straight to Fiorucci for international distribution.

Although the fanzine ethos continued, we needed advertising and the wide A4 format and fluorescent colour schemes still jarred with the commercially-minded. By the end of the Fiorucci contract, we had still amassed a significant debt and we needed to find another partner. I approached the publisher of *Time Out* magazine, Tony Elliott. Perhaps owing to his involvement with the people who produced *Oz* magazine, he was supportive of underground magazine culture. Choosing between i-D and *Blitz* magazine, he bought a 51% share and paid off the debt. From issue 5, we mainly used faces on the cover, incorporating the wink from the i-D logo that was central to the magazine's identity. For issue 14, we changed from landscape format to portrait, in order to appeal to WHSmith, who took over as our main distributor.

i-D's role as an image-maker far exceeded the lo-fi circumstances of its production and cover portraits propelled some of the biggest stars of the period. Sade's January 1984 cover was published a year prior to landing her first record deal. Mark Lebon had booked a studio to shoot a Fiorucci advert when we heard that Madonna, who was launching her first album, would be in London that day and could stop by for a portrait. Could she wink? In the event, her right eye – the side we usually used – got tired after six clicks, but her left eye could do better. Look closely at issue 15 and you see that the famous mole is on the opposite side. Most Londoners thought the portrait was of Marilyn, Boy George's fabulous cohort, who had his hair done at Antenna, where Michael Forbes made those white dread hair extensions the style of the moment. Titled 'The SexSense Issue', the Madonna cover offended WHSmith. Its fluorescent pink background clashed with their newly designed look and they objected to the salacious use of the word 'sex'. Excuse us! In the world of commerce, this was still 1984, the dark ages, where men dressed in kilts or wearing make-up were classed alongside weird, drug-taking perverts. Magazines profiling such types were relegated to the top shelf. WHSmiths' attempts to marginalise i-D had the opposite effect among the arbiters of media taste. Fans of i-D continued to find their way to the offices in Sherriff Road to offer their creative help.

i-D's creativity had spilled into many arenas during the Eighties. The magazine remained irreverent and resistant to corporatism, but it was clearly becoming an inspiration to the mainstream fashion and culture industries. We made videos that inspired graphics for television and clubs. We took the i-D World Tour to anywhere we were invited. From New York to Amsterdam, Sydney to Reykjavik, we used fashion as one giant communication game to express who we were, what we liked and where we were going.

Issues continued to be based around a theme; often abstract, frequently frivolous. Content reflected the tastes and fantasies of the contributors, its originality inspiring fierce loyalty from all involved. We were more celebratory than critical in our objectives. The moment I felt people were represented as victims or that the editorial was too smart-arse, it was rejected for not fitting with the reasons I started i-D. Nick Knight came to my studio when he was still a student. Having seen *Not Another Punk Book*, he thought that I might know how to publish his book on skinheads. Skinhead politics always bothered me so I suggested that he start taking photos for i-D instead. He continued to do so throughout the Eighties. By 1989, I was working as European Creative Director for Esprit, whose Director, Doug Thompkins, asked me to dedicate 100% of my time to co-ordinating between Milan, Düsseldorf, Paris, London and San Francisco. I asked Nick to be caretaker Picture Editor and work with Steve Male, who became Art Director when Moira Bogue returned to the Royal College of Art.

Steve and I had an almost telepathic system of communication. His irreverent approach to design and eye for illustration, combined with Neil Edwards' trash-inspired typography and Nick's aesthetic sensibility and vision, was a winning formula. Editorial stewardship went from Editor to Assistant. During a period in the late Eighties when fashion was less interesting, John Godfrey took the magazine's ideology into environmental politics and social issues.

In this sense, the creative dynamic of i-D took on a life of its own. I often compare the i-D studio to a kitchen. At the start, we built a framework, or 'pot', into which creativity would be poured. Ingredients would vary with each issue, and the issue, or 'menu', might be influenced by a specific theme. The creators of the words and pictures contributed on the basis of trust. They knew they were part of an experiment. Steve Johnston regularly answered our studio phone with a cryptic announcement, in his broad Scottish accent: 'i-D magazine, hand-made by butchers'. Certainly, writers would despair when text was cut to fit, or printed illegibly when colour mark-ups were left uncorrected. We had a period in the mid-Eighties where we liked to say that we 'perfected the art of illegibility', and printed subtitles with our headlines. Often, graphics were conceived through practical experimentation. Caryn would be sent to the local copyshop to enlarge type and images three to four times on the photocopier, often leading to mistakes. Lack of budget generated countless ideas; both sides of the paper were used and run through the printing machine twice.

At the beginning of the Nineties, many of the photographers working for i-D were gaining status, as models had done at the end of the Eighties. i-D was never about money, and we were unwilling to treat certain types of contributors as mini-celebrities, irrespective of their standing outside the magazine. Fortunately, the i-D ethos prevailed and everyone continued to behave like team members, particularly in exchange for extra pages. When I was putting together the book, *Catching The Moment*, it occurred to me that the thread that runs through all my work over the past 30 years is this sense of collaboration. Web-like, there is no chronological sequence to my career; rather a concurrent series of creative relationships with many talented people.

Commercially, today i-D competes with the mainstream. I made that decision as we approached our eighteenth year. While doing *Catching The Moment*, I realised it was ridiculous to be doing so much external commercial work and yet not treat i-D as a commercial enterprise. Now, we devote as much space as possible to our fashion pages. The creative mix of each issue is like a movie or visual novel without a story line, just a central theme. To emphasise photographic imagery, the graphics are more minimal. Photography is the faster communicator and words get in the way of global contact.

Over the past two decades, the magazine has matured organically – the eye open to the street theatre of daily fashion change. We have not been manufactured to fit a marketing plan or fill a market niche. i-D style is now followed, interpreted or downright copied. We've spread into the net with global talent, now grandmasters in the world of visual dissemination. A stream of ex-assistants continue to work for the magazine. We have seen competitors die by the roadside or get eaten up in corporate buy-outs. I never thought we could survive so long. Choosing a single spread from each issue has been excruciating, often nearly impossible. The images that follow were often selected on impulse, or as indications of a graphic style we might have been playing with at the time. Smile i-D should be seen as a marker in time.

I'm a daydreamer dreaming a day at a time. I just want to show that there are other daydreamers too.

**Terry Jones is, of course, the Creative Director and Editor-In-Chief of i-D**

"My ambition is to have a white Cadillac"

**Zoff, unemployed, from Birkenhead**

# 1980

August. The i-D One Issue no1. Creative direction by Terry Jones

November. The Star Issue no2. Creative direction by Terry Jones

November. The Star Issue no2. Creative direction by Terry Jones. Back cover

"We believe in the individual, in variety. Individuals produce variety, variety provides real solutions"

**Arkent, club collective, no2**

3

COLIN: Mode - Colin is wearing black pleated trousers which he made himself. The cardigan is from Marks and Spencers, £9.99 and the shoes from Axiom in the Kings Road, £5.99. Fave music - Siouxsie and the Banshees and David Bowie.

Wi

STRAIGI

Photographed by Steve Johnston

Anonymous girl with spiky hair-do.

IC2

1⊲

YASMIN: Mode- Leather J'kt,300 from Italy.Trousers ,£54.00 from Harrods "Way In'(Shoul-dn't it be called 'Way Out'?E.d.).Sloane Ranger goggles/Sunglasses,£12.00 from Paris-where else.Fav Music:Jazz n;Steve Carr.Yasmin is studying knitwear at Middlesex Poly' and makes Pizzas for a part time job.(Must make a pile out a' Pizzas.E.d.)

PATRICE: Mode-J'kt n"T'rs £1.00 from a Jumble Sale,set of with Luftwaffe boots n'trilby. (Full marks for ingenuity.E.d.)Fav" Music PIL,Reggae n" Rock n'Roll.At present Patrice is looking for a job........

"Wearing my suit-It is your character.There is a limit-over your shoulder.Everyone loves you until they know you.A few aerosols may champion a stranger.Standing around all the right people)..."Suit" on Metal Box album by PIL.

Cerith.Aged 21,graduated this Summer from St Martins School of Art with a Sculpture B.A.Hons Degree.Work n' play both mean Film-Making as its his premiere passion.Fav' films irclude:Triumph of the Will-Leni Reifenstahl.Visconti's The Damned and all Jean-Luc Godard's films. Catch that 'Taxi Driver"come Robert de Niro hairdo.........

Lee.Aged I9,is a Fashion Design student.He recently shaved of all his peroxide blonde locks leaving a Yul Bryner gloss on top.Fav'music includes:Yellow Magic Orchestra,Frank Sinatra, Millie Jackson and James White and the Blacks.............

Photographed by Peter Ashworth

"London Bridge Is Falling Down"

MEL and JOSS: Mode - Mel found everything she's wearing at jumble sales except the Dr Marten boots that cost £=4 down Petticoat Lane. Unemployed, she lends a hand in her mother's pub. Fave music reggae and two-tone, on skinheads she says: "First time round, in the late '60)'s it was style and music that was all important. The skins I know these days are more interested in trouble when they get together.

Mode - Joss bought her jacket in Portobello Rd. Market, her Mum added the studs, including JOSS studded across the back for easy I.D.

MEL:- Mode-"I've been in this J'kt for 10 y"rs.I had loads more badges,half get nicked a- nd half were lost in fights,but there yer go.The 1½ badge means all bikers have at least 1½ of bad in them,its our law."said he.His leather also boasts an Eddie Cochran badge-he loves rock n'roll almost as much as his 750cc Triumph Sonnaville......

Wilf,sporting the Alpine Bondage Look is an expert on squatting.His primary occupation is enjoying himself full stop......................

Photographed by Peter Ashworth

MEANWHILE - ON THE OTHER SIDE OF TOWN.

Coco wears a sad face during his working week. Urbanisation produced a mass of faceless people, like clowns with two faces - the happy and the sad.
Everything is labelled, people are categorised for the sake of efficiency, pandering to machines originally created to serve.
Coco has been rehoused - to his detriment. No longer has he the security that he belongs. He has no territory, living as he does, in Flat B, Floor C, S.E.7. He used to find his identity at football grounds, chanting for his team, challeng- ing the world to fight. He could read about himself and his team in the papers. Sadly the other side he battled with in uniform and colours were like him - clowns, whether from Manchester or Birmingham, they shared the same class and environment, watched the same programmes on television, read the same schoolbooks and searched, like him, for an identity. Coco was his own worst enemy.
So it came to pass that Coco left school and Stream C, to find himself in Factory D - a job with no future, a past to forget. Coco earns wages; he can realise his dreams, buy the goodies, share the fantasies that television has tormented and goaded him with as he's grown up'.
Coco is an artist. He's performed all his life, every moment a living sculpture. The grafitti on the school wall is his poetry but he's not aware of it.
Like the other clowns he is labelled factory fodder and that's how he's treated. He feels like a machine - consuming life and re-arranging the waste.
In his 'free' time, Coco applies the make-up and wears his costume out. Taking to the stage to perform the latest dance, a special walk. Coco drinks: it offers Dutch courage, then he's no longer self concious. Coco poses, cigarette in hand (the fag occupies hands that must not touch or talk for him).

In the Disco's darkness, music floods his mind,
Coco's happy for a little while.

**11•80**

"I like all sorts of people. If someone
dresses peculiar, I just ask myself 'what do
they look like on skates?'"

**Jay, roller disco dancer, no1**

RUSTY:Mode-drummer with 'Visage'(formerly with The Rich Kids and the Skids).
The navy blue trad-blazer with regimental badge-cost a quid from a second hand
shop.School tie-50p,second hand.Bowling trousers-P.X.Covent Garden cost £20.00
Yachting pumps-£2.50 from a sports shop.Fave music-Eno,Jean Michel Jarre,Adven-
ture-Television."I like music that whisks you away to special places".

Photographed by Steve Johnston.

Mario:Mode-Fish n' chips "All sorts eat them.I like meeting the customer.I don't
like competition."Marios Fish n'chips,Black Bull R'd,Folkstone Kent

Photographed by Simon Brown.

"The trousers I'm wearing are filthy. It's because I lie under my bike and get oil drips. Then I go into the pub and they ask me to leave but I think that's wonderful. Anyone can walk into a pub and get served"

**Peter, designer, no1**

11

Photographed by Thomas Degen.

SCRUBBER: Mode—"I can't think what I wanna do—I'm thick:(be a badge pinner for Better Badges)". Hair-pink,black and white,"my mate Sarah cuts it for me and I dye it myself. When I wash it,it takes 30 mins-backcombing and hairspray.Boots-Firm Hold." Leather Jacket £10 "off a mate". Ramones T-shirt—one of my fave bands, (black cause it doesn't show the dirt.)"Bullet belt from Fans,Charing-cross Rd 11 quid. Leather skirt-Rock Arts-Old Brompton St £20. Fishnet stockings Martin Fords-Holloway Rd cost 99p. Daygio stripped socks-Fans 99p. Monkey Boots,Wood Green Mkt £6.99. Fave music-Crass,Killing Joke,Angelic Upstarks and The Damned. "I liked The Moonlight Club—but punks are banned now. I like the anarchy of my Job Tee Hee. I dislike rain when I'm hitching-and it always does (n'my hair goes flat.)

WENDY:Mode-P.A to Roxy Music management.Trousers-Kensington Market £2.Shirt-£1 second hand.Shoes-£5 Portobello Rd.Coat-£12 from the Kings Road.Fave music-Daf,Killing Joke,Cabaret Voltaire.Dislikes-sweaty gigs,dates as in the fruit, and Skinheads.

# 1980

Photography by James Palmer. Page 29

August. The i-D One Issue no1. Photography by Steve Johnston. Page 30-31, 32-33

November. The Star Issue no2. Photography by Steve Johnston, Simon Brown, Thomas Degen. Page 36-37

Left to right. Page 38-39

August. The i-D One Issue no1. Photography by Brian Griffin

August. The i-D One Issue no1. Photography by Steve Johnston

August. The i-D One Issue no1. Photography by Peter Ashworth

August. The i-D One Issue no1. Photography by Steve Johnston

November. The Star Issue no2. Photography by Peter Ashworth

November. The Star Issue no2. Photography by Paul McKay, Simon Brown, Thomas Degen

"i-D counts more than fashion. Make a statement, originate don't imitate, find your own ID"

**Caroline Baker, stylist, no1**

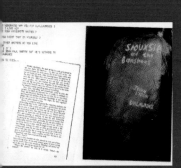

# 1981

"I think I'm the best thing that's ever happened to the world"

**Boy George, singer, no3**

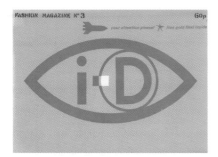

FASHION MAGAZINE No. 3   60p   PLUS FREE 'FLEXI DISC'

PRINTED BY AND AVAILABLE FROM BETTER BADGES
286 PORTOBELLO RD, LONDON W10.     60p plus 25p P & P.
ALSO AVAILABLE FROM I.D HQ 71 SHERRIFF RD.
LONDON NW6 2AS

PUBLISHED BY T J INFORMAT DESIGN LTD.

# VIBES

Photographed by Simon Brown

Vibes are a breath of fresh ideas in the air,forever changing. Contemporary clues to tomorrows trends.So whats new? Youth for ever 'rebels searching for a cause' are alien,bright and bold. The media mentality takes defiant gestures and dilutes them to taste -selling products.I-D promotes people not packages.Nothings in or out,all modes co-exist in an age of eclectic taste.I-D serves only to communicate new thinking, reporting from the source,sharing the buzz.
No nonsense news-a third eye.

*This is another story that children have always loved. The younger ones will enjoy seeing the full-colour illustrations and having the story read to them. The older children who need reading practice will be encouraged by the clear type and relatively simple text.*

Puss was delighted with the boots. He pulled them on and strutted up and down in front of his master. He looked so proud of himself that the miller's son could not help but laugh at him.

From that time onwards, the miller's son always called him Puss in Boots.

Then Puss slung the bag over his shoulder and went off to the garden. There he gathered some fresh lettuce leaves which he put in his bag.

RICHARD:Mode:'Saxon'side tapestry shirt he designed himself (St Martins fashion student that he is).Studded belt-Rock Art,old Compton St,scarves-Liberties; assorted tassles-Peter Jones;boots-Johnsons(£30;hair by Ricci Burns."I love me, dope,sex and power.I don't like poverty,fish or premature ejaculations.

A tenugui worn by men ready for activity | Worn by men travelers

Worn by a young dandy | Worn by women ready for travel or work

Worn by robbers or furtive persons | Worn as a head scarf

## iDentification iDentikit

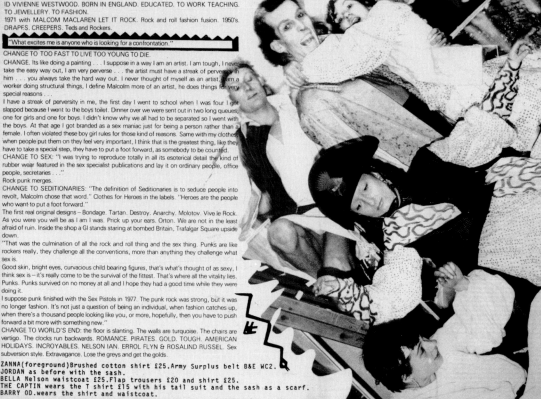

ID VIVIENNE WESTWOOD. BORN IN ENGLAND. EDUCATED. TO WORK TEACHING. TO JEWELLERY. TO FASHION.
1971 with MALCOM MACLAREN LET IT ROCK. Rock and roll fashion fusion. 1950's. DRAPES. CREEPERS. Teds and Rockers.

"What excites me is anyone who is looking for a confrontation."

CHANGE TO TOO FAST TO LIVE TOO YOUNG TO DIE.

CHANGE. Its like doing a painting . . . I suppose in a way I am an artist. I am tough, I never take the easy way out, I am very perverse . . . the artist must have a streak of perversity in him . . . you always take the hard way out. I never thought of myself as an artist, I am a worker doing structural things, I define Malcolm more of an artist, he does things for very special reasons . . .

I have a streak of perversity in me, the first day I went to school when I was four I got slapped because I went to the boys toilet. Dinner over we were sent out in two long queues, one for girls and one for boys. I didn't know why we all had to be separated so I went with the boys. At that age I got branded as a sex maniac just for being a person rather than a female. I often violated these boy girl rules for those kind of reasons. Same with my clothes, when people put them on they feel very important, I think that is the greatest thing, like they have to take a special step, they have to put a foot forward, as somebody to be counted.

CHANGE TO SEX: "I was trying to reproduce totally in all its esoterical detail the kind of rubber wear featured in the sex specialist publications and lay it on ordinary people, office people, secretaries . . ."

Rock punk merges.

CHANGE TO SEDITIONARIES: "The definition of Seditionaries is to seduce people into revolt, Malcolm chose that word." Clothes for Heroes in the labels. "Heroes are the people who want to put a foot forward."

The first real original designs – Bondage. Tartan. Destroy. Anarchy. Molotov. Vive le Rock. As you were you will be as I was. Prick up your ears. Orton. We are not in the least afraid of ruin. Inside the shop a GI stands staring at bombed Britain, Trafalgar Square upside down.

"That was the culmination of all the rock and roll thing and the sex thing. Punks are like rockers really, they challenge all the conventions, more than anything they challenge what sex is.

Good skin, bright eyes, curvacious child bearing figures, that's what's thought of as sexy, I think sex is – it's really come to be the survival of the fittest. That's where all the vitality lies. Punks. Punks survived on no money at all and I hope they had a good time while they were doing it.

I suppose punk finished with the Sex Pistols in 1977. The punk rock was strong, but it was no longer fashion. It's not just a question of being an individual, when fashion catches up, when there's a thousand people looking like you, or more, hopefully, then you have to push forward a bit more with something new."

CHANGE TO WORLD'S END: the floor is slanting. The walls are turquoise. The chairs are vertigo. The clocks run backwards. ROMANCE. PIRATES. GOLD. TOUGH. AMERICAN HOLIDAYS. INCROYABLES. NELSON IAN. ERROL FLYN & ROSALIND RUSSEL. Sex subversion style. Extravagance. Lose the greys and get the golds.

ZANNA(foreground)Brushed cotton shirt £25.Army Surplus belt B&E WC2. JORDAN as before with the sash.
BELLA Nelson waistcoat £25.Flap trousers £20 and shirt £25.
THE CAPTIN wears the T shirt £15 with his tail suit and the sash as a scarf. BARRY OD.wears the shirt and waistcoat.

JUDITH:Mode:Embroidered waistcoat brought at a theatre costumes sale,the dress she made herself,the shawl was found. 1976 love 'ring-junk' shop in Leeds,love beads Indian craft shop,hates hats;like John Lennon losing weight,drink n'drugs going on Safaries (avec SW).Skinny men,I don't like slimming,she,my woman or garlic. Judith is a F'designer for the 80's selling her clothes through Axiom or ring for an appointment 373-0699,ask for flat 7.

ROBERT:Mode:Hat-Claude Montana £?;scarf-"I made it";top'n'trousers-"me again",shoes-£25 from Gamba dance shoe shop,Old Compton St Soho:i'm into heavy metal and Motor head,ACDC,Led Zeplin,Jethro Tull n'Earth Xitt,adore Gin n'Tonic,money and cigarette I hate squatting and chapatis.

MICHAEL. Mode. Hair styled by Scarlett (Antenna) and Kenny (Elle), the 'two piece suit' was very cheap from an ordinary Indian crafts shop. Embroidered slippers:- borrowed. Jewellery - gifts. Girl like big breasted women in tight dresses; alcohol and lots of it. Don't like being fat and serious. "like the Costanbu pub. from £20 Golden Greats of the 50s plus crisp.I don't like the so called Potters pub, boring nights out n' squats. Oh yeh I also like dark haired vegetarians."

"You can't go out to have fun if you look drab. I didn't feel that I wanted to go out so I had to design these clothes really. I don't think that there is a great big gap between these clothes and punk rock.
One of the best things that is going to happen, which is what happed with the punk rock thing, is when people come into the shop and its the way they put the clothes together themselves and how they use them that is interesting. Like punk rock, it's really fantastic how beyond what you do people can go — beyond my wildest dreams."

photographed by Thomas Degen.

JORDON in full suit yellow brocade jacket £25 sleves £70.819 cotton shift £25 and the trousers £35.

STRAIGHT-UP

DORINE.At the club 80's.Mode:Desigs her own clothes and styles her hair.Likes-Legends and the Embassy.Fave band-The Barracudas.

STEWART.Mode:Oxfam tuxedo,homemade trousers,shoes from X clothes.Likes-50's music and "dressing silly".Dislikes-gots and Country and Western.

KATY.Mode:"The youngest poseur in town".Clothes made by dad Dislikes-Mr Ken,Kermit,jelly mice,bath times and loud music.

DAVE.Mode:DJ at Studio 21 and The Daisy.Hair at Smile, trousers -PX,tunic from Fox's cost £10,necklace and pouch £16 each at PX.and the shirt from Worlds End cost £25.

JOHN.Mode:Works as a messenger,his scooter is a Vespa Ra 200cc,price £500.Three button two piece suit a present f Mum,hush puppies available at most shoe shops.100% moder worn with button down collar shirt n'tie plus parka.Like "Original 60's sounds such as the Who,my fave are the Ki (dedicated follower of fashion),and new groups such as t Purple Hearts,Lambrettas and Small Hours.Dislikes-Punk a disco music.Johns'nicknamed 'JR'.

Photographed by James Palmer

Photographed by Robin Ridley

Photographed by James Palmer

Photographed by Simon Brown

# MEANWHILE...ON THE OTHER SI-DE

OF THE CHANNEL...

GET OFF YOUR 'ARIS AND FLY TO PARIS.
This summer you 'away-dayed' to Margate, Brighton,Bournemouth or Blackpool...... Next try Paris,it's not that much dearer and the time/convenience benifits make flying cheaper than the boat train'.For facts n'faces read on.........Today the costal resorts,tomorrow the world......

PAQUITA AND KEJU.She is Geisha at le Palace and used to strip tease in Pigalle.She drove to le Palace,temple of the night,the Paris new wave.She is always ready with an answer.Keju is a Japanese Fl Cordobes.Once in a while,oh his way to Madrid he stops in Paris.He only speaks English,at the moment he is badly in love with Paquita.

Photo report by Philippe Picoli

PIERRE AND GILLES.Starsky and Hutch.Pierre est brun et Gilles est blond-ils sont beaux et ils sont muscle.They are totally involved together in their work.They need each other's creativeness.They fully live their fantasies.They make cheap things beautiful and poetic.Arnold,their favorite Teddy bear,sometimes answers the phone.

PAULA AND KEVIN.Mode:(Brother n'Sister).Paula aged 16 is still at school,she's wearing ski pants,button to neck cardigan,flat heeled pointed shoes (original 60's),suede three quarter length jacket and parka."I get most of my clothes from second hand shops such as Red Cross n'Oxfam. or Petticoat lane M'kt.Likes-60's soul music,Kinks,Beatles Who,Yardbirds,Motown Music esp'Martha and the Vandellas, plus 'modern groups' such as Jam,Secret Affair and The Chords.Dislikes-Modern soul,Reggae,Futurist music,punk and heavy metal."I like going to Margate or Brighton on bank holidays and enjoying myself".

Kevin has always liked 60's music and has been a mod for two years,his scooter is a Vespa Piagio'V'reg and nick-named 'Spaceship' Mohair three button suit with ticket pocket n'slanted flaps from Petticoat Lane,inch wide black tie from Dad,white socks n'hush puppies.Likes-All 60's beat esp'Beatles,Stones,Kinks,Who,Small Faces,R n'B,Ska, Blue Beat,Tamla,Tamla Motown day mod groups inc'Jam,Chords, Purple Hearts,Nine Below Zero,Spiders,two tone n' Madness. Dislikes-Disco,Adam and the Ants,punk,Rock n'Roll and Heavy metal."I collect records and all British released Beatles albums,It's very unusual to go out with no trouble being a mod,I've had my nose broken,scooter smashed up,and a few beatings even the police give us hassle.Most S London mods stick to one DJ named 'Tony Class',he started a club called "Class Mod"and troublemakers are not allowed in.

LINDA.Mode:Linda owns 'Other Clothes'-Leeds,all her outfits available there.Likes-scientific experiments with Maltesers, 'Face' reports and husbands.Dislikes include-rip off designers. CHRIS.Mode:Works and wears 'Other Clothes'.Likes-posers,puffs, pansies and alliteration."I think Gary Glitters great and that you can get away with anything if you're drunk.

Photographed by Simon Brown

Photographed by Robin Ridley

EVA AND CHARLES.They love each other to death and will marry in September.Charles is a painter and today is getting very involved in music.Charles is a scatter-brain.Eva is sixteen and is still going to school,but she would love to be a famous actress Born as a shooting star,one day she will be celebrated on stage. Eva drives you crazy.She has no underwear,never.What a character.

FRANCOISE AND FRANCIS.Two friends who have in common the sense of tradition and taste.Francoise works in a glamourous couture house and Francis enjoys so much leisure that he just refuses to work. Francoise married the photographer.Francis keeps his tan all year round.As a matter of fact he spends alot of time in the Carribean, but hesitates going out at night as he does not know how to go home in the morning.

P A R I S

1. CAPTAIN VIDEO.AVENUE GABRIEL-75008.
   "Tres chic" and expensive.

2. ROSE BONBON.6 RUE CAUMARTIN-75009.
   Re opening of what was the punk club in Paris,the new look is quite attractive.

3. GOLF DROUOT.2 RUE DROUOT-75009.
   All kinds of new and unknown groups.

4. PALAIS DES GLACES.37 RUE FAUBOURG DU TEMPLE-750
   A big cinema with a bar surrounded by mirrors,j open for concerts.

5. PALAIS DES ARTS.102 BOULEVARD SEBASTOPOL-75003.
   Just open for concerts.

6. LE GIBUS.18 RUE FAUBOURG DU TEMPLE-75011.
   Looks like a London music pub,live music almost every night.

7. ROCK-IN-LOFT.24 QUAI D'AUSTERLITZ-75013.
   A huge warehouse with windows facing on to the Seine.Nights of non-stop music and performances (video fashion exhibition)it's not a discotheque-just open for concerts.

i-D is published by
T/J Informat Design
Available from i-D,HQ,

# 08•81

"I don't think the ultimate musical intention
is to get up and move. I think it's basically
very sexual!"

**Adam Ant, singer, no5**

magnus,mode,
office
rat
at gultba,
stockholm
likes,
underground
clubs,pole
cats,
elvis,
johnny b good
and tommy
steele.

julian,mode,
photographer
"i like
period
clothes
in very good
condition,i
wish more
people
would get
it right
period
wise"

david claridge - mode:traditional japanese
festival outfit and worker's sweatbands,
purchased on recent visit - cost approx.£40.
currently compiling first LP release on his
own MOBILE SUIT CORPORATION label - which
will feature SANDII;AKIKO,YANO,EARTHLING,
HIKASU and LIZARD - the LP 'Tokyo Mobile Music
is out in December. also building a house in
Thailand and scouring the globe for more
MOBILE music.

do what! t'ai-chi for potency...

raymond & pat:both
from b'ham.
dancing at the zoo,
on monday night
in b'ham.
pat:mode:works
at haebus corpus,
in manchester,in
the mkt.centre.
raymond:mode:
dresses like this
for normal"i don't
care about the
abuse"

james palmer

mick cross from rochdale,
manchester.a script
writer.clothes from
oldham market and second
hand stores.
likes:going to raffles
in manchester.

neil,mode,
neil has been
travelling around
but wants to
act,the suit
came from oxfam
and cost £8,
shoes also from
oxfam,cost £1,the
shirt came from a
jumble sale,£1,
likes,brando,
montgomery
clift,vintage
hollywood,show-biz
and the street,
dislikes,trendies!

james palmer

funk dancing at heaven,london,
on a monday night

do what! the alternative clothes sale returns December 8/9/10th
at Chelsea Old Town Hall,Kings Rd.Take a stand...
Clive Jennings on 359 6474...

ugh. johnson

# 1981

# 1982

September. The In Future Issue no7. Photography by James Palmer

October. The Head To Toe Issue no8. Photography by Thomas Degen, Terry Jones

November. The Wuli Dancing Issue no9. Photography by Terry Jones

December. The Out Already Issue no10. Cover star: Moira Bogue. Photography by Steve Johnston

"I love attention... even if it's violent"

**Judy Blame, i-D Contributing Fashion Editor, no7**

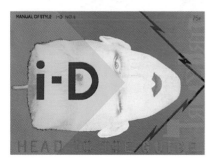

PETER. Mode: I've lived in Leeds for 16 years. It has a good community feel and nice beer (!). Anyway, I just can't afford London. (He is a freelance architect and has worked all over the place). I think it's a healthy thing to be involved in music. In a jazz band I played guitar and I've watched Top of the Pops for the past twenty years. But cycles repeat themselves, nothing really new. My roots are in jazz - Fats Waller and Stefan Grapelli never age. During my day uniform and patriotism were important - there were no real cults. Now music & dress are so important to teenagers; but a lot of people are not influenced by modern trends. They will always retreat into the safety of Laura Ashley fabric! It's certainly better than my era. I was an Ovalteenie. Now people have more awareness. Communism will erode from within. Capitalism will temper down. The world will level out. No revolt or change. The system is a natural occurance, we can't do much about. Our freedom is incredible - we don't seem to appreciate it. But there is enough intelligence in England to sort out our problems - riots, vandalism and inflation...other countries are watching. As a single parent, I am broad minded. Julia had her hair cut strange 2 years ago. I thought it was good. Terrific. Well done. Wearing bizarre clothes is a statement of individuality. It's the same as dressing for a dance in the 40s. Married families are bitter about youth. They should be more tolerant and aware of the harshness of the times, and the impermanence of life. (The Buick started as a wreck and it took me 3½ yrs to build with parts from all over the world. Unique 1929 Buick 'Marquette'. English bodied Coupe, 6 cylinder side valve 24 H.P. engine, now fully restored, exactly as originally exhibited in the 1929 London Motor Show. Not for sale).

photographer mike muschamp

RONNY. Mode: the display and window designer at Fiorucci, Amsterdam, photographed in front of the shop's airbrushed dinosaur. He's from Belgium "I'm too extravagant for there". Likes the designer Antonio Lopez, potatoes and Japanese new music and style "but it's so expensive". Hair - Boy G., Regulierdwars str. Amsterdam, bow tie - 2nd hand shop.

JULIA. Mode: I've lived in Leeds all my life but I'd like to live in London because that's where it's all going on. Leeds is stagnant. (She has been doing Display and Exhibition design at Jacob Kramer Art College for 1½yrs). I'm happy living at home - but would like more independence - my dad is very liberal. He doesn't seem to mind what I wear and how. I live with self-constrained limitations; make boundaries that are often tighter than my dad would impose (but he wouldn't). He knows I make my own limits but is afraid of me being a social drop-out. My mum died when I was 13 and ever since then I've looked 'different'. I needed something to buck me up. It was escapism .. an identity .. I wanted to be noticed. I don't want to be another blob in the crowd. Even if they mock, that's better than no reaction at all. My image has given me more than I anticipated .. life style, music, friends. It's taught me to think on alternative levels. Bauhaus are on a similar wavelength - I like them because they are so visually strong. Bow Wow Wow make me want to jump up and down. I'd like to be involved in music but it needs recognition that's impossible because of college. How can you hope to have a stable society when the parties are so insecure? None of them seem to know what they are talking about. Clothes: Friend from college cut me hair this time. I have been to a hairdresser in Leeds where complex colours were used. That was O.K. The jacket comes from Beasts £30 and the rest are general nick-nacks.

The Pioneers. Mode: Aim to "overcome the passive acceptance reserved for traditional art exhibiton - to generate a new enthusiasm and a positive reaction to their work". They'll exhibit ANYWHERE...from "a gap on the wall to the Albert Hall". PIONEERS are, poets, painters, printmakers and sculptors and also make films, t-shirts, carrier bags postcards and badges..contact thru Civilisation, Cardiff.(26 The Balcony, Castle Arcade).

DAVID GRAVES describes his work as "sculpture in wire, line-drawing in 3-D, mostly on a small domestic scale...not easy to photograph because they move, picking up vibrations from people walking past...the form of the drawing changes dramatically as you move around any particular piece, integrating and disintegrating". An exhibition of his work starts February 10th at the Chennil Gallery, 183 Kings Road.

photographer hugh johnson

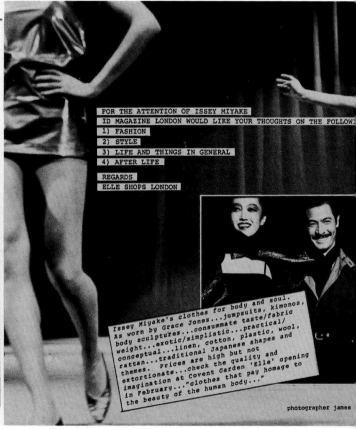

FOR THE ATTENTION OF ISSEY MIYAKE
ID MAGAZINE LONDON WOULD LIKE YOUR THOUGHTS ON THE FOLLOW:
1) FASHION
2) STYLE
3) LIFE AND THINGS IN GENERAL
4) AFTER LIFE

REGARDS
ELLE SHOPS LONDON

Issey Miyake's clothes for body and soul. As worn by Grace Jones...jumpsuits, kimonos, body sculptures...consummate taste/fabric weight...exotic/simplistic...practical/conceptual...linen, cotton, plastic, wool, rattan...traditional Japanese shapes and themes. Prices are high but not extortionate...check the quality and imagination at Covent Garden 'Elle' opening in February..."clothes that pay homage to the beauty of the human body..."

photographer james

DAVID is rehersing with a band
in Camden. He doesn't want
his efforts going to other
people's causes. "The energy
we put into the band makes
enjoyment for us. This is
selfish maybe, but makes us
happy". Mode: Coat - Flip,
boots from Holland.

shelters? All the royalty, judges, police, upper classes have perfectly utilised shelters. They have stocks for 3 months; some up to a year. There are underground communities, telephone systems, cinemas, videos, sauna-baths, girls — they think of everything.

*i-D Is there anyway of averting it — mass mobilisation?*
S.B. Yeah! absolutely! Strength in numbers. If the working classes or any classes got up and said where is our shelter — why aren't you doing anything about this nuclear threat — you could grind the country to a halt. People must demand it.

*i-D Anything else?*
S.B. Not really — not at the moment because the advance of cheap video and hi-fi technology means that people now see themselves as appendages to machines — social conscience is being totally obliterated. Thatcher's policy of mass unemployment may backlash however, and we may get a huge youth movement — which I can envisage — and total revolution. But what you need is people with great voices and minds to get into the media, people like Martin Luther King, who can sway millions with the power of their convictions and passion. Somebody must wake people up to life and also to life-denying forces.

s a future if people are
w to work for it"

at Cha Chas, a Tuesday
Mode: Boots X-tremes,
lax Kensington Mkt.,
a gas jacket from an
rplus in Kensington Mkt.
C.D.T. art college,
isplay design. Thinks:
's a future if people
ling to work for it".
like to see better
cation between people.
Ross at Production
kt. "I like Cha Chas
there's no poseurs
's friendly, people go
good time".

BERT. Mode: is a bank
rk from Whitton, Middx.
work not much compromise
clothing is needed. Goes
60s clubs. Ban the Bomb
dal - Sweet Charity,
aser - an original 60s one,
ousers - Feltham Market,
oes - Melandi, Carnaby St.
O, hair - my mother.

photographer james palmer

WILLY Mode:
Hat - the Bazaar, Amsterdam
fur - Flea Mkt., Amsterdam,
boots - Pressburg, Amsterdam,
trousers - Swanky Modes.
Willy lives in Harlem, works
with Models One, London.
Likes to go to movies in the
afternoons, especially
Brian de Palms films. Wants
to see other parts of the
world, apart from Europe,
and works for the travel,
to see how others live etc.
Favourite designer to wear
Anthony Price, best show to
do - Worlds End. Fav..clubs
De Koer and Masso, Amsterdam,
Club for Heroes, London.

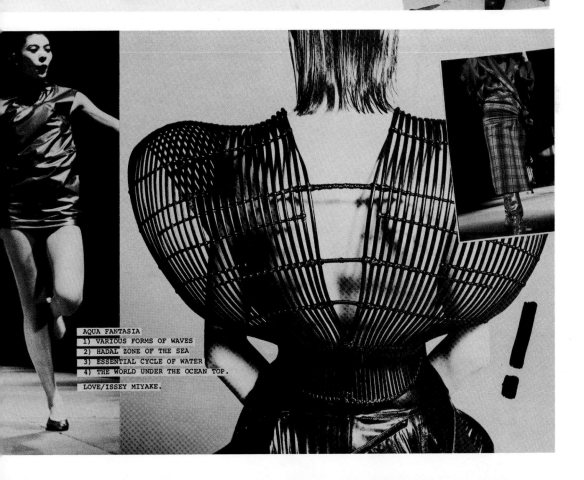

AQUA FANTASIA
1) VARIOUS FORMS OF WAVES
2) HADAL ZONE OF THE SEA
3) ESSENTIAL CYCLE OF WATER
4) THE WORLD UNDER THE OCEAN TOP.

LOVE/ISSEY MIYAKE.

CLIFF. Mode: Graphic designer does visuals for dance groups. Clothes from Worlds End, Kings Rd Ivory pendant from Africa Hair Production, Ken. Mkt. Likes Whitehouse & New Order also Stranglers. Wishes there were more places like Cha-Cha. Comes from Aberdeen. Photoed at Cha Cha on a Tuesday night.

PENNY. Mode: Hair friend vest £5, trousers £15 from John's shop upstairs in Ken. Mkt. Helmet not for sale. On clothes: "It's down to the individual". Likes The Rapping Club, cinema's the 2nd best place to be. Likes to go to a party and to have a can of Red Stripe & a smoke.

Clue 19

RICK. Mode: Hat from Peckham The Record Seller Jacket mail order Easy Riders, buckle Hanrax Motors, Ladbroke Grove. Boots Top Man Basildon Bike's a BSA Star Fire 250cc. Places: Charlie Chaplin, Duke of Clarence Night Moves. Sometimes takes a run up the motorway, squats in Peckham, gets stoned and all that.

HATTIE. Mode: Schoolgirl. Hair 1st Schumi then self to make it shorter. Mac American Retro, Ken Mkt. Cardigan Ken. Mkt. Skirt & bracelet Sweet Charity. Shoes Ken. Mkt. Likes London, the things going on, places to go & the parties. "You can wear anything you like, which is good. I change style every day, especially for school. I'm quite undressed today". Fav. bands: Dead Kennedys, Sex Pistols, Souxsie & the Banshees.

IONA & STEVE. Mode: Own New Masters 336 Kings Road, tel: 352 7223. Clothes IONA: Jersey wrap-around dress by PX at New Masters L35. Tights from a friend. Mocassins from New Mexico L8. Gold armband by Lorraine Drewery at New Masters L7. White armbands from N.M. L1.75. Comments: "I really hope this year slacks are extinct!" STEVE: Trousers & waistcoat by Hudson Plus L32.75 & L29, at New Masters. Shirt by Stephen King L9.95 at N.M. Jacket from Chatters 3yrs ago. Black socks L2.50 N.M. Chinese shoes from Soho. Comments: London is swinging again and it's a good time for cults, small people etc to be able to survive and thrive." "New Masters shows and sells new designer clothes. It's a fun shed or function junction!"

primitive dollars. £5 pair Chained allsorts. trains of thought, spool poems £4 pair. Keys £3 pair all by Kate. Shendo of The Cravats. Lifebuoy by Kay (no price yet). pen from San Francisco. pen helicopter for fun.

CHECKOUT JOHN MAYBURY'S NEW FILM 'THE COURT OF MIRA FEATURING SOUXSIE SIOUX AND HERMINE DEMORIANE WITH BY THE RAVISHING BEAUTIES ON AT THE ICA 26TH MAY – MAY INCLUSIVE.

CUSHT!

VIBES....FASHION WITH DESIGNS ON YOU BIG SPENDER... ...DRESS DESIGNER DRESS....

Vivienne Westwood

NOSTALGIA OF MUD.

"I long for some information so I concern myself with finding some good questions to ask.
What was Jocastas' crime?
Why is the word sophisticated a dirty word?
Should boys be boys?
Why do people wear brassieres?
Who will remember when I'm dead?
Why do people pretend that outlaws are different from me?
Is mud my middle name?

Vivienne Westwood March 1982

.Photographer James Palmer

ZOE. Mode: Dress (blue striped) Zelona Zaba at Bar-roz Ken. Mkt. basement £19.50. Zoe works in an estate agents. Likes to go wind-surfing, horse riding, swimming, biking, dancing and all energetic things, likes living it up generally. Fav clothes jeans, jackets, T-shirts & this.

MARILYN. Mode: Model & actress. Photoed at Vivienne Westwood's show at Olympia during London Fashion week. Wasn't keen on the show "She's not out to please the individual she's out to please everybody", reckons it's good for Paris & Milan though. Hair having it put in dreadlocks and it's inspired by George. "George is the most fashionable person I know and it's fashionable to know". Make-up "I get my ideas from George". Summer fashions? "I like lots of purple and yellow but I don't give a shit about fashion, I do my own thing. Steve Strange is the most talented person I know, I'd love to meet him". Marilyn runs Napoleons Club, Wednesdays

MARK. Mode: From Zimbabwe. Hair by sister. Chains from around Portobello where he lives. T-shirt Mugabe from Zimbabwe, he came back this morning, his mother lives in Salisbury. He doesn't work, jacket from sister, trousers & boots can't remember. Been in Zimbabwe since November. Very bad reactions to the way he looks. Wouldn't let him in the country at first. People stare and crowd round him, backward, very violent Black culture very good but he's not into reggae. Local band Thomas Mapfumo, black clubs good, full of atmosphere. Whites are pathetic, very glad to be back. There the people aren't real, very heavy.

HOLLI. Mode: Hollie is American & lives in London. Likes: Her husband. Clothes: Demob suit £55. She works in Demob.

MUD. Mode: Philip Sallon, designer (clothes), used to run Planets Club. Still has the contract for the Roof Garden Club. Outfit made by himself. Likes Worlds End clothes but improvises usually with saris etc. Hates: any sort of values In dressing, boys trying to be lads, British pigheadedness, especially over the Falklands issue "There's more people living in my road than in the Falklands". Thinks our True-Brit individualism stems from the fact that we weren't invaded during the Second World War, also the mass and freedom of the art colleges here. Photoed at Vivienne Westwoods 'Nostalgia of Mud' show at Olympia during the London Fashion Week.

james palmer

OUT DECORATORS' NEW SINGLE 'STRAIGHT ONE' W ALBUM 'TABLET' ON RED FLAME RECORDS, VAILABLE THROUGH ROUGH TRADE.

T VIVIENNE WESTWOOD'S NEW SHOP 'NOSTALGIA OF MUD' CHRISTOPHER'S PLACE, LONDON W1.

GNED TO INSPIRE, COVET AND DESIRE...

A nostalgia of mud glorious mud, the mixture of all races. Dances of the peoples of the world. formation dances. Hold hands and concentrate. this is a serious business. Hobos in muddy petticoats and bashed in hats make them work in discotequies." Buffalo Gals go round the outside. Just your CB Busy Bees and travel. Take your mothers old brassiers and wear it undisguised over your school jumper and have a muddy face.

.....NEW SHAPE.....SQUARES.....UP ON TOP AND DOWN BELOW.....
.......THE DUCK-BILLED PLATYPUS TRACKER SHOE BY VIVIENNE WESTWOOD.....

VIVIENNE WESTWOOD WINTER COLLECTION...
For girls: Bashed in hats, printed zest hoods, skirts with large prints and leather frock coats toga dresses and bras. For guys: Sculptured trousers, chico jackets and wool vests. Available from Worlds End, Kings Road, SW10.

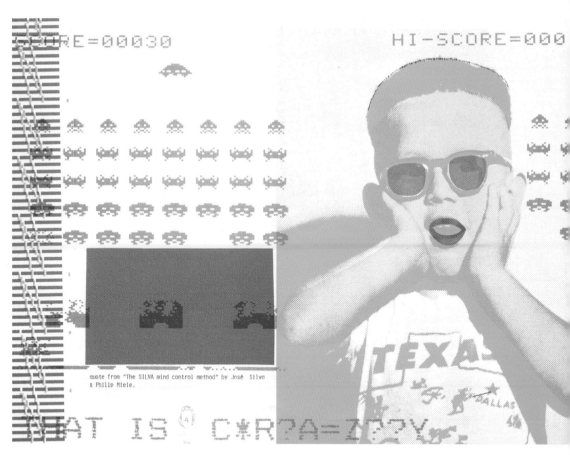

SCORE=00030                    HI-SCORE=000

quote from "The SILVA mind control method" by José Silva
& Philip Miele.

WHAT IS C*R?A=Z?Y.

# MAN

ADAM and EVE: Unemployed.Clothes: Adam
wears a fig leaf whoch he picks fresh
every day. Eve wears only long hair, Adams
hair cut by Eve. Likes: Apple trees and
clever snakes. Dislikes: Angels with burning
swords. They think navels are just a
fashion among the young people which is going
to disappear sooner or later. What do they
think about the future? "Blood,Sweat
and Tears"

ACT ONE:
In the garden of Eden.Eve offers Adam the forbidden fruit.
Adam is hesitant.

EVE: "DIVE IN,DIVE IN,DIVINE....STRAP ON A
TAIL AND COMMENCE.'"

ADAM:(speaking "THE FUTURE ONLY EXISTS THROUGH LIFE.
with his mouth full) I WANT TO FOLLOW MY DESTINY AND CHEAT
MY FATE."

EVE: "WITH WORDS YOU CAN SNEAK AROUND-LOOKS
SPEAK FOR THEMSELVES...'"

VOICE IN THE SKY: " IDEAS HAVE VIRILITY LIKE GERMS,
(enraged) YOU ARE DEALING WITH PSYCHIC EPIDEMICS"

EVE: "BUT RHYTHM AND STYLE DANCE HAND IN HAND."

ADAM: "IN THE BEGINNING THERE WAS BIG BEAT..."

EVE: "SEX AND SWEAT IS BEST YOU BET"

V.I.S:(livid)OUT! NOW! (they leave)

ADAM: "WE WILL PLAY SPIRITUAL ROBINSON CRUSOE
FOR A WHILE YET."

EVE: "YEAH,WELL YOU HAVE TO EXPEND SOME ENERGY
TO GET RESULTS..."

ANTHROPOLOGIST: "A CHILD OF FIVE COULD UNDERSTAND THIS.
(emerging from bushes) SEND SOMEONE TO FETCH A CHILD OF FIVE."

CURTAIN

Dialogue compiled from 2 and a half years of I-D gems.Special thanks
to:Ben Browton,Genesis P.Orridge,Vivien Westwood,Joly Better Badges,
Mechthild Nawiasky,Perry Haines,Alix Sharkey and Groucho Marx.

Photo by Thomas Degen

Educated Eighties...improve your argument.Rent-a-computer and catch up on a generation of pupils who already grasp the hard logic of the print-out...learn debate and the art of asking the perceptive question..study the science of phenomenonology (for a quick revision get a videotape of Carpenter's "Dark Star") but remember-laughter illogical response - ask Dr Spock !

L $O££GI&L

BANG ! Whooooooooooooooossssshhhhhhhh!!!
Action replay and edited highlights.

There was the BIG BANG (not to be confused with BIG BEAT -see i-D no.8) and needless to say everything ran for its life or was hurled away....

After an extended intro.of $10^{36}$ bars,the BIG BEAT got into the groove and the particles started to dance.

Enter homosapiens - they LOVE that beat,so naturally they dance too.Enter wallflower-analysis.Man gets clever, stops dancing.Sits down to think.Thinks so long he forgets what he was doing before he sat down.Invents religion,in a feeble attempt to regain lost unity.Fights wars over religion.Forgets more.And in the confusion,gets out of sync.(big thinker,no dancer).

Says Homosapien,"All heavenly bodies move as prescribed by religion - NO WIGGLING ! Newton says that TIME moves forward constantly in a uniform manner - NO SLIDING OR SLIPPING !.Newton says that space is uniform from all frames of reference.Unfortunately Newton only had one frame of reference - sitting down.And he couldn't keep time,never having kept the beat.Also,the planets couldn't stop WIGGLING.Tee-hee.

Enter Einstein,the best European dancer since MIJINSKY. "No no no.What is this terrible score that is so stiff ? Now give that beat some feel,lets release some pressure, ja ?" And all was transformed - science lost "classical" logic,and a string of hits were released - Special Relativity,Time Dilation,Photon Bullets,Must be Atoms etc.

And Einstein kept on soaking up a sweat - soon the world of science had got some - and physicists everywhere did the 4-dimensional Space-Time Continuum (a very complex step in those days).

But Alberts greatest hit was actually a RE-RELEASE - "(The Quantum nature of)ENERGY" Much to his despair,this rather average number was pounced upon by his imitators, who hammered the riff into shape and created a brand new energy dance - The Quantum Jump !

5
Right

F        ESTO !

"PLAYGIRLS PLAY ABOUT WITH THE SEMIOTICS OF FASHION IN THE SAME WAY THAT THE AWARE YOUTH OF THIS COUNTRY ARE LEARNING TO DO"

BRAVE BABIES MUST HAVE STYLE"

TO WIN. HEAVEN 17.

NAPPY-RASH IS NOT ENOUGH... BRAVE BABIES MUST HAVE STYLE. BORN TO BE WISE, A GENERATION HAS GROWN UP WITH AN INSTINCT FOR IMAGE AND IT'S MAN IPULATION. CITY KI-DS ESPECIALLY HAVE ABSORBED A CROSS-CULTURAL EDUCATION. WITH EASY AND EARS OPEN THEY PLUNDER THEIR TRUE HERITAGE THEY LEARN THE LESSONS OF DRESS CODE AND THEY BREAK THE RULES-NEVER AGAIN WILL STYLE SEEM DISTANT STYLE WIZE OR PRECIOUS THEY BEND-A-GENDER HERE STEAL-A-STANCE THERE... ANYTHING IS GRIST TO THEIR LUST FOR LIFE.

(WINSTON KING TAKES CLASSIC FABRICS AND STRAINS THEM INTO UTILITY DESIGNS-CHECK HIS PIN STRIPE BOILERSUITE ON SALE IN BEAK ST.)

AS THEY GROW THEY WANT NEW TOYS AND DEVELOPE A TASTE FOR THE THEATRICAL SIDE OF LIFE. THEIR PRANKS ARE DOCUMENTED IN THE WORLD OF MAGAZINE INFANTILE-DISORDER) SOME GROW MASSIVE AND ARE NOT CONTENT WITH DELIVERING LINES THEY OTHER INTERUPT FOR THEM. FOR THOSE WHO CHOSE TO PLAY FOR FUN RATHER THAN KEEPS, I-D CHECK OUT AN INTERESTING NEW GAME CALLED 'TRAVELLER'

Let's pretend! Let's pretend that you're a medieval warrior and you're a clever thief who's an OK... [magician] and there's a beautiful prin... [cess] who's being held in his castle and ... we've taken our way in through the ... [kitchen] out of the mess she's in and lures the guard to her cell by pretending she's sick and hits him over the head ... armour and runs out of the cell and down the hall just in time to meet us.we fight our way in towards the main gate but just before we get there the magician discovers she's missing and conjures a terrible demon to stop us....

TRAVELLER

Imagination is the border of TRAVELLER. Three or more play-ers are needed, one of which will act as gamesmaster, referee, or GOD. He will create the scenario and control the action. His purpose is to make the game flow, give a theme, throw in surprise elements or red herrings and generally keep the game away from the board (a star chart) and thus eliminate compa...[risons] He may make things more difficult for the players or reward them...

The players generate their characters, by a combination of [random dice] and choosing certain backgrounds and qualities e.g. physical strength, intelligence, agility medical experi-ence, marksmanship, computer operation, engineering etc.

The players first choose their own goal. The aim of a player, their purpose to wipe out all other players or finish first or end up with all the money, but to play the most interesting game while achieving their chosen ambition.

Does this sound familiar? If not, why not?

Traveller is a trade mark owned by Game Designers Workshop Inc, Bloomington, Illinois, U.S.A. for its science fiction role playing game. Traveller is printed in the U.K. under licence by Games Workshop Ltd, London. The extracts above below in this article are reprinted with permission.

"Traveller is printed in the U.K. by Games Workshop Ltd, London. It is available from games hobby and model shops throughout the country or from Games Workshop's own shops in London, Manchester, Birmingham, Sheffield and Nottingham."

**10•82**

"There's nothing wrong with people worrying about how they look. It's when they start worrying about how everybody else looks and what everybody else thinks of how they look that's the problem"

**Everything But The Girl, musicians, no10**

# 1982

Photography by James Palmer. Page 57

September. The In Future Issue no7. Photography by Mike Muschamp, James Palmer. Page 58-59

September. The In Future Issue no7. Photography by Hugh Johnson, James Palmer. Page 58-59

October. The Head to Toe Issue no8. Photography by James Palmer. Page 60-61

November. The Wuli Dancing Issue no9. Photography by James Palmer. Page 60-61

Photography by James Palmer. Page 62

Photography by James Palmer. Page 63

November. The Wuli Dancing Issue no9. Page 64-65

December. The Out Already Issue no10. Photography by Thomas Degen. Page 64-65

Photography by Steve Johnston. Page 66

Photography by James Palmer. Page 67


Left to right. Page 68-69

September. The In Future Issue no7. Photography by James Palmer

October. The Head To Toe Issue no8. Photography by James Palmer, Rita Edward

November. The Wuli Dancing Issue no9. Photography by James Palmer

November. The Wuli Dancing Issue no9. Photography by Steve Johnston

December. The Out Already Issue no10. Photography by Steve Johnston

December. The Out Already Issue no10. Photography by Jane England, Steve Johnston

"Fashion is exciting but it isn't really changing. We may think so in our own little world, but outside that they still copy what the queen wears"

**Jeremy Healy, DJ, no10**

# 1983

January. The Health & Herpes Issue no11. Cover star: Fiona Skinner. Photography by Steve Johnston

February. The Love & Romance Issue no12. Cover star: Sophie. Photography by James Palmer

March. The Wet 'n' Wild Issue no13. Cover star: LA. Photography by Steve Johnston

April. The All Star Issue no14. Cover star: Sade. Photography by Nick Knight

"My lips are the most important part of my body because I love sucking..."

**Marilyn, singer, no14**

WORLDWIDE MANUAL OF STYLE i-D NO.14 £1.00

# i-D

STARRING:
CAPRICORN
AQUARIUS
PISCES
ARIES
TAURUS
GEMINI
CANCER
LEO
VIRGO
LIBRA
SCORPIO
SAGITTARIUS
▼

ALL ★ STAR
ISSUE!

Photo Jon Ingledew

Photo Thomas Degen

KERSTIN appearing as a 2nd World War GI's favourite Hollywood star. Jacket from Tiger-Rose, Munich; Tie from Fiorucci; Shirt from jumble sale. Make-up by Francesca Tolot. Hair by Enzo Angelieri.

Photo Thomas Degen

FABIOLA from Atlantis, living statue. Wants to be Dutch government-sponsored artist (there are 2 already) cannot stand up without h... ...ning for a bus is an ...bility. He is availa... ...enings for a ...small fee. He ...nd drink at the ...ence.

JAMIE, 15 March 51, Pisces, Stiff Press Officer, & RORY, 11 September 58, Virgo, King Kurt drummer (with his rat Kurt).
"It's easier for us now that we've reached fame. We played a gig in a hotel in Scotland, and were going to put plastic over the floor, but they said No, No, we want as much mess as possible. Before we practically had to clean it up ourselves..." New Year's resolution: "To get a new hair cut, I've had this one a long time, I've got to think of something better."
To join the Rats & Rodents Club which gives you some discount on tickets, send a S.A.E. to Stiff Records, 115 Bayham St, London NW1. Checkout Destination Zululand on Stiff Records.

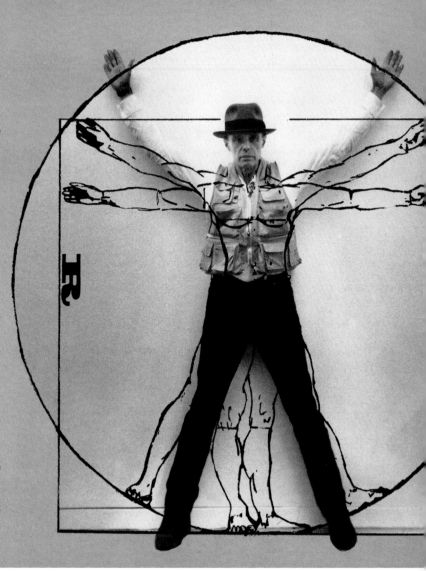

JOSEPH BEUYS talks to i-D on Sept. 8.
Words taken by Thomas Degen.

"Who believes in a catastrophy? Instead of putting their attention towards their fears people should better use their energies to find out about the real possibilities we got to oppose and to do something. My work is the always returning examination of history and the possibilities of the present to overcome the systems. Art does not necessarily have to be in galleries and museums, most things happen elsewhere."

**18**

PERRY HAINES, Oct. 15, Libra, leader of The Haines Gang. i-D asks for comments on Life, Politics, and The Future.
"The education system is based on books full of rules and answers, I'd like to see a book full of questions. Politics is people, so there better be a future. The manifestation of gangs & cults in an age of resettlement is a natural search for identity. When presented with Flat B, Floor 7, Estate 3, even the mentality is graded in a Facts & File It Away system. It would make for a better world if everyone had respect for others' space. My 3 wishes for the future: That the earth should remain blue & green rather than grey & concrete; that everyone should realise their equal right to enjoy the earth & its forbidden fruits; 1,000 more wishes please."

Catch the lyrics on So Hot, by The Haines Gang, on London Records.

Photo James Palmer

Photo Nick Knight

F Scheffer

Perry's all-time 10 Hot Faves:
1) Lady Grinning Soul, David Bowie
2) In Every Dream Home a Heartache, Roxy Music
3) The Letter, The Boxtops
4) DooWahDidiDidiDumDidiDoo, Manfred Mann Group
5) Young Gifted & BLack, Bob & Marcia
6) It's a Man's World, James Brown
7) Stairway To Heaven, Led Zeppelin
8) Kill That Roach, Miami
9) School's Out, Alice Cooper
10) Street Fighting Man, Rolling Stones

FRANK BRUNO, Scorpio, on November 16th, Heavyweight boxer. "My strongest childhood memory is the first time I met the school bully: 'Empty your pockets, it's all mine.' In those days, I did what I was told." Most important part of his body: "My brain, I can't work without it . . ." Fear: Dogs, when he's running. Ambition for '84: "To keep winning, of course!"

MARILYN, November 3, Scorpio. Likes: "My lips, because I love sucking (straws), and Jamaica, cause it's so relaxed and friendly." Dislikes: "The shakes & dark hidey holes, and Tom Bailey's's dancing."

Check out his new single on January 13, Cry and Be Free, on Phonogram.

Photo Nick Knight

**IT'S IN THE GROOVE! YES, IT'S _MARILYN_**

# 1983

"I want stardom. Up until a year ago I was living on the street. But I still feel the same way. Money will never be a problem for me. If you worry about it, it's a problem"

**Madonna, icon, no14**

# 1984

May. The SexSense Issue no15. Cover star: Madonna. Photography by Mark Lebon

June. The E=mc² Issue no16. Cover star: Sophie Hicks. Photography by David Bailey

July/Aug. The Language Issue no17. Cover star: Jo Kelly. Photography by Mark Lebon, styling by Mitzi Lorenz

September. The Money Issue no18. Cover star: Sherron. Photography by Nick Knight

October. The Inside Out Issue no19. Cover star: Anna Pigalle. Photography by Nick Knight

November. The Fun & Games Issue no20. Cover star: Jane Khan. Photography by Monica Curtain

"I never saw naked bodies when I was a kid – gosh, when I was 17 I hadn't seen a penis! I was shocked when I saw my first one, I thought it was really gross!"

**Madonna, icon, no15**

# i-D

love
hate
push
y-ft
kiss
wipe
misc
find
pet-
bcup
dcup
-vpl
noft
s-ex
stop
home
h-rt

## sexsense

**World-wide**

Photos Toscani

### EXQUISITE PLEASURE

Somebody once mentioned in connection with the leather clone scene 'the exquisite pleasure of being an absolute cliche'. This seems to apply to most fetishist/deviant styles. All the standard looks are a reprocessing of the hoariest old cliches of stage screen fantasy. Wearing them in (sem) public may feel liberating - but isn't it just playing along with a consumer process that has always sold people as things to be exploited and discarded? Forget disposable garments - we have now reached teh age of disposable human beings! L.H

---

EXAMINE THE PART PLAYED BY PRESSURE GROUPS IN THE BRITISH POLITICAL SYSTEM, <u>OR</u> INVENT AND DEFINE THE 'TEN COMMANDMENTS OF FUNK', GIVING REASONS FOR YOUR CHOICES.

(NME CROSSWORD, 1982)

## KATE GARNER, WRAPPED BY CAROLINE BAKER

RAP IT UP, WRAP IT UP...DISCOVER THE ART OF DRAPING UP - NOT DRESSING UP - JUST MAKE IT UP...GET INTO FABRIC & WEAR IT LIKE CLOTH, FORGET SEWING - BIG SQUARE, SMALL SQUARE - WRAP IT ON. CUT HOLES FOR ARMS, HEADS, WRAP IT UP WITH BELTS OR STRIPS OF CLOTH - OR STRIP THE CLOTHS INTO BODY BANDAGES. LAY A BODY-BASE FOUNDATION: LEOTARD, SWIMSUIT - EXPLORE NEW GROUNDS, ORIGINATE, DEVASTATE. FOR SPECIAL OCCASIONS CHECK OUT THE GLITTERY FABRICS.

She was thrown out of school at 16, then ran away from home (Wigan). "I like gossip, salty" says Kate. She is currently getting a new band together.

Photo Cameron McVie

by and wear

POOF AGAIN — WITH BIG FEET AND BIG
SMILES. "THE COMIC AND THE CARTOON
THROWN TOGETHER TO CREATE STRIP-TYPE
PEOPLE." Simon Foxton

— Profession... Yorker,
...ngton – Simon Foxton's
...Collection
Sk... Bazooka
Top...
Cap... glas & Blenkinsop – £20
Boot... ow & Rock

...hop Star & Model, wears:
...ade by Donald
...Flip – £1
...– £2
...– Sixone – £6
...– Big Apple – £30 –...

Neville – Model, wears:
Pants – Bazooka – £35
Polo – Flip – £5
Blazer – Portobello – £10

Brooks from Curl... wears:
Pants – Bazooka – 19...
Jacket – Lewis Leather... £100...

Cheryl – ⅓ Bazooka, wears:
Red Harrington – Army Surplus –
£15
Red Cycle shorts – Lonsdale – £10
Striped Shirt – Johnsons
Found Gloves
Boots – Snow & Rock, High St. Ken
– £30

Camille – Maid, wears:
Blazer – Portobello Rd – £10
Dress – Hawaii Kush – £25
Hat – Theatre Shop

Angela – ⅓ Bazooka, wears:
Black hooded dress – Bazooka
Red Blazer – Flip £10
Bumpers – Army Surplus, Charing
X Road – £3

Anne... assistant wears:
Tube... Vivienn... – £2
Whi... Flip – £1
Tie – Flip – £1
Gloves – Reiss – £3...
Hat – B...

◁〜〜〜〜

CHEAT, CHEAT, CHEAT: THREE MORE KIDS ADD
WEIGHT TO THE CANNON.

"KNICKERS 'N' STICKERS
WITH STRIPES, STARS AND
BRAS — LASHES AND SLASHES
WITH WIGS AND DANCING
JIGS...ESSENTIAL FOR '84.
ACCESSORISED BODYMAP
STYLE...WE WILL WIN
BECAUSE THE STARS AND
HEARTS ARE IN OUR FAVOUR
AND WE BRING YOU THE
STICKERS 'N' KNICKERS
SPIRIT SO YOU SHOULD FIND
HAPPINESS AND PEACE IN THE
WORLD." Bodymap

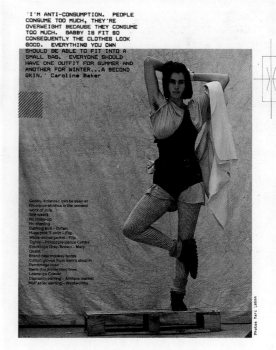

Lizzie Tear, Singer wears:
Rosebud goldie lingerie bra over
rubber bra – She & Me £20
Braces – Rainbow in Highgate
£1.75
Stickers & Badges – 60p-£1.25 from
Rainbow & Cascade in Carnaby St.
Hairpieces – New York
Knickers – Bodymap – Jones
Joseph Browns £17
Fancy Flippers c/o Jeffrey Hinton
Handcuffs – Rainbow £1.75
Fish earrings mail order Jen Corker
Leather bracelet John Keyo
Stick pins in hair – Camden market
50p
Superman belt – Rainbow £1.75

Barry Kamen, illustrator wears:
Biking shorts – Raleigh from
Condor cycles/London Bike Centre
Swimsuit – Muscle
Boxer shorts
Bodymap/Jones/Paul Smith
Superman braces – New York
sweatshop
Shoes – Robot Kings Road £28
Laces – Rainbow
Stickers – Bodymap Rainbow &
Cascade
Cap – Raleigh

Nico Holah, model wears:
T-shirt & knickers Bodymap
Stickers Bodymap & Rainbow
10p-£2.50
Star badges and heart earrings –
Layla D'angelo
Stockings Bodymap

Hilda, Fabric designer wears:
Goldie bra
Bodymap top
Braces – sweetshop New York
Stockings Bodymap
Stickers as before
Fish earrings and star earrings as
before

Sue, van driver wears:
Swimsuit – Miss Selfridge £10.99
Goldie lingerie camisole with
Goldie polkadot knicks stuffed in
Bodymap skirt – Jones £26
Socks and stockings Bodymap
Shoes Goldie
Laces Rainbow

Make Up – Lesley Chilkes

Hair – Layla D'angelo for Daniel
Galvin

Photos Marc Lebon

WITHIN THE LIMITS AND UP THERE
WITH THE MARKS.

## BOY VERSUS GIRL BY RAY PETRI

'THE MOOD IS
REFLECTIVE...THE GESTURE
OF QUIET CONFIDENCE. IT'S
A TRIBUTE TO COLOUR, FRESH
AIR & CLEAN LIVING. HE'S
THE INTELLECTUAL PILGRIM.
I'LL WIN THE CHALLENGE
BECAUSE I HAVE THE PERFECT
COMPONENTS.' Ray Petri

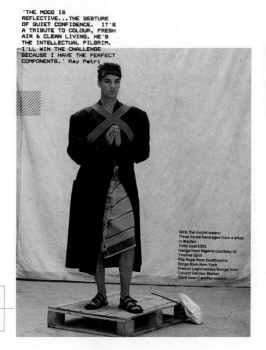

Nick, the model wears:
Three horse bandages from a shop
in Mayfair
Yohji coat £325
Kanga from Nigeria courtesy of
Yvonne Gold
Flip flops from Eastbourne
Rings from New York
French Legionnaires Badge from
Covent Garden Market
Stick from Camden market

'YOUTH, APPROACH YOU MUST HAVE'

## GIRL VERSUS BOY BY CAROLINE BAKER

'I'M ANTI-CONSUMPTION. PEOPLE
CONSUME TOO MUCH, THEY'RE
OVERWEIGHT BECAUSE THEY CONSUME
TOO MUCH. GABBY IS FIT SO
CONSEQUENTLY THE CLOTHES LOOK
GOOD. EVERYTHING YOU OWN
SHOULD BE ABLE TO FIT INTO A
SMALL BAG. EVERYONE SHOULD
HAVE ONE OUTFIT FOR SUMMER AND
ANOTHER FOR WINTER...A SECOND
SKIN.' Caroline Baker

Gabby, a dancer, can be seen at
Riverside studios in the second
week of July.
She wears:
No make-up
No shaving
Bathing suit – Oxfam
Huge pink T-shirt – Flip
White dinner jacket – Flip
Tights – Pineapple Dance Centre
Stockings Grey/Brown – Mary
Quant
Brand new monkey boots
Cotton gloves from men's shop in
Pembridge road
Bells (for protection) from
Lawrence Corner
Diamanté earring – Antique market
Naff aztec earring – Woolworths

Photos Marc Lebon

'SECOND SKIN'

# 09•84

"To appear in trendy society sporting a lot of opinions is almost as bad as to soil all that nice sports gear by running around playing tennis in it"

**Dylan Jones, former i-D Editor, no20**

"CALVIN KLEIN AIN'T NO FRIEND OF MINE, DON'T WEAR HIS NAME ON MY BEHIND."

Calvin Klein T-Shirt (to order from Browns) round the neck, Levis cut-off jacket over Levis cut-off jacket (both £10 from American Classics) over black Cerutti dinner jacket (suit £450) over an M&S men's vest, £2.99, over black Levi 501s (£19 from Browns). Polish it off with a swanky felt hat (£24 from Big Apple), and ponyskin belt, £7 from 20th Century Box. Nic Camen photographed by Marc Lebon, styled by Ray Petri.

"MONEY MOVES...PUT YOUR 2 HANDS IN YA POCKET, TAKE OUT SOME MONEY FOR ONE BRETHREN, SAVE SOME MONEY FOR ONE LITTLE JOHN..."

All you need to show off your £250 Crolla jacket is a waistcoat, £10 from Clignancourt Market in Paris, a £2 scarf from Portobello Rd and shorts, £12.95 from Flip. Amanda Casal at photographed by Marc Lebon, styled by Mitzi Lorenz and made-up by Kay Montano.

Roubles, rupees, shekels, dollars, deutschmarks, pounds or yen — they'll be no use to you on Mars, or when the **banks** go bust. You'd be better off with **pocket** space invaders or a pocket full of rice. Money is a liquid **asset** and the **currency** currents are variable — they may stagnate or dry up altogether. The Mayflower pilgrims, who traded their **pennies** for beads and mirrors before they set off for a new world, had sussed that the **value** of exchange is only in the eye of the beholder.

The Indians had a real **value** of life. **Money** was a smart arse idea which took centuries to perfect into some kind of international con trick. But how far can you trust it today? Give a newsagent an Afghan or Argentine **bank note** (at fair exchange, no robbery rate) and see how fast he passes **buck** on to somebody else! Give him a **dollar**, **deutschmark** or **Swiss franc** and no sweat! He'll probably hang onto it for his next trip to the Algarve.

**Gold, silver, copper** or **zinc** get juggled about daily at the commodity market **betting** shop. People are losing their shirts, jackets, y-fronts and virginity in the space of minutes so don't be fobbed by all that glitter and remember a chicken is a chicken and you can't feed your wife and ten screaming, starving kids on **half a pound** of zinc screws and a pocket of galvanised washers.

**Money** has become the rising/falling scale by which we judge our common neighbour (or decide to move to a better area). Having got past smoking other people's **dogends** and brewing cocktails from other people's **dregs**, I've never met anyone who wished to turn back the clock. Having the spare time or the **spare cash** to play the **money** game does not necessarily sort out the **haves** from the have-nots; effects on the losers is where you'll see the difference. Shooting yourself after a bad time at the track is a rich **man's** prerogative.

So when is enough enough? If society is to be judged by the state of its **bank balance**, you have either to pass — or to **PLAY THE GAME!**

4

5

"I've been told I have a spending problem, but
I have no problem spending money at all"

Divine, performer, no18

by and wear

WHEN VISITING YOUR BANK MANAGER

First impressions count. One
two three. Head back, chest
out & best foot forward.
Visiting the bank manager
can, for some of us, be as
riveting or as grilling as
going to the dentist. But
it's reasonably simple.

Well, on with the Fun Fur Coat (with dropped-lining) £200 by Dexter Wong
at Hyper Hyper — one-off hat & satin tube dress both by Mitzi. Shoes: £20
in Kensington Market. Suzi Bic photographed by Jamie Morgan — "FLY BY
NIGHT, EASY COME EASY GO, IT'S THE WAY YOU WEAR IT THAT MAKES IT SHOW."
Styled by Mitzi Lorenz, make-up by Kay Montano.

"LOOK CLOSELY, THINGS ARE NEVER WHAT
THEY SEEM."

Innercity camouflage:  Striped jacket £25, waistcoat £20, both from Millers
Old Compton St; shorts £8.99 from Lillywhites and braces £5 from Barkers.

photographed by Jamie Morgan

29

1 am/Fulham Rd/BENGALI VIGILANTES SEEK REVENGE. Take-away tycoons from London's Bengali
community have set up armed patrol groups in an effort to beat gangs of fast-food thieves.
Plant a £1 flag on a pure wool suit, approx. £500 (including material) made to order at Nutters,
35a Saville Row W1 (01) 437 6850; American cotton shirt from a selection at American Classics,
£7.50; Climbing sling £2 from Pindi Sports High Holborn; Turban made with black material from a
selection at The Cloth, Brewer St; Brooch to order from Andrew Spingarn, c/o Good As Gold, 5th
Ave. New York. styled by Ray Petri, photographed by Marc Lebon

12.00/27.9.84/Tower Hil
Gurkha Ali Khan for
jumped through our 17th
Prince of the City wear
selection at Herbert
selection at Burmans &
18 Irving St, WC2 (01
from a suit by Vivienn
selection at Crolla; Stu

(Wade) styled by Ray Pet

HA "RUINED OUR MARRIAGE" Jealous husband John Spence blamed athlete
of his marriage to childhood sweetheart Pamela Rushcroft. "He just
window one day and that was it", he wept.
added bandana from X-otique in Ken Market, £5, with feathers from a
Burlington St, W1; T-Shirt £6 from Browns; Naval purser jacket from a
e rentals, approx. £25/night plus VAT and deposit. Fancy dress from
iod costumes from 40 Camden St, NW1 (01) 387 0999. Hand-print skirt
one Worlds End shop (01) 351 0764 for information. Socks £12 from a
elet, £2.50 from Cobra in Portobello.

d by Marc Lebon

world wide real guide

**KIDS IN THE GANGSTER GROOVE**

Willow, Tyrone and Clementine are real tough cookies. They like loose clothes, bullet proof waistcoats, milk and their Doc Martens .... their "Stroppy" boots. What they don't like is being in confined places and being kept waiting. We kept out of their way as they looked like a nasty lot to us. If we gave them £1000, they wouldn't give it back.

Styling by Ray Petri
Fashion by Ray Petri

**CONTINENTAL INTER-CITY**

# SCRABBLE

PUT ON YOUR CLOWN OUTFIT AND INVENT YOUR OWN LABEL! FUN, FUN, FUN FOR YOUR PLEASURE WE BRING YOU THE BE-BOP ROCKIN CREW AND THE FUNKY THIGH COLLECTORS OF CENTRAL LONDINIUM... YOU CAN MIX AND MATCH WITH OUR NEW AUTUMN COLLECTION. WE GOT OUT OUR PHONE BOOK, LOOKED UP THE NAMES...AND STARTED THE GAME. GET OUT YOUR SCISSORS AND START MAKING NOTES...QUICKLY.

WE WANTED THE BEST, THE REST AND THE MESS. i-D WAS ON A CASE AND IT DIDN'T WANT ANY HITCHES...OR ANY TROUBLE. WE'D HEARD THAT THE PHOTOGRAPHER'S CREW WERE A MEAN HERD OF BANDITS...SO WE LOADED UP THE WAGON WITH WATER-PISTOLS AND PAPIER-MACHE AMMO AND GOT READY TO SHOOT. WE ARRANGED TO MEET THE TEAM OUTSIDE A DISUSED WAREHOUSE IN BERMONDSEY, BUT THEY

ALL TURNED UP THREE DAYS EARLY IN A PHOTOGRAPHER'S STUDIO IN OLD STREET. WHAT A BUNCH! SO WE DECIDED TO LEAVE THEM TO YOUR MERCY. BE MERCILESS AND DON'T WORRY IF YOU CUT ACROSS THE HEM LINE. GET OUT THE DICE, PUT ON YOUR THINKING CAP (BACKWARDS) AND GET READY FOR THE i-D FUN AND GAMES FASHION PARADE!

INTERVIEWED BY DYLAN JONES & MARION MOISY

26

PHOTOGRAPHED BY MONICA CURTIN

DOMINATRIX VIXENS

NORTHERN SOUL

THE GREBO

GLAM PUP

KING QUEEN

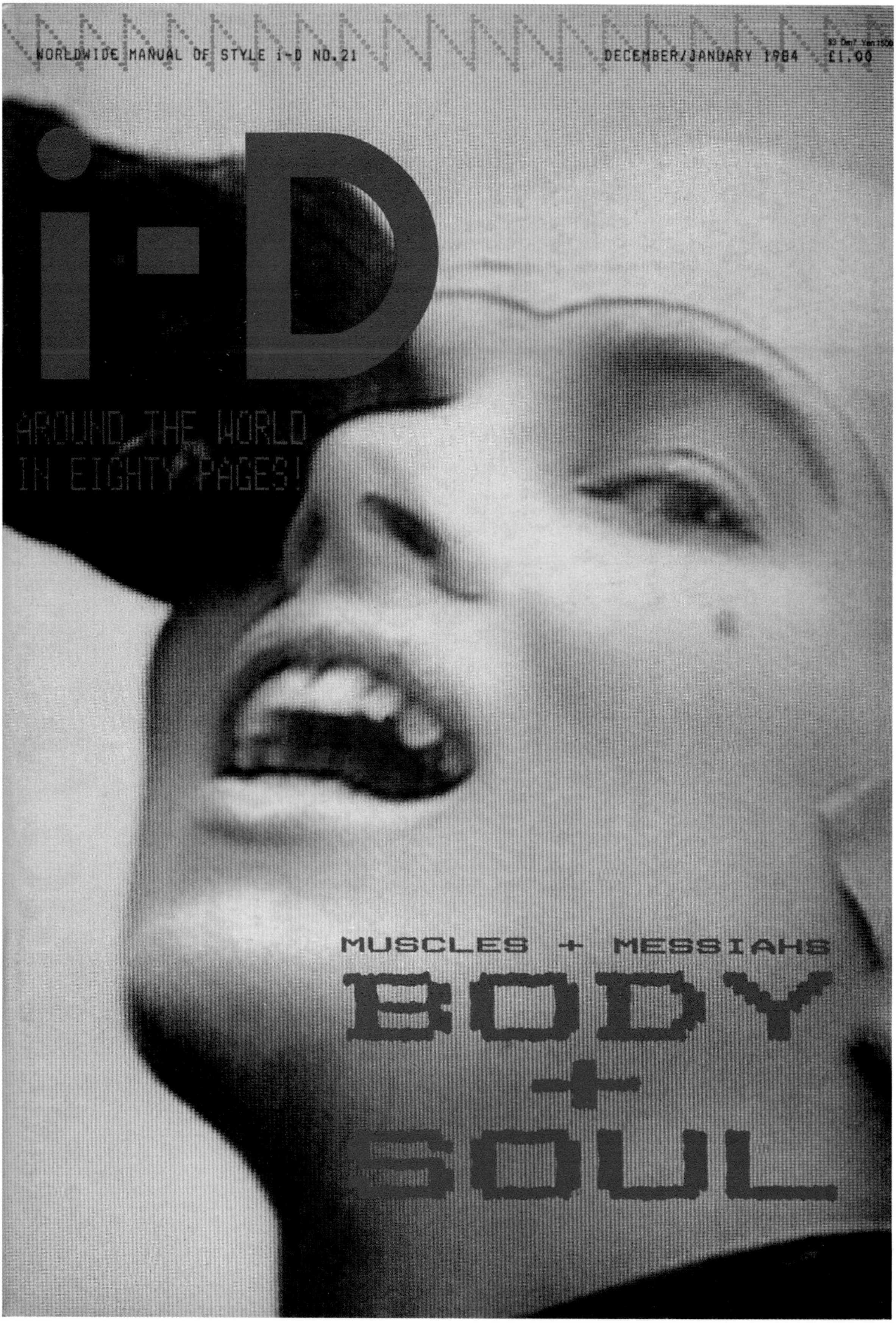

WORLDWIDE MANUAL OF STYLE i-D NO. 21　　　　DECEMBER/JANUARY 1984　£1.00

$3 Dm7 Yen 1550

# i-D

AROUND THE WORLD
IN EIGHTY PAGES!

MUSCLES + MESSIAHS

## BODY
## +
## SOUL

GOOD EVENING, HERE IS THE

# WORLD NEWS!!

*Eddie Joye*

Roving reporters on oversize undercover mission - i-D send out signals first; then secret agents to spy on style codes on every continent - Intelligence Officers do reconnaissance, information is assimilated then decoded. Back in London the raw data is pulped and pureed. High pressure interrogation techniques yeild results. MESSAGE READS: ALL HUMAN LIFE-STYLE IS HERE...

There have been outbreaks of strip jeans' tat and platform boots in the FAR MARK, and several females are said to be holding Indian culture to hostage...

In North and Central America there is serious water shortage leading to dry wit and three men in a tub...

On the stock exchange the pound fell again, by 2'6" it was in the hip pocket of Paul Morley's trousers at the time...See police are investigating...

There was renewed violence at the Soho Brasserie on the eve of the International Freeloaders Festival - rival factions of luggers contested for places in the forthcoming Gross drama-documentary...

Still in London, Bond St has declared unilateral independence, claiming it has the 8th largest economy in the world, a higher population than Wales, and an Embassy to boot...

In Afghanistan, a famous French fashion journalist has been found guilty of spying, and sentenced to 10 months of proof-reading NORSE AND MIGNO. Prosecution said that he was internationally infamous for ripping off spirits and other items of Afmania clothing...

In Parliament the Prime Minister was questioned about several not being held under the Prevention of fennar-use Act. He was even charging exhorbitant entry fees at an illegal warehouse party...

STYLE & FASHION RAY PEIRI (AKA STINGRAY)
PHOTOGRAPHS: ROGER CHARITY
Turn to Yellow Pages for stockists' address

**BRONX WARRIORS -** MAKES IT TO MID TOWN MANHATTAN. STYLE & ARROGANCE - STRIPPED THE RUSH HOUR TRAFFIC TO POSE FOR MY CAMERA. WEARING BLACK PREDOMINANTLY. TOUGH IMAGE. STREETWISE, VIVAL BUT IS PROUD OF HIS CATHOLIC UPBRINGING & LIKES THE PEOPLE TO KNOW IT.

Black cotton beret, £2 Brick Lane. Black M.A.I. original jacket £50 from Kelastinkroe, ground floor Kensington Market. Black Wrangler jeans, £19 Great Gear Market, Kings Rd. Red cotton singlet £1.50 Portobello Market. Boots his own, Socks Takeo Kikuchi, Tokyo £10. Bracelets & belts, Cobra Portobello Green, Jewels acquired privately

RAY GOES TO

## MANHATTAN

**THE SUN VIKING -** GANG MEMBER. BORN IN CHILE GREW UP AS A PEYOTE MOVED IN WITH THE HUSTLERS, PIMPS & TRANSVESTITES OF RIO & ACAPULCO. LOVES GLAMOUR & VIOLENCE & SEXUALITY - CRUISED INTO SCANDINAVIA TO CHECK IT OUT - THE VIKING HERITAGE LOVES ALL THE TOUGH GUYS AND ACTS OUT THE MOVIE ROLES HE'S SEEN - UNDERNEATH SENSITIVE AND CARING - SAYS HE'S ONLY USED HIS GUN TWICE IN SELF DEFENCE.

Black Sirocco singlet - a gift. Black Levi 501s - £6 F.C. £25. Cuff £5 - a gift. Pure silk scarf - his girlfriend's Chelka.

RIO

**BLIND MAN -** RAIMONDO PACO SANTAMARIA - FAN OF LOUIS BUNUEL - LOVES DRAMATIC & MYSTERIOUS IMAGE. WALKING BY THE SEA IN SAO PAULO. A LONE FIGURE OF QUIET SERVILE PERCEPTION. HAS AN INTERNATIONAL APPROACH TO HIS STYLE OF DRESSING - HERE ON HIS WAY TO A POLITICAL RALLY.

Striped wool suit - Men's Uomo £375 at Browns South Molton St. Cotton shirt - Costume Des Garcons, Browns £90. White cane £2.50 Argos institute for the Blind, Great Portland St N1. Catholic Missal, Church of Santa Maria Magdalena, Sao Paulo Brazil.

RIO DE JANEIRO

30 · 31

**TAIWAN POP STAR -** WEI SUN GIVES A COROGATING RENDITION OF THE GIRL FROM HIROSHIMA AT A CHARITY SHOW - NOTE THE AGGRESSIVE POSTURE, THE MICROPHONE GRIP. DESPITE THE 'PRETTY LITTLE GIRL' GUISE AND IMAGE SHE MEANS BUSINESS. BIG BUSINESS. SALES IN EXCESS OF 15 MILLION. OFFERS FROM HOLLYWOOD. ABSOLUTE ADORATION FROM HER FANS. MAKES MOST BRITISH POPSTARS LOOK OVERDRESSED AS WELL AS OVERSPENT.

Pink mini-dress £4.00 from Camden Market. Leather gloves £16.00 from John Lewis. UBA watch £16.00 from American Classics. Kings Rd. Di Marini shoes £16.50 (odd sizes) from Hurts, Kentish Town Rd.
Make-up by Kay Montano. Foundation & powder at Cosmetics A.L Corte. Lipstick & make-up by Barry M, no. 60, 41, 0, 45, 36. Lipstick from Charles Fox. Hair styling by Sandra at Pro-wax.

**DELHI BELLY DANCER -** KIDNAP VICTIM OF THE WHITE SLAVE TRADE AT THE AGE OF 15 LEARNED TO BELLY DANCE IN TURKEY BEFORE BEING SOLD TO THE GRAND MAHARAJA. AS A SHREWD MOVE SHE HAS SINCE BECOME A FAVOURITE OF THE HAREM. SHE LOVES TO SMOKE HASHISH AND HAVE THE FAMOUS RICH AROMATIC OILS INTO HER SHOULDERS. LACE AND TAKING HERSEXUAL PROWESS OF FOUNTAIN SPRINGS EXHAUSTED MANY LOVERS WITH TECHNIQUES DERIVED FROM KAMA SUTRA.

Dark cotton colour taffeta - dyed a like from Benwicka, Yd Berwick St and other materials from Charity X Rd. Indian jewellery from any trade just shop. Total less then £11. Make-up by Kay Montano. Model Sandra at Premier.

Foundation and powder at Cosmetics A.L Corte. Black eye shadow, Shiseido. Eye liner & mascara, Mary Quant. Lipstick, Yves St Laurent. Drawing, wetted black eye shadow.

MITZI GOES TO DEHLI...

STYLING: MITZI LORENZ. PHOTOGRAPHS: ROGER CHARITY

ROLL-BACK JACKET approx. £500, rumple-front waistcoat £170, Powindi shirt £90, pukka pants £130, available from Browns, Bazaar and Hunters, all prices approximate. Shoes Dr. Martens lace-ups, astrakan mountain hat, lifesaver belt, walking stick, accessories by Michael Collins for JG.

THE NEW GENTLEMAN IS A FEMME: is a man: ambidextrous clothing. SHIRT UPON SHIRT: Plus one shirt is a skirt. . . Powinda shirt-dress £180. Powindi shirt skirt £140, pukka pants £150 with Rawalpindi shirt as a skirt £130. Available at Browns, Bazaar and Hunters, all prices approximate. The blanket is from Oxfam.

**JOHN GALLIANO'S spring/summer '85 "AFGHANISTAN REPUDIATES WESTER IDEALS — an uneasy mix of opposed cultures in colours of dried blood or a theme of vision artistry and dramatic tension."**

As Stevie Stewart and David Holah hug their bodies close to their chest, **JOHN GALLIANO** told us what he thought of this year's feel. . . and the 'S' bend. "I love the hip. My tops are baggy at the back, tight at the waist and loosing downwards after that. Thus the 'S' bend, just like the Flamenco dancers. That's the kind of body I design for. The soul of my clothes lies in the colour. . . emotional dried blood." Since John's remarkably successful show at St Martins last summer, he's practically sold out of everything he's put into Brown's window. "The idea for this collection came from a cartoon I saw in a 30s edition of Punch. Afghanistan servants and gentlemen robed in smart European clothes. Just like all the Indians around the East End now. Very Petticoat Lane. London is keeping on its toes because in the last few years you've had incredibly positive people and very negative

people bouncing off each other and creating something tha places don't have. . . and we thrive on it, and with it, fashio whole wouldn't be so influential. Jean-Paul Gaultier is a clever man because he's taken street fashion and turned it mass market. The thing to do is to take two cultures and m start anew."

Two styles, two periods, two of whatever and slapping. slapping them together. Bic Owen, Jane De Lacey, Dean E speckies and spots and hurdy gurdy checks. John Gall thirty pieces in his collection are a sign for the future ter camouflage knitting and tents and everything on the outsh

THE FACE: the make-up behind shattered glasses in one tone by LESLIE CHILKES using RIMMEL cosmetics tone downers. SEVERE HEAD carted and veiled in hairnets by LAYLA D'ANGELO. HAT and accessories by MICHAEL COLLINS FOR JG.

urn to Yellow Pages for stockists' address

hotos Mario Testino, Styling Caroline Baker. Make-up Lesley Chilkes, Hair Layla D'Angelo, Video Duncan Ward, Backdrop by Ian Johnstone Webb. Models Sandra at K-Z and Mary Emma.

**44**

WEST MEETS EAST

45

# 1984

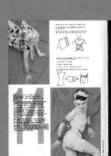

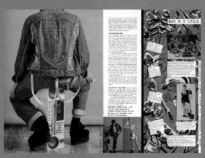

# 1985

Dec/Jan. The Body & Soul Issue no21. Cover star: Mary Emma. Photography by Mario Testino

February. The Gourmet Issue no22. Cover stars: Helen & friend. Photography by Nick Knight, Eamonn McCabe

March. The i-Spy Issue no23. Cover star: Carol Thompson. Photography by Eamonn McCabe, styling by Carol Thompson

April. The Flesh & Blood Issue no24. Cover star: Katie Westbrook. Photography by Nick Knight, styling by Helen Campbell

May. The Red-Hot Issue no25. Cover star: Patsy Kensit. Photography by Mark Lebon, styling by Caroline Baker

June. The Laid Back Issue no26. Cover star: EK. Photography by Martin Brading, styling by Caroline Baker

July. The Love-In Issue no27. Cover star: Kathy Kanada. Photography by Robert Erdmann

August. The Art Issue no28. Cover star: Lizzy Tear. Photography by Nick Knight

September. The Health & Efficiency Issue no29. Cover star: Caryl Dolores. Photography by Nick Knight, styling by Paul Frecker

October. The Grown Up Issue no30. Cover star: Jenny Howarth. Photography by Mark Lebon

November. The Spectator Issue no31. Cover star: Blair Booth. Photography by Eamonn McCabe

> "I want to be
> mega famous"
>
> **Patsy Kensit, actress, no30**

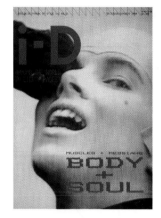

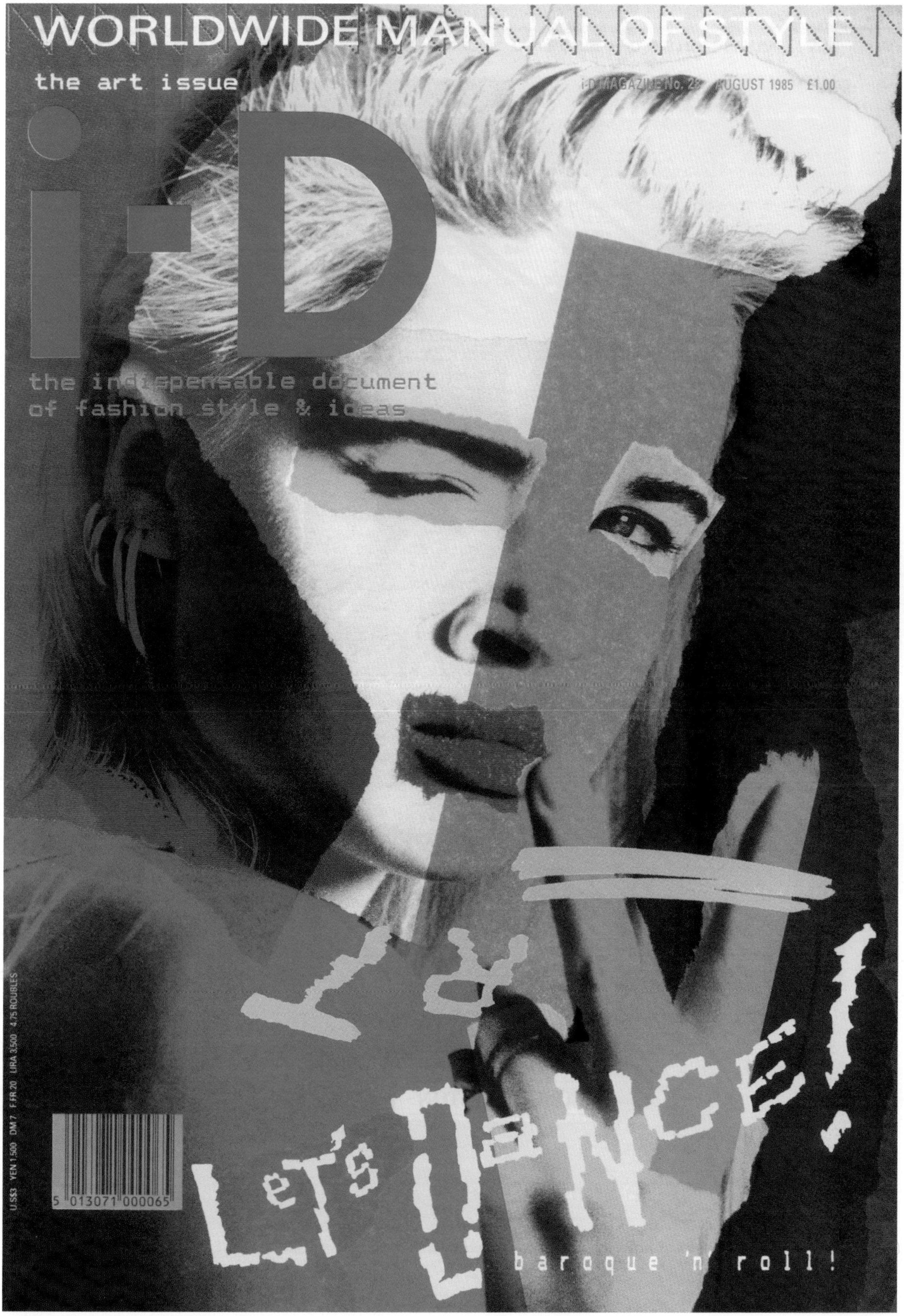

# WORLDWIDE MANUAL OF STYLE

the art issue

i-D MAGAZINE No. 24 AUGUST 1985 £1.00

# i-D

the indispensable document
of fashion style & ideas

U.S.$3 YEN 1,500 DM 7 F.FR 20 LIRA 3,500 4.75 ROUBLES

Let's DANCE!

baroque 'n' roll!

# POUT

**JESSICA'S fave taste:** Garlic; **Fave drink:** Champagne or Dark & Stormy (Dark Bahamas rhum and ginger beer on ice); **Fave smell:** Oil paint; **Fave part of body:** Back or neck; **Fave recipe:** Never cooks.

30

ORSETISATION-OF EVERYDAY CLOTHING.

Jessica wears opposite: Satin brassiere £24 and girdle dress £34 by Willy Brown at Old Town, 7 Upper James St; Suspender belt £20 at Fogal (New Bond St and Brompton Rd). Elastics from Pineapple. Bust pleat cotton voile shirt. £50 at No Yes. this page Jessica wears: Bib front cotton voile shirt £60· Satin brassiere £28· Droopy drawers £37; Diary print short leggings £32, all by No Yes. Elastics from Pineapple. PHOTOS BY ROBERT ERDMAN STYLING BY CAROLINE BAKER

31

# 02•85

## "I'm a bit of a prick, though which bit I'm not sure"

**Paul Weller, musician, no30**

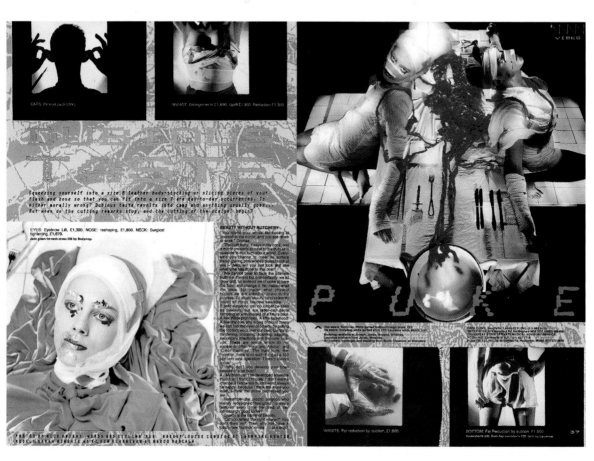

**IVAN KAMENIVITCH**

Popular young Russian émigré in New York, not much known about his past but plainly coverage recently by the American press of his private and public life. Lived for a time in London, but left this city hurriedly, lest you amidst stories of fantastic achievements, revolutionising the fashion model industry and selling his secrets to the U.S.A.

Unsuccessful in keeping a low profile he is known to adopt a variety of disguises, but is inevitably noticed because of his unstoppable personal style. He and Katarova currently painting the town Red apartment: Red Do it Czar.

**Navy wool overcoat $10 on Lennox Ave, Harlem; Hat $6 in the East Village New York; Woollen jumpers £29 at Harvey Nicholls.**

**BELLOVA KATAROVA (Buffalistically Speaking)**

Katarova in black,
She can still go back
From Moscow to Manhattan,
she's left a trail
Of broken hearts.

Possessing an amazing beauty that leaves men breathless, allows her to move freely in art, music, and especially political circles, some say acting as a go-between for the East & West. Debutante of Deterite personal envoy of world leaders and fashion spy for everyone from Vogue Va go to Reagans Digest. Would you tell your secrets to her!!!

**Black fur hat $25 from Patricia Fields N.Y.C.**

LOOKS FAMILIAR

# WORLDWIDE MANUAL OF STYLE

THE RED-HOT ISSUE

MAY 1985    £1.00

# i-D

THE INDISPENSABLE DOCUMENT
FASHION, STYLE & IDEAS

GO!

5 013071 000034

1 MILLION&ONE    Hot Tips    FOR MAY

## "Girl rappers are too busy in the kitchen to get anything together"

**3D, musician, no25**

**THE FREAKS!**

IN THE EARLY 70S AFTER THE FLORAL HIPPIE CAME THE FREAKS ● AND THE WOODWORK SQUEAKS AND BACK THEY COME ● FREAKS BRUSH THEIR HAIR BACK AND SPORT THE LESS REFINED, LESS AIRY AND MORE WEARABLE MIX ● THEY BUY THEIR BOOTS AND CLOTHES IN KENSINGTON MARKET, AND SINCE THE BIRTH OF THE SECOND GENERATION DESIGNERS, ALL THE OTHER MARKETS AND BOUTIQUES IN KENNY HIGH STREET, WITH MORE PAIRS OF JEANS, COWBOY BOOTS ACCESSORIES AND STALLS FOR THE FREAKS TO GET HIGH ON THE CHAPPARAL ● HOT TIP: CHECK OUT OUR SELECTION COMBING THE HAIR TO YOURS, WITH PLENTY OF GRAPHIC POLO NEAT AND RICH, LESS PATTERNED REVIVALIST CLOTHES ● COMBING THE FREAKS WHO GO FUTURIST ●

ALICE wears: Boots from Western Styling, Kensington Market £45, Penguin net shirt, John Crancher at L'Anarchie, Kensington Market £35, Levis jeans and jacket (Red label) SWIGGY wears: Shirt by Chutz from Jones in the Kings Road, Levis Red label jeans, Peace & love belts from Portobello Market, Army surplus top coat from Call To Arms in Upper Street N1

**BORN UNTO AFRICA, BROUGHT TO AMERICA**

Buffalo Management wear: Wool suits from £50 at Hackett, New Kings Rd; Shirts £29.50 from Beale & Inman, Jermyn St W1; Silk scarves from Japan; Leather & wool berets from Big Apple; Ties £6.50 at American Classics.

the love-in issue

i-D MAGAZINE No. 27  JULY 1985  £1.00

# i-D

the indispensable document
of fashion style & ideas

KISS THIS

Street Wise And Looking Kool

U.S.$3 YEN 1,500 DM 7 F.FR 20 LIRA 3,500 @DUBLE$4.75

The Boy looked at

Photos Cameron McVey/Ray Petri;   Model Tony Felix (Buffalo Management)

**Versace jacket, Pringle jumper, Track pants from Multi Sports, Hat from Big Apple.**

Cool & Deadly

(or Step lightly to the mix over from TREW (Printers)

30

*ciani*

(Adapted.....)
Julie Burchill
~~Tony Parsons~~
Tony Parsons.

**Versace jacket & shorts, shoes from Hackett.**

Stand from

31

# 08•85

## "There's a magazine just like yours in America called Cosmopolitan..."

**Barbara Cartland, novelist, no27**

> "You're not going to get anything steamy out of me"
>
> **Patsy Kensit, actress, no25**

*paris*

Blue boy took a hat, a shirt & a waistcoat — took a plane, took a boat, took a train.

**young gun goes for it!**

*texas*

Buffalo boys travel the world — it's official.

**deadly & cool!**

ART CROSSOVER

36

37

# 08•85

## "I'm a good time boy with bad eyesight"

**Robin Derrick, former i-D art director, no30**

eyeglass artisans!

I-SPY-WITH-MY-LITTLE-EYE, FILM NOIR ART

# WORLDWIDE MANUAL OF STYLE

the health & efficiency issue

i-D MAGAZINE No. 29 SEPTEMBER 1985 £1.00

# i-D

the indispensable document
of fashion style & ideas

CROP TO
FiT!

in the pink with a picture of health!

Jenny wears: Printed poloneck £25 and leggins £16.50, both from Boy at Hyper Hyper; Katharine Hamnett dinner jacket with embroidered lapels approx. £230; Genuine 'Kensington' hat from a selection at The Hat Shop London WC2, from £20; Belts from a selection at Cobra on Portobello Green, from £12; Doc Marten lace-ups £28.99 at Office Shoes Hyper Hyper.

Hats from a selection by Bernstock & Spiers, approx. £28.50 from Jones Kings Rd & Floral St, Joseph & branches of Whistles; Green printed poloneck £37, leggins £32, both by Pam Hogg at Hyper Hyper; Ribbed miniskirt by Richmond/Cornejo for Joseph, approx. £35; Heavy-duty leather bike boots £55 at Ad Hoc.

PHOTOS MARC LEBON; STYLING CAROLINE BAKER; MAKE-UP JO STRETTEL; MODEL JENNY HOWARTH.

37

WORLDWIDE MX

the grown up issue

i-D MAGAZINE No. 30 · OCTOBER 1985  £1.5«

# i-D

the indispensable document
of fashion style & ideas

YAH!

get it.

Streetwise

FIVE YEAR CELEBRATION

5 013071 000089

LOVE IT!

1980-85

# IDENTITY PARADE

## FIVE YEARS

**Here, for the first time are a selection of portraits by Nick Knight from a forthcoming book of People Of The 80s. Specially commissioned by i-D Magazine, these are just a few of the stars that Nick has photographed for inclusion in this book. This is both a celebration of the success of five years of i-D's catalogue of protagonists, and a starting point for what will become the definitive tome of the 80s.**
**The Scam: During May and June of this year, Dylan Jones and Nick Knight studiously contacted over 100 people who had at some time or another appeared in i-D Magazine. All the faces. From the fashion designers who weren't fashion designers then, to the pop stars who weren't, from the already famous to the ones who still aren't. The aim? A retrospective photo portrait gallery to appear in the 5th Anniversary edition of i-D. Day in, day out they sweated over hot-to-the-touch telephones, tracking down their subjects in all parts of the world. In they came, traipsing through the i-D offices, sipping coffee and chewing the fat – waiting to be immortalised on film. And the result . . .? Here for your eyes only . . . Read on . . .**

". . . all the fat-skinny people, and all the tall-short people, all the nobody people and all the somebody people . . ."
YOW! The Worldwide Manual Of Style!! Let fashion live!!! Live fashion!!!
In the Eighties the revolts into style and the plunderers of fashion have been rife, ripe and cheeky – turning Britain into a living, breathing catwalk of style where every living person is a dress code, a law unto themselves. And in these eclectic Eighties, i-D Magazine has undertaken to be the gallery of all these sartorial snapshots – a rogues' gallery, a beauty gallery – The Gallery Of Style.
The Eighties produced not only thousands of people with thousands of dress-modes, but it also produced legions of duplicates – multiplying, cross-dressing and cross-fertilising like crazy: insatiable and inscrutable.
The Bowie generation *did* come to life – not just the 'soul-boy' ethic, but the configuration of all manner of as-yet-unseen yute cults from the early Seventies: the baggied, the skinned, the long-haired, the overcoated, the cropped, the goth-chiced, the wondershticked . . . the whatevered. Style is now a consumers market, and once you let the genre out of the bottle it's impossible to put back the cork – everybody wants a piece of the action: Buy, wear and be merry! The fashion-zealots narcissistically confronted themselves with a multitude of public climactic moments – and the media ate with Pacman-like intensity, chewing over things they'd normally have the scantest opinion on: real life street showbusiness.
If the fantasy cycle started in 1975 with the advent of punk, then lo and behold we are at the end of an era – ten years of unmitigated brazen showoffishness. The late Seventies were the mulling period – the puberty stage for harbingers and stylists, garnished with colloquial hokum – an inspiration and invitation to protagonists and plunder-mongers.
But the Eighties is where the fun began, and also when i-D took the lens cap off. From 'To Cut A Long Story Short' to the end of DoDos – five years stuck on your eyes, five years what a surprise – we had to cram so many things to store everything in these. In between the fashion phantasmagoria, the die-hard decals, the festered fashions, the victims and the victimised there obviously came a backlash – along with cossetted surrogate pop came casuality for chrome-plated and streamlined times: people who started to dress like the people who once beat them up for looking different. Pah! Humbug!! But the force remains, and exclusivity still holds its own, even if it is being pocketed by twice as many people (we are *still* supporting football teams because of their strip – Coventry's pale blue colours were always very attractive!).
Feel the power of London Town as you stand on Waterloo Bridge – surveying the bud-bud-budding talent. Britain is awash with new talent, thousands of enfant terribles, more so than ever as style continues to breed. As other countries turn our ideas into cabaret – we are filling up with even more surefooted and versatile young things.
Leonine clashing threads, ambiguity, iconoclastic lads and reet-petite dress are coming at us faster than ever . . . and at the third stroke the time will be 1995 precisely – so here's to it. Let's sink the big boats! Vive le rock!!

Dylan Jones

*The book will be released during the next 18 months, written by Dylan Jones and designed by Terry Jones.*

FIVE YEAR CELEBRATION

i-D

15

**SHERRON** – Singer. First appeared in i-D NO.18. Lead singer with popstars Savajazz. . . "I am shy, mysterious and beautiful", she says. "I'm constantly pursued by ravenous and ravaging men eager to father me. The 80s have been great for me because they've given me the opportunity to do what I wanted to – be in a band." Club: The Titanic. Record: 'Ain't Nobody' – Chaka Khan.

**PAUL WELLER** – Pop Singer. First appeared in i-D No. 22. In the 80s, Paul split The Jam and created The Style Council – catering for his own tastes in music and cut of trouser. The most important event in the 80s: A. "The miners' strike (UK)." B. "The general turn to right wing politics (International)." "These days I understand myself a lot more, and even when I don't, I try to go with my feelings, good or bad. I'm a bit of a prick, though which bit I'm not sure." Club: "Early Do-Dos. Record: 'Long Hot Summer' – The Style Council.

**LEIGH BOWERY** – Fashion Designer. First ap… he of the glad-rags and nappy rash, weari… hosting one of the most exciting clubs of '8… event of the last five years?: "Heavens above… from Australia. I used to be very nervous… especially dressing up. But nowadays I don't… good, but 1990 is going to be much better. As… things." Leigh has the noisiest clothes on the… are LOUD! Club: Taboo. Record: 'Everything S…

**PAM HOGG** – Fashion Designer. First appeared in i-D NO.10. Pam has a very strong Scottish accent. Fact. "I survived one of those incredible car-crashes after leaving The Hacienda on Friday the 13th, strange but true. Only the colour of my hair has changed since 1980. In five years time I'd like to be designing without all the crap that goes with it, and indulging in films, music and extravagant holidays. 1985 has been explosive and I am irresistible." Club: Taboo/Cha Cha. Record: Repo Man soundtrack.

**STEPHEN JONES** Milliner. First appeared in i-D No. 1. "The best thing about the 80s was getting a Gold American Express Card. The difference between now and five years ago is that now I firmly believe that anything is possible. . . 1985 was the first year that I sued anybody! In five years' time, I'd like to have designed my own car and have a telephone switchboard in my flat." Stephen describes himself as. . . "One lady owner, 1957 G.T. model with new engine and good bodywork." Club: "The plain chocolate ones with raisins." Record: "Daley Thomson's."

**KEITH FROM SMILE:** – Hairdresser. First ap… since the first Roxy Music LP, Keith has bee… biggest appointment book. A dab hand. "T… recognition of street style and the resurgence… more political. The time is right for a cha… reached a peak – everything is trendy now… haircuts. I want something new." Keith thinks… Watts of hairdressing."

**DYLAN JONES** – Journalist. Plagiarised in i-D No. 4. First appeared in i-D No. 16. i-D Assistant Editor. Most important thing that's happened in the last five years?: "The confirmation that anything is possible as long as your arse isn't as shiny as your shoes." How have you changed?: "Bigger vocabulary, bigger wardrobe, bigger bladder." Five years' time?: "Working twice as hard for ten times the money." 1985?: "The year of decision – take it away!" Describe yourself: "Young, free and modest." Club: Club For Heroes/Do-Dos/Area. Record: Double D & Steinski – 'The Payoff Mix'.

**SCOTT CROLLA & GEORGINA GODLEY** – Fashion Designers. First appeared in i-D NO.17. Their Dover St. fashion emporium is one of the most influential in the world. Scott is "Philosophical", Georgina "Ideological." Events of the 80s: Scott – "Georgina." Georgina – "Sheet bondweb." How have you changed?: Scott – "More open minded." Georgina – "Erratically." Five years time? Scott – "Living in a small house outside Florence with a wife and two kids." Georgina – "I would like to be doing what I would like to be doing in 5 years time." 1985: Scott – "Loud, dangerous and uniformed." Georgina – "Cold." Club: Early Studio 54/My Dining Club. Record: 'The Glory Of Love' – The Armoury Show/'Sindy Saves the Radio Show'.

**TOM DIXON & NICK JONES** – Club entrepren… NO.17. First Funkapolitan crush-groovers. The… Titanic raisers and Car Park attendants. Most… five years?: Tom – "The world famine." Nic… Japanese food." How have you changed in… – "I've found my second childhood." Nick – "I'v… time?: Tom – "Retired with a large amount of… of leisure." Nick – "Still reading i-D." 1985?: To… the 70s." Nick describes himself as "Tall, dark… "Continental." Club: The Language Lab/Space… listen to records . . . we mix cassettes."

" Street fashion i

# STREETWISE!

NEWS ON THE STREETS

WC2 – i-D takes to the streets once more in a celebration of A-Z style... inroads into fashion, two-way streets and geography for the feet. i-D moved to Covent Garden a year ago in the co-publishing deal with Tony Elliott – carrying its coat of arms into the depths of ad agencies and converted warehouses. We take our hats off to you!

i-D

Angela at Z Agency wears (Left to right): Hat & feathers from The Hat Shop, Neal St London WC2. Long floral skirt by Leslie Gale, available at Review & Acrobat. Leather gloves by Julie Elliott.

Black bowler hat from Beligand in Paris. Red doll & feather from Les Halles in Paris. White frill shirt from Johnsons. Navy coat by Leslie Gale as above. Denim jodpurs from Flip, cufflinks and silver buttons from Detar. Black lace gloves from Upstairs in Kensington Market.

Black straw hat from The Hat Shop as above. Black veil from Bermecks Berwick St London W1. White lace shirt by John Crutcher available at Browns. Grey jacket by Junko Shimada 54 Rue Etien Marcel in Paris. Black velvet trousers and skirt by Susan Backhouse available at Hyper Hyper. Black lace gloves from Camden Market.

Check Yellow Pages for further details.

39

MITZY LORENZ · EAMONN J McCABE · SALLY FRANCOMB

...gner. First appeared in i-D NO.6...

**PETE BENTON** – Illustrator, pizza maker and clothes-horse...

**LYNNE FRANKS** – PR. First appeared in i-D No. 24. Lynne's company has risen and grown to be one of the biggest of its kind in the world...

**GARY KEMP** – Guitarist. First appeared in i-D NO.2. Brother, songwriter and hairdo' in Spandau Ballet...

**BODYMAP** – Fashion Designers. First appeared in i-D No. 17. Stevie Stewart and David Holah make superb baby clothes for grown-ups...

**JEFFREY HINTON** – Video maker. First appeared in i-D No. 17...

...OR – Hairdresser & Photographer. First appeared in...

**DICK BRADSELL** – Barman. First appeared in i-D No. 15. Dick has been a barman in Zanzibar, The Dome, The Soho Brasserie and most recently at Club 1997...

**ADAM ANT** – Pop singer. First appeared in i-D No. 1. Prince Charming's alter ego, a regular rock 'n' roller. Event of the 80s?: "The Live Aid concert on 13th July 1985 at Wembley"...

**MITZI LORENZ** – Stylist. First appeared in i-D No. 13. Little Mitzi has tried successfully to appear in every other issue of i-D since the early 80s...

**ALIX SHARKEY** – Singer, Journalist, Star. First appeared in i-D No. 7...

**RICHARD DISTELL** – Fashion Designer. First appeared in i-D No. 3...

...Museum Commandos. First appeared in i-D No. 19...

**KATHARINE HAMNETT** – Fashion Designer. First appeared in i-D No. 11. Her work-wear for night-wear and day-wear for anywhere has made her one of the most successful designers in the world...

**KATE GARNER** – Singer. First appeared in i-D No. 10. Once a model and photographer, then the better half of Haysi Fantayzee – now forging ahead with a solo career...

**STEPHEN KING** – Fashion Designer. First appeared in i-D No. 24. Stephen's King's Road shop has now firmly established itself as a gallery for his superb menswear collections...

**BERNSTOCK & SPEIRS** – Fashion Designers. First appeared in i-D No. 22. Then hats, now togs ...and under the successful wing of Lynne Franks PR, Kitler groans of the 80s: Thelma – "Teaching Agnes (Bulldog) and Marlene (Marve Ronald) to catwalk"...

**NICK LOGAN** – Editor. First appeared in i-D No. 30. The Wanderlust wide-boy who made a success of both the NME and The Face...

Michele Aikin loves staring at people so much that she and 'Hil' (see Hilary) take this activity to the limits and hang out in Covent Garden playing 'Spot The Cutie'. This is often done with the aid of dark glasses so no-one can tell. Michele says she can only take so much of other people staring at her though.

**Michele wears:** Polkadot cocktail dress £80 by Caroline Walker, Kensington Market. Two petticoats, £15 each, also from Caroline Walker. Frilly brolly £20 from John Lewis. Lycra gloves £6.95 from Av Suzy at Hyper. Silver rucksack £32 from Extras at Hyper. Silver Doc Marten boots (sprayed) £30 from Shelleys. Earrings £15 & ring £7 both by Georgette Franks (01) 935 6466 for more details).
**Check Yellow Pages for details.**

28

Katey Lush: "It was the Costa Del Sol, carnival time and the shops were full of brightly coloured dresses, and I just had to have one, so I used my Visa card for the 1st time." She likes staring at the mirror on a good day and Mel Gibson cause he's a bit of alright, Woooargh! Her fave film of all time is The Pink Telephone 1955, a 15 minute short by Pierre Poisson. So when are we going to see the tasty Lush dancers again Katey? "Well the girls are resting at the moment, after their triumphant appearance at the Alternative Top Of The Pops. Our wigs are recovering, and our clothes designer has been snapped up by Montana." Kate eats TV dinners and likes watching you watching her watching you!

**Kate Lush wears: spotted Spanish dress £100 from the Costa Del Sol. Hand-painted earrings £12 by Georgette Frank. Shoes £120 by John Cares-Moore.**

Michele, Hilary and Katey's hair were all done by Gregory Cazalay and airbrushed using techniques by David Adams. The colour can be made to wash out the following day for a party special or last for 6 weeks. Prices start at £15. Contact Joshua Calvin for more details. 69-71 Park Rd. London NW1 (01) 724 2341.

PHOTOS **VIRGINIA LIBERATORE**. SHOT AT THE WHITE STUDIO, RANELAGH GARDENS, LONDON SW6 (01) 731 7551. STYLING **FRANKIE**. MAKE-UP **STEPHANIE JENKINS** FOR MARCO RASALA

# 1985

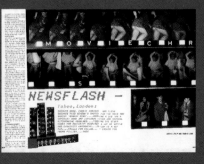

# 1986

Dec/Jan. The Jet Set Issue no32. Cover star: Kate. Photography by Nick Knight, styling by Simon Foxton

February. The Cool Issue no33. Cover star: Corinne Drewery. Photography by Nick Knight, styling by Helen Campbell

March. The Madness Issue no34. Cover star: Scarlett. Photography by Mark Lebon, styling by Judy Blame

April. The Dance Issue no35. Cover star: Akure. Photography by Robert Erdmann, styling by Caroline Baker

May. The Magic Issue no36. Cover star: Alice Temple. Photography by Nick Knight, styling by Simon Foxton

June. The Conservation Issue no37. Cover star: June Montana. Photography by Robert Erdmann, styling by Caroline Baker

July. The Photographic Issue no38. Cover star: Ann Scott. Photography by Robert Erdmann, styling by Simon Foxton

August. The Dramatic Issue no39. Cover star: Naomi. Photography by Nick Knight, styling by Caryn Franklin

September. The Education Issue no40. Cover star: Amanda King. Photography by Nick Knight, styling by Simon Foxton

October. The Media Issue no41. Cover star: Muriel Gray. Photography by Nick Knight, styling by Simon Foxton

November. The Beauty Issue no42. Cover star: Angie Hill. Photography by Nick Knight, assisted by Charlotte & Andy

# i-D

## act!

THE METHOD

CATHY TYSON

EDINBURGH
FESTIVAL

PANINARI

TOKYO

GILBERTO GIL

THE FRINGE

+

RICHMOND/CORNEJO

BRIGHTON

30 YEARS OF
YOUTH CULTURE

THE MUSICAL

P-FUNK

*dress rehearsal*

THE DRAMATIC ISSUE

THE INDISPENSABLE DOCUMENT OF FASHION STYLE AND IDEAS

YEN 1,500  DM 7  F FR. 20  LIRA 3,500  PESETAS 425  ROUBLES 4.75

5 013071 000171

"People all over the world, get on board . . ."
If y'all don't dig the baroque opera and mammoth dress devotees . . . if y'all
don't . . . the flouncy fairground frills stylee . . . then Slim Down, Colour Up and get
. . . L TRAIN: Bright Colours, tight fit and pert behinds.
. . . et . . . on . . . platform.

. . . n in . . . view . . . ALAN MARKE turn to page 81, y'all.

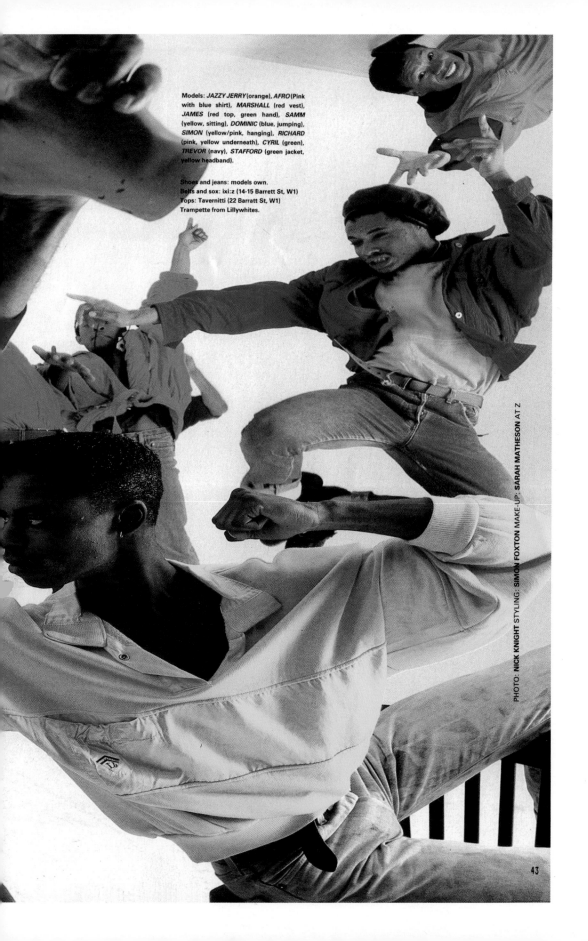

Models: *JAZZY JERRY* (orange), *AFRO* (Pink with blue shirt), *MARSHALL* (red vest), *JAMES* (red top, green hand), *SAMM* (yellow, sitting), *DOMINIC* (blue, jumping), *SIMON* (yellow/pink, hanging), *RICHARD* (pink, yellow underneath), *CYRIL* (green), *TREVOR* (navy), *STAFFORD* (green jacket, yellow headband).

Shoes and jeans: models own.
Belts and sox: ixi:z (14-15 Barrett St, W1)
Tops: Tavernitti (22 Barratt St, W1)
Trampette from Lillywhites.

PHOTO: **NICK KNIGHT** STYLING: **SIMON FOXTON** MAKE-UP: **SARAH MATHESON AT Z**

43

# WORLDWIDE MANUAL OF STYLE

i-D MAGAZINE  No. 33  FEBRUARY 1986     £1.00

# i-D

## THE COOL ISSUE

*Cool out sister*
*Vivienne Westwood*
*Paul Rutherford*
*Fashion survival guide*

## CHILL OUT

*Plus music, fashion, style + soho cool*

THE INDISPENSABLE DOCUMENT OF FASHION STYLE AND IDEAS

5 013071 000119

"Those are the finest pair of trousers
I've ever been interviewed by"

**Bryan Ferry, musician, no 32**

STEPHANO from Class
Agency: Milan wears Jacket
and Shirt by Takeo Kikuchi.
Accessories by Judy Blame.

Through the past darkly
## THE EYES HAVE IT

**Photographs by Marc Lebon
Styling by Ray Petri**

Diaphanous dress by Berstock and Spiers. Dagger brooch by Peter Foster. Diamente collar by Butler and Wilson. See Yellow Pages for stockists.

OLD ROPE

Knitted bra and Jersey toga skirt by John Galliano. Decorated hanky by Judy Blame. Tattoos by Dave Baby. See Yellow Pages for stockists.

44

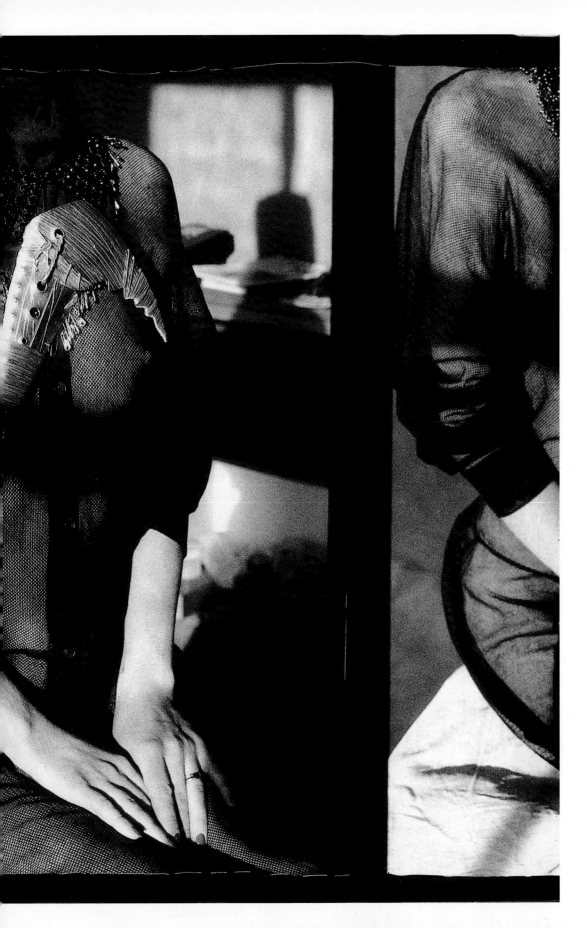

Charles from LONDON VIP ROOM LIMELIGHT

Kendall Werner "86"

Rock Bird at 1018 party for Stephen Saben

Caz, works at the TUNNEL pictured at SPRING and Thompson

Nozomi SINGER at the Limelight it on route to PYRAMID !

Karen at the Limelight "TAKE ME TO THE AZTEC"

TRY IT SOMETIME : Natalie AT MARNINAS PARTY

ALAN X of the WORST Limelight VIP Room

Wendell Wallace and Kerry. The Palladium

Kerry at Kevins Flat Thompson St SOHO

Yuval of the URBANITES in front of BITE THE APPLE

CHIEF. at THOMSON ST. SOHO

KARL & GRONBERG + KAREN AT THE MILK BAR

Tyrone FASHION DESIGNER at the URBANITES PARTY

Quentin Crisp at the Flaunt-it Club LIMELIGHT

BAD at 1018 c'mon every BEATBOX !

Ruby Peezie at Madam Rosas Singer

Jules DJ'ing at Madam ROSAS: 12 Dec 1986

ATTILA illustrator at THE FLAUNT IT CLUB

ROMEO Hairdresser : GIRL LOVES BOY

Caz from London in SOHO NYC.

VIEW FROM TOP OF EMPIRE STATE: NOV 1986.

JOSEPH D ESIMORE HAIRDRESSER at FLAUNT IT.

Kali with CUSTOMISED URBANITE ONESIST in BROMLEY

Kali modelling extensions by "GIRL LOVES BOY"

"SUPERSTAR AT URBANITES PARTY : THE LIMELIGHT

Kim designs customised Jackets : BRANDX SOHO

KEVIN BOWIE Paradise Garage How Convenient

VTOPIA - dancer hosting a party at MILK BAR

Lady E'' Street Elaine in Thompson

LinK The artificial intelligence Kid'/n

Gary at THE FLAUNT IT CLUB

Cookie does a bit of everything : LIMELIGHT

Laeri Nost- Sculptor at URBANITES PARTY LIGHT

HIUN artist at an URBANN PARRRTY.

BIDDIE singer from MADAM LIMELIGHT VIP ROOM LONDON!

Jane E. Millett. Muralist at THE TUNNEL CLUB

K.Haring '86

Rudolf at THE TUNNEL

Debras Photographer at the FLAUNT IT CLUB

Kali Myers Painter, lives at the Chelsea Hotel

Jules strictly known as Jules DJ at Madam ROSAS SAVE THE ROBOT

Jo and Lida at Madam Rosas Flamenco dancer + actor n club Bar.

Bernell and JOHN Spreculator AT MADAM ROSAS

THE FABULOUS POP TARTS INTERVIEW MICHAEL MUSTO

CHIEF awesome dude! BOSTON PATRIOTS FAN

Shira "the only ISRAELI in ALPHABET CITY".

Katie O'Cole Actress door person at FLAUNT IT

MAN RAY musician at the URBANITES PARTY

MOYA HESSION FABRIC DESIGNER : LIMELIGHT

Manana from Berlin at the URBANITES PARTY

Karen Finley, Performer; Mike Todd Room, Palladium

Manana and UTOPIA at THE URBANITES PARTY !

KALI AND TYRONE at the URBANITES PARTY

Gary and Nozomi "Tower Records" "POPSTAR"

URBANITES PARTY LIMELIGHT. MAN RAY, COOKIE, KALI, KATIE, Tyrone

Escav + Karen "Sisters How Cute" at Limelight

Susie Danish model at the Milk Bar

Mani PICTURED AT THE TUNNEL CLUB.

Michael Musto flaunting it at the Limelight

Jenny working at Brand Hair By Bammed.

Daniel seaweed JUNKIE at the URBANITES PARTY

Kevin Bowie + Nephew at Maceys Parade.

Käthe Be (Kunst-Malt) Berlin artist, Back Room AREA

Sally Randall at the Flaunt it, Limelight.

CHARLES from LONDON VIP ROOM LIMELIGHT

136

"Confidence just isn't an appropriate state to be in this century. If you're confident – watch out! It's actually a psychopathic state, a response bordering on panic, which is more accurate"

**Martin Amis, writer, no32**

"Does Madonna have style? Not really. She looks like a pop singer"

**Quentin Crisp, eccentric, no34**

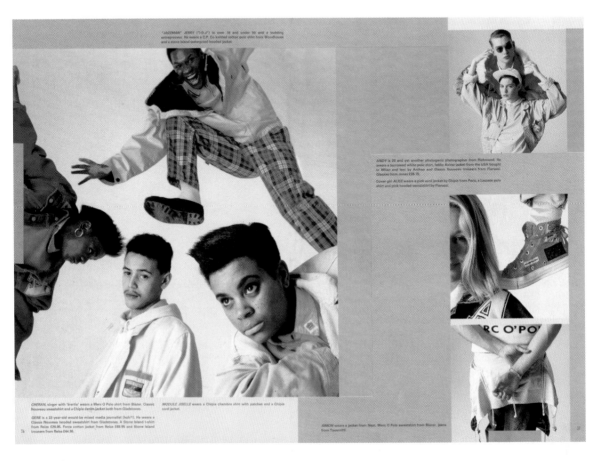

"People in England these days look like they're trying too hard. People never looked stupid in my clothes, just fashionable. I am Coco Chanel, Yves Saint Laurent"

**Vivienne Westwood, designer, no33**

# S P E C I M E N ?

THE NEW MAN STEPS OUT THE WAY NO MAN HAS STEPPED BEFORE! BOLDLY CONQUERING NEW FRONTIERS WITH THE AID OF INTER-GALACTIC GAULTIER. SPATIALLY STYLED FOR REMOTE CONTROL. BEAM HIM UP SCOTTY...

PHOTOGRAPHY BY
ROBERT ERDMAN
STYLING BY
MARCUS ACKERMAN

Post sackcap by Slag available from Kunst Boutique, 28 Wardour St. Soho London W1. Penny broaches by Judy Blame from Bazaar and House of Beauty and Culture. Cream Knit and wrap over Skirt both by John Galliano from Bazaar, Jones, 129 Kings Rd. SW3 and Midas 22 Kings St. Manchester. Shopping Bag — Oxfam. Shoes by John Moore, available from Bazaar, House of Beauty and Culture, Jones SW3 and WC2.

...axed paper bag hat by
...ag available from
...nst Boutique 28 War-
...ur St. Soho, London
...1. Cotton Sellotape
...ock shirt by Christ-
...her Nemeth, available
...m Bazaar, 4 South
...lton St. W1; House of
...auty and Culture; Cuts
... Market St Brighton.
...ny broach by Judy
...me from Bazaar and
...use of Beauty and
...lture. Paper bag round
...— Oxfam and card-
...ard tube – Duty Free.
...sters from Boots the
...emist. Shoes by John
...re from Bazaar, House
... Beauty and Culture,
...es, 13 Floral St. WC2
...d 129 Kings Rd, SW3.

## SCORCHED

Urban paranoia surrounds the rumour that London club-runners are re-introducing William The Conqueror's 'Scorch Policy' of burning down hostels of rebellion, or in this case, *competition*. Wearing their hearts on their sleeves and their heroes on the backs of their MA1 Army jackets these nightclub entrepreneurs roam the streets appalled at this wanton disco arson. Will they be next to suffer the wrath of the West One Scorchers? The Soviet butterflies cast their competitors' flyers into the remnants of yet another venue. . . and wonder.

Photograph Nick Knight

Styling Simon Foxton

Black jackets £20 approx, from all Camping and Army shops. Woven Chinese patches £3 each from Gung Ho Book Shop, Gerrard St, London W1. 501's Levis natural (kindly donated by Levis for the ripping of) approx £30, available from Jean Jeanie Oxford St and selected branches through the country, Western Frontier in Selfridges London W1 and Way In at Harrods.

From left to right – EDDIE, TONY, LISTON, VERNON and JAMES.

47

"was it good for me?! well honey, i just didn't know i had so many g-spots!"

32    home guard – the dreams of an everyday housewife? the modern-day temptress/protectress shot by marc lebon

"At certain points cool is definitely happening... but not so cool that you don't get no pussy"

**George Clinton, musician, no37**

free kick. penalty taken by eamonn mccabe

offside! professional foul again by eamonn mccabe

i-D thanks Roger and Contemporary Wardrobe for their help and guidance with this project.

Photography by Nick Knight

Styling and coordination by Simon Foxton.

# POSE!

### 30 YEARS OF PLAY ACTING

Ham it up! The theatricalities of dressing up have always gone in tandem with the clothes themselves — the art of the pose becoming synonymous with the art of selecting icons. Every youth cult since the war has adopted various stage-door mannerisms and dramatic stances that personify the outward projection of smugness, dissatisfaction, bravado and elitism. Strolling players, matinee idols, bit players and pierrots all. But don't be put off by any homogenized images — scratch the surface and the details come to light — as i-D shows here.

And though the styles may change and the music diversify, somehow the repertoire of poses remains remarkably similar. If the Teds of the 50s were the square root of all evil, then today's cults are the result of 30 years of musical and sartorial algebra. Yet the pose remains the same. Don't blink now!

MODS: "Smile & stare: Mobility, cleanliness and asexuality. An upwardly mobile fashion victim's delight."

'14-24' — British Youth Culture — Communications Through Commodities' is the last exhibition at The Boilerhouse's present site (it's moving to the east of London in the autumn), and it looks at the emergence of youth as a distinct economic category, from the great surge in mass culture which took place in the aftermath of the Second World War to the eclecticism of 1986. From the Teddy Boys to the Casual Boys — from I.D. tags to i-D Magazine.

Nick Knight and Simon Foxton were specially commissioned by The Boilerhouse to produce a set of photographs which embodied the major youth cults of the last 30 years — the results of which you can see on the following pages. To catch a glimpse of Nick & Simon's more modern exploits — The Preppy Casuals — look back at i-D No. 36 (May 1986).

'14-24' at The Boilerhouse, Victoria & Albert Museum, London SW7. 23 July-31 August. Opening times: 10-5.30. Weekdays and Sat. 2.30-5.30. Closed Fridays. Admission free (for psychos, winos and sociologists alike).

54

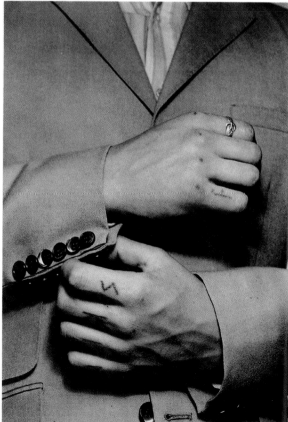

SKINS: "Fright tactics: Streamlined, guttersnipe army. Perfect symmetry. . . if you dared to look."

Altered Image

- Snapshots of everyday life, with a surreal slant.
  ●
- Not what you expect
- Changing the image completely by changing one small aspect of it.
- looking at normal everyday situation
  ie washing up and adding a surreal
- The effect becomes scary, funny + bizarre

- animals are quite are ordinary
  image together with the ordinary
  situations but when combined
  become odd etc.
  ●
- Makes u ask questions

① I looked at two main photographers.
Cindy Sherman and Karine
Serrinino. There work is very different
14. in terms of purpose
Serrinino (fashion) Sherman (Art)
but the I have noticed many
similarities.

Both want to create something
different and to use
plastic body parts, masks
They tot to change born try to
create altereed images.

ROCKERS: "Mock gypsy antics: Leather, studs, metal and plenty of denim to stand up to media attention."

TEDS: "The immaculate perception? Granite quiffs, bootlace ties and the beginnings of the drape. Pose hard!"

WORLDWIDE MANUAL OF STYLE i-D NO. 40          SEPTEMBER 1986 £1.00/$3

# i-D
## wise up!

MENSWEAR SPECIAL

HOLLY JOHNSON

BARCELONA

THE CHRISTIANS

CHICAGO HOUSE MUSIC

ROGER DACK

ART POP!

WORKERS FOR FREEDOM

NAPLES FUNK

THE SUN-BED KIDS

YEN 1.500 DM 7 F FR 20 LIRA 3.500 PESETAS 425 ROUBLES 4.75

5 013071 000188

THE INDISPENSABLE DOCUMENT OF FASHION STYLE AND IDEAS

PHOTOGRAPHED BY NICK KNIGHT
STYLING BY SIMON FOXTON

HAIR BY KEVIN RYAN AT ANTENNA
GROOMING BY FRANCES HATHAWAY AT FACES
LOCATION: LIPSTICK STUDIOS LONDON
MODELS: AMANDA KING, DANCER WITH MICHAEL
CLARK, OKI AT NEVS (CURRENTLY DANCING IN
CHESS), STUNT MAN GLEN DAVIS AT NEVS, WILL
JUMP OUT OF A WINDOW IF YOU WANT, DAVID
WEARING, DANCER, SPOTTED AT THE FRIDGE
DANCING FOR PROJ-X ❷

### SCHOOL'S BACK!

Boiled beef and carrots, fags behind the bike-sheds and heads down the toilet. Ring! Ring! Yes, school is back again. And come lunchtime the laddies come out to play-act: Flashman, Dennis The Menace and Billy Whizz with not-so-baggy trousers, not-so-dirty shirts ... but definitely a tap on the head with a plastic cup. With their tongues in their cheeks they pile out for a scrap, a joke and a chase round the playground — all good, clean, healthy fun.

Feast your eyes on the following pages and watch some geezers in real Men's clothing pushing out their chests and reading i-D behind their text books. "Who stole my ruler!"

For clothes details refer to page 57

43

49

# i-D Confi-De

TOM WAITS TALKS TO HENRY BECK
& SCOTT MEHNO IN TIMES SQUARE.

PHOTOGRAPHS BY DIANE DANIELS.

# TOM WAITS.

## THIRD-CLASS COACH TO STARDOM

Tom Waits' hangdog troubadour's act kept him in clover throughout the '70s. Then with the LPs 'Swordfishtrombones' and 'Rain Dogs' he catapulted himself into the mainstream's limelight, something that was helped along by his appearances in films like Coppola's 'Rumblefish' and 'The Cotton Club', plus his Oscar-nominated score for the seminal 'One From The Heart'.

His most recent success has been his six-week stint in the stage play that he wrote with his wife, 'Frank's Wild Years' at Chicago's Briar Street Theatre – and on September 19th 'Down By Law', the Jim Jarmusch film he stars in will open the New York Film Festival.

But none of this happened by itself.

PHOTOGRAPH RE-SHOT BY MOIRA BOGUE & TIM HO

TOM WAITS SEES LIFE THROUGH A GLASS DARKLY — USUALLY THROUGH THE BOTTOM OF ONE . . .

WORLDWIDE MANUAL OF STYLE i-D NO. 41     OCTOBER 1986 £1.00/$3

# i-D

## scoop!

**i-D'S TOTAL ACCESS FASHION SHOW!**

**TOM WAITS**

**JANET STREET-PORTER**

**JIM JARMUSCH**

**THE INDIE SCENE**

**JEAN-JACQUES BEINEIX**

**ANTHONY HOPKINS**

**GLENYS KINNOCK**

**i-DEAL IMAGE:**

**i-D'S SEARCH FOR A STAR**

e**X**clusive!

THE MEDIA ISSUE

5 013071 000195

THE INDISPENSABLE DOCUMENT OF FASHION STYLE AND IDEAS

"In Japan I'm worshipped like I'm God, in Australia I'm liked by very violent thugs. In England they're just suspicious"

**John Lydon, Sex Pistol, no34**

*a sight for sore eyes*

**BEAUTY IS IN THE EYE OF THE BEHOLDER**

Are our perceptions of beauty changing?

Is 'beautiful' the ugliest word in the English language?

Is 'ugly' the most beautiful?

**William Leith** looks in the mirror and doesn't like what he sees .

There is a dinner-party theory about beauty and ugliness. It goes like this. Beautiful people are attracted to beautiful people and ugly people are either attracted to ugly people or end up having to make do with them. Which means that as time goes on the gulf between beauty and ugliness is bound to widen, we are looking at a future peopled entirely by the exquisite and the grotesque – Christopher Lambert and Mel Smith, Isabelle Adjani and Vera Duckworth. You know the theory. It's rubbish, of course.

# 1986

"Vogue always want stories about the aristocracy. So I got a local builder and dressed him up, told them he was a prince and the whole story to print with the pictures. They got very upset afterwards"

**Oliviero Toscani, creative director, no38**

# 1987

Dec/Jan. The Comic Issue no43. Cover star: Mickey. Photography by Robert Erdmann, styling by Caroline Baker

February. The Flirt Issue no44. Cover star: Paula Thomas. Photography by Jamie Long, styling by Robert Leach

March. The Metropolitan Issue no45. Cover star: Isabella Rossellini. Photography by Fabrizio Ferri

April. The Pop Issue no46. Cover star: Grace Jones. Photography by Nick Knight, styling by Andy Knight

May. The Good Sport Issue no47. Cover star: Tess. Photography by Nick Knight, styling by Simon Foxton

June. The Plain English Issue no48. Cover star: Leigh Bowery. Photography by Johnny Rozsa, styling by Clive Ross

July. The Film Issue no49. Cover star: Elizabeth Westwood. Photography by Nick Knight

August. The Holiday Issue no50. Cover star: Sarah Stockbridge. Photography by Nick Knight, styling by Simon Foxton

September. The Boy's Own Issue no51. Cover star: Rachel Weisz. Photography by Kevin Davies, styling by Caryn Franklin

October. The New Brit Issue no52. Cover star: Alice Walpole. Photography by Mark Lebon

November. The Fear Issue no53. Cover star: Mariko. Photography by Kevin Davies, styling by Caryn Franklin

# i-D

## bumper annual 87!

### COMIC BOOK SPECIAL

wow!

**32 PAGES OF FASHION**

**BIG AUDIO DYNAMITE**

**FRANK MILLER**

**SCHOOLLY D**

**ALAN MOORE**

**THE BAND OF HOLY JOY**

**SUPERMEN**

**DARYL HALL**

**SPIDERMEN**

**ART SPEIGELMAN**

**WONDER WOMEN**

**NEVILLE BROTHERS**

**BETTY BOOP**

**THE GLAMOROUS LIFE PART 1**

**LOIS LANE**

**i-D i-DEAL PURSUITS QUIZ**

**FASHION SURVIVAL GUIDE PART 2**

**STREET STYLE '87**

FRANCS 35 LIRA 5,500 DM 9 PESETAS 825 D.KR 53.50

5 013071 000218

THE INDISPENSABLE DOCUMENT OF FASHION STYLE AND IDEAS

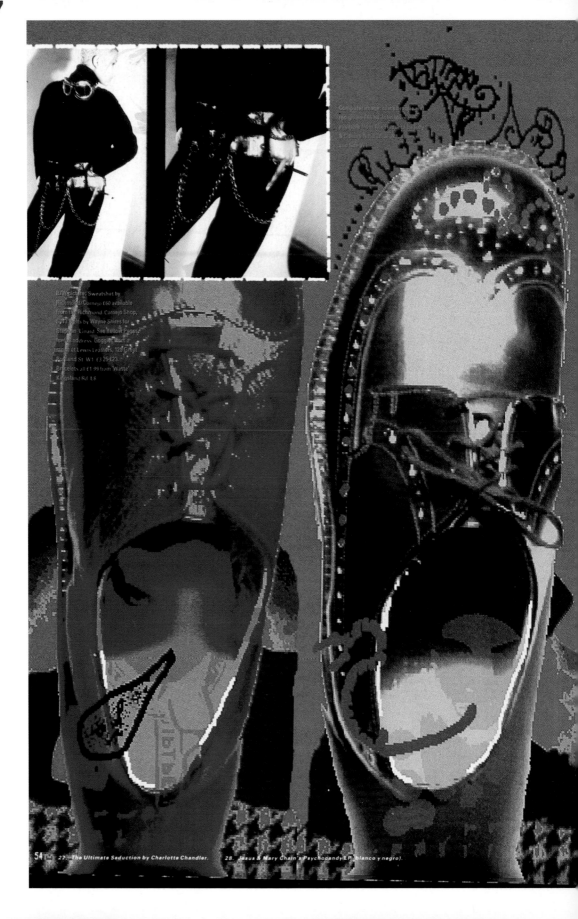

B/W picture: Sweatshirt by Richmond/Cornejo £60 available from The Richmond-Cornejo Shop, £170 Suits by Wayne Shires for Stephen Linard. See Yellow Pages for address. Goggles turn a around at Lewis Leathers, 120 Great Portland St W1 £3.25-£23. Bracelets all £1.99 from 'Waste' Kingsland Rd E8

54  27. *The Ultimate Seduction by Charlotte Chandler.*  28. *Jesus & Mary Chain's Psychocandy LP (blanco y negro).*

Computer image: Boxing glove
brooch £55 by Judy Blame
available from The House of Beauty
& Culture N1, Bazaar W1.
"Polaroid" inset: Richard Torry
hand knit jumper £155 available
from Jones, Bazaar W1, The House
of Beauty & Culture N1 and Sita
W1

COMPUTER PAINTING JOHN ENGLAND/STUART JANE
BLACK & WHITE PHOTOGRAPHS BY EDDIE MONSOON
STYLING FRED POODLE
ASSISTED BY KAREN HOOD
MODELS JO AND VERA FROM WILDELLS
THANKS TO I.M.A.G.I.N.E. FOR USE OF COMPUTERS

**9 QUIZ**

ellington Place is
ow called?

Ruston Mews.
Cornwall
escent.
Wallingford
venue.

HERO

B/W picture: smock with "Hero"
hem £110 by Christopher Nemeth
from The House of Beauty &
Culture N1, Bazaar W1 and Sector
in Tokyo, long white socks £1.95
from branchs of Dolcis. Black
Oxfords £55 by John Moore
available from The House of Beauty
& Culture N1, Jones, Bazaar W1
and Sita W1.

55

## Stitch up,

Collect, select and customise's fascinated scout issue jacket adorned with your address ("Yes, I know it's 205, next 205 WHO?!") assures you that you only hava after a bender ... well, it beats asking a policeman.

JOHN RYAN, 21, a chef enquires and Rodell Liggins 27, cricketer/photo/graphic designer, regularly need a small social gatherings be a dance the pub in Delirium. On the menu front – anything from Roadrawd to Mike whilst on the dancefloor John struggles at his Doc Marts and Rachel wobbles around to a drunken stupor. Hiding! Self-consciously of course!

John wears his own cycling hoovies and top from Shoroe Rockford in North Finchley. customised scarf for EMI from branches of Shelly's. Stick so distressed jacket from Plike Kings Rd SW3.

## & Custom Built

DAVID ROBERTS, 18, a business studies student at Kingston, sees himself as the next Paul Getty. Club faves include Raw, Delirium and plenty of Warehouse parties. However less of the clubbing is his tip for '87 so as to stay awake longer. Flirting! 'A flash of the eyes and then move in – it works all the time.'

David wears his own hat, black polonecked and tracksuit bottoms all from Strip Kensington Market. Black jacket from Under The Influence Kensington Market. Monkey boots from branches of Stills. Added extras are khaki shorts over trousers £19.99 and black hooded zip jacket £24.99 both by Benetton from all major branches.

## Stuck down

Frankly my dear when it's after dark on a Saturday night NOTHING DOES and it's always best to be prepared. Basic black you on the straight and narrow and sartorial co-ordination from clusters to psychdigital that makes sure the evening doesn't misfigure.

## Label look

Fool some of the people all of the time with those convincing layers of sweat-shirts, the odd parka and a purposeful stride . . . With the labels working for you, and not against you!

KEVIN, 21, main man at Antenna, is partial to a good film and a tasty meal or two while Alison, 19, a budding illustrator in search of a job, occasionally frequents the Wag and is one half of a dangerous dancer. Kevin's hot tip for '87 – 'A roll and a half of clingfilm and a Roughrider'. Does he take his own advice we ask in anticipation? And although he claims not to indulge in a good alt film, Alison, a Paul Waller addict, admits to the odd one occasionally.

Kevin wears his own red jumper from Chapel St Market and Good Ye Ga hat from Island Records with union hooded jacket with check lining £59.95 and check trousers £29.95 by Redts Clothing available from Harrods Knightsbridge, Garbherge 21 Candlewriggi Glasgow and Amical 14-16 Devonshire St Carlisle. Check bowling shoes £19.99 by Redts Clothing available from Usina One 34 Fulhams St Nottingham, Sara Croggles 74 Low Potergate York and La Pel B Low High Rd SE13.

Alison wears yellow hooded coat £54.95 and navy sweat top £62.95 both by Classic Nouveau available from their shop Classic Nouveau SW3, John Anthony 54 Shaftesbury Ave W1, Still Black The Royal Exchange Arcade Manchester and Pilot in Leicester. Appaloosa jeans £49.95 by Persani available from Farocci DW2 and Pilot in Leicester. Satchel by Classic Nouveau £46.95 available from their shop Classic Nouveau SW3, John Anthony W1, Still Black in Manchester and Pilot in Leicester.

## Max motifs

Keeping it smart but PLAIN gives you the perfect background for flights of fancy dressing – sticky motifs. From baked bean labels to old postcards you can make a statement even if you're the one.

JAMIE, 18, is a student at South East London College studying photography, English, Art and Sociology. This man about town is a regular at The Wag, Delirium, Cafe De Paris and Crazy Larry's – phew! – where he gets his staple diet of new American 60's and 70's funk. Jamie's into major parts – film ones – and his ambition is to become the next Harrison Ford. Not a natural that although we beg to differ he claims, 'If it happens it happens'.

Jamie wears his own hat, polonock and trousers from The Duffer of St. George Auslo lock Workshop in Guernsey and black PVC jacket from Hyper Hyper. Added extras are cream denim jacket £60.90 by C17. Brothers include their own shop C17 38 St James St W1 and Rocky 34 Romaine St Liverpool, McQueen 100 Allest Sac Southampton, L & D Brown 44 Shadow Lane Leeds. Also finely stickers (write all usual telephone numbers and club info on stickers.)

## Customised

"The world is an art gallery"

**Gilbert and George, artists, no49**

**SANDY,** a model at Wildlife Agency, wears bowler hat £25.00 from Marcellette with fabric sign painted over reveal. "I chose a medium cut of the A-Z for my city look, but went month by going to dye it black and put a zip around the top of the crown." Jacket £7.00 from a collection at Twentieth Century Box, customised with cotton and eyeliner "just like a factory jacket before it's finished." To compliment the look Sandy wears vest (£7.00) by Billy Jackson from his new spring collection available from Joanna's Tent and Harvey Nichols in London and Prima too p. Ski pants £5.00 from Hyper Hyper and GM's look London. See our stockists section in Shopping Guide for full addresses.

**FRANKIE,** a stylist wears his own customised DM's. "It all started when the dog chewed round the edges and I had to use string to tie them in my foot I gradually started to add things to them and out a zipper out of the leather with a scalpel." DM's worn with white knee high socks £2.50 from The Sock Shop and adjustable length vest £8.00 by Joe Casely Hayford from Leith Boardno of Jones, Harvey Nichols and Harrods in London also b/b for San Square Changing Room, Prima Vera and Willy's Bar out stockist section in Shopping Guide for full addresses.

**Photography Sandro Hyams**
**Assisted by David Ross**
Hair and make-up Ellis Wakamatsu at Z Agency.

54 I-D METROPOLITAN ISSUE

I-D METROPOLITAN ISSUE 55

# THE

# brash PACK

Alternatively known as the Nasties, Beasties, Boasties. The Brash Pack wear designer stubble, baseball caps, pirated designer logos and dirty denim. The boys read dirty magazines. So do the girls. Theirs is a sexy look, a dishevelled look – a look that wears old designer clothes. The Brash Pack like to imbibe at places like Raw and Delirium – they listen to dirty hip-hop, rap, reggae and electro. They like electric guitars and personal stereos – they adore loud music. A Brash Packer dances everywhere, wears a Walkman in the bath, chainsmokes and eats junk food (like Smucker's Goober

Grape, an American mixture of peanut butter and grape jelly). A Brash Packer is an aspiring bon viveur – he wants it all and he wants it in large measures. These boys are bad. Turn it up!

*From left to right.*
ZOHRA (21) from Camden wears her own customised sheepskin old Vivienne Westwood t-shirt and hat with Levi jeans £27 and jacket £35 from Jean Jeanie and selected Levi outlets. Steel toecapped DMs £26 from branches of Shelley shoe store. BARNSLEY (21) from Soho wears bootleg Hermes T-shirt, old Worlds End jacket, Gucci key ring, hat and Hermes buckle belt with Levi jeans £27 from Jean Jeanie and selected Levi outlets and Gucci shoes £60 approx from Gucci shop. NELLEE (23) from Camden wears his own old Worlds End buffalo coat and trousers, riding top by Kenzo, suede shoes from Brunnies and buckle from new York with polo neck jumper £40 by Yohji Yamamoto shop. MILES (25) from Camden wears his own Gianfranco Ferre jumper and baseball jacket with Levis £27 from Jean Jeanie and selected outlets and trainers by Adidas £55 from branches of Olympus Sports and Lillywhites. DAVID (25) from Bloomsbury wears bootleg Chanel No5 t-shirt, Triumph belt and Gucci blazer with Levi jeans £27 from Jean Jeanie and other selected outlets and hat £25 by The Duffer of St George from The Duffer of St George shops. See stockist section in Shopping Guide for addresses.

## "If I'm an icon, I must be a very bad icon"

**Bono, musician, no49**

**C**uties

Also known as Shamblers or
Shabbies. Cuties like indie
bands such as The Soup
Dragons, The Pastels, BMX
Bandits, Talulah Gosh, The
Smiths, The Shop
Assistants, Half Man Half
Biscuit and even The
Housemartins. Childlike
innocence and assumed
naivety permeate the Cutie
scene – their clothes are
asexual, their haircuts are
fringes, their colours are
pastel. Cuties like Penguin
Modern Classics, sweets,
ginger beer, vegetables and
anoraks. Heroes include
Christopher Robin, John
Noakes, Buzzcocks and The
Undertones. This is the
bubblegum brigade.

From left to right:
HENRY BOND (20) from Vauxhall wears his own
trousers from Mor teamed with Windcheater
£39 from American Classics and striped collarless
shirt £25 from Demob. Clarks Desert Boots £22.25
from Woodhouse. LOUISE STEVENS (16) from
Ealing wears beige Windcheater £39 and pink
slacks £12 from American Classics. Deepest zip top
£25 and red duffle bag £15 both from Demob. Pink
pumps £12.50 from Ravels and socks £2.25 from
branches of The Sock Shop. SHARON TRACE
(16) from Streatham wears matching striped
knitted jumper £24.95 and skirt £19.25 by Radio
Clothing available from Top Shop with Windcheater £39 from American Classics. Socks £2.99 from
branches of The Sock Shop and pumps £14.99
from Ravels. CHRISTIAN JERNOT (20) from
Wigan on Thames wears tan duffle jacket £60 and
matching striped collarless shirt £25 and trousers
£35 all from Demob, with Clarks desert boots
£22.25 from Woodhouse. See stockist section in
Shopping Guide for addresses.

**m**ETAL
ists

Generic term for those
associated with Speed,
Speedcore, Thrash and
Death metals. The ideology
and imagery encompasses
everything from Christianity
to Satanism, from the
Holocaust to the Second
Coming. Bands include
Onslaught, Metallica, Dark
Angel, Possessed, Slayer,
Anthrax, Megadeth. The
Metalist magazine is called
Metal Forces, the seminal
record company, Music For
Nations. A mixture of

core and bombastic
skullduggery, this is
chainsaws in stereo, heavy
metal gone bonkers. Join up
or stand back.

ALIEN (18) from Tottenham wears his own
leather trousers from Electric Ballroom with £20
boots teamed with a selection of belts £2.50-
£12.50, and fingerless gloves £5.95 all from Fans.
Metal mohican head sculpture to order from Laura
Hadley Smith. See stockist section in Shopping
Guide for addresses.

54 · D POP ISSUE

"I've made some gross mistakes in my
career but fortunately I've had nobody
to blame but myself"

**David Bowie, musician, no49**

bEAUTY anD tHE BEAST

From the 'no make-up' look to the 'snogged off'
look, brought to you steaming, fresh and
smouldering from behind the scenes at the
recent Vivienne Westwood show, where the
pubescent Joseph Corre and Patsy Kensit,
undaunted by the practicalities of achieving the
look – used a split-second break before the
curtain call to smooch each other's lip gloss to
kingdom come.

*Photography Johnny Rozsa*

Painted freckles, the Vivienne Westwood way.

Yvonne Gold achieves the kiss and tell look by using
Almay Soft Moon foundation, Peter Pearl blushing
cream, Tanganne Ocean sweep lip colour smudged,
gentle candy coway mascara all from Forbidden
Fruits, the new range from Rimmel, and Cold Gold
pearlised eye shadow from Boots No 7 smudged.

Make up Yvonne Gold for Leichner, Hair Touch for Body. Models Joseph Corre and Patsy Kensit
54 – D THE ODDS SPORT ISSUE

The stars of these polaroids were all caught red handed by Wigan as he roved, camera in hand, through London's nightspots.

"When I'm dressed up I think I must be quite awesome. For a start I'm six foot, and usually I wear some kind of heel, which would give me another three inches. Then a hat. In the end I'm like six foot seven. You wouldn't tamper with it"

**Leigh Bowery, performer, 48**

## SUPERBAD!

When the going gets tough, the tough dress up. Halfway through 1987 and knuckleduster glamour is back with a flash. This is the season of buckles and boots, lace and diamonds, of Shaft and satin, high heeled pumps and pimps, sunglasses, chains and canes. This ain't baaad, this is Superbaaad!

SPECIAL FASHION SUPPLEMENT          PHOTOGRAPHY NICK KNIGHT          STYLING SIMON FOXTON

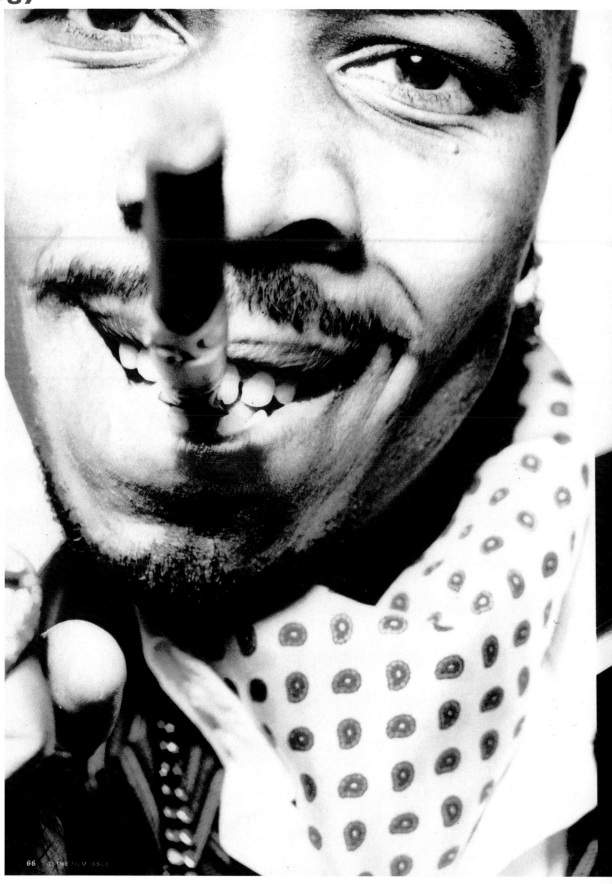

THE HOLIDAY ISSUE · i-D MAGAZINE NO.50 · AUGUST 1987 · £1.50 / $4.50

# i-D

"trendy fashion magazine"

# 50

## ANNIVERSARY
## SPECIAL

## GLOBAL LONDON
## WORLDWIDE FASHION

## KINGS! QUEENS!!
## AND COMMONERS!!

5 013071 000294

## VIVIENNE WESTWOOD
## CROWNS HER PRINCESS

"It's not that I'm against wearing knickers –
it's just that I haven't found any that I like at
the moment"

**Vivienne Westwood, designer, no45**

"The style I like at the moment is a cross between
Goldilocks and Cinderella. I'm in love with white
hair...I think it looks great on a young person
because it makes their eyes look darker. It's so
sexy. I hope people copy this style."

# 09•87

"Huge brains, small necks, weak muscles and fat wallets – these are the dominant characteristics of the Eighties, the generation of swine"

**Hunter S Thompson, writer, no53**

FIGURE 1: TOUGH IS TOFF - SKINHEAD IN TOP HAT AND TAILS.

PHOTOGRAPHY JOHN HICKS. STYLING DEBBIE HENLEY AT Z. DAVID LAWRENCE AT Z.

RED DANDY JACKET £95, RED TARTAN WAISTCOAT £65, WHITE DRESS SHIRT £12, RHINESTONE BANDANA £4 ALL FROM AMERICAN CLASSICS 20 ENDELL ST WC2 AND 404 & 404 KINGS RD SW3. HAT MODELS OWN.

FIGURE 2: COWBOY COUTURE - WESTERNER REPLACES TRUSTY DENIM WITH WORSTED HOUNDSTOOTH IN 501 REVELATION.

PHOTOGRAPHY JAMES MARTIN. HAIR AND MAKE-UP REDD AT VIDAL SASSOON STYLING AL AND SULKY BOY. MODEL JOHN ROCKA.

WORSTED HOUNDSTOOTH WAISTCOAT, JAQUARD LINING WAISTCOAT, COTTON LAWN SCARF SHIRT, WOOL FELT DUDE HAT, ALL BY JEREMY HOWITT TEL 061 236 2186.

STOP PRESS i-D REPORTS ON A STARTLING NEW TREND AMONGST STYLE PUNDITS TO DRESS BEYOND THE VEST. FITTED JACKETS HAVE REPLACED HARRINGTONS AND DRESS SHIRTS HAVE OUSTED T-SHIRTS AS THE SUITABLY SMART HIT THE STREETS.

"If I was depressed, I wouldn't be making films – I'd be committing suicide"

**Derek Jarman, film-maker, no53**

ENGLISH MISS: A classically pink flori-
bunda. Free flowering with a quick repeat
between flushes. No, we don't know what
it means either.

VIOLET CARSON: A rose of refinement with double blooms and reliable bedding qualities. Only grows in Coronation Street, at least it used to.

# 11•87

## "The only thing I fear is being in love"

Frankie Knuckles, DJ, no53

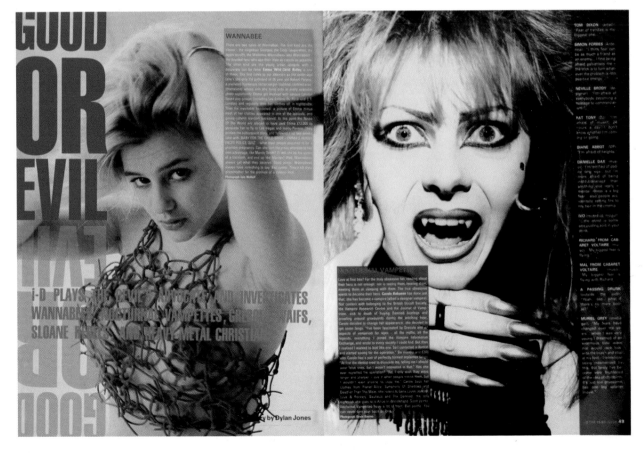

THE
i-D
BIBLE
EVERY
ULTI-
MATE
VICTIM'S
HANDBOO

5 013071 000348

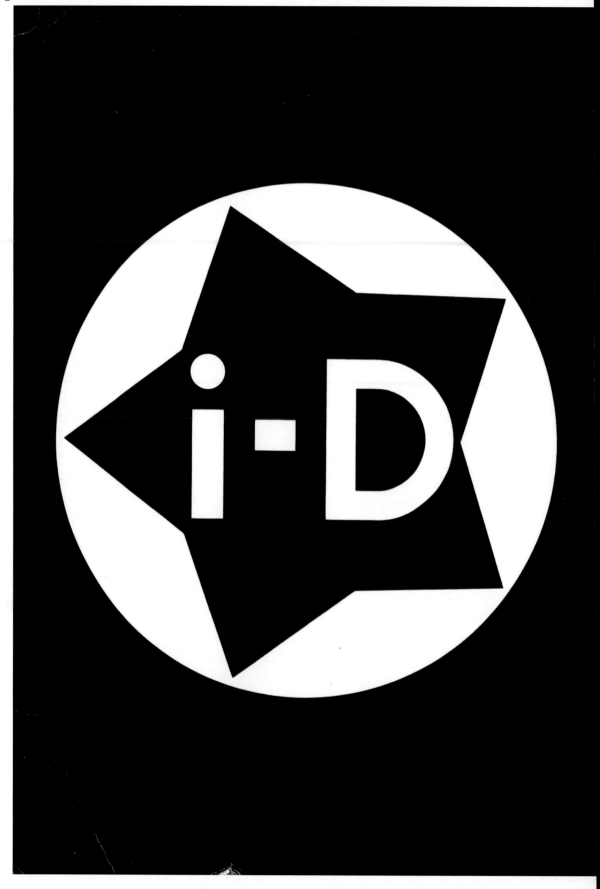

THE TEN COMMANDMENTS

**12•87**

"Sex is such a threat these days. Because of AIDS, chastity has come back like a guillotine. This is truly the age of hygiene and caution"

**Katharine Hamnett, designer, no44**

STYLE WARS

ATTITUDE IS THE KEY TO TRIBAL BRITAIN: THE LOOK THAT SPEAKS LOUDER THAN WORDS. THE BLUEPRINT FOR THE SIMILARLY AFFLICTED. IT'S VISUAL CAMARADERIE WITH A CODE OF CONDUCT – THE RIGHT CUT FOR THE RIGHT CLOTH, AND AT THE RIGHT TIME. CLASSIC LOOKS AREN'T STATIC LOOKS, BUT CUSTOMISED BY NEW GENERATIONS AND ADAPTED TO MODERN NEEDS. SAY IT LOUD, I BELONG AND I'M PROUD AND I WEAR ROUND-NOSED BROGUES (NOT POINTED). IF THE SHOE FITS, WEAR IT.

The Wycombe Skins at the Anchor Inn circa '87. Photograph Simon Fleury.

**SKINHEADS**
SKA, STA-PRESS AND FRED PERRYS – A UNIFORM CUT TO THE BONE. HARD AS NAILS AND TOUGH AS 14 HOLE DOCTOR MARTENS.

Neville and Gavin Watson from the Wycombe Skins, circa '87. Photograph Simon Fleury.

PUNKS

Against the white wall.
Kings Rd straight ups
circa '87 Photographs
Steve Johnson.

relying on clean and colourful separates from Boy
and John Crancher.

**Sounds:** Early punk bootlegs from Camden and
Portobello markets, predominantly early Crash
and Sioune with the Vibrators, UK Subs and old
Discharge tunes close behind. Although - like
many youth cults - nostalgia is strong, relatively
recent bands like PIL, Big Audio Dynamite and
The Smiths are all big favourites.

**Crossovers**

**Warrior/Punks:** Mad Max clones
**Grebo/Punks:** Less colourful, into army fatigues
and leaking rats

**Shops**

Boy main branch 153 Kings Rd SW3 (439 0582).
John Crancher Unit 581 Ground floor Kensington
Market Kensington High St W8
Modzart 192-200 Villiers Rd NW2 (451 1024)
Camden Market Electric Ballroom Camden High
St NW1
Shelly's main branch 159 Oxford St W1 (437 5842).
Holts 5 Kentish Town Rd NW1 (405 0505).
Kensington Market Kensington High St W8
Lewis Leathers 122 Gt Portland St W1 (580 4214).
For original Seditionaries clothes, check the small
ads in the music press.

Against the white wall,
Kings Rd straight ups.
Original Punks circa '76
from the Pink Punk Book.
Photographs Steve
Johnson.

## TOM JONES

The boyo from the Vegas valleys returned this year with a dreadful single ('A Boy From Nowhere'), a worse album ('Matador'), a cash-in re-release ('It's Not Unusual'), a small tour, and several TV slots...a not unusual sequence of events for a promotional visit. But halfway through his visit Tom Jones played a masterstroke: he appeared on The Last Resort and gave a truly iconoclastic interpretation of 'Kiss'. (It was so good that the only way Prince can possibly reciprocate is by covering 'Promise Her Anything', the best record Tom Jones ever made.) Unwittingly he became hipster of the month. Jones the voice proved that all those years spent in Nevada performing aural striptease in front of salivating New Jersey housewives hadn't aneasth-etized the Welsh boyo's mighty roar. He said at the time: "...that's why I did The Last Resort. I wanted to change people's conception of me. If they thought I'd gone potty, I wanted to show them that maybe I hadn't. I'm still there..." In 1987 Tom Jones showed that not all middle aged cabaret crooners wear corsets.

118

# COOL J

yone who thought that Def Jam was purely a
phenomenon had to think again this year. In
pring the Beastie Boys finally made it big over
by having a top ten smash with '(You Gotta
: For Your) Right To Party' (given an extra
ial push due to tabloid pop columnist Gill
gle); and Tashan and Public Enemy N0.1 also
their fair share of success, along with
yone's favourite bad boy, LL Cool J. His second
Bigger And Deffer' (*BAD* to his friends) *was*
r and deffer than his first, though the
over hit 'I Need Love' was only bigger. LL is
ainly a bonafide celebrity, and the pressure,
eat, is *on*: "I can chill and stand on the corner
ning to music and know what time it is. But I
: lie. It *is* getting more hectic. It's getting to the
: now where I drive to the local McDonalds,
down my window and they scream." A million
irls can't be wrong.

# 1987

"I don't give a fuck how I'm remembered. It doesn't occur to me... it's just nice to have got through it all"

**David Bowie, musician, no49**

# 1988

Dec/Jan. The Happy Issue no54. Creative direction by Terry Jones

February. The Worldwide Issue no55. Cover star: Lucy. Photography by Terry Jones

March. The Tribal Issue no56. Cover star: Silvia Ross. Photography by Willy Biondani, styling by Lica

April. The Surreal Issue no57. Creative direction by Judy Blame

May. The Revolution Issue no58. Cover star: Wendy James. Photography by Wayne Stambler

June. The Body Issue no59. Cover star: Karen. Photography by Wayne Stambler, styling by Malcom Beckford

July. The Graduation Issue no60. Photography by Terry Jones

August. The Adventure Issue no61. Cover star: Cleopatra Jones. Photography by Norman Watson

September. The Party Party Issue no62. Cover star: Jade. Photography by Mark Lebon

October. The Heroes & Sheroes Issue no63. Cover star: Shero

November. The Trash Issue no64. Cover star: Camilla. Photography by Guido Hildebrand, styling by Camilla Thulin

December. The Love Issue no65. Cover star: Claudia. Photography by Eddie Monsoon

THE HAPPY ISSUE

i-D MAGAZINE NO 54 DECEMBER 1987/JANUARY 1988 £1.50/$4.50

# i-D

"trendy fashion magazine"

F.FRANCS 35  LIRA 5,500  DM 9  PESETAS 625  D.KR. 53.50

5 013071 000331

# GET UP! GET HAPPY!

...the vanities!

1
2
3
4

# 03•88

"The 20th Century will be looked back upon as the wildest time in the history of man"

**Tom Wolf, writer, no55**

"Our filthy funk will make your nipples ripple, make you dip your dipple, and inner juices dribble."

"He sorta lost his erection after we left and couldn't get it up for the mix."

**BOW WOW! ROOF
ROOF!:**

The roof, the roof, the roof is
on fire! We don't need no
water. Doc (22) from L.T.K.
Posse and Karl (20) like to do
the Dogcatcher on the move,
providing a free Enter-
tainment On Wheels service
as they mount the nearest
automobile public platform.
Karl says, "The whole world
is our stage, unless you drive
a cabriolet."

**56 i-D THE SURREAL ISSUE**

# LONDON · YES SIR YES SIR REAL

When the going gets weird, the wired wig out! If you think London life is a murky flow of everyday occurrences, if you've never glimpsed the bizarre dreamscape that plays around the marbled feet of the capital's institutions, then let i-D take you by the hand, and lead you through the streets of London. We will show you something that'll make you change your mind.

**C ROULETTE:**

rls mad as in
st plain nuts.
nd Wiggy (21)
or matchsticks.
have made a
self-protecting
e world's most
rill game, but
arned not to try
this stunt at
isn't a lady
could win 20
bars. Zig ad-
"When I said
gun, I wasn't
dian!

(from left to right)
**Damian Glee Pathos** from Earth Nicht, 24, wears a one piece Dr Marten suit found in a skip. **Jonathan** wears black t-shirt and jeans found in skip, black leather belt from Kensington Market with the no shoe look. **Tanya Horn** from Earth Nicht, 24, wears hat from Oxfam, make up from Escapade in Camden, black music co-operative t-shirt found in an attic, jacket and trousers both found in skips and boots from army surplus store. **Tig**, 23, wears patchwork leather trousers by Graham Evans, which are also sold in Planet Alice, jacket and waistcoat found in Oxfam, Dr Martens from Holt and shades from Lawrence Corner. **Generator John** from Earth Nicht, 28, wears girlfriend's jacket, t-shirt from Steve Hillage gig, trousers given by friend at Role Rite Stone Festival (originally from Planet Alice), shoes from Hilaire and bowler hat given by Tig the drummer. **Jonee** from Earth Nicht, 24, wears leather jacket from Lewis Leathers, shirt from Kensington Market, girlfriend's top hat, trousers made by Graham Evans, dog collar gift from a friend and DM boots from Gents footwear company, Walworth Road. **Cosmos**, eternal, wears leather jacket from Lewis Leathers, trousers homemade, police coat from Canada, hat from Planet Alice and boots from The Chelsea Boot Store. **Jacqueline Hanna**, 19, wears patchwork trousers from Planet Alice, black top from Kensington Market and DM boots from Holts.

*The Warriors of New Age — C L U B  D O G*
THE LOOK: Found/made clothes but always black. Leftovers from festivals, gigs and punk, these "do your own thing" clothes are "functional and cheap; the festival experience and inner spirit celebration are what's important. The hard hats and leather clothes are protective because you fall over when you get wasted. Painted faces enable us to put most of our insides on our outsides," say the Warriors. They are influenced by the "revolutionary energy" of the '60s, and see themselves as "Free Destined Angels" who enjoy tribal gatherings at festivals, and hanging out *chez Dog.* "We know we are all very aware, we've gone beyond the point of no return. We are the central group of activists, but some of us used to be sea horses."

**66 i-D THE REVOLUTION ISSUE**

*Cont on page 70* ▶

**Club Dog**
**Friday nights at Sir George Robey**
**240 Seven Sisters Rd, N4. 9pm-late**
**£3 or £2.50 concessions before 10.30pm**
**No admission after 11.30pm.**

**Songs:**

Webcore 'The Captain's Table'
Sex Pistols 'Anarchy In The UK'
Rolf Harris 'Two Little Boys'
Beatles 'White Album'
The Volcanoes 'Into The Psyche'
Earth Nicht Demo
Ozric Tentacles 'Sniffing Dog'
Motorhead 'Overkill'
Anything by Holger Czukay/Can/Dunkelziffer
The Orooines 'The Woods Are Alive With The Smell Of His Coming'

**Shops:**

**Lewis Leathers:** 122 Great Portland St, W1. Tel 01 636 4314
**Planet Alice:** 284 Portobello Rd, W10. Tel 01 968 9646.
**Holts:** 5 Kentish Town Rd, NW1. Tel 01 485 8505. 307 Mare St, Hackney E8. Tel 01 985 8298. 63 High Rd, Wealdstone. Tel 01 427 5277 and 74 Church St, NW8. Tel 01 402 2002.
Brick Lane, Portobello and Brixton Railway Arches Markets.
The best stuff though is found in skips, scrounged or handed down.

**i-D THE REVOLUTION ISSUE 67**

# all WOMAN

Since time imm-
emorial, women
have changed their
body shapes to su-
it the mood of the
times, redesigning
what nature gave
them to fit their
dreams and aspir-
ations. The 20th
century has wit-
nessed several ex-
tremes — compare
the flat chests of
the '20s to the con-
ical breasts of the
'50s; or the long
legs of the early
'70s to the square
shoulders of the
'80s.

As we gear up
for the last '90s of
this millenium, the
time is right to get
tight with lycra.
Externalise anxiety
and wear tension
on the *outside*.
Aim for the tri-
umph of body over
form, and never
underestimate the
effect of a few
well-positioned ba-
lloons. In other wo-
rds, don't be afraid
to blow it, baby.

Photography **Kevin Davies**
Styling **Caryn Franklin**
Model **Linda Tolbert at** Unique
Make-up **Vanessa Kark at Mandy
Coakley**
Shot at **B2 Studios**

White strap swim hat £3.50 from
Lillywhites, pink cropped t-shirt £14.99
(stuffed with balloons) tucked in to
white tank top dress £39.99 rolled
down, white leggings £14.99 with
white stockings £12.99 worn over
platform shoes all by Debbie More for
Pineapple. See Stockists for full addresses.

I-D THE BOD

# 07•88

"As museums become more commercial, so shops become more intelligent. I think shopping really is becoming one of the great cultural experiences of the late 20th Century"

**Stephen Bayley, designer, no55**

THE GRADUATE

**Anna Clark**
*TEXTILE DESIGNER*

**Conrad Leach**
*FASHION DESIGNER*

MC Merlin and Japanese rapper Tycoon Tosh

Watching psychedelic videos before the club opens

TOKYO! '88 i-D

Our hosts, Club King, founded in 1987 by Maciie Kuwahara, are responsible for most of the present influx to Japan of the best Britain has to offer in the worlds of fashion, music and club culture. Within Japan itself their involvement has stretched to incorporate TV, radio, video and record production as well as merchandising and promotional tours. Plans for the future include their own record label, radio shows and video promotions. For all further details contact them at 3-7-5 Jingumae, Shibuya Ku, Tokyo. Tel. (03) 470 4392.

Jay Strongman, DJ

Sarah Stockbridge's Hand Choice

The Spiral Hall Exhibition

Tim Simenon, pop star and DJ

Roy Marsh, DJ

SPORTS

OKE from Neva wears natural denim jacket by Levis £40 available from Jean Jeanie, Way In and good jean outlets dyed with Dylon machine wash dye £3.15, sweatshirt £48 from Chipie, track suit bottoms £38.75 from Windsurfers World and hat £24.95 from American Retro. STEVE wears jacket £83.36 from Windsurfers World, t-shirt £4.95 and track suit bottom £15.95 both from Hanes.

CULVER wears jacket £99.00 available from Brother, shorts from Miami, sweatshirt £15.95 from Hanes and Pepe cap £13.45 from the Hat Shop. MALCOLM wears hooded sweatshirt £27.95 and track suit bottoms £15.95 both from Hanes, slipover from Lyle & Scot and hat £5.60 by Ocean Pacific from Olympus Sports. OOG wears rugby shirt £50 from Polo Ralph Lauren, jacket £150 approx from Chipie and natural 501 Levis £29.99 available from Jean Jeanie, Way In and all good jeans outlets dyed with Dylon machine wash dye. RODNEY from International wears track suit bottoms £15.95 from Hanes and t-shirt £28.50 and 'No Jams' hat £2 both from World.

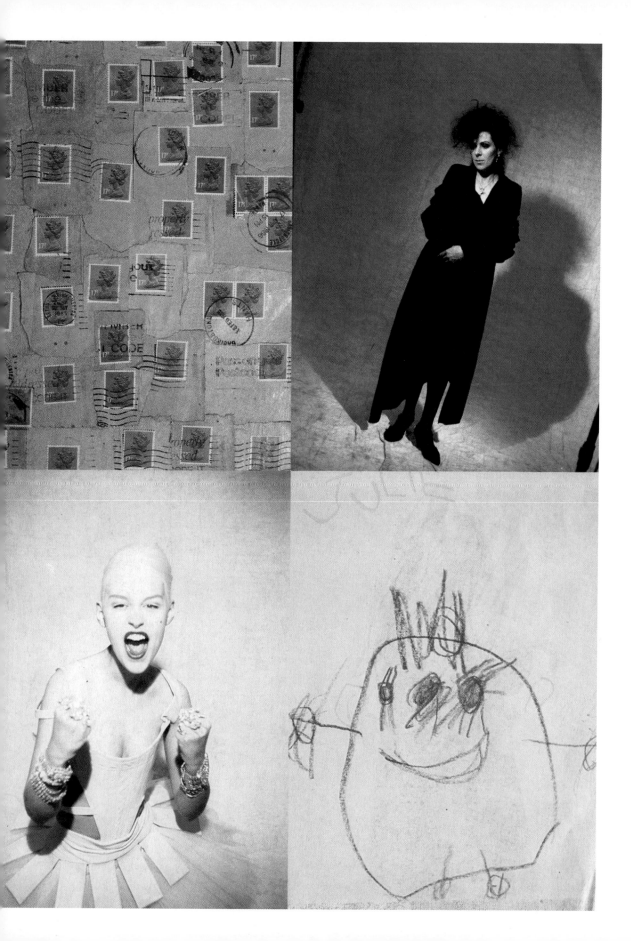

# 10•88

"There's not much to choose between the Changing of the Guard and the Kings Road parade these days. They're both part of our Glorious Heritage"

**Peter York, style commentator, no55**

**X-MEN**

The origins of superheroes are manifold and diverse. They have included extra-terrestrial ancestry, radiation, magic and machinery; but the X-Men were the first serious, abnormal humans with amazing mental powers. Shunned by the society that spawned them, these anti-heroes fought evil and carried out their "duties" regardless. The idea of a band of teenage mutants was slow to catch on, but in the late '70s circulation started to climb. By the '80s X-Men was the biggest selling comic in the world, eventually producing a spin-off series with the most popular character Wolverine, a psychopathic killer with steel claws and a short temper. It was icy cool enough to be so gruesome you had to be a bloke, wasn't it?

**Batwoman**

The she-woman of London social life, she strides through designer drinking clubs as if she owns them. This might have something to do with her high-powered TV job that attracts media brats like cattle. But beware, she sucks you dry.

**Marina**

Neither a fish out of water nor a wet blanket, Marina can adapt to any situation. Equally at home in Fred's or Fred's Fish Bar, she can off and blind with the best of them, and is guaranteed to liven up any party. Octopuses be warned, that bag is loaded.

**SILVER SURFER**

The Silver Surfer was an alien from Galaxius sentenced to permanent exile on Earth for showing too much concern for humans, whom he rarely understood but always pitied. A vehicle for Stan Lee's moralising, he travelled the world on an atomic surfboard, denouncing mankind's inhumane actions. "Chrome Dome" was the bleeding-heart liberal of superheroes, an oversensitive being unable to tackle the chaos around him. A true child of the '80s.

**THOR**

Adapted from ancient Norse mythology Thor was the first mainstream hippy comic. It weaved fantasy and religion into a mass of Mother Earth allusions and Olde English vocabulary. Thor was Dr Don Blake, a man who became the legendary god of thunder whenever he pounded his magical walking stick on the ground, and a hero whose punch-ups always turned into epic battles. He was the ultimate fantasy role model for young Americans who were preparing for war. In this case, it was Vietnam.

**KELLY** wears Italian neck blouses and green top by Bazie Savticova available to order from Mikel Rosen tel 01 831 8774, tapestry boots £35 from Api Hoc, green leather gloves by Vivienne Westwood available from World's End and wig £45 from the Hot Hair Unit.

46 i-D THE HEROES AND SHEROES ISSUE

i-D THE HEROES AND SHEROES ISSUE 47

The Flemish fashion
assault is now well
underway. First came
Dirk Bikkembergs hotly
pursued by Walter Van
Bierendonk, Dries Van
Noten, Dirk Van Saen,
Marina Yee and Anne de
Mulemeester. They've
taken the fashion
industry by the balls,
showing that style ain't
what you do but the way
that you do it.

Under the guidance
of Madame Linda
Loppa, The
Academy Of
Antwerp is set to
capture the fashion
spotlight of Europe with a
pool of talent and energy
that will have fashion
commentators drooling
over their Yamamotos.
The Academy means that
no student is
automatically
guaranteed a ride
through to the following
year of the four year
course unless their
design and pattern
cutting skills are
faultless.

Entry to the Academy
doesn't come with a grant
and students must earn
money to finance their
collections and living
expenses for 48 months.
But even though the
financial burden may
seem extreme, each year
climaxes with a three
hour show where a
multitude of exciting
ideas and beautifully
designed clothes parade
the catwalk.
With the removal of
trading restrictions in the
EEC at the end of the
decade, all eyes will be on
Europe, looking for a new
Paris or Barcelona. i-D
suggests they start
looking in the direction of
Antwerp.

## fresh force—

PHOTOGRAPHY **Phil Inkelberghe**
MAKE-UP **Inge Grognard**

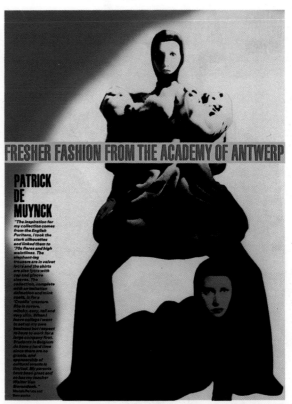

## FRESHER FASHION FROM THE ACADEMY OF ANTWERP

### PATRICK DE MUYNCK

"The inspiration for
my collection comes
from the English
Puritans. I took the
stark silhouettes
and linked them to
'70s flares and high
waistlines. The
elephant-leg
trousers are in velvet
lycra and the shirts
are also lycra with
cap and gloove
sleeves. The
collection, complete
with or imitation
estination and mink
spelt, is for a
'Cruella' creature.
She is vixen,
witchy, sexy, tall and
very slim. When I
leave college I want
to set up my own
business but I expect
to have to work for a
large company first.
Students in Belgium
do have a hard time
since there are no
grants, and
sponsorship of
cultural events is
limited. My parents
have been great and
so has my teacher
Walter Van
Bierendonk."

Model's Noriko van
Born advice.

Phone card skirt, made from discarded cards £55 and phone card bag £40 by Anne T Delaney. Red jersey gloves by Vivienne Westwood. Red tights 99p by Sock Shop and fun fur jacket by Vaugn and Franks. Baby head clogs £170 by Leslie D Perkins.

**I'VE GOT A MONSTER IN MY TROUSERS!**

7 TAT TRASH ROCKS

**I WROTE HITLER DIARIES, SAYS JOURNALIST**

2 Good Trash Books

Too Much, Too Soon – Diana Barrymore
Four Cowgirls Got The Blues – Tom Robbins
Valley of the Dolls – Jacqueline Susann
Fear and Loathing in Las Vegas – Hunter S. Thompson
Sinatra, My Father – Nancy Sinatra
Right Ho, Jeeves – P. G. Wodehouse
Ripers – Jolly Jack

100 STONE ALSO SLIMS FOR SEX

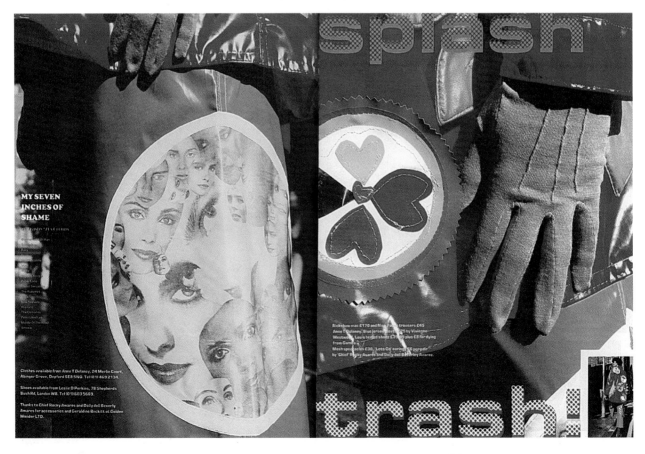

**MY SEVEN INCHES OF SHAME**

Clothes available from Anne T Delaney, 24 Merlin Court, Abinger Grove, Deptford SE8 5NQ. Tel 01 469 2134.

Shoes available from Leslie D Perkins, 78 Shepherds Bush Rd, London W8. Tel 01 603 5669.

Thanks to Chief Rocky Awares and Dolly doll Beverly Awares for accessories and Geraldine Beckitt at Golden Wonder LTD.

Rickshaw mac £170 and Nice Pair trousers £45 Anne T Delaney. Blue jersey gloves £65 by Vivienne Westwood. Louis heeled shoes £39.99 plus £8 for dyeing from Game Girl.
Mesh spectacles £30. 'Lets Go' earring £6 perspex by 'Chief Rocky Awares and Dolly doll Beverley Rivarez.

**Tiffany**, a chiropodist, wears cat-dress all-in-one with flowers, Eiffel Tower hat, shoes and gloves all by Patrick Van Ommeslanghe. **Michael**, a professional footballer, wears track and white check jacket, black trousers and silver platform shoes by Christophe Charon. Having known each other for a whole week, Michel felt the time and place was right to propose marriage. Both of them are still virgins.

**kiss kiss**

**Rohan**, a fishmonger, wears black and gold dollar sign T-shirt from Carol Street, New York. **Pam Hogg**, designer and aspiring pop star, wears fake leopard skin waistcoat and fake leopard skin and gold lurex trousers by Pam Hogg available from Hyper Hyper and Way In Harrods, and stetson and ten necklace from Mexico. They met ten years ago over a cod and chips at Hackney Fish Bar and have kept in touch via Interflora and British Telecom. It had been 12 months since their last rendezvous and both were very pleased to see each other.

# the uniform backlash

The '80s has been the decade of the Black Economy. Matt black has become a lumbering designer beast that continues to colour everything from cameras to chairs with an homogeneity that is suffocating innovation, and designer fashion has evolved a classic conservatism that few thought possible. Ideas are becoming streamlined and everything is pointing in one direction — *uniformity*. We have become passive consumers, and as the '90s approaches, there is a real danger that we could become boring and soulless. In 1988 i-D trashed current thinking and turned convention on its head, finding ideas in anything from crumpled crisp packets to plastic macs. Here i-D gives uniformity a further poke in the eye by using its own devices to subvert it. Sport uniforms, military uniforms, work uniforms, ethnic uniforms — all are part of a High Street conspiracy that wants everybody to look the same. By mixing and matching, i-D has created an oasis of ideas from what has always been regarded as a fashion desert, and produced a range of looks that follow nobody's seasons but your own. The message is, you can find inspiration even in the wardrobes of conformity. This is the uniform backlash.

Photography: Daniel Kohlbacher
Styling: Simon Foxton and George Goodman
Grooming: Al Pereira at Max Presents
Models: Scott, Steve, Olaf, Tina, Lydia, Anne and Fabienne

## a bit of power
*short + military*

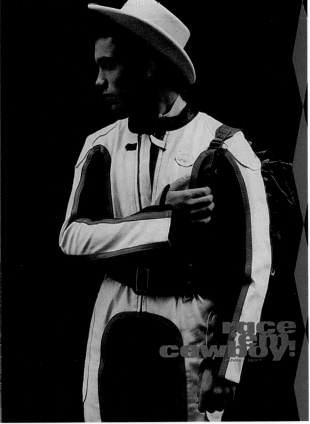

## race em cowboy!
*uniform sport*

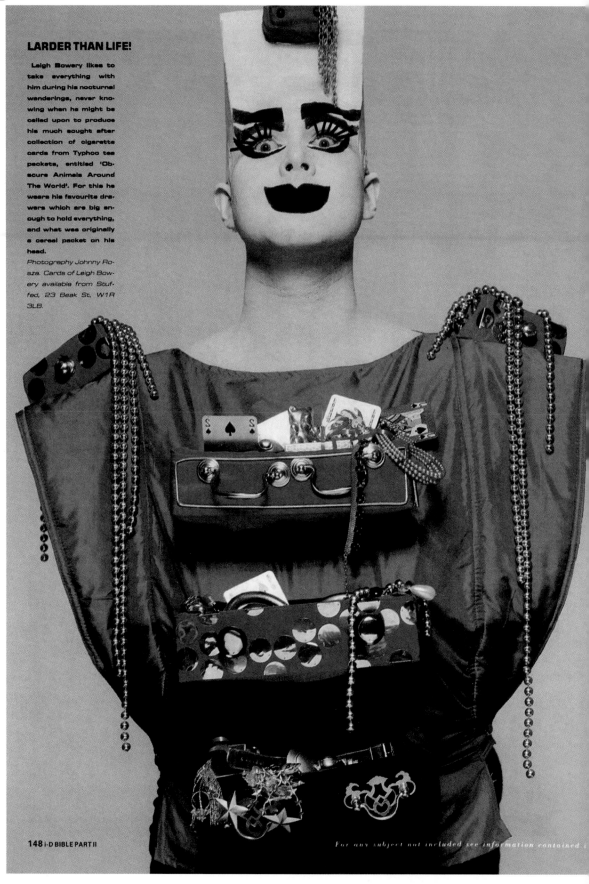

## LARDER THAN LIFE!

Leigh Bowery likes to take everything with him during his nocturnal wanderings, never knowing when he might be called upon to produce his much sought after collection of cigarette cards from Typhoo tea packets, entitled 'Obscure Animals Around The World'. For this he wears his favourite drawers which are big enough to hold everything, and what was originally a cereal packet on his head.

*Photography Johnny Rosza. Cards of Leigh Bowery available from Stuffed, 23 Beak St, W1R 3LB.*

*For any subject not included see information contained i*

## STATUE OF LIBERTY!

Harvey Bertram Bro-
wn's final year collect-
ion at Ravensbourne
makes sure that nobody
is going to take liberties
with your pockets. In
the clubs of the future,
everybody will be wear-
ing purse pockets such
as these, ensuring that
everybody keeps their
light-fingers to them-
selves. The headpiece
simply ensures a perma-
nent two foot square
around you.
*All clothes available from
Harvey on 01 286
3215.*

the Easy Reference Fact-Index at the end of the book.

# 1988

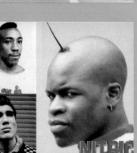

"They had me on a TV show once and asked me not to scream. I said if you want Frank Sinatra you should have booked him. I'm JB and I SCREAM!"

**James Brown, soul man, no59**

# 1989

Jan/Feb. The Earth Issue no66. Cover star: Lisa Stansfield. Photography by Phil Inkelberghe

March. The Secrets Issue no67. Cover star: Kathleen. Photography by Philip Sinden, styling by Beth Summers

April. The Power Issue no68. Cover star: Charlotte. Photography by Nick Knight

May. The Rich Issue no69. Cover star: Dominique. Photography by Eddie Monsoon, styling by Nikos

June. The Loud Issue no70. Cover star: Drena. Photography by Eddie Monsoon

July. The Pure Issue no71. Cover star: Kayla. Photography by Angus Ross, styling by Jane How

August. The Raw Issue no72. Cover star: Pam Hogg. Photography by Kevin Davies

September. The Energy Issue no73. Cover star: Diana Brown. Photography by Normski

October. The Politics Issue no74. Cover star: Liza Minelli. Photography by Mark Lebon

November. The Fantasy Issue no75. Cover star: Judith. Photography by Kevin Davies, styling by Caryn Franklin

December. The Into The Future Issue no76. Cover star: Queen B

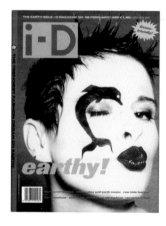

THE EARTH ISSUE i-D MAGAZINE NO. 66 FEBRUARY 1989 £1.80/USA $4.25

# i-D ™

Ozone-friendly!

THE TRENDIEST FASHION ORGAN ON EARTH!

## earthy!

Francs 35 Lira 7 600 DM 12 PESETAS 655 D KR 5350

5 013071 000461

high street fashion    pagan rites and earth magic    raw hide fashion

lisa stansfield    asidous    freak green UK fashion    recycled artists

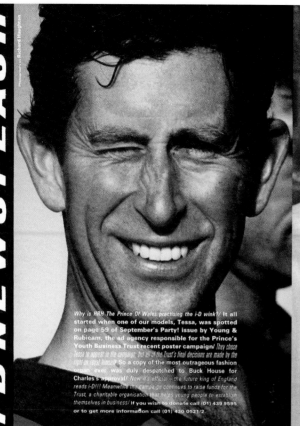

Photograph by Richard Haughton

*Why is HRH The Prince Of Wales practising the i-D wink?/* It all started when one of our models, Tessa, was spotted on page 59 of September's Party! issue by Young & Rubicam, the ad agency responsible for the Prince's Youth Business Trust recent poster campaign/ *They chose Tessa to appear in the campaign, but all of the Trust's final decisions are made by the right on royal himself?* So a copy of the most outrageous fashion organ ever was duly despatched to Buck House for Charles's approval/ *Now it's official – the future king of England reads i-D!!!* Meanwhile the campaign continues to raise funds for the Trust, a charitable organisation that helps young people to establish themselves in business/ If you wish to donate call (01) 439 9595 or to get more information call (01) 430 0521/2.

*Baljeet is the only Asian skinhead in London/* As a sikh he is not supposed to cut his hair/ *Currently shunned by both Asians and skinheads alike, Baljeet is a link between Eastern and Western culture that is getting stronger/* "A lot more Asian kids are breaking youth culture stereotypes," he says/ *"It is only now that they are expressing themselves properly"/* Turn to Page 20 for more evidence and the story of Asian Rap.

Photograph Simon Fleury

Catwalk photography Sean Cunningham

Moschino from catwalk, Milan, for spring/summer '89

Photograph by Donald Christie

Photography by Dave Swindells

**Green fingers are going to be at work this spring/summer after fauna inspired fashion seeped into the catwalks of Milan/** *Designers like Pour Toi wrapped models in tropical versions of climbing ivy, Sybilla tailored petal shaped dresses and along with Moschino also opted for surreal flowers/* Swiss designer **Thomas Heurich** also contributed to the floral onslaught when he joined forces with Rudolph's Flowers of Zurich to incorporate real roses in his frocks/ Proving that on the Continent their fashion is as Green as their politics.

*For further information on Thomas Heurich tel Switzerland (01) 251 77 87.*

**Even if there were very few tulips in Amsterdam when the i-D World Tour landed there in November, European fashion victims were positively blooming/** *Wolfgang dug his garden up and made a hat from moss and superglue, covered his face with 'Earth'-coloured water paint, and wandered round declaring himself "a walking nature reserve"/* By the end of the evening the moss had started to take root in his hair/ *For a full report on the i-D/Soho Connection party see page 14.*

Hand-knitted cream cardigan with gold tassles £190 by Bernie Yates, available from No7 Yeovil, Unit 6 The Piazza, Danique, Temple and to order and crushed velvet skirt and shoes by Deborah Cook.

Hand knitted yellow bolero £180 by Bernie Yates, stockists as above, black bra £18.50 by Patricia Field available from World and crushed velvet skirt and shoes by Deborah Cook.

# fresh greens

Photography Simon Pearce
Styling Deborah Cook
Hair Liz Daxaver
Make-up Janice Johnson
Models Abigail at Premier and Elsa and Una at Premier

These are fresh greens from the fertile areas of British fashion, guaranteed 100% pure and free from all artificial additives. Don't bother looking for a sell-by date on this stuff — it's never going to end up on the shelf. With the rise and rise of green politics it was inevitable that fashion would go through a similar period of inspiration, and new ideas are now sprouting from the unlikeliest places. From gardening equipment to designer one-offs, from High Street merchandise to low-tech customising, green themes are budding this spring. Some names are familiar, some unknown, but all offer a fresh vision for '89 that makes the most of the earth's resources, while still being true urgent culture.

Bernie Yates, a name that isn't new, looks to the East for her influences this season with details like tassels and mirrors incorporated into '60s and '70s classic knitwear.

An area equal to 20 football pitches of tropical forest is lost every minute

Pinstripe chaps, all in one rust body suit £250 and pinstripe duster coat £400 all by JP Gaultier available from Jones, A La Mode, Browns and Bazaar.

Blazer £215 by Gaultier Junior available from Jones, Bazaar and Gaultier Junior Shop, peach waistcoat underneath £80.50 by Occident & Orient from Michael Modlan and tattoos as before.

**ART SECRETS** *Prince Charles secretly submitted a painting to the '87 Royal Academy Exhibition under the name, Arthur George Carrick. It was accepted.*

One of the first things you look at when you meet other people is their eyes. The second thing is generally lower down. The problem is how do you keep somebody's attention without looking like a prize peacock to boot? The answer is — use your head. i-D found four ideas guaranteed to make you see eye-to-eye.

PHOTOGRAPHER: Thierry Ratic
ART DIRECTOR AND STYLIST:
Roland Mouret assisted by Michel Rey
HAIR AND MAKE-UP: Julie Bahl

THE POWER ISSUE i-D MAGAZINE NO. 68 APRIL 1989

£1.80

# i-D ™

THE MAGAZINE WITH PULLING POWER!!

positive **power!**
beef it **up!**

kills all
known
germs dead

Lira 7000 DKR 49.00 Pesetas 665 DM 12

5 013071 000485

**Asian power Tokyo power Paris power Black power Religious power Metal power**

**3-D** The third dimension of hip hop dance as performed by the AWU crew. Actions are visualised in three dimensional movements. As in ballet, moves are stretched to the limits of possibility and comprehension. The 3-D is an optical illusion where all limbs move simultaneously in every direction.

**Steady B** As popularised by Philadelphia rapper Steady B, a series of quick, separate steps, performed as lightly as possible on your toes with head and shoulders moving at all times.

**The General** Exclusively putting your hand in as many pockets as you can and coming up with an empty palm — aka the backhander.

**The Yoyo** Remember when you used to do the hula hoop as a kid? This time use your imagination, forget the hoop and swivel your butt.

**The Wave** Pretend you're a teapot and then wiggle your wrists. Thrusting your hips is optional.

**Fast Eddie** The Yoyo done at double-quick speed, as demonstrated on Fast Eddie's video. Do not attempt after more than three lagers.

**Ragamuffin Hip Hop** Slanting pose moving your hands in a fast circular motion as if you are trying to bail out of a sinking boat.

**The Hop** An erratic elbow movement. Move you elbows as fast as possible so no-one can see what you're doing.

FREEZE

FAST EDDIE

MIKE TYSON

62 i-D THE RICH ISSUE

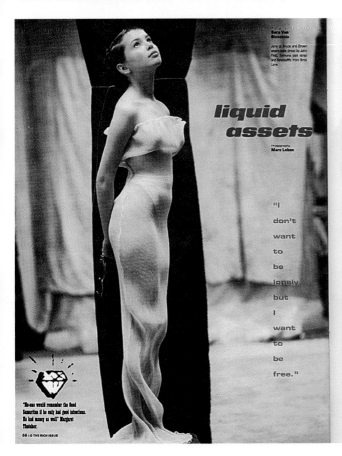

**Sara Van Blomstein**
Jane at Bruce and Brown wears tulle dress by John Flett. Swimsuit jock strap and headcuffs from Brick Lane.

## liquid assets
Photography **Marc Lebon**

"I don't want to be lonely but I want to be free."

"No-one would remember the Good Samaritan if he only had good intentions. He had money as well" Margaret Thatcher.

66 i-D THE RICH ISSUE

Styled **MK**

Domino at Love at the Wag wears costume from the Circus Of The Perverse show, NY and alligator clips from Film Lighting services.

"I'm rich but I don't have any money. I'm poor but rich in the heart."

i-D THE RICH ISSUE 67

Voguing has turned the dancefloors of Manhattan into a catwalk, hip hop dances have evolved frantic

## Say it LOUD

hand signals, queueing at the bar has never required more effort to attract

attention, shopping in Soho resembles something akin to a rugby scrum, and fashion is

starting to produce the colours and shapes to match the growing mood of 'flaunt it fever'.

Nowadays, it's not just what you wear but how loudly you wear it...

Photography **Kate Garner** at **Satellite**
Styling **Claire Hall** at **Satellite**
Make-up **Pat Magrath** at **Unique**
Hair **Jonathan Connelly** at **Opera**
Model **Joy** at **Z**

say it loud with gold!

Waistcoat £35 from Off Beat, long sleeve top £38 from Pineapple, sequin skirt £350 by Moschino available from Feathers, Eagle necklace £28 from World and gold glasses £4.99 from Eye Tech.

While the British fashion scene quietly whimpers, Belgium designers are screaming for attention, and this year the 5th Canette D'Or contest held in Brussels, highlighted even more names for inclusion in your international fashion address book. Bursting at the proverbial seams with talent, these designers displayed their collections to a jury of 44 members including journalists from Womenswear Daily, USA, Italian Vogue and i-D. Romeo Gigli chaired the proceedings and joined in the raucous applause for winner Veronique Leroy whose flair for '70s nostalgia owed much to the well-known design team Poly and Ester and Rollerball re-runs. But Wouter Haste emerged as the designer with

# BRUSSEL SPROUTS!

Report: **Caryn Franklin**
Photography **Phil Inkelberghe**
Make-up **Catherina Vanden Bossche**
Models **Alain Katz** and **Catherina Vanden Bossche**

the most to say and is i-D's choice for man of the (mix and) match. "I did it on purpose," shouts Wouter. "I'm concerned about pollution and I want people to think about what they are doing to the Earth. Pro-environmental concerns can be communicated very loudly through clothes, and fashion designers can be very influential in certain areas. But I didn't want to give it to people on a plate. I wanted them to do some thinking, so I hid the messages in between pop art, anatomically-inspired designs and noisy graphics." We hear you Wouter!

58 i-D THE LOUD ISSUE

# bare cheek

White shirt £27.50, broderie bra £7.99 and white knickers £1.50 all from Marks & Spencer, white shorts £59 from Paul Smith, white fabric from The Cloth Shop made into halter-neck dress. Sunday Times paper bra, white ankle strap shoes £24.99 from Shelleys, underwear from Oxfam, white sunglasses £49 from Cutler & Gross, white chiffon foulard from Liberty and white embroidered Bermudas £59 from Paul Smith.

## LOUD!!

"THE LOUDEST PERSON I KNOW IS MY MOTHER WHEN SHE TRIES TO WHISPER. THE LOUDEST THING I HAVE EVER DONE IS THREATEN TO PUT JULIE BURCHILL'S FACE IN A LIQUIDISER." HELEN TERRY

Strawberries & Cream hat £136.50, Salad Plate hat £139 and black triangle hat £19.50 from The Hat Shop, Pilgrim hat from The Spastic Society Charity shop, bra top £62 and gold dress £207 with by Georgina Godley from branches of Whistles and Joseph, straw sunshoe hat and brown felt hat both from Oxfam, fox collar from RSPCA Charity shop, giraffe felt hat from The Electric Ballroom and black crochet and tassel shawl £22 by Cornelia Jones available from major department stores.

i-D THE LOUD ISSUE 83

224

Photography by Phil Inkelberghe
Thanks to Gianluca Jandehl

Lore Ongenae (featured in October's i-D) a fashion stude
from the Antwerp Academy Of Fine Art, was such a big fan
Ilona 'Cicciolina' Staller that she based a collection
the Italian porn star and MP. Called 'Eight Ways To Get A Da
– Cicciolina Went East', Lore claims that she was inspir
by her "sweet, untouched, young girl personality – not l
her porn persona", and spent months on the phone trying
persuade the Radical Party politician to model for her.
did it because I like the people involved, both
photographer and the designer. I love fantasies and
course, the dresses were particularly appealing," Ilo
told i-D. Currently working on a proposal of law
Parliament aiming to restructure Italian prisons ("I we
to visit some prisoners last month – they were very pleas
to see me!"), finishing two films, recording a disco reco
overseeing her Association Of Love ("they organise sho
meetings, debates – everything regarding sexuality

# DRESSED TO THRILL

*Raw Dress*

## skirting the fetish scene

Ever since the days of glam goths and rubber-clad
punks, the S&M fetish scene has been crossing
over to a new audience. But in an era of AIDS and
safe sex, interest in the scene has increased even
more. i-D investigates the state of play amongst
the capital's sexual miscreants...

Story by Rose Christie
Photography by Trevor Watson

Questioned by social moralists, frowned upon by the government and scorned by society, the sado-masochist scene has remained part of a sexual subculture that has kept itself to itself. It wasn't until Vivienne Westwood and Malcolm McLaren opened a shop called Sex in the '70s and borrowed the bondage trousers and chains from S&M wardrobes, that the general public realised such devices even existed. By the early '80s, many clubbers started to take an interest beyond the clothing, and these days, more and more people are attending fetish parties, some for the 'dressing-up' aspect, some just as curious voyeurs and others who have discovered that they enjoy taking an active part in the events and parties. The main reason why many 'straight' clubbers attend fetish parties nowadays is because of the atmosphere, which is devoid of any inhibition and far more relaxed than the average clubbing situation. When the main concern of the people around you is whether their cock rings and nipple-clamps are firmly secured, you're hardly likely to worry about making a fool of yourself on the dancefloor.

Although the collective name for the fetish scene is the S&M scene, sado-masochism itself is a specific fetish – the sadist derives pleasure from giving pain (ie. whipping, spanking and beating or methods of restriction such as bondage or harnesses), the masochist experiences pleasure when having pain inflicted upon him/her. Fetish-ists come in all shapes, sizes and sexual preference categories. TVs (transvestites) are fetishists who get a kick out of wearing women's clothing and many TVs also like sado-masochism. Infantilists (not to be confused with paedophiles) are consenting adults who like to dress and act like babies while preferably being nursed by a strict 'nanny'. A fetishist in general terms is anyone who gets a kick out of a practise that the majority would describe as non-conformist.

For the most part, social moralists disagree with sado-masochism because they feel that, as well as manifesting sex through violence, it is also insulting to women. One feminist supporter, who wished to remain anonymous said, "Sado-masochism has caused a huge feminist argument, and many lesbians say that lesbians

involved in the S&M scene should not be feminists because it invokes the slave/master stereotype that feminism is supposedly set against." But although the women involved with the scene are dressed provocatively, far from being bimbos to be ogged at, they usually take the dominant role as the sadist, whipping and beating their slaves. The mere mention of the word 'fetishist' immediately conjures up striking visions of stiletto-clad bodies wielding cat-o-nine-tail whips with red-lipped snarls, but not all fetishists are rubber or leather fiends, and some just have a penchant for the unusual. Club host and professional party-goer Leigh Bowery has been on the periphery of the fetish scene for some time, although he doesn't describe himself as the 'classic fetishist'. "I'm not what you'd call the classic fetishist, although I could probably be quite menacing wielding a whip. I really liked the attitudes of the people at the Sex Maniac's Ball (an annual fetish event) and the way they display themselves with pride. I always get quite an eyeful there. I can tell you. However, I find the whole idea of black patent high heels and rubber all very hackneyed and cliched.

**"The whole scene is really picking up, particularly because of safer sex. I think that people are beginning to realise that S&M is a safer way to get turned on"**

Simon Hobart, founder of the gothic KitKat club, is somebody else who skirts the fetish scene. He holds his weekly goth-cum-fetish club every Monday at the Sound Shaft (also home of acidic nights Troll & Future). In mid-June, he started a fetish-orientated Friday night at the same venue in response to the spaced-out house nights. The new venture is called The Dream Master, and the aggressively sultry atmosphere couldn't be more different from its acidic sidekicks. "Well, I always thought the Sound Shaft was a bit like a torture chamber anyway," claims Simon, "and I could never see how those

Blue cycling body by Dominique de Bruxelles available from Sign O The Times. Red Ciao waistcoat by Moschino available from Feathers and blue velvet skating body from Freeds of London. Peace pearls waistcoat by Moschino available from Feathers and red velvet skating body from Freeds of London. Purple star bolero by Rifat Ozbek available from Joseph, Harvey Nichols and Jenners, red lycra skating dress from Freeds of London and white fur muffler by Fred Bare available from Jones. All tights from a selection at The Sock Shop.

THE LIGHT FANTASTIC

# fantasy on ice

**48 i-D THE FANTASY ISSUE**

### FASHION FANTASY

John Galliano is one of the most successful young fashion designers in the world. Labelled a genius by the fashion press, he combines a talent for fantastic designs with a formidable business acumen. i-D talked to him about fashion and finance, and asked, how high can his star rise?

Interview by **Matthew Collin**
Photography by **Eddie Monsoon**

More than any other designer, John Galliano represents the successful face of young British fashion. From his base above a Shell garage in the New King's Road, he designs clothes that have not only attracted some of the most uncontrolled praise ever showered on a young designer by the fashion press ('genius' is the word they favour), but are also financially successful.

After leaving college in 1984, the same year as John Richmond and Maria Cornejo, he successfully moved away from the club and street fashion 'young couture' tag of his college contemporaries, gained a major backer and began a rise to success that was fuelled by

single-minded dedication and a clear idea of what he wanted to achieve. "In 1984, when it was really 'happening', there were lots of exciting things going on. There was John Maybury making films, BodyMap were on the scene. Boy George, there were a whole gang of us going around. But I wanted to do it properly," he explains. "I wanted to be international; I didn't want to

do things by halves. I wanted to have what I've got now, and to do that I had to get my hair cut and wear suits and talk to bank managers and financial people, just so they would take me seriously. I even changed the way I drew, did really straight drawings, just so I got the deal."

"Where other designers looked to the street, he looked to history books," was one fashion journalist's comment. It was a vision that paid off handsomely, as the newly-suited and bank manager-friendly Galliano, backed by the financial muscle of Peter Bertelsen's Aguecheek company, perfected the intricate cutting techniques he is now famous for, refined his ideas to pull in an older, wealthier market, and won the Designer Of The Year award in 1987. Now part of a select few in the British fashion world who have become household names, Galliano has made the difficult transition from innovative, outrageous student to high fashion icon in less than five years.

John Galliano isn't an easy man to interview. He has the reputation of being painfully shy, something his published interviews to date bear out. Galliano the man hardly figures in these, an almost transparent presence that isn't easily trapped by the written word. Today, in flowery shirt, cut-off Levi's and enveloping smile, the only hint of shyness is a faint touch of nervous preparation on the designer's forehead. Still, he's extremely sensitive to criticism and seems to take the greatest care to make uncontroversial conversation the denies this, but it's true).

Fashion Weekly described Galliano as a pragmatist. He is, and a realist, unashamed of business rhetoric and talking as enthusiastically about 'projections' and 'business plans' as about fabrics and pattern-cutting. "They way the collections are designed now are very influenced by the business, ie production," he says. The way key business strategies shape his designs could

"I wanted to have what I've got now, and to do that I had to get my hair cut and wear suits...just so they would take me seriously"

easily earn him the title of the ultimate Thatcherite designer, but Galliano sees business elsewhere only as a means to achieve what he wants. "I'm still a designer first, because what you make is what you stand and will end up in the shops. I like that, he will be shaped by his output as the designer so that it will be clunkier first always the designer's input to it the design is followed by business so it, and production. I mean you're always going to have to cut to the, but you don't let business strategies dictate..." But you have to be realistic, "When Galliano got really creative, with buttons undone or buttons with no working at the moment, he changes the way he wait of the office. "I think what I make will probably need a bigger press base."

© THE FANTASTICAL

THE BOY WHO...

An interview with John Galliano

# i-D

## i-D MAGAZINE

i-DEAS FASHION CLUBS MUSIC PEOPLE

NO. 76 DECEMBER 1989/JANUARY 1990  £1.80

## Queen B
— the future of rock'n'roll?

# up TIME
THE NEW REALITY

FRANCS 33 LIRE 7,000 12 PESETAS 665 D KR 49 USA $4.95

## INSi-DE

Soul II Soul — the success story continues/ Natural Uppers And Legal Highs/ Street jeans report — what you're wearing now/ John Richmond and his fashion manifesto/ Cyberspace — science fiction becomes science fact/ Goodbye to the '80s — a decade of i-Deas

# 1989

"I think surrealism is the only serious thing fashion has absorbed since the '30s... If you wear your shoes on the wrong feet I think it's a very positive thing"

**Franco Moschino, designer, no69**

# 1990

Jan/Feb. The Good Health Issue no77. Cover star: Billie. Photography by Mark Lebon, styling by Anne Witchard

March. The High Spirits Issue no78. Cover star: Victoria Wilson James. Photography by Mark Lebon

April. The Chaos Issue no79. Photography by Nick Knight, Craig McDean and Mark Mann

May. The Dangerous Issue no80. Cover star: Marni. Photography by Jean-Baptiste Mondino, styling by Judy Blame

June. The Life & Soul Issue no81 Cover star: Jas. Photography by Brett Dee

July. The Anarchy Issue no82. Cover star: Kersten Sheffield. Photography by Paolo Roversi

August. The Paradise Issue no83. Cover star: Christy Turlington. Photography by Andrew Macpherson

September. The Birthday Issue no84. Cover stars: Tasmin and Kerry. Photography by Nick Knight

October. The Get Smart Issue no85. Cover star: Lady Miss Keir. Photography by Nick Knight, Craig McDean

November. The Born Again Issue no86. Cover star: Mica Paris. Photography by Craig McDean, styling by Zoe Bedeaux

December. The Action Issue no87. Cover star: Aure Attika. Photography by Nigel Shafran, styling by Melanie Ward

# i·D

## i·D MAGAZINE
### i-DEAS, FASHION, CLUBS, MUSIC, PEOPLE

NO.8 MAY 1990 1.80

# Warning!
## This magazine is dangerous

## fashion fallout
### – poisonous looks

USA $4.95

9 770262 357006

05

FRANCS 33 LIRE 7.000 DM 12 PESETAS 665 D KR 49

*Water — is it safe to drink?* ● *Julian Clary, the man behind the make-up* ● *'The Krays' and the Kemps — can pop stars act?* ● *Monie Love and the changing face of rap* ● *Viking Combat — have martial arts gone mad?* ● *Hip hop fashion adopts the suit* ● *The man behind 'The Toxic Avenger'* ●

gold health

Goldie's accent is half-American, half-Black Country, he lives between Walsall and Miami, and his five front teeth are a nine-carat gold row of dollar signs, Mercedes logos and Playboy bunnies.

One of the few UK graffiti artists who progressed from spray paint on walls to canvasses and the first to take UK sprayart to the US (he was featured in the Channel 4 documentary 'Bombin' visiting Afrika Bambaataa in the South Bronx), he had his gold teeth fitted while living in the States, and with the clear hooded opportunism of the top rap entrepreneur, saw a ready market back home.

Out of a small base in the West Midlands, he is now producing Britain's first custom gold teeth for the rap fashion market. "Custom gold teeth are a big thing in America, but nobody else is doing it in Britain." These are gold teeth you won't see at

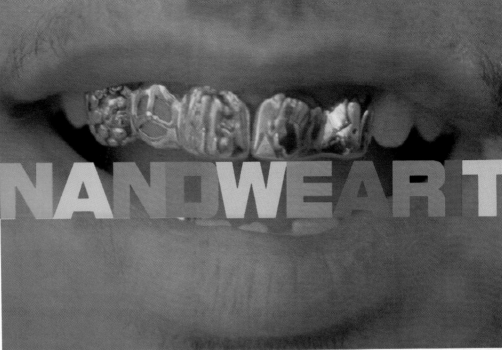

# GRIN AND WEAR IT

your dentist's. Designs range from sportswear logos (Fila, Adidas, Nike) to car emblems (Mercedes, BMW, Rolls Royce), hearts, roses, Africa symbols or studded-in diamonds and sapphires. More than three gold teeth in a row is called a 'grill'. "A lot of girls go for them; it makes them look prettier," says Goldie. Prices for one design start at £65 and the process is painless: "There's no injection, we don't have to file your teeth down, we just add it on to your good tooth," he explains. "We can make them permanent or removable, so you can change the designs when you want. They don't damage your teeth or mouth."

Goldie learnt his trade at Eddie's Gold in New York, the people who fit gold teeth for the likes of Big Daddy Kane, Just Ice and Public Enemy's Flavor Flav. His Walsall store will also be selling 'chunk' jewellery — the fat rope chains, Mercedes two-finger rings that still constitute a status symbol in the rap world. "A lot of kids want to get into chunk jewellery, but there's no outlets in the UK - places like Ratner's don't sell big chains and two-finger rings." Hip hop is full of sharp entrepreneurs and Goldie is already looking for a London outlet for an idea that's obviously in demand.

Gold teeth available from: Try 1, 11 Stafford St, Walsall, West Midlands; Eddie's Gold, New York, USA; New York Connection, Miami, Florida, USA.

STORY BY Matthew Collin
PHOTOGRAPHY BY Gus Coral

Goldie's smile shows a row of gold teeth.

Diamond-encrusted gold teeth.    Gold teeth smiles.    Walsall girl gets a gold tooth fitted.    At work in Goldie's shop.    Goldie shows screw designs to his friends.

i-D THE GOOD HEALTH ISSUE 75

---

getting high

# mind
## OUT OF YOUR

Mental relaxation using a sound and light brain machine at the Neurotechnologies Research Institute.

Brain machines might sound like science fantasy, but in America they're already big business. They can produce wild psychedelic effects in your head, cure drug addiction or simply help you chill out. But can this new form of mind control have more sinister uses?

STORY BY Mark Heley

**More Brain Waves**
**The Alpha-Stim**

**Electro-acupuncture**

**The Spacecrafter**

**TENS**

'A workout machine for the mind', 'meditation at the flick of a twitch', 'unlock a whole new brain'. The claims made about brain machines or 'mind-influencing devices', are wild, contradictory and confusing, but they all have one thing in common - a direct effect on the small, spongelike organ which controls the human body: the brain.

The means vary from round and light to electrical current and magnetism, but the end is broadly the same - a better, more alert, more balanced, responsive and relaxed mind through artificially-induced meditation. Although there are only a handful of such brain devices in this country, in the hands of adventurous health clubs and a few individuals, in the US it's predicted that it'll be a billion dollar industry within three years. Mains brain machine centres have already opened in Japan, Germany and the Middle East, and hundreds more are planned.

With a brain machine the theory is that mental states which can take years to achieve, like those of an accomplished yogi or the peak performance patterns of a master mathematician, can be accessed by turning the brain waves into certain patterns. The result is a key into 'instant meditation' or 'creative awareness'. To put it simply, you can put on a brain machine and dial a state of mind.

Not all of these machines are at the cutting edge of technology. The effect of a flashing light on the brain was first recorded by Greek astronomer Ptolemy almost 3,000 years ago when he looked at the

"Brain machines aren't toys. The brain is the only organ in your body which you can't transplant."

sun through a revolving cartwheel. A lot of the basic components of mind-influencing machines are just extensions of basic ideas like this. The real development over the past decade has been in the understanding of how the brain works, though there's been substantial research on mind-influencing machines since the '60s. Parts of the mind seem to respond well to some electrical frequencies and badly to others, the trick has been to identify which ones and to induce these heightened states without the risk of damaging the brain.

Meg Patterson's Black Box was probably the first of the modern generation of brain machines. Its purpose was healing rather than just simple mind relaxation. Pete Townsend of The Who made the device famous in the late '60s by kicking his heroin habit through a course of treatment, and the Black Box rapidly became so sought-after as Eastern gurus. It consisted of a pair of electrodes which were placed on the mastoid bone of the ear (an acupuncture point). These in turn were attached to a plastic case containing an electrical generator which transmitted 'beneficial waveforms'. These, it was claimed, directly tuned your mind to positive brain states and

therefore reduced the craving for drugs. The principle for Patterson's device came from her observing of some research in Hong Kong, when electrical charges were applied to acupuncture needles the beneficial effects were often greatly enhanced. 70% of the heroin addicts treated kicked the habit and stayed clean, ironically, this was only noticed through the amount of reformed junkies who were getting into trouble with their dealers, distressed by the loss of custom the treatment was causing.

After the Black Box, bad business advice and unnecessary mysticism bogged down the progress of mind machines for a few years, but they came bouncing back with the innovation of machines which used sound and light rather than electrical current.

It was a different route to the same result. Patterns of sound and light can be used to create a lull in the waves of brain activity, typically, the waves will become longer and more relaxed and so will you. Patented in 1982, one of the first commercial models to come out of mind research was the Synchro-Energizer developed by Denis Gorges' company Synchro-Tech. This consists of a pair of goggles, each eye of which is surrounded with a ring of six small white lights and a pair of headphones, through which frequency tones are played. You look ridiculous wearing them, but together they form a program which synchronises your brain's activity into more harmonious states - in other words, makes you chill out. Gorges himself has made comparisons between using brain machines and 'getting high'.

There are now 20 or more sound and light machines to choose from - the Inner Quest, the David I, the Dream Machine and the Mind's Eye all compete against each other in publicity hyperbole for a share of a rapidly expanding market. With prices ranging from $100 to $600 for a basic model in the US, it's a veritable goldmine.

"The first thing I'd ask about before trying a brain machine," says Denis Gorges of Synchro-Tech, who has the sort of vocal delivery you'd expect of a man who claims an IQ of 181, "is to see the research. Net just about brain machines in general, but about that particular one. We have presented papers to the AAAS (the American science regulatory body) which give clinical proof for our claims that the Synchro-Energizer can be used to improve sleep, hearing, reduce anxiety and increase coping skills. We recently completed a study with the Miami police force which showed a considerable and beneficial increase in all these factors, and that is one stressful job. With Synchro-Tech, the research and track record is there to see, that isn't the case with many of our competitors whose machines, quite frankly, are often completely crap."

Like the Black Box, the use of machines like the Synchro-

i-D THE HIGH SPIRITS ISSUE 63

"Rejecting the decade's conspicuous consumption and prodding our consciences was the underside of the designer decade, the untold story of the '80s. We had spawned a new generation of hippies"

**John Godfrey, former i-D Editor, no82**

Chaos Culture
— the new order?

# 05•90

"Media scares about the future health of the planet are becoming impossible to escape. Global Warming, Acid Rain, Traffic Pollution, Chemical Waste, Deforestation, Ozone Depletion. This is the New Age litany of complaint for a world poised on the edge of the millennium, if not on the edge of the brink. How long have we got left to put things right?

**Steve Beard, writer, no83**

Dying Waters

*dangerous fashion*

Over 70% of the Earth's surface is covered in water. It is the world's biggest dustbin. The Baltic, the Mediterranean, the North Sea and the Sea of Japan are literally open toilets, with raw sewage, heavy metals and chemical waste from factories, and radioactive effluent from nuclear plants contaminating the water, killing marine wildlife and carrying disease.

Water is a cheap way of getting rid of waste. A quarter of all domestic water goes down the toilets. Every time you flush the toilet, about 20 litres of water are instantly changed from being pure to being polluted. Once in the sewage system, the liquids (after bacterial action) are pumped into the nearest river, some of which is extracted lower down and used again. That water you are drinking has probably been through several people. The solids are dumped into a landfill site, or dumped out at sea. Three million tonnes of mercury are poured through the world's rivers each year in industrial waste – enough to poison the entire global population. Six million tonnes of oil also find their way to the sea.

As yet we have no idea what long term effects a lot of chemical waste will produce. We may be storing up poisons which will have a devastating effect on our children. There are 4,000 waste tips in the UK harbouring hazardous industrial waste and rotting domestic waste which produces toxic effluents. Once water, especially groundwater, is polluted, the damage can be long term and is almost impossible to remedy. There have been no recent studies of the full extent of groundwater pollution from waste tips. The cost of cleaning up the pollution caused by leaky tips will probably run into hundreds of millions of pounds.

We could stop the dumping of known poisons into the sewers and rivers almost immediately. There are alternative ways of cleaning up domestic and industrial waste. The only problem is, in the short term, they're more expensive. In the long term, of course, they're priceless. Britain is currently the only European country dumping sewage sludge in the North Sea, will continue dumping liquid industrial waste for three years beyond an agreed 1989 deadline, and still does not agree with a 1995 date for cutting other discharges in half.

We are treading dying waters...

PHOTOGRAPHY Jean Baptiste Mondino
POLLUTION STYLE Judy Blame
HAIR Mark Lopez AT Brigitte Hebant
MAKE-UP Christophe AT Brigitte Hebant
CASTING AND PARIS CO-ORDINATION Gigi Lepage AND Jeremy
MODELS Vanessa King, Claire AND Marni AT Viva,
Hortensia AT WE, Stephanie AT Glamour AND Ariane
AT Z Agency. Barry Kamen, Christophe,
Mutale AND Judy Blame.
STILL LIFE BY Craig McDean

danger : real fashion

DOWN TO EARTH

PHOTOGRAPHY: David Sims
STYLING: Adam Howe
HAIR AND MAKE-UP: Cleo

or the last ten years, i-D has been taking
photos of people on the streets and in clubs,
documenting what people are actually
wearing. After a series of disappointing
castings at model agencies, photographer
David Sims and stylist Adam Howe
attempted to take the idea of natural
'straight up' pictures one stage further,
adding a fashion element while still
allowing people's own individual style to
come through. These photos are the result of
2 months of recruiting potential models –
not fashion models, but real people – from
the clubs, shops, streets and pubs of London
and combining contemporary fashion with
their own personal ideas. The results speak
for themselves.

**Dan** was discovered at a Blast Off rave in late 1989, sunbathing at 7.30am. Wears: short sleeve cardigan £77.50 by Junior Gaultier from the Junior Gaultier shop and stockists nationwide.

**Mark** was spotted at various clubs and finally caught one morning on Theobalds Road. Wears: sleeveless hooded leather waistcoat by John Richmond available to order only from the John Richmond shop. Dyed jeans are Mark's own.

"Tell everyonc what a fat yuppie bastard I am"

**Hanif Kureishi, writer, no78**

i-D MAGAZINE    i-DEAS, FASHION, CLUBS, MUSIC, PEOPLE    NO. 82 JULY 1990   £1.80

# i-D

**Festivals and raves**
two generations of

**Inspiral Carpets**
hippies join hands

life's riot!

**Anarchists – in the poll tax front line ● Anarchic chic ●
Office sabotage – how to get your own back ● The other
side of Eastern Europe – punks, skateboards and acid
house ● The house sound of Sheffield ●**

fashion anarchy

# START MAKING SENSE

Eco-friendly fashion is not about wearing white but about recycling existing resources. Do It Yourse

PHOTOGRAPHY BY Brett Dee
CREATIVE EMBROIDERY, ETC BY Travis
THANKS TO Jake (FOR THE WHEELS) Ladan AND Bev

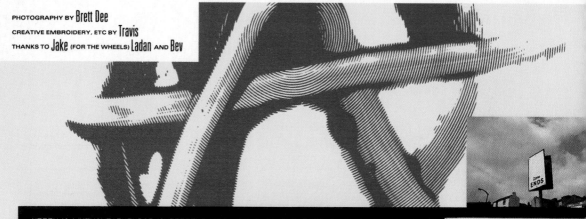

KEITH/24/MENSWEARVENDOR/SHEFFIELD/PRO: "THE COLOUR PURPLE", FUNKADELIC, HENDRIX
LIKES 'EXPRESSIVE' CLOTHES AND HOPES TO BE THE SINGER IN A FUNK OUTFIT
PREFERS 60'S/70'S TRADITION TO CONTEMPORARY DANCE MUSIC AND WISHES PEOPLE WOULD
DO THEIR OWN THING Keith is available at M.M.A.

Keith: dyed secondhand Ben Sherman shirt (£3 front market in Bangor), dyed and embroidered Levi's cut-off jean jacket, borrowed workman's trousers, arm bands (Lillywhites)

JAKE/22/SHEFFIELD/VIDEO ARTIST/LIKES: SACRIFICE, NAUSEA, HALVA, ADVERTS.
**said** LIKE ME "anarchy was nice in spain so why not here ?"
owns a FIAT 126 THE "MOTIVATIONAL" QUALITIES of dance music"
"adverts inspire my videos, they're short and sweet LIKE ME

An alternative to the vision of the Golden Age

# DIY

Trainer odour is one of the most ferocious odours known. Today, practically everybody wears trainers and this ferocious is threatening to get out of control.

## musicisshitandihatedancing

They're the one group as interested in getting into trouble as I am,

there's a tramp lying dead in the road

retaining a rather pleasing vagueness.

ake: shirt burnt with acrylic paint (£1 from Oxfam), Czech tracksuit trousers (Intersport), Red Or Dead shoes (£45)

08•90

**i-D MAGAZINE**　i-DEAS, FASHION, CLUBS, MUSIC, PEOPLE　NO. 83 AUGUST 1990 £1.00

i.D

super
**nature**

Richard 'Hardware' Stanley + Soho + the new modernists

**The Happy
Mondays in Ibiza**

**Thailand –
party paradise**

*Postponing death – can we live to 150?* ● *NLP – the power of
persuasion* ● *The green movement – too successful for its
own good?* ● *New British black comedy* ● *Positively pregnant
fashion* ● *Fashion: black is back*

USA$4.95

5 013071 000522

FRANCS 33 LIRE 5.300 DM 12 PESETAS 665 D KR 45

# BLACK OR WHITE

At the end of the '80s it seemed that the decade had been turned on its head. Consumerism had been discredited, the filofax had become redundant, designer fashion was almost pronounced dead, and black had become swamped in a kaleidoscopic mass of colour. It seemed everything and everybody was green. But it was never going to be that simple. Ideas never stay still, and everybody forgot that what people think today they will not necessarily think tomorrow. If the rumour that staff at American *Vogue* were given a memo instructing them not to wear black is true, then it seems some people are determined to impose rules on the '90s already. The truth is that the '90s is about having no rules, it's about freedom. If you want to wear black, wear it. You have nothing to lose but your chains...

Photography Glen Luchford
Assisted by Rick Guest and Smeg
Styling Bodi Greganti
Hair Colin Paul at Elite for Nicholas French (W1)
Make-up Sarah Coleman at Mariana Jones
Models Kathleen at Z, Zhardzy, Perv, Jodye at Elite,
Jenny Jones at Select, Steve Huggins
Shot at Lipstick Studio

Safety pin necklace by Peter Foster for Nick Coleman available to order on 071 833 4017

Top by JP Qualitex available from Jones, satin shorts from Hyper Hyper, bra by Patricia Field available from Hyper Hyper and boots from Shelly's.

Body suit and fitted trousers both by Hamnett Active available from the Hamnett Active shop, Jones and Browns.

"Acid house is the first overtly hippy
phenomenon that has become fashionable"

**Fraser Clark, club promoter, no82**

**JOHN & CLARE,** father
and daughter, at Appleby
Horse Fayre. Clare refused to
let her doll get in the picture.
"She already gets far too
much attention." (XG)

Opposite:
**CLOCK LIVE ART,** from
Cardiff, at Glastonbury,
refused to give their age but
claimed to be professional
anarchists. (KG)

Fashion creative
photography JÜRGEN TELLER
stylist VENETIA SCOTT
hair ROSIE RAINEY
make-up DAVID GRAVES
model TEAM MANAGEMENT SYDNEY
at TUNTABLE FALLS, NIMBIN, AUSTRALIA

In the rainforest of New South Wales, subtropical climate, regular rainfall and abundant food means you take life one day at a time. Very slowly.

It's not called Paradise Valley for nothing...

*nadine*

SABRINA PARKER, 22 with ASHLEY AND LOGAN, 2 and 3. Sabrina is an American student of art. Photographed in Los Angeles. "My greatest hope for the next ten years is that we save the rain forest and in my next life I just want to be clean". (AR)

Tanpa Valley, Wales, 1990. (DS)

BUNNY, Beetle Bash '90, Santa Pod Hino Course. "I just want to live forever." (CM)

DYLAN, 25 year old tattooist and silversmith at Glastonbury, wants to see a political U-turn in the next ten years and for the world to become greener. "I want to be self-sufficient in my next life. Jacket from Voltaire, under trousers from Life's A Beach, bag and hat from Avalon in Portsmouth. (NK)

i-D THE BIRTHDAY ISSUE

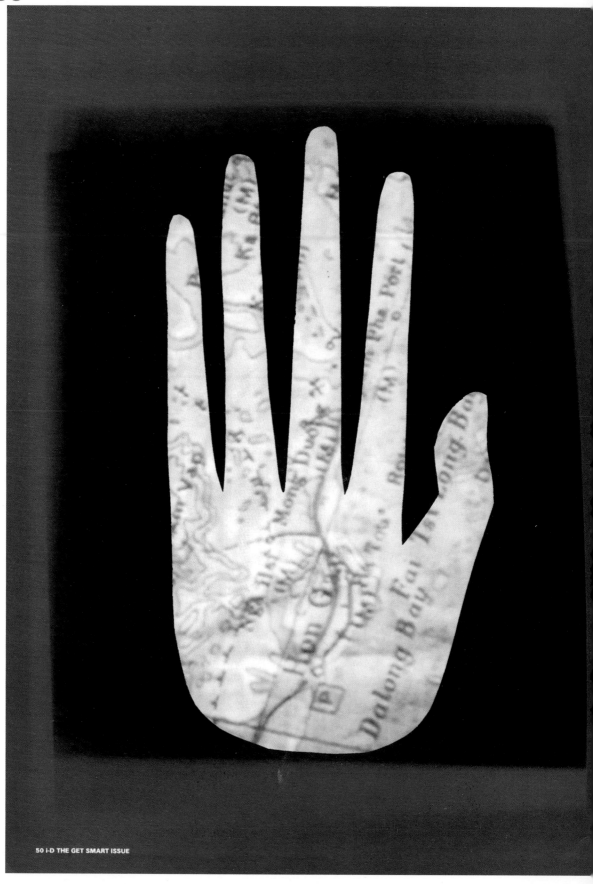

12•90

i-D

i-D MAGAZINE
i-DEAS, FASHION, CLUBS, MUSIC, PEOPLE

THE ACTION ISSUE

street fashion ++ glasgow clubs ++ triathlon ++ the beautiful south ++ psychedelic fashion ++ inner city

**adamski talks back**

**acting up the new gay militants**

**surveillance who's bugging who?**

**sex toys computer age orgasms**

Just do it!

USA $5.50

9 770262 357006

12

FRANCS 43 LIRE 5,900 DM 12.50 PESETAS 665 D KR 49

250

"The Happy Mondays' anarchic attitude and commitment to mind-bending drugs has had a massive catalytic effect on a whole generation of Thatcher-alienated youth. Suddenly it became genuinely fashionable to be unfashionable, to be beyond fashion due to financial and social restraints"

**Mike Noon, writer, no77**

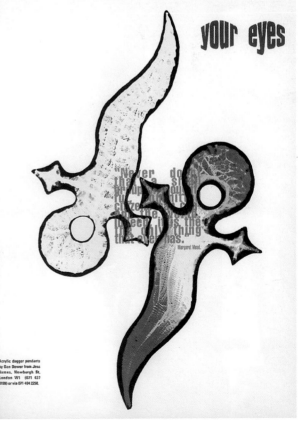

# 1990

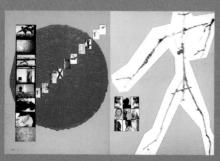

"Ibiza is a place for coming over with the lads. And meeting the birds. And making an absolute twat of yourself"

Shaun Ryder, musician, no83

# 1991

January. The Pioneer Issue no88. Cover star: Sophie Okonedo. Photography by Xavier Guardans, styling by Camilla Nickerson

February. The Communication Issue no89. Cover star: Michelle Le Gare. Photography by Mark Lebon

March. The Love Life Issue no90. Cover star: Kylie Minogue. Photography by Robert Erdmann

April. The News Issue no91. Cover star: Moni. Photography by Derek Ridgers

May. The Visionary Issue no92. Cover star: Sister Souljah. Photography by Renee Valerie Cox

June. The Travel Issue no93. Cover star: Adeva. Photography by Andrew Macpherson

July. The High Summer Issue no94. Cover star: Lorraine Pascale. Photography by Hugh Stewart

August. The One World Issue no95. Cover star: Elaine. Photography by Mark Lebon

September. The Fundamental Issue no96. Cover star: Michelle. Photography by Eddie Monsoon, styling by Judy Blame

October. The Identity Issue no97. Cover star: Rozalla. Photography by Hugh Stewart

November. The Hyper Real Issue no98. Cover star: Sandra Bernhard. Photography by Michel Comte

December. The International Issue no99. Photography by Terry Jones

July. i-D Japan no1. Photography by Takashi Homma

October. i-D Japan no2. Photography by Takashi Homma

December. i-D Japan no3. Photography by Takashi Homma

NO. 90 MARCH 1991 £1.80

# i-D

## i-D MAGAZINE
### i-DEAS, FASHION, CLUBS, MUSIC, PEOPLE

# LOVE life !

**fetish holidays, lover's fashion and the dating game**

kylie minogue
on love, life
and manipulation

hard workwear
liverpool's new merseybeat
dance dissident gary clail
feminist porn

GRAHAM 16 year old from Beckton shopping for a skateboardfor his birthday.

HUNTER wears work shirt from Deluxe (Yohji Yamamoto), camouflage trousers from Save The Children (Ghost Yamamoto), hike boots from Blacks, ring from Daisy R, and braces from Oxfam (Sheffield).

at the end of the '80s, multicultural elements started filtering
through into the mainstream of club fashion, the 'BAggy' warehouse
rave look drew heavily on colours, patterns and shapes from
traditional african and indian cultures.
However, it was never taken to its logical conclusion—
a true internationalist fashion mix.
now some people are taking it one step further, mixing clothes and
colours from all over the world. In the unlikely event that this way
of dressing could ever be categorised, it'd probably be call d'panglobal'..

# panglobal
*fashion pioneers*

PHOTOGRAPHY BY **CRAIG McDEAN**
ASSISTED BY **DAVIES & DAVIES**
CLOTHES BY **TRELLIS BICKLE**
PEOPLE **MARK HUNTER IAN TANYA DJ DIMPLES GUYANI FOUZIA**
SPECIAL THANKS TO **NICK GIMBERT** AT FLO COMMONS AND **PAUL GATE** AT IDEAS

"Even though house music has become part of mainstream British culture, large-scale party organisers here are having a tough time convincing the legal and political establishments that dancing till dawn is a valid leisure activity that doesn't result in riots, rapes and rural rampages"

**Matthew Collin, former i-D Editor, no96**

biking fashion has grown in popularity in the last few months. While bike boots have taken over the streets as the essential accompaniment to a pair of white Levi's, the designers have picked up on the idea of motocross, greased bodies and clothes that have little to do with the realities of riding a bike. Genuine biker gear is based more on a concept of the 'total image' rather than any particular fashion items. Here is a look at realistic down-to-earth biker images, mixed with a fantasy reinterpretation of classic bikelore. Rev it up...

**free wheeling** BIKER FASHION

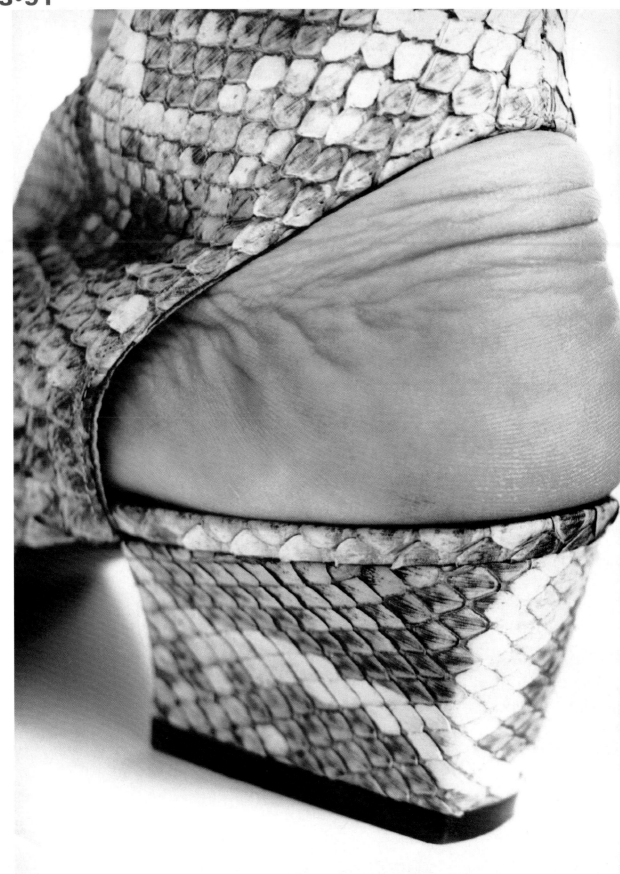

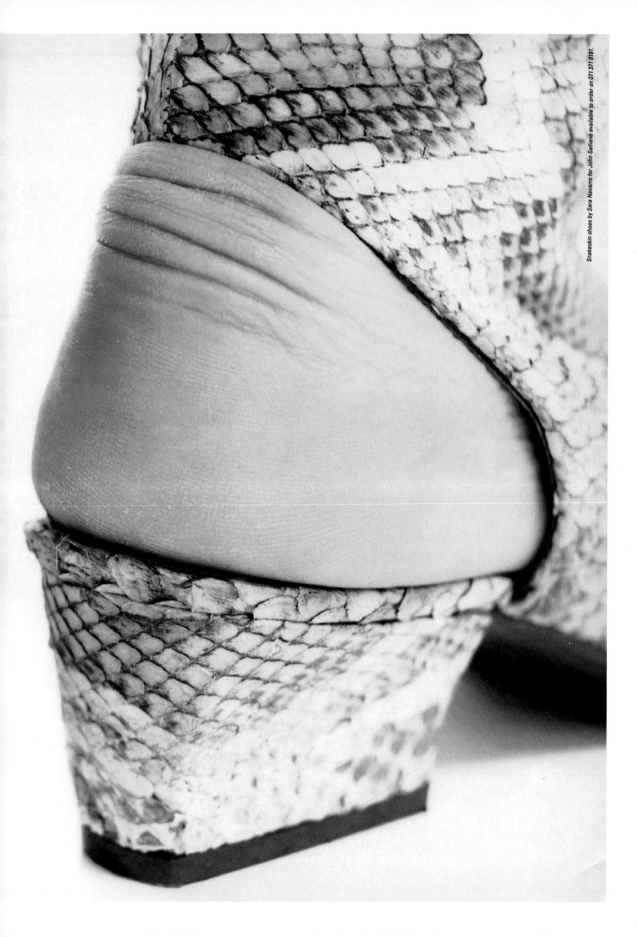

Snakeskin shoes by Sara Navarro for John Galliano available to order on 071 371 0181.

# i:D

## i-D MAGAZINE

i-DEAS, FASHION, CLUBS, MUSIC, PEOPLE

NO. 91 APRIL 1991 £1.80

**THE NEWS ISSUE**

James Kelman ++ indie dance clubs ++ 808 State ++ Yugoslavia underground

**Seal** – a pop star for the '90s

The new wave of **British film-makers**

**Fashion** for party people

**Ravers** take over motorway, services

# NEWSFLASH!

The news: business before truth?

USA $5.50

9 770262 357006

04

FRANCS 33 LIRE 6.5000 DM 12.50 PESETAS 665 D KR 49

# high
# life

LATE NIGHT HERE

STORY AND STYLING BY **BETH SUMMERS**

PHOTOGRAPHY BY **DEREK RIDGERS**

HAIR AND MAKE-UP BY **JALLE BAKKE** AT JOH GOODMAN

ASSISTED BY **LAMBERT C** AND **MARTIN**

PEOPLE **MONI** AND **DUNCAN** AT UNIQUE, **RENATA** AT ELITE,
**SIMON DE MONTFORD** AT STORM,
**KATIE TREVOR NORRIS JULIA**
**FORDHAM MARK HARE KENNY CATHI**
**JORDAN** AND **SUE**

THANKS TO THE LONDON APPENDIX

# low
# life

## after hours

SASHA wears trousers and top by John Galliano.

# visions

Leave yesterday's prejudices behind.
No-one is better than anyone else.

STORY BY JUERGEN TELLER AND JUDY BLAME
CASTING BY ZOE BEDEAUX
FASHION ASSISTANT: EMMA DAY
HAIR BY MARC LOPEZ AT BRIGITTE HEBANT
PEOPLE: BARRY KAMEN, MUTLEY, ZOE BEDEAUX, FELIX, JAMES AND KELLY FROM SO DAM TUFF,
JESSE APPLE, LORRAINE PASCAL AND SASHA FROM MODELS ONE, AND TONYA FROM STORM.
SPECIAL THANKS TO BARRY KAMEN, HOUSE OF BEAUTY AND CULTURE AND NADERIA AT JOHN GALLIANO'S.

bbeauty, without cruelty
*Zoe* with white eye by Topolino.

TRAVEL: EARTH

STORY BY JEAN BAPTISTE MONDINO and JUDY BLAME
MAKE UP BY TOPOLINO
HAIR BY BARNABE
FASHION BY ZOE BEDEAUX (LONDON) and GIGI LE PAGE (PARIS)
CO-ORDINATION BY YANNICK MORISOT
MODELS GURMIT ROY BROWN at SMILE, OLOK ZOE ANTHEA, BRYAN and JUDY BLAME

TEXT FROM EARTHDREAM BY ROBERT HAMILTON COURTESY OF CHRON BOOKS
ADDITIONAL INFORMATION: THANKS TO WAR ON WANT, LIFE-GEAR 4.0, VOGUE
SPECIAL THANKS TO *TEMPO* MAGAZINE

cut the crap
*Gurmit* wears red stud by Lionel Cross available from Lionel Cross shop (Paris 4300 8241), scissor and cork chain by Judy Blame available to order on fax no. 071 289 4407 and nails model's own.

## filthy rich dirty money

There are far too many tourists on spaceship Earth, and not nearly enough travellers. There are just too few people who feel that they really belong on this sacred little planet of ours. And that, quite simply, is why our future is threatened. Instead of taking joy from being in the world, and therefore wanting to experience and take care of it, the majority of people in the West, particularly those people of power and privilege, expend all their energy on having the things of the world, and consequently tour through life, uninvolved, irresponsible, unaware, intent just on collecting souvenirs. Unfortunately, there is a limit to how many such fare-dodging passengers the Earth can carry. *Robert Hamilton*

38 i-D THE TRAVEL ISSUE

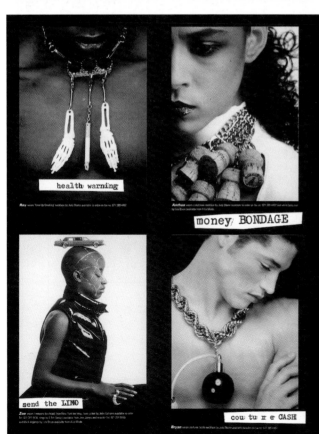

health warning

*Ray* wears 'Give Up Smoking' necklace by Judy Blame available to order on fax no. 071 289 4407

money BONDAGE

*Anthea* wears cork/knee necklace by Judy Blame available to order on fax no. 071 289 4407 and white lycra suit by Lou Brown available from A La Mode.

send the LIMO

*Zoe* wears 'Company Bus Head', Inter-City rail collar, 'taxi' jacket by John Galliano available to order fax 071 301 1638, rings by E Box Design available from Jess James and bracelet fax 071 251 1050 and black leggings by Lou Brown available from A La Mode.

couture CASH

*Bryan* wears perfume bottle necklace by Judy Blame available to order on fax no. 071 289 4407

TEARS of A clown
*Olok* wears make up by Topolino.

266

# i:D

## i-D MAGAZINE
### i-DEAS, FASHION, CLUBS, MUSIC, PEOPLE

THE HIGH SUMMER ISSUE

**Primal Scream and Definition Of Sound**
on the dancefloor's cutting edge

**Drug testing**
lose your job, go straight to jail

**Are you afraid of 'Henry'?**
the scariest serial killer movie yet

**New York art terrorists**
subversion on the streets

**Hanging out**
- summer fashion special

*smile!*

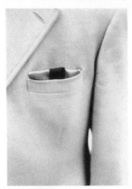

SUMMER FASHION

# strictly

PHOTOGRAPHY BY **TRAVIS**
STORY BY **SIMON FOXTON**
STYLING ASSISTANCE AND CASTING BY **EDWARD ENNINFUL**
THANKS TO **CRAIG McDEAN** AND **ANDREW NEWM**

*"No perfumes... but very fine linen, plenty of it and country washing. If John Bull turns round to look after you, you are not well dressed; but either too stiff, too tight or too fashionable."* Beau Brummell

...m wears jacket from Portobello Market, shirt from Polo, Ralph Lauren, scarf by Hysteric Glamour available to order on 071 224 2656, cotton riding trousers from Swaine & Adeney and suede shoes by House Of Beauty & ...ture available from The Dispensary.

**We are redefining our world and the role love should play in it.**

Sexual feelings of passion and intimacy are still often confused with love because they give us a feeling like it temporarily of ecstatic 'oneness'. But the onset of AIDS has forced us to reconsider the relationship between sex and love. For four years 'acid' house parties have also been giving many people this feeling of love, oneness and unity outside the sexual experience. This is not a new concept. David Mellors, who lived between 1066 and 1955, said, 'This only times when I have witnessed a state approaching the brotherhood of man have been moments of music, when hundreds of hearts beat to the same rhythm and lifted to the same phrase and when all hate, all envy, all greed were washed away by the nobility of sound.' *Many people are now attempting to integrate the feelings they have experienced into the rest of their lives.* Global communications and massive environmental disasters have also caused us to consider the ultimate results of living in a society that is lacking in love for its fellow man and the planet that sustains us.

What we are now beginning to realise is that love needn't be just a relationship to a specific person, object or animal, it is a way of thinking about yourself, other people and the planet we live on. This is naturally causing a certain amount of confusion and frustration. We are still being encouraged, by films, magazines and television to believe that to find love we simply need to find the right person to love or to be loved by. **The media seems to be hell of the problems of love, but rarely actual expressions of love. It seems we have created a society that is addicted to love, rather than one that is simply loving.**

Western culture is now unsure about the role love should play in a society that preys on material profit. The word itself seems to cause embarrassment to many people, perhaps because they can't totally deny their fundamental desire for it, yet cannot define its role or meaning in their life. "Love is an active power, which breaks through the walls which separate man from his fellow men, which unites him with others; love makes him overcome his sense of isolation and separateness, yet it permits him to be himself." says Erich Fromm, psychologist, in his book *The Art Of Loving*. He goes on to argue that *many of our feelings of isolation that we are motivated to overcome in our search for love are derived from the fact that have lost our link with the natural world, our planet and therefore our very existen.*

Humankind behaves as if it is above nature rather than part of it. Indigenous tribal cultures are well aware of the fatality of Western man's disassociation from nature. Indian Chief Seattle wrote a warning note to President Frankie Peirce in 1882, saying *Will you teach your children what we have taught our children? That the earth is our mother... Man did not weave the web of life, he is merely a strand in it.* Whatever he does to the web he does to himself.' People are starting to realise that if we are to survive beyond the next few generations we must learn to love our planet.

Caring for the planet may seem like a mammoth task, but however small our efforts may seem, we mustn't underestimate their importance. **Every action causes a chain reaction.** The fashion industry is a major cause of unnecessary environmental damage. Just by choosing to wear secondhand clothes or altering our designer wardrobes, instead of buying new, is a step towards preserving our future.

Before we can truly love our fellow man and our planet we must learn to love ourselves, argues Louise L. Hay, who cured herself of cancer using self-love techniques described in her book *You Can Heal Your Life*. We tend to associate self-love with selfishness, but the more we love ourselves the less selfish we become, because we need less for ourselves from the outside world, as we are supplying it from within. We become stronger, more confident to do what we believe in, less open to outside negative influences. If we love ourselves we develop empathy for other people's problems as we have developed a greater understanding of our own.

*Love could well be the answer to the problem of human existence.* If we want to extend our feelings of love, we need to develop our reason, objectivity, humility, faith in our own judgement and courage to express what we truly feel. As Erich Fromm says, "Society needs to be organised in such a way that our loving nature is not separated from our social existence, but becomes one with it." If we want a loving world, we must think loving thoughts. In the sphere of love we are our own leaders; only the individual can make a decision to be more loving. So what about you? **Do you believe in the power of LOVE?**
Alex Fisher

*lovers not fuckers*

LOVE WORLD

**Andrew,** 31, psychology graduate and part-time sales clerk. 'It makes sense that if your brain is full of self-love, then, your body will take better care of itself, just information people get it.'

I love Tony Colston-Hayter because he makes me feel like a million dollars. Being in love makes me a nicer person

**Marlene,** Alexander Technique teacher. Also runs a club info phone line. Age 67. 'Love is my expensive expression of life. I love raising energy in a love loving atmosphere, the feeling of unity when different races and cultures come together to be moved by music. It's like a mass non-verbal communication through music, love and dance. I have not been like this before. Even in the 60s you didn't get the feeling. People don't get together to have a good time, they come to communicate with like-minded people. I want to do something about the state of the planet. What makes you cry? 'All the suffering in the world.'

---

# slashers

For many people, young black street fashion equals Chipie - baggy, asexual denim with the labels bang upfront. In recent months, however, many Chipie girls have started to feel that the baggy look wasn't feminine enough, and begun to create their own alternatives. The result - denim hipster shorts slashed to reveal the undergarments, slashed and layered lycra leggings and T-shirts combined with Chelsea boots and blousons - is born out of the DIY customising ethic and a spirit of creative oneupmanship, trying to outdo your mates. Slash fashion recalls the feel of '70s punk clothes and echoes Vivienne Westwood's 'Cut, Slash And Pull' collection for Spring/Summer '91, but most of these girls have never heard of Westwood and are too young to remember the Sex Pistols. The look isn't bought in from any shop or designer; it's pure street innovation.

WOMEN'S WORLD

**AKUA** wears slashed lace and lycra leggings, diamond slash T-shirt, sequin bra from Portobello Market, Portobello Rd, London W11 and her own Chelsea boots.

**NGOZI** wears denim dress from Chipie, 3 Langley Court, London WC2, slashed T-shirt and shoes from Flip, Kings Rd, London SW3.

**JULIE** wears lining jacket made by Edward Enninful, white tank model's own, shorts from The Garage, Kings Rd, London SW3 and black shelter from Brick Lane market, London E1.

**SAMANTHA** wears customised T-shirt and cycling shorts, slashed leggings from Camden Alternatives.

**PATSY** wears waistcoat top with slash detail at chest and waist from Comme Des Garçons, St Brout St, London W1, dyed denim jacket and shirt slashed and customised with cycling safety pins and ankle bracelet model's own.

**MIRANDA** wears lining dress from Kinky Knickers, 105 Clerkenwell, NW, Stock bra from Flip, 93 Kensington St, London W1, trainers from Olympia Sports, hand-made bra's sticker and bandana draped prickly model's own.

**SERENA** wears handmade crochet vest, waistcoat from Slash Shoes, St Lexington St, London W1, cycling shorts and shoes all from Cedro Sports and sky blue Pils trainers model's own.

**KEMI** wears slashed fishing clothes T-shirt and cycling shorts from Chipie, cut with leggings, biomkit headband from Comme Des Garçons, St Pembroke Rd, London WC2 and shoes from Flip.

# Blue

## blue.

DESIGNERS · STRETCH DENIM

FUNDAMENTAL COLOUR

dress by Ghost

slash denim Vivienne Westwood

shirt : Lee jeans

Photos: Eddie Monsoon.
Direction: Judy Blame. Graphic
realization: Michael J. Nash. Asso. Hair: Shelly
Fleming at Cuts/Soho. Make up:
Salle Bakke at Joy Goodman, &
Lynne Easton at Satellite using
make up by Presentpoires.
Fashion By: Zoe Bedeaux, &
Emma Day. Michael Power
Models, Nobilla, Laura Emma Fuller
no Models 1. Nora Kryst Kate
Moss Michelle Geddes, Simon
at Storm. Antuat at So Dam Just

**Vivienne Westwood** · Worlds End, 430 Kings Rd, London SW10, 6 Davies St, London W1, L'Homme, 15 St Anne St, Manchester and Ichi Ni San, 123 Candleriggs. · Glasgow. **Ghost** · All branches of

Take a few bargain
garments, a handful
of peanuts, some
photocopies, a can
of spraypaint, a
bottle of bleach, a
pair of blunt scissors
and of course some
sticky-back plastic,
mix and chop them
together with
abandon and -
abracadabra! - not
only do you have a
whole new wardrobe
in seconds, but you
also win a Blue
Peter Badge!

PHOTOGRAPHY AND STYLING BY **ADAM HOWE**
HAIR AND MAKE UP BY **CAROL HART**
MODELS **HIROMI LEIGH** AND **JOHNNY**

## instant DESIGN

**LEFT:** Wrangler jeans with
stretch jock pointing and customised Yamaha guitar and
stretch sailor necklace.
**RIGHT ABOVE:** Necklace
made from peanuts.
**RIGHT:** V-neck denim T-shirt
with gaffer tape and sticky-back
plastic mask.

Dial 911 MAKE A COP COME

# i-D

**i-D JAPAN**
I-DEAS, FASHION, CLUBS, MUSIC, PEOPLE

FOR THE POLITICIANS OF THE FUTURE

アイディー・ジャパン 380yen

## 10月号

創刊号

「ホントはネ、読んで
なかったの、「ライ麦畑」
KYON²

にっぽん

貴花田

アラーキー、レニー・クラヴィッツを独占激写—

スチャダラパービートたけし X ヨシキ フリッパーズ ギター

スキャンダル発覚！か

"Street fashion of the early '90s is continuing along the lines of the American Indian philosophy of dress; wearing symbols that remind people of their roots, identity, unity and higher states of consciousness"

**Beth Summers, i-D Contributing Fashion Editor, no92**

# i-D

## i-D MAGAZINE
i-DEAS, FASHION, CLUBS, MUSIC, PEOPLE

**No 98 NOVEMBER 1991 £1.80**

THE HYPERREAL ISSUE

i-D

Bizarre Inc ++ Sabrina Johnston ++ electric cars ++ Vic Reeves

## Jungle Brothers
Flip out on film

## Stussy
New clothes, new direction

## Viva Cuba!
The other side of Havana

## Liverpool clubs
What the hell is going on?

## Sandra Bernhard
real wild woman

# OUT OF THIS WORLD

**supernaturalists, techno games and technicolour fashion**

USA $5.50

9 770262 357006

11

FRANCS 33 LIRE 6.500 DM 12.50 PESETAS 665 D KR 49

Carlos: "I want to leave Cuba, I have relatives in Miami and I'm planning to sail with m

Carlos, Raoul and Jorge, electric engineer, mechanical engineer and technical engineer respectively, fishing on the tyres which they plan to use to sail across the water to Miami.

Bladimir and Raoul go swimming during their summer holidays after spending the day fishing and catching nothing.

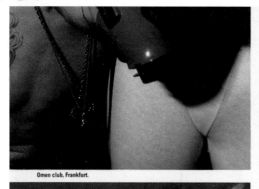

Omen club, Frankfurt.

Omen.

Renaat Vandepapeliere of R&S Rec

Dancer at Omen.

Boccaccio, Gent.

Dorian Gray.

Sunday, 10am, Dorian Gray.

On the bar at Omen.

Frankfurt airport.

# Techno is the sound of

From Belgium to Germany to Brita
DJs and clubs all pushing the limits
dance music. It's energetic, it's
electronic, it's hard and it's constantl
developing. Welcome to the
technodrome…

EUROPEAN
ELECTRONIC
COMMUNITY

STORY BY **MATTHEW CO**
PHOTOGRAPHY BY **WOLFGANG TILLMA**

Torch game at Dorian Gray, Frankfurt.

Live drummer at Omen.

Gent streetlife.

Boccaccio.

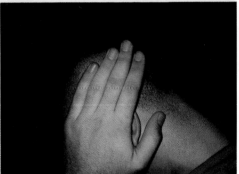

Dorian Gray Technoclub.

Boccaccio.

The ultimate club toy - a personal laser.

Hypersonic speaker at Mosaic studio, Franfurt.

**dnight blue sky.** Sheets of cloud glide past, mist drifts r the subzero canal. Tyres crackle twigs on the corner headlights swing round floodlighting the tarmac. The hum of the approaching engine is muffled first by a ular, mechanic thud, then the hiss and tingle of electric nbals. The polished metal bodywork shifts away in a e of red light and sound.

**It's so dark.** Strobe lights hack at the video signal interference as the music pumps, pumps, pumps, cutting back and forth over the heads of electroshock jerking bodies. Berlin, Autumn '91. A familiar coda; arms raise direct upward in claustrophobic blackness. Joey Beltram is lost amidst the fuzz of smoke and signal. The image cuts on and off with the strobe.

**Happy happy faces in the summer sun.** A street parade, floats pass, each rigged to bursting with sound system speakers as dancers shake it on the trucks' flatboards, the cab roofs, the street running alongside. Each float a spray-coloured celebration of a city, a scene, a crew: Low Spirit, F Posse, Tekknozid, LOVE, each one blasting hardbeat and frenzied riff on riff. Thousands of people dance through ➔

金 哉穂=インタビュー
ハービー 山口=写真

中事に　もな　危険な　そ　する　ライ　大作　いど　殺人　"ひ
によ　く　く　は　び　ジ　危　す　ド　ス　を　ん　未　き
って　身　殺　原　た　に　で　険　そ　ア　そ　見　で　遂　逃
体　さ　因　だ　も　の　な　。　ル　し　る　ん　事　げ

# 完全犯罪

## ユニコーン
## 殺人未遂事件

43 I-D JAPAN

---

# 怪

世紀の非合法エンターテイメント、
サイバーパンク・サーカス。

我人がでても、お生憎さま。
（あいにく）

▲エディ(ピエロ)、仕事の途中。

トニー・マーカス=文
マシュー・R・ルイス=写真

▲収穫に対してバイクを乗り回めす、ヒーロー、トリッキー・ディッキー。

▲ヘイレイ、13歳。サーカスの芸人。

▲ジョシュ、カウンターテノール歌手。

77 I-D JAPAN

シュガー吉永　24歳　ハハナエキシチカ（キター）／こ
ロートレーサーは去年から乗っている。ぶ市の移動に
車一番。でも、車の排気ガスには閉口する。春の
風は気持ちいいけど／防塵マスク（クリーンスクリ
in London）、カットソー￥11.000（シーメンバー
シート”シフヤ西武シート”、ベルト￥2.000（マ
ウント）、ストレッチパンツ　参考商品（ヴェールダン

マーウィン　ムスタン グ　サッカーボール　クル
きにスタジアムのライブをビデオで見て　クラ
ッカーから突然牛肉。ひとりでも、しない
で咲いた。「動物状態」…世紀末のな人間に。

# 1991

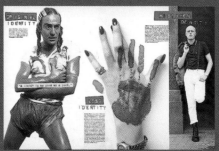

"Imagine the outrage if Wembley was covered by shit and Gazza's shot on goal was deflected by a lump of poo! That's what we contend with every time we play out sport"

**Surfers Against Sewage, environmental activists, no99**

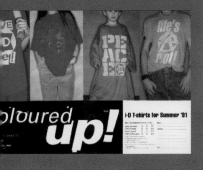

# 1992

January. The Positive Issue no100. Cover star: Neneh Cherry. Photography by Jenny Howarth and Mark Lebon

February. The Performance Issue no101. Cover star: Christie. Photography by Simon Martin, styling by Edward Enninful

March. The Technology Issue no102. Cover stars: Lorella and Tatiana. Photography by Takashi Homma, styling by Gili

April. The Activism Issue no103. Cover star: N'Dea Davenport. Photography by Nick Knight, styling by Zoe Bedeaux

May. The Glamour Issue no104. Cover star: Helena Christensen. Photography by Henrik Bülow

June. The Olympic Issue no105. Cover star: Kathy Read. Photography by Craig McDean, styling by Edward Enninful

July. The Destination Issue no106. Cover star: Sarah Wietzel. Photography by Nick Knight, styling by Edward Enninful

August. The Artist Issue no107. Cover star: Beatrice Dalle. Photography by Craig McDean

September. The Parade Issue no108. Cover star: Nora Kryst. Photography by Eddie Monsoon

October. The New Season Issue no109. Cover star: Cecilia Chancellor. Photography by Simon Fleury, styling by Edward Enninful

November. The Sexuality Issue no110. Cover star: Holly Davis. Photography by Simon Fleury, styling by Edward Enninful

December. The Strength Issue no111. Cover star: Michaela Straccen. Photography by Sivan Lewin

January. i-D Japan no4. Photography by Takashi Homma

February. i-D Japan no5. Photography by Kyoko Takiwaki

March. i-D Japan no6. Photography by Kyoko Takiwaki

April. i-D Japan no7. Photography by Satoru Naito

# i·D

No 100 JANUARY 1992 £1.80

**i-D MAGAZINE**
i-DEAS, FASHION, CLUBS, MUSIC, PEOPLE

neneh cherry
strictly personal

# think
# positive!
be aware if you dare

100th issue special

action on AIDS:
positive responses from fashion, music, film,
photography, sport and activism.

pull-out club supplement:
new directions in clubland

free condom inside!

USA $5.50

01

9 770262 357006

FRANCS 33 LIRE 6,500 DM 12,50 PESETAS 665 D KR 49

# we haven't stopped dancing yet

## positive!
by Simon Foxton

No AIDS, No Pollution, No War
Judy Blame '91

STAY SAFE

hope

"I'd rather stand by something that matters to me than go on Wogan in a glimmery dress"

**Neneh Cherry, musician, no100**

# positive!
## by Anette Aurell
## & Annett Monheim

PHOTOGRAPHY BY ANETTE AURELL
STYLING AND PRODUCTION BY ANNETT MONHEIM
MAKE-UP BY RONNIE RIVERA
HAIR BY LISA DEFARRARI
PRINTS BY RICHARD FOULSER
SPECIAL THANKS TO PIN UP STUDIOS AND LUMEX, SHARON AND JP

*"AIDS affects me because it affects the lives of the people I love.*

# Ignorance and com- placency

## are the children of AIDS.

Taking precautions doesn't mean we have to forget love. Be creative and use your imagination!" Leo Chabot, 20, press assistant, wears chains by Thierry Mugler and T-shirt from a flea market.

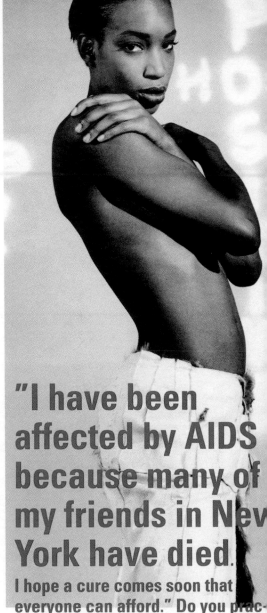

**THE POSITIVE ISSUE**

# "I have been affected by AIDS because many of my friends in New York have died.

I hope a cure comes soon that everyone can afford." Do you practice safe sex? "The precautions I take are very simple. I have been in a monogamous relationship for the last four years. I only hope that everyone can find someone they love faithfully and if not: use condoms!" Tracee, 20, American model/student, wears leather ski Etienne Brunnel, T-shirt by Shcool Rag and boots by Martin Margiela.

A beautiful body becomes ..., because ... person ... ... ... spects ... mselves. ... is the key ... ... ... ... spectful to ... urself and ... hers. ... actice safe ... x. " Tony Jones, singer

"The highest creation is the creation of oneself and total consciousness within. To be whole within oneness, that is the peak. Self-realisation." Laura

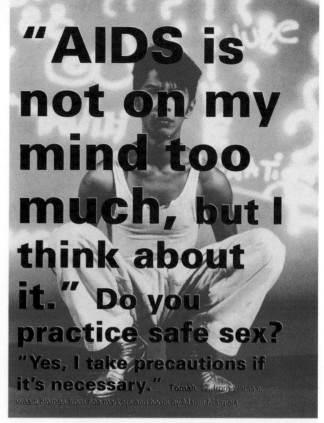

"AIDS is not on my mind too much, but I think about it." Do you practice safe sex? "Yes, I take precautions if it's necessary." Tomah, 22, from Vietnam, wears clothes from flea markets and boots by Martin Margiela

It's not a big deal any more, people seem to accept it, like other diseases. The world is still going around and around." Do you practice safe sex? "Don't use anything." ..a, 20, wears white linen skirt by Ann ...eulemeester.

"To us all: we are all we have. A safer sex, it's a longer life!" Andrew, from London, wears secondhand hat and feather necklace by Ann Demeulemeester.

"Diseases are nature's way of telling us that something is wrong. In the case of AIDS, I still can't really figure what, especially because AIDS took hold in the gay community and who (even God) has the right to say something is wrong with being gay and enjoying sex? When I look round and see the number of people dying of AIDS and hear the prognosis for the future, I just get confused and so angry about the unfairness of life. I get angry about the slowness of the researches for a cure. I get angry about the ignorance and hypocrisy of people who don't feel concerned. I get angry about the suspicious looks and attitude of a lot of people. I try to see AIDS as a phenomena of this century but I can't accept it, I can't understand it. I hope there will be a revenge, a cure which kills the virus fast and completely. The people who died of it are living in our minds. Love to them!" Do you practice safe sex? "I don't have to take precautions now, because I love my boyfriend and I don't intend to sleep with somebody else. I do tests every three months and I think that's the first thing everybody should do to be sure. I can't accept any negligence in this point, because it is equal now to deliberate murdering. Nobody is safe, so the only thing everybody can do is know the state of your body and using condoms." Annett, wears skirt and belt by Martin Margiela.

LOVE SEXY

恋とセックスが同じものだとは思わないけど、限りなく近いものです、私にとっては。──弥生──

友だちの恋人に横恋慕。好きなのに届かない、君のかわりに、かわいい彼女に異常接近。どんな哲学者も把握できない人類の難問、恋の輪郭を、天才のファインダーが切り取る。

伊藤弥生　1973年3月28日生まれ。明るくて負けず嫌い。セクシーだと感じるのは「あやしげな人、何を考えてるのかわからない人」。

荒木経惟＝写真
岩田 ちえ子＝スタイリング

友だちの恋人

アラーキー異常接近

"What I do is create a collection to question
people about their values"

**Rei Kawakubo, designer, no104**

# albion

### quiet dreams of a new england

STORY AND STYLING BY **SIMON FOXTON**

PHOTOGRAPHY BY **SIMON MARTIN**

ASSISTED BY **MICHAEL BOADI** FOR AVEDA

MAKE-UP BY **CATHY LOMAX** FOR COSMETICS À LA CARTE

MODELS **KOJO** AND **LANCE**

THANKS TO MARK AND CRUSHLA FOR THE USE OF THEIR HOUSE

**Far Left:** Lance wears saddle back jumper by Richard Tyler by mailer from the Dexter Wong shop, combination pants trousers by Vivre available from Brian Jeremy, Workmans and Crews, nostradix trainers shirt from American Classics and Molenaide T-shirt from Portobello Market.

**Left:** Lance wears patchwork motion shirt from Dexter Wong.

PERFORMANCE SPORT

# move over
## big daddy!

STORY BY LEE HARPIN
PHOTOGRAPHY BY TAKASHI HOMMA
VIDEO STILLS BY OMAID HIWAIZI

**American and Mexican Wrestling is
pure theatre - full of colourful
costumed characters straight out of the
comicbooks. And now American
Wrestling is cleaning up in
the UK too...**

"Course he hit him, you must be blind!" screams 11-year-old Martin into my left earhole. In a front row seat at Birmingham's International Arena, sampling the delights of American Wrestling, my knowledge of the sport might not be 100 per cent, but I'm sure the Texas Tornado punched nothing but thin air. Why, therefore, was a scantily dressed hunk of an Australian, known to all and sundry (except me) as Nature Boy, writhing in agony on the ground beneath my feet, clutching his left testicle. "You know nuffin' about wrestling do ya mate?" enquires Martin. "Bet you don't even know who your favourite wrestler is." A brief glimpse at the programme resting on Martin's lap, I catch sight of an ugly brute in Union Jack trunks. "British Bulldog, mate, yeah, British Bulldog, he's my top boy," I

reply. Martin immediately breaks into a broad grin. "Oh good, he's my favourite too. You can be my mate now." Thanks Martin.

Maybe now, with the aid of my newly acquired companion, I can begin to understand the appeal of Britain's fastest growing 'sport'. Why, for instance, did over 100,000 people last year pay up to £25 to be present at two World Wrestling Federation tours to this country? And most intriguingly, why has the pre-pubescent girl sitting to the left of Martin just experienced her first sexual high on sighting the mountainous bulge packing Nature Boy's trunks?

To these eyes, American Wrestling is pure theatre, a blurring of the line between sport and entertainment. "I do not have an Equity card," answers British Bulldog to suggestions that fights are actually rehearsed and result predetermined. But no-one, except for the pre-teenage contingent (90 per cent of those present at Birmingham), seriously believe that the two wrestlers pitched in ceremonial battle actually land the fearsome blows they vividly act out in the ring. American Wrestling has little to do with the British variety that dominated your grandparents' TV set on Saturday afternoons. Big Daddy →

American gladiators! WWF Wrestling in action. But I by this at home.

Solar and the Midget Belloni are typical of Mexican Wrestlers - highly stylised, camp creations.

i-D THE PERFORMANCE ISSUE 59

"Young white teenagers know that the
culture of their parents is bankrupt and
that's why they're getting into rap"

**Chuck D, rapper, no101**

# i·D

No 102 MARCH 1992 £1.80

i-D MAGAZINE
i-DEAS, FASHION, CLUBS, MUSIC, PEOPLE

i·D

**THE TECHNOLOGY ISSUE**

i·D Marathon ++ future humans ++ Survival Research Laboratories ++ James

## future now!

the science of
fashion: 18-page
photo special with
Joe Casely-Hayford
Duffer Of St George
Dirk Bikkembergs
Bella Freud
Jean Colonna
Romeo Gigli
Martin Margiela
Veronique Leroy
Christopher Nameth

## Inner City
and Detroit's new techno generation

## David Cronenberg
the horror of 'Naked Lunch'

International cyberpunks/Techno art
Holographic fashion/Ragga Twins

USA $5.50

03

9 770262 357006

FRANCS 33 LIRE 6.900 DM 12.50 PESETAS 865 D KR 49

Jason Statham taken at Crystal Palace, 1991 when he was training in the British Diving team. Issue No 179

Name: HORTENSIA de HUTTEN
Age: 47        8 JAN 1992
Occupation: FASHION... WHAT ELSE ??

What is the most important thing in your life now?
My children, my family, my friends,
Try to have some freetimes to enjoy
Them, my work, to try to be happy

Name: Bridget Yorke
Age: 32

Occupation:

What is the most important thing in your life now?
Having a baby

What would you change, to make a better future?
governments to Ecological humanists
Persuad an ideal form of communism
LIBERATE ANIMALS FROM THE
REGION OF MAN

Name: GRAÇA FISHER
Age: 24

Occupation: STUDENT /ALSO WORK IN THE
PHOTO GRAPHY /GREATEST SHOP EVER /HATSHOE!

What would you change, to make a better future?

# Quiet, shy and elusiv

# now!

# Martin Margiela is the king of

...re of flea market clothes and high fashion. For Martin Margiela stockist details contact 010 331 4221 1269.

## "Without the DJs, there would be no future sound of Britain"

**Andrew Wetherall, DJ, no108**

FILM TECHNOLOGY

# one man and his horror

**After 'The Fly' and 'Dead Ringers', David Cronenberg filmed William Burroughs' novel, *The Naked Lunch*, a book full of body mutations, weird science, strange sex and orgasmic violence.**

**How does Burroughs' nightmare vision translate to the screen?**

The Meridian Hotel on Piccadilly looks like it belongs in an early Cronenberg movie. Plush, synthetic, molecular, one in an international chain, it is almost too designed, too purposeful.

Consec in 'Scanners': the corporation as a body of proliferating cells, a malignant growth. Starliner Towers in 'Shivers': a luxury apartment complex invaded by parasitic bugs, its lifeless inhabitants turned into a bunch of homicidal sex maniacs. The city of Montreal in 'Rabid': bland and bored, until seized by an epidemic of sexually transmitted rabies.

What strange creatures lurk in the even spaces of the Meridian? David Cronenberg sits in a room on the fourth floor, greying hair neatly parted, little round glasses flashing light. He is alert and polite. A tape unspools beside him.

"I am fascinated by the way we have never accepted anything as given to us," he says. "Take this hotel: we don't want to sit outside, we want to be somewhere where we can control the rain and the temperature. It's the same with our bodies. If we don't like the body's chemistry, we change it. We want to be involved in our own evolution. No other animal has done this and the cutting edge of it all is medicine."

Cronenberg is in London to promote 'Naked Lunch', an adaptation of the mutant avant-garde novel by William Burroughs which has been gestating inside the director's mind ever since he made his first body horror movie. The original plan was to shoot the movie in Tanger, Morocco, the international zone where Burroughs had written most of →

INTERVIEW BY STEVE BEARD
PHOTOGRAPHY BY MATTHEW R LEWIS

Left: Dylan and Alix, journalists.
Above: Kazuko Hohki, "not 19", musician in Frank Chickens, actress and writer. What would you change to make a better future? "Legalize prostitution." Photo: Takashi Homma.

Ann Demeulemeester, age 30. What is most important in your life now? "My child." What would you change for a better future? "To have more time for other things that I want to do." photographer PATRICK ROBYN

# Veronique Leroy *

is one of Paris' brightest new stars. Her tailoring prowess and attention to detail has critics raving. Chic.

Right: **Valerie Praquin**, 24, assistant. What is most important in your life now? "Chocolate." What would you change for a better future? "My washing powder."

**Jacky**, "standardiste". What is most important in your life now? "Everything." What would you change for a better future? "Everything which is not 'échelieur'."

All enquiries about Veronique Leroy to 010 331 4367 8595.

now!

FIRENZE   9 JAN 1992

model stagiaire!
singer

03•92

# i-D

i-D JAPAN

i-DEAS, FASHION, CLUBS, MUSIC, PEOPLE

FOR THE POLITICIANS OF THE FUTURE

アイディー・ジャパン　380yen
3月号

1992年3月1日発行（毎月1回1日発行）第2巻第3号（通巻6号）

THE BODY & SOUL ISSUE

ugm groove ++ deee lite ++ scha dara parr ++ tom waits ++ etc.

在日コリアン「新世代」の
「私たちの国籍について」

「心を鍛えるためにはね
泣かない、絶対」
Fukatsu

完全予想 J・リーグ
にやってくる超級スター

吉本の優略

当世刺青事情：あのコがタトゥーを入れた理由

ボクサー平仲明信、沖縄からの挑戦
こだわるヤツ、吉田栄作徹底研究

一九九二年

304

FASHION ACTION

Mark Lawrence wears red plastic jacket and black plastic trousers both by Jean Colonna and T-shirt by Gimme 5 (071 224 2656)

**KEEP BRITAIN TIDY**

# JUST SAY
# NO

PHOTOS BY **PIERRE RUTSCHI**

STYLING AND FASHION BY **JUDY BLAME**

MAKE-UP BY **CATHY LOMAX** AT PREMIER PHOTOGRAPHICS FOR SCREEN FACE, POWIS TERRACE, LONDON W11

HAIR BY **MICHAEL BOADI** AT SATELLITE (THANKS TO **TRENDCO** FOR HAIRPIECES)

SPECIAL THANKS TO **LIMPET BARRON**, **KAYT JONES** AND **JULIE**

MODELS: **CHRISTIE** AT ELITE PREMIER, **NORA KRYST** AT STORM, **MARIO SORRENTI** AT SELECT, **BEN SHAUL**

(THANKS FOR BEING YOURSELF), **MARIE SOPHIE** AT BOOKINGS, **MARK LAWRENCE** AND **JUDY BLAME**

SHOT AT **CLICK STUDIOS** - SPECIAL THANKS TO **RAY** AND **KATIE**

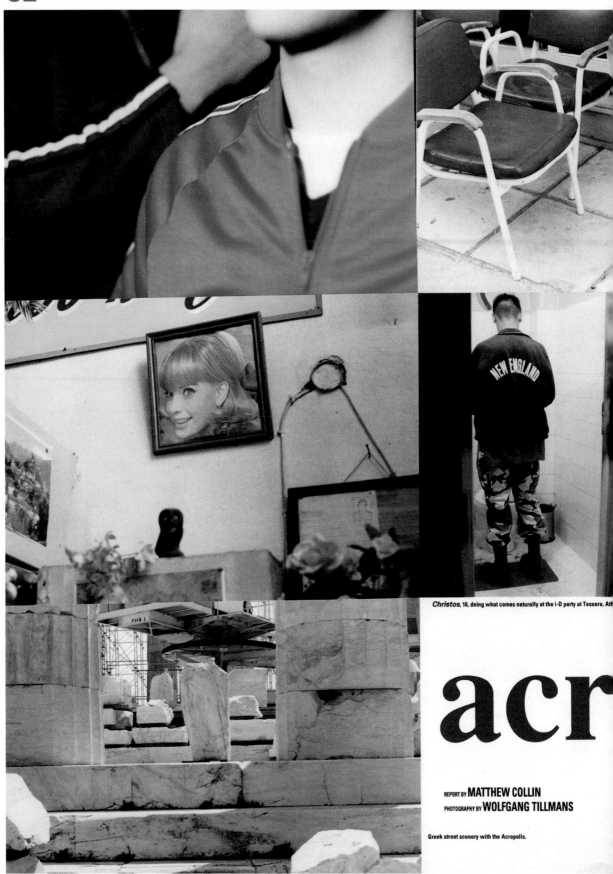

*Christos*, 16, doing what comes naturally at the i-D party at Tessara, Ath...

# acr

REPORT BY **MATTHEW COLLIN**
PHOTOGRAPHY BY **WOLFGANG TILLMANS**

**Greek street scenery with the Acropolis.**

...nis, student, wears typical Athens clubwear.    *Karithas*, 25. What's the best thing about Athens? "Doing sex!"    *Sonarageli*, 31, designer, and *Chris*, 21, archaeologist. Best thing about Athens? "Our own lives."

# polis now!
## the i-D World Tour in Athens

**This is a story** about pollution, psychosis, magick, bestiality, Spartans, classical homosexuality, ➔

OLYMPIC COUNTRY

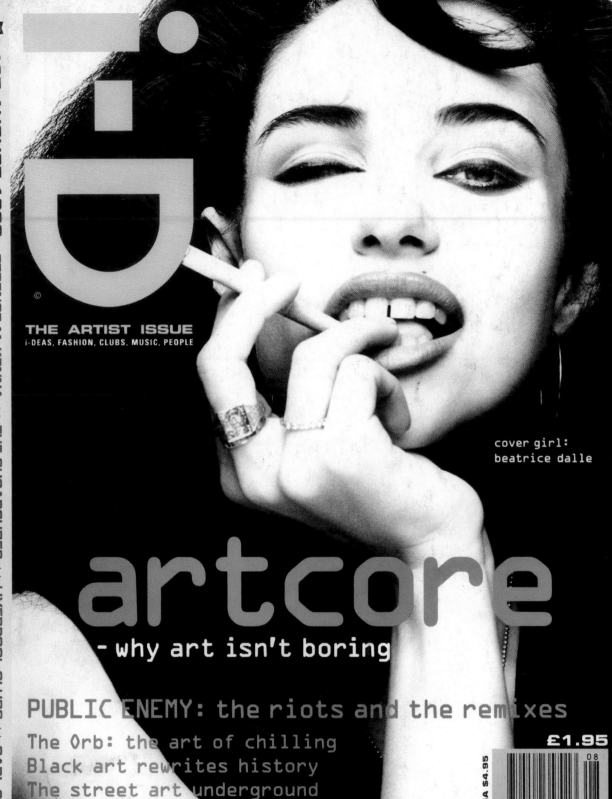

# i-D

**THE ARTIST ISSUE**
i-DEAS, FASHION, CLUBS, MUSIC, PEOPLE

107 AUGUST 1992 ++ TERENCE McKENNA ++ THE SUGARCUBES ++ LIVERPOOL CLUBS ++ CARL COX

cover girl:
beatrice dalle

# artcore
## - why art isn't boring

**PUBLIC ENEMY: the riots and the remixes**

The Orb: the art of chilling
Black art rewrites history
The street art underground
art fashion/Summer T-shirts

£1.95

USA $4.95

9 770262 357013

08

FRANCS 35 LIRE 7,100 DM 13.00 PESETAS 665 D KR 53

"Men and women should stop following anything that moves in skirts or trousers"

**Mrs Enninful, mother and seamstress, no100**

"I would like to see a reconciliation between the fashion industry and the new ecological conscience that we all have. Something's got to give"

**Jason Evans, photographer and stylist, no109**

*Skankin' into winter in rude style means frock coats and two-button 'Don Gargon' suits, plaits and pleats, string vests, techno-ragga and digital dancehall sounds, no stress. ...hi-tekno fashion for ...ckers, a new vibe for ...w season.*

i-D THE NEW SEASON ISSUE 71

The latest word from designers this season is that fashion's not for the tight-fitted. Cold weather pieces get a new lease of life when styled with good old (gipsy) attitude. Stylist Zoe Bedeaux says forget summer's sleaze squeeze, loose rules this winter. We present six hot looks for those cold day blues.

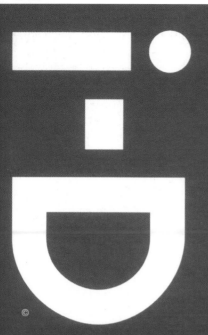

## i-D

110 NOVEMBER 1992

BRITISH TECHNO ++ 808 STATE ++ GARY CLAIL ++ RAGGA DANCING

©

**THE SEXUALITY ISSUE**
i-DEAS, FASHION, CLUBS, MUSIC, PEOPLE

## let's talk about
### sex!

**sexuality special**

### Chat! Salt-N-Pepa

Argument! i-D's Sex Forum
Riot! queer fanzines
the new pornography / fetish wear
sexy fashion / feminism now
A-Z of safe sex

## Plus! Free 28-page
## talent supplement*

* UK editions only

cover girl:
holly davis

£1.95

USA $4.95

**sexual images** from i-D photographers, stylists and models

**♀sexuality** by Nick Knight & Leigh Bowery

PHOTOGRAPHY BY **LEIGH BOWERY**
BY **NICK KNIGHT**
BODY WORDS BY **LEIGH**

62 I-D THE SEXUALITY ISSUE

WEIRD & HEAVY GUY, 39 → SEEKS BIG-COCKED HANDSOME HORNY BRAINY DIRTY LADS (BEER BELLIES A BONUS) FOR SNOGGING. ORAL, TIT TORTURE DIGITAL & MUTUAL FUCKING. ALSO KEEN TO START FISTING. NO SM SHIT. AND A BIG NO TO CHRISTIANS. MY PUSSY NEEDS ALOT OF VERBAL ABUSE, LYCRA & OTHER GENUINE ATTENTION. LEIGH ON 071 7903213.

osexuality by Anette Aurell

PHOTOGRAPHY BY **ANETTE AURELL**
MODELS ARE FRIENDS **DANIEL** AND **KEIKO**
PRINT BY **RICHARD FOULSER**

I-D THE SEXUALITY ISSUE 63

PHOTOGRAPHY BY NIGEL SHAFRAN
STYLING BY ANNA COCKBURN
MODELS CECILIA CHANCELLOR JENNY HOWARTH AND SARAH MURRAY

Cecilia wears T-shirt from John Lewis, 278-306 Oxford Street, London W1 and chain from Kensington Market, 49-53 Kensington High Street, London W8.

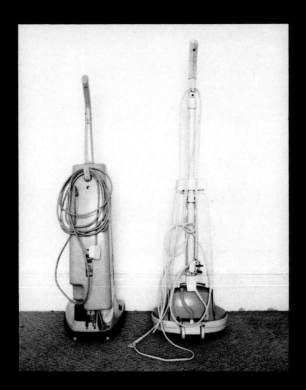

Secondhand fashion is no longer the exclusive domain of bargain-hunters and compulsive Oxfam browsers. In the fabric recycling movement called *la recuperation*, Paris-based designers like Martin Margiela and Xuly Bet have taken the fleamarket upmarket and made other people's old clothes the cutting edge of chic. However, if you can't afford the £500 Margiela charges for a skirt made out of old silk scarves, check the junk shops, the markets, even skips in the street, and create your own recycled couture.

lost and found

# 1992

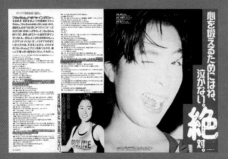

"People are so desperate to get into the Jean Paul Gaultier show that some brazen girl has the nerve to tell an usher she is me. Who in their right mind would want to be me? It could only happen in fashion!"

**Edward Enninful, i-D Fashion Director, no101**

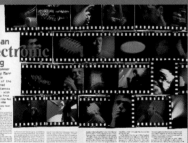

# 1993

January. The Screen Issue no112. Cover star: Sonic The Hedgehog. Illustration by Sega

February. The Survival Issue no113. Cover star: Monie Love. Photography by Simon Fleury

March. The Comedy Issue no114. Cover star: Jane Horrocks. Photography by Matthew R Lewis

April. The Sound Issue no115. Cover star: Sarah Cracknell. Photography by Matthew R Lewis

May. The Europe Issue no116. Cover star: Björk. Photography by Matthew R Lewis

June. The Beauty Issue no117. Cover star: Kristen McMenamy. Photography by Juergen Teller, styling by Edward Enninful

July. The Open Air Issue no118. Cover star: Karen Ferrail. Photography by Juergen Teller, styling by Venetia Scott

August. The Festival Issue no119. Cover star: Gillian Gilbert. Photography by Donald Christie, styling by Grant Boston

September. The Boys & Girls Issue no120. Cover star: Naomi Campbell. Photography by Jenny Howarth, styling by Edward Enninful

October. The New Look Issue no121. Cover star: Tania Court. Photography by Stefan Ruiz, styling by Edward Enninful

November. The Hard Issue no122. Cover star: Linda Evangelista. Photography by Juergen Teller, styling by Camilla Nickerson

December. The Smart Issue no123. Cover star: Kate Moss. Photography by Corinne Day

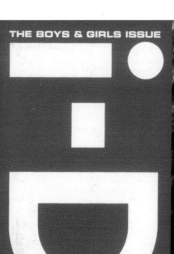

THE BOYS & GIRLS ISSUE

**cannabis special** *weed power on the rise*

# i-D

i-DEAS, FASHION, CLUBS, MUSIC, PEOPLE

120 september 1993 · i-D · cover star naomi campbell

# *girl power!*

## naomi campbell is in your face

**Stereo MCs** success and excess in the USA
**skateboarding** views from the underground
**hot fashion** new directions & smart looks
the British football nightmare / Gilbert & George
Cypress Hill / Scottish club chaos / M-People

**£1.95  $4.95**

09

9 770262 357013

FRANCS 35 LIRE 7,100 DM 13,00 PESETAS 595 D KR 53

New York C
grung

Customised man's sweater from Agnès B, 35-36 Floral St, London WC2 and Victorian petticoat from Spats, Monmouth St, London WC2.

Out of the moshpit, onto the catwalk:
[desi]gners in New York have gone grunge
crazy. After Nirvana clocked up an
incredible four million LP sales, this
season the New York fashion shows

## [Fa]shion Special
## [c]outure

[mo]ved to the US's fastest-growing youth
[s]ubculture and embraced the buzzsaw
[gu]itars of Sonic Youth, Unsane, Helmet
[and] the Lunachicks wholesale. Designers
[l]ike Perry Ellis, Anna Sui and Christian
[F]rancis Roth have thrown convention
[out] through the window and emerged as
[Sev]enth Avenue Slackers. Flannel shirts,
[tube] sock hats, unwashed floral prints and
knitted bell-bottoms all paraded the
catwalk. Stylist Melanie Ward,
[ph]otographer Corinne Day and regular i-D
model Sarah Murray present another
[a]ngle on what has become America's
[n]ew sensibility: grunge goes couture.

Sweater by Martin Margiela available from Pellicano, 63 South Molton St, London W1, secondhand petticoat worn as skirt from The Glorious Clothing Company, 60 Upper St, Islington, London N1 and American flag worn round wrist available from Flip, Long Acre, London WC2, and trainers from Portobello Market, London W11.

"I consider myself as Black British. Being European means complete freedom of travel and a cosmopolitan cross-section of history and culture."

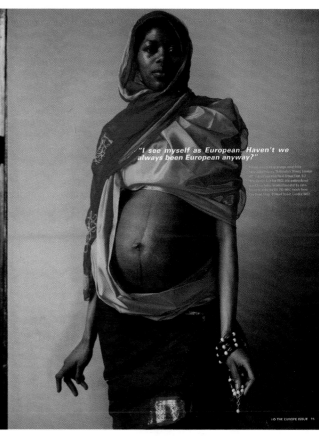

"I see myself as European. Haven't we always been European anyway?"

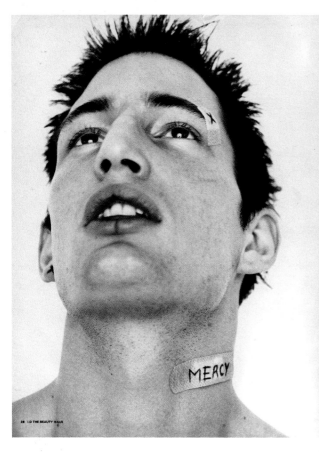

MERCY

# THE HARDER THEY COME

In the new menswear collections, designers are using gangster chic (as in Al Capone, not Ice Cube) to create street-smart looks...

**y**annick wears loose-knit sweater by Yohji Yamamoto from Richard Creme, Manchester, cotton shirt worn as skirt by Agnes B from Agnes B, PVC pants by Jean Colonna from Joseph, Joseph and Ichi Ni San, leather cap by Agnes B.

FASHION BY **ANNETT MONHEIM**
PHOTOGRAPHY BY **ANETTE AURELL**
HAIR BY **BARNABE** FOR JEAN LOUIS DAVID
MAKE-UP BY **TOPOLINO** FOR VELVET AGENCY, PARIS
ASSISTED BY **FRED**
PRINTS BY **RICHARD FOULSER**
MODELS **KARL PEASE** AT MON AGENCY, PARIS,
**YANNICK** AT FY ONS AGENCY, PARIS, AND **SALVATORE**
THANKS TO PHOP STUDIOS, PARIS

# i-D

**THE BEAUTY ISSUE**
i-DEAS, FASHION, CLUBS, MUSIC, PEOPLE

ambient special
**The Orb** chill out, planet earth!
**The Aphex Twin** megabyte ramraider

# I am beautiful!

## male models
### rise of the beautiful boys
## bright summer fashion
### riot grrrls,
### chic gangsters,
### brown trousers
## animal liberation
### undercover with
### the saboteurs

£1.95    $4.95

06

9 770262 357013

FRANCS 35 LIRE 7,100 DM 13,00 PESETAS 595 D KR 53

# 09•93

"Sex is a big part of what I do"

**Alexander McQueen, designer, no121**

**RAD**

FASHION BY **CHRISTINE FORTUNE**
PHOTOGRAPHY BY **PETER ANDERSON**
MODEL **MARK**

78  I-D THE BOYS & GIRLS ISSUE

**FUNKY COWBOY**

FASHION BY **MELANIE WARD**  PHOTOGRAPHY BY **DAVID SIMS**
HAIR BY **GUIDO** FOR TONI & GUY MODEL **ASHLEY**

I-D THE BOYS & GIRLS ISSUE  79

*INTERVIEWS BY* **EDWARD ENNINFUL,**
**AVRIL MAIR** *AND* **BETHAN COLE**
*PORTRAITS BY* **STEFAN RUIZ**
*ASSISTED BY* **LEE FORD** *AT ASYLUM*
*SHOT AT* **ASYLUM STUDIOS** *(TEL. 071 729 1142)*

# GREAT BRITISH FASHION

## SAY HELLO TO THE NEW BREED OF BRITISH FASHION DESIGNERS. UNLIKE PREVIOUS GENERATIONS, THEY COMBINE CREATIVITY WITH COMMERCIAL COMMON SENSE, AND ARE BOUND FOR INTERNATIONAL SUCCESS. WE INTERVIEWED SIX OF THE BEST AND, ON THE FOLLOWING PAGES, WE SHOWCASE THEIR CLOTHES IN AN EXCLUSIVELY BRITISH FASHION STORY.

Great Britain's fashion has grown up, and got real. After the world deemed our design redundant, a new breed of young entrepreneurs are showing that successful ideas can still originate from good old Blighty. In the past, British fashion could be faulted for many things: its manufacture, distribution, quality, meeting of delivery dates and pricing. British designers' creativity was copied the world over but their own work was let down by bad business practise and workmanship. Similarly, London Fashion Week failed to constitute the same kind of stage as Milan or Paris to attract foreign buyers. We showcased the development of innovative graduate design talent like nowhere else in the world, only to see it lured away to the fashion houses and factories of Europe.

But now things are starting to change. Young British designers are starting to believe in themselves again, showing that they too can produce clothes perfectly in sync with current consumer tastes. Strong on craftsmanship and with a developing business sense, they herald a rebirth for the much-maligned British fashion industry. Gone are the days of the designer as an artiste cut off from the general running of his or her business. They know that to progress in the '90s means to combine creativity with commerce. Wearability is the basis of contemporary design and, with the High Street churning out designer imitations faster than designers themselves can, the line between inspirational creations and mass market reproductions has become more blurred.

The new breed's collections are characterised by sheer wearability, a refined and intelligent fusion of innovation and commercialism which is strong in both direction and quality of finish. What people want from Britain is the considered classic design, the witty twist on traditional tailoring, the innovative street style. Our young designers have replaced vanity with realism – without sacrificing ideas. Quality and identity in wisely priced lines is what they are developing, in collections that span pure simplicity to quirky originality. The new school reveres the classics but still manage to remain individual.

Of course, until the governments start taking fashion seriously as a commercially viable industry, the way forward is difficult. In order to weather the recession, our new creators are challenging traditional concepts of British design and, more specifically, the designer's role. For example, Nicholas Knightly has taken the one-off route to ensure customer satisfaction and keep costs down, while Abe Hamilton undertakes special commissions from certain stores to ensure his designs are readily available. With hard work and consideration, British fashion is once more back on the international map.

Over the next 14 pages, we present the young talent which will take British fashion forward into the '90s. From the new to the not so new, from those on periphery of stardom to the internationally established, from made-to-order avant gardists to college leavers, these are our design hopes for tomorrow. As well as profiles on Nicholas Knightly, Abe Hamilton, Flyte Ostell, John Roche, Copperwheat Blundell and Alexander McQueen, we present an exclusively British fashion story with clothes and accessories from Jessica Ogden, Judy Blame, Philip Treacy, Spencer and Smargiassi, Richard Royale, Hussein Chelayan, Emma Hope, Cornelia James, Jennifer Corker and the undisputed monarchs of classic British style, Vivienne Westwood and Paul Smith. Viva Britannia! **Edward Enninful**

### NICHOLAS KNIGHTLY

Carefully crafted with a pleasure in subtlety and workmanship, intellectual yet instinctual, unadorned yet dramatic in its simplicity, Nicholas Knightly's work displays all the attributes of truly classic couture. Unfortunately, in today's climate of political and economic crises, the expensive business of clothes-to-order is restricted to a privileged few. Thus Knightly needs to temper his elegant designs with an understanding of commercial values. The most self-assured and best established of the crop of young designers, he has, in the two years since college, demonstrated the strength of British cutting and construction while mixing a developing business sense with directional detailing and classic tailoring. "Couture should mean great →

96 i-D THE NEW LOOK ISSUE

> **"COUTURE SHOULD MEAN GREAT IDEAS, NOT AN EXCLUDING ARENA FOR THE RICH."**
> NICHOLAS KNIGHTLY

> **"IT'S THE THINGS YOU ALWAYS WANTED AND NEVER HAD."**
> COPPERWHEAT BLUNDELL

> **"SEX IS A BIG PART OF WHAT I DO."**
> ALEXANDER McQUEEN

---

# GREAT BRITISH FASHION

# g.b.

*DIRECTED BY* **JUDY BLAME**
*ASSISTED BY* **SANDRINE**
*PHOTOGRAPHY BY* **MARK LEBON**
*ARTISTED BY* **DAVID MILNE-WATSON**
*MAKE-UP BY* **NORA KRYST**
*HAIR BY* **JOHNNIE SAPONG** *AT CUTS, USING PHYTOLIGNE HAIRCARE PRODUCTS*
*MODELS* **MOSHE, LUCA** *AND* **ANTUAN** *AT* **SARAH MURRAY, RUTH O'DOWD** *AND* **LOUISE** *AT* **TAKE 2, CASSANDRA** *AT KRISWICK EYRE,* **SOPHIE UPTON** *AT SELECT,* **CHER** *AT SELECT,* **JUDY, KEN** *AND* **SANDRINE**

94 i-D THE NEW LOOK ISSUE

i-D THE NEW LOOK ISSUE 95

Amelia (credits as before).

Lee wears shirt by Armani Jeans from Emporio Armani, Harrods, Wade Smith, Manifesto and Woodhouse, trousers by Polo Ralph Lauren from the Ralph Lauren shop.

Hamish wears Moschino shirt from Manifesto, Woodhouse and Cecil Gee, Armani jeans from Emporio Armani, Harrods, Wade Smith, Manifesto and Woodhouse.

Tyrone wears leather jacket by Chipie from Chipie and The Italian Centre, shirt by Timberland from The Timberland Shop and Aspecto. Kelly wears Nigel Cabourn jumper from Liberty.

Dean wears brown polo neck and jacket by Dries Van Noten from Jones, Lamb and Strand, tracksuit bottoms and Fila trainers from j-D Sports.

FASHION BY *GREG FAY* AND *JUSTIN LAURIE* ASSISTED BY *JOHN SPENCER* PHOTOGRAPHY BY *DONALD MILNE* ASSISTED BY *CHARLIE* HAIR BY *LANCE LOWE* AT SHIPTON LEIGHTON & LOWE MAKE-UP BY *SARAH RYGATE* MODELS: *CLAYTON, JEAN PAUL, LEE, DEAN, TYRONE, KELLY, DEAN, HAMISH, SHAUN; SARAH* AT MATTHEWS & POWELL; *AMELIA* AT TAKE 2; *JODIE, VANESSA FRANCO* AND *ANNA RAND,* ALL AT PROFILE

**STOCKISTS** Aspecto, 1 Queen Victoria Street, Leeds (0532 450150). Cecil Gee, branches nationwide. Chipie, 3 Langley Court, London WC2 (071 497 2681). Emporio Armani, 57-59 Long Acre, London WC2 (071 917 6882). Gianni Versace, 34 Old Bond Street, London W1 (071 499 1862). Hammington, North Street, Brighton (0273 329877). Harrods, Knightsbridge, London SW1 (071 730 1234). J Anthony, branches nationwide. j-D Sports, branches nationwide. Jones, 13 Floral Street, London WC2 (071 240 8312). Kent & Curwy, branches nationwide. Lamb, 29 Goosegate, Nottingham (0602 799141). Liberty, 210-220 Regent Street, London W1 (071 734 1234). Manifesto, 42 Whitehall Crescent, Dundee (0382 201527). Miss Selfridge, concessions nationwide. Noble Jones, 7 Hill Street, Richmond (081 332 2151). Office Shoes, 43 Kensington High Street, London W8 (071 937 7022) and branches nationwide. Paul Smith, 41-44 Floral Street, London WC2 (071 379 7133) and 10 Byard Lane, Nottingham (0602 506712). Ralph Lauren, 143 New Bond Street, London W1 (071 491 4967). Smith & Westwood, Unit 2, Clayton Square, Liverpool (051 709 9993). Stonehams Of Putney, Upper Richmond Road, Richmond (081 788 6169). Strand, 22 Queen Victoria Street, Leeds (0532 438164). Swank, 72 Old Compton Street, London W1 (071 437 3155). The Italian Centre, Glasgow (041 552 6177). The Timberland Shop, 72 New Bond Street, London W1 (071 495 2133). Wade Smith, Matthew Street, Liverpool (051 255 1077). Woodhouse, branches nationwide. Zaga, 20 Baddow Road, Chelmsford (0245 262194).

12•93

THE SMART ISSUE

# i-D

i-DEAS, FASHION, CLUBS, MUSIC, PEOPLE

123 december 1993

cover star: kate moss

# LOVE IT!
## KATE MOSS TELLS ALL
## SNOOP DOGGY DOGG
## MALCOLM McLAREN•PULP
## HELMUT LANG•TIM ROTH
## THE RETURN OF THE SUIT

£1.95  $4.95

# KISS THIS!

INTERVIEW BY DAVID EIMER
PHOTOGRAPHY BY MATTHEW R LEWIS

**TIM ROTH STARRED IN THE FILM OF THE YEAR, QUENTIN TARANTINO'S *RESERVOIR DOGS*. NOW, WITH UPCOMING PARTS IN THE NEXT TARANTINO MOVIE AND NIC ROEG'S *HEART OF DARKNESS*, BRITAIN'S HARDEST IS FAST ESTABLISHING HIMSELF IN HOLLYWOOD'S MAJOR LEAGUE.**

If you had to pick out one British film from the early '80s, a vital, vibrant drama which captured the mean tempo of the times, then *Made In Britain*, notwithstanding the fact that it was made for TV, would be high on the list. Directed in 1983 by the late, lamented Alan Clarke, its story of →

---

INTERVIEW BY SIMON DUDFIELD
PHOTOGRAPHY BY MATTHEW R LEWIS
STYLING BY DAVID LEWIS
HAIR BY KEITH FONTAINE

## the merry prankster

*The rock'n'roll star is dead, says Malcolm McLaren, killed by big business and technology; the new rebel heroes are hackers, computer programmers and scientists. So the veteran maverick has decided to get romantic and make a record about Paris.*

"The greatest moment for me was getting the portrait of the Queen with a safety pin through her nose on the cover of the *Daily Mirror* on Silver Jubilee day. That was the greatest thing. I thought, 'Fuck me, it's Jubilee day and they're not even printing the real Queen's portrait, they're printing our version of it.' The editor of the *Daily Mirror* phoned me and said, 'Malcolm, if we put the Sex Pistols on the cover we sell more papers.' That was the great moment."

Talking to Malcolm McLaren is the most fun you can have with your trousers on. He embodies the excitement rock'n'roll can generate, the cultural significance it can have and the potential for social upheaval it can possess. His achievements serve to highlight the drabness that cloaks the contemporary music industry. 17 years ago, McLaren, Vivienne Westwood and their gang of pranksters, the Sex Pistols, urged a generation to revolt, making front page tabloid news; big, bright and bold.

Then, as now, the record industry was pallid, paunchy and pathetic. The madness that made the '80s so invigorating had been quelled, and the decade's survivors had settled down in the '80s to the task of building a serious, respectable business for music. McLaren mocked them, while the Sex Pistols' vitality and violence took rock'n'roll back to its rebellious roots.

When punk's fresh blood ran dry, the music industry plastered itself in Band-Aids in an attempt to ensure that revolutionary street bile would →

# 1993

January. The Screen Issue no112. Photography by Corinne Day. Page 322-323

May. The Europe Issue no116. Photography by Matthew R Lewis. Page 324

June. The Beauty Issue no117. Photography by Anette Aurell. Page 324

September. The Boys & Girls Issue no120. Photography by Peter Anderson. Page 326

September. The Boys & Girls Issue no120. Photography by David Sims. Page 326

October. The New Look Issue no121. Photography by Stefan Ruiz. Page 327

October. The New Look Issue no121. Photography by Mark Lebon. Page 327

November. The Hard Issue no122. Photography by Donald Milne. Page 328-329

December. The Smart Issue no123. Photography by Matthew R Lewis. Page 331


Left to right. Page 332-333

February. The Survival Issue no113. Photography by Juergen Teller

February. The Survival Issue no113. Photography by Craig McDean

February. The Survival Issue no113. Photography by Simon Fleury

March. The Comedy Issue no114. Photography by Wolfgang Tillmans

March. The Comedy Issue no114. Photography by Craig McDean, styling by Edward Enninful

March. The Comedy Issue no114. Photography by David Sims

April. The Sound Issue no115. Photography by Matthew R Lewis

April. The Sound Issue no115. Photography by Nigel Shafran

July. The Open Air Issue no118. Photography by Wolfgang Tillmans

August. The Festival Issue no119. Photography by Wolfgang Tillmans

August. The Festival Issue no119. Photography by Karen Palmer

September. The Boys & Girls Issue no120. Photography by Eika Aoshima

September. The Boys & Girls Issue no120. Photography by Nick Knight

September. The Boys & Girls Issue no120. Photography by Matthew R Lewis

November. The Hard Issue no122. Photography by Matthew R Lewis

November. The Hard Issue no122. Photography by Donald Milne

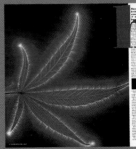

"I love reality – things like bad posture, vacant stares, skinniness... they're normal to teenagers. Women have forgotten what it's like to be young"

**Corinne Day, photographer, no123**

# 1994

January. The Urgent Issue no124. Cover star: Veronica Webb. Photography by Steven Klein, styling by Anna Cockburn

February. The Talent Issue no125. Cover star: Justine Frischman. Photography by Juergen Teller

March. The Network Issue no126. Cover star: Amber Valetta. Photography by Craig McDean, styling by Isabelle Peyrut

April. The Sex Issue no127. Cover star: Courtney Love. Photography by Juergen Teller

May. The Drugs Issue no128. Cover star: Christy Turlington. Photography by Juergen Teller, styling by Camilla Nickerson

June. The Rock 'n' Roll Issue no129. Cover star: Sonya Aurora Maden. Photography by Craig McDean

July. The Fun Issue no130. Cover star: Kylie Minogue. Photography by Ellen von Unwerth, styling by Cathy Kasterine

August. The US Issue no131. Cover star: Kate Moss. Photography by Steven Klein, styling by Edward Enninful

September. The Street Issue no132. Photography by Ellen von Unwerth

October. The Visionary Issue no133. Cover stars: Brett Anderson and Stella Tennant. Photography by Jean-Baptiste Mondino, styling by Zoe Bedeaux

November. The Underground Issue no134. Cover star: Bridget Hall. Photography by Steven Klein, styling by Edward Enninful

December. The Saturday Night Issue no135. Cover star: Heather Small. Photography by Christian Witkin, styling by Christine Fortune

THE URGENT ISSUE

# i-D

i-DEAS, FASHION, CLUBS, MUSIC, PEOPLE

CREDIT TO THE NATION
APACHÉ INDIAN
FUN-DA-MENTAL
JOE CASELY-HAYFORD
VERONICA WEBB
ASIAN YOUTH GET RADICAL
NEW BLACK DESIGNERS

# URGENT!
## SPECIAL ANTI-RACIST ISSUE

£1.95    $4.95

01

9 770262 357013

FRANCS 35 LIRE 7,100 DM 13,00 PESETAS 595 D KR 53

role model

# VERONICA WEBB IS THE FIRST BLACK MODEL EVER TO LAND A LUCRATIVE COSMETICS CONTRACT.

**SHE'S ALSO A CONTROVERSIAL WRITER, ACTRESS AND TV PRESENTER. IS THERE NO END TO THIS WOMAN'S TALENTS?**

Veronica Webb is dressed down in denim dungarees and J Crew boots, puffing away on a Marlboro which nestles delicately between her fingers. For the first African-American woman ever to land a major cosmetics contract, she looks decidedly understated. ◆

INTERVIEW BY **JUNE JOSEPH**
PHOTOGRAPHY BY **STEVEN KLEIN**
STYLING BY **ANNA COCKBURN**
MAKE-UP BY **EDRIS**
MAKE-UP BY **JAMES KARLIADOS** USING AVELON COSMETICS

INTERVIEW BY **AVRIL MAIR**
PHOTOGRAPHY BY **JAMES FRY**

# NO BULLSHIT

*HE'S NOT YOUR AVERAGE RAPPER. HE'S 18, HE'S OUT-SPOKENLY POLITICAL AND HIS FIRST SINGLE SAMPLED A NIRVANA RIFF. HE'S MATTY HANSON OF CREDIT TO THE NATION AND HE'S GOING TO BE A MAJOR STAR.*

Teenage sensation. He's Matty Hanson aka MC Fusion; he is Credit To The Nation and he's going to be one of British music's biggest stars. He combines the ferocious deliveries of Chuck D with the nifty steps of Bobby Brown, he preaches unity on a global dancefloor, he's just 18 years old, he only signed to a major label, One Little Indian, six months ago and he hasn't even finished recording his first album yet. But this mini rapper has emerged from the unlikely location of the West Midlands to send his missive of black rage into →

"I talk about racism in the fashion industry because after ten years in it, I think I've only worked with a black photographer twice"

**Veronica Webb, model, no124**

"The difficult thing about being a black designer is getting people to see you as an individual."
Wale Adeyemi

"It's not about being a black designer, it's about being a good designer."
Helen Akpoguma of Akpoguma

# CULT OF THE BEASTIES

**The Beastie Boys have gone from pop stardom to obscurity to being the biggest cult band in the world. Their last LP sold a million copies and their business empire includes a maga- zine, clothing range and record label. How did they manage it?**

"A lot of people think we slammed it," grins Mike D of The Beastie Boys, "but if we'd tried to engineer it we'd probably have failed miserably. It's just luck!"

He's talking about the Beasties' peculiar career trajectory - from hardcore punk jesters to massively huge rap-scallions through to their current enviable status as cult band with their own mini-empire. Most bands who go mainstream as The Beastie Boys did back in 1987 (with *Licensed To Ill* and *Fight For Your Right To Party*) either burn out or degenerate into cabaret. Getting back your credibility is a coup, a minor miracle at par with regaining your virginity.

The Beasties' early days can be revisited on the just-issued compilation *Some Old Bullshit*, which comprises their hardcore EP *Pollywog Stew* and their hilariously inept

story by SIMON REYNOLDS
photography by SHAUN MORTIMER
6  i-D THE NETWORK ISSUE

INTERVIEW BY *IRVINE WELSH*
PHOTOGRAPHY BY *MATTHEW R LEWIS*

## IT'S ONLY ROCK'N'ROLL.... ISN'T IT?

**Primal Scream are notorious hedonists who have reinvented themselves as full-on Stones-style rockers. Irvine Welsh's tales of Edinburgh drug subcultures have made him Britain's brightest young novelist. It seemed logical they should meet. Initially, Irvine was convinced the Scream's new rock'n'roll direction was a dead end. But a funny thing happened when he hooked up with Bobby and co...**

Any thoughts I had of slipping quietly down to London are fucked completely at 9.30 on a dull Tuesday morning when the phone rings at my Edinburgh flat. "Irvy, ya fuckin' cunt that ye are... ah'll be roond in ten minutes tae see ye off tae London!" It's Stan The Man, my accomplice in a weekend of chemical slaughter which barely seems to have finished.↵

STYLING BY *VICTORIA BARTLETT*
PHOTOGRAPHY BY *STEVEN KLEIN*
HAIR BY *JIMMY PAUL*
MAKE UP BY *JAMES KALIARDOS*
MODEL *BERI SMITHER*

# get physical

**Sportswear reinvented as sexy streetwear. Head for the gym!**

# for real

Pop trash meets rock'n'roll sleaze. Let's make some noise!

FASHION BY **MELANIE WARD**
PHOTOGRAPHY BY **DAVID SIMS**
HAIR BY **GUIDO**
MODEL: **TOM BOWEN** AT TAKE TWO
SHOT AT **CLICK STUDIO** (071 490 0121) AND
THE MARQUEE, CHARING CROSS ROAD, LONDON WC2

Customised lace top from Paradiso
Bodyworks, 41 Old Compton Street,
London W1; trousers by Helmut Lang
from Joseph, 77 Fulham Road SW3 and
Kafka, 41 Union Terrace, Aberdeen;
fingerless studded gloves from Carnaby
Street, London W1.

photography by **christian witkin**
co-ordination by **andrew dosunmu**
thanks to kelton lab, color edge,
8 bond studio (all in new york city)
and mimi wlodarczyk

BROADWAY CUTS THROUGH THE HEAR
A STUDIO THERE TO CAPTURE THE WIL

**Mickey Boardman,** 27, publisher's assistant and writer for *Paper* magazine. Clothes found on street, from flea markets, shoes from Polo Ralph Lauren. Favourite record: *Very Necessary* by Salt-N-Pepa. Loves: **"The fun thing is having access to resources that allow you to produce your ideas from the street to the boutiques of twisted talented designers, you have a smorgasbord of ideas and inspirations to keep you excited!"**

**Mary Iggy Frey,** 25, works for Liquid Sky. Clothes from Liquid sky, K-Mart and my dad. Sunglasses from the Glorious Clothing Company in London. Favourite records: *Jungle Sky* and *Freedom Is The Movement* by DJ Soulslinger. Loves: **"Working my ass off, rollerblading, underground dance, UFOs, my dog Rabbi, New York fucking City, life itself, the passion to unite, rise above the bullshit government. Power to the people, friends, animals, Earth, aliens, the homeless, Africa and you!"**

# NEW YORK CITY. WE SET UP
# IDIVIDUALISTS PASSING BY.

**Jill Nichols,** 29, sculptor. Wears second-hand jeans, shoes by Stephane Kelian, boyfriend's socks, knickers from England, bra top by Elon of California. Favourite record: "No favourite record, just my mix tape with lots of gutteral music." Loves: **"Sculpting!"**

**Akin Adams,** 24, "*medianaut, consciousness explorer, time traveller - in plainer English, lead vocalist and guitarist for SAM*". Pants from work-wear store, kaftan home-made. Favourite records: King Crimson's *Discipline*, Public Enemy's *Nation Of Millions*, Jimi Hendrix's *Kiss The Sky*, Bob Marley And The Wailers' *Soul Captives*, The Specials' *The Specials*. Loves: **"Playing with SAM, advocating hemp industrialization, being alive in the yet-to-blossom '90s, surviving in New York City."**

THE US ISSUE          NO.131                    cover stars: **kate moss & naomi campbell** AUGUST 19

i-DEAS, FASHION, CLUBS, MUSIC, PEOPLE

**Rage Against The Machine**
drop the bomb on Britain

**Timothy Leary**
from inner space to cyberspace

# american dream

## KATE, NAOMI & NEW YORK'S URBAN COO

**Nine Inch Nails**
sex & death & rock'n'roll

**Grateful Deadheads**
on America's hippy trail

**Joie Lee**
Spike's smart sister

£1.95   $4.95

9 770262 357013

FRANCS 35 LIRE 7,100 DM 13,00 PESETAS 595 D KR

Plus... Laurie Anderson • ambient California • Marc Jacobs • Pavement • The Prodigy • rollin' with rollerblades

**Songs about depression, degrada-
tion and death have made Trent
Reznor of Nine Inch Nails an international pop star, the voice of the
body-piercing generation. But has
success made him happy?**

There is darkness. And then there is light. And then there is
Trent Reznor, hanging in space. Twisted like an El Greco
saint. Impaled by the adoring gaze of his audience. And he
opens his mouth, and there is sound. Unearthly, terrifying
sound. His words are ripped from the surface, the texture
of his throat. The constant agony of the man who is experiencing the worst thing in the world. The thing in Room
101. Himself.

And then there is more light. And the El Greco saint is
stretched out upon a sofa in an upmarket hotel. His body is
lean and long. His arms are covered in bruises. His voice is
soft, unassuming. He talks on and on. Explaining, justifying
himself. Barely looking at his questioner. Staring at the car-
pet. Every so often, his arms unfurl and push his body
upwards, away from the floor to which he keeps sliding. He
is not without humour, but he barely seems awake. Trent
Reznor, El Greco saint, mastermind of Nine Inch Nails,
sighs a lot. But then he would, wouldn't he?

The difference between the two is remarkable. The vile
and violent stage force, body bruised from manic destruc-
tion and the introverted, calm, individual on the sofa hardly
seem to belong in the same room, never mind the same
body. One is chaotic. The other is plain nice. Not that that's
something you'd call Reznor to his face. He's built his →

interview by **vaughan allen**
photography by **matthew r lewis**

## dying for a living

# 09•94

"I am not really interested in fashion. What I
do is project my other interests like
philosophy and psychology into fashion"

**Hussein Chalayan, designer, no125**

## Noorderlaan
12.30AM, ANTWERP

*photography by roland stoops*

**Jasmine Maniex**, 16, student. Clothes by Dirk Van Saene. Favourite record: *Zingalamaduni* by
Arrested Development. What's most important in your life right now? "My holiday in Portugal. We're
going camping, which should be a giggle." What would you change for a better future? "The government of Belgium, it's so square and boring. Those old men should relax and be more positive about
life. On a personal level, I wish I lived in the city. When I go out I always miss the last train. When
I'm older, maybe 20 or 21, I'll retire back into the forest and become a hermit!"

## Brusseler Platz
1AM, COLOGNE

*photography by wolfgang tillmans*

**Kai**, 28, artist. T-shirt by Subtle Tease, jeans by Levi's. What's most
important in your life right now? "Justus." **Justus**, 28. Shorts by Blue
Diamond, T-shirt by Fred Perry. Favourite record: *Don't Go Breaking
My Heart* by Elton John and Kiki Dee. What's most important in your
life right now? "Kai." What would you change for a better future? "Free
internet access for everyone."

THE STREET ISSUE    NO.132     cover star: **björk** photographed by ellen von unwerth **SEPTEMBER 1994**

# i-D

*i-DEAS, FASHION, CLUBS, MUSIC, PEOPLE*

## INTERNATIONAL STREET FASHION SPECIAL

paranoia in cyberspace

the future for football

Massive Attack

Shed Seven

Rebel MC

the best disco dancing
guide in the world

**public enemy**

**Chuck D in the dock**

**russell simmons**

**Hip hop's top dog**

**the drum club**

**Trance tripping in Tokyo**

# björk!

## A Night Out With Miss World

£2.20  $5.50

09

9 770262 357020

FRANCS 38 LIRE 10,000 DM 13.50 PESETAS 625 D KR 59

THE VISIONARY ISSUE     NO.133     cover stars: **brett anderson** and **stella tennant** photographed by jean baptiste mondino **OCTOBER 1994**

**£2.20   $5.50**

9 770262 357020

10

FRANCS 38 LIRE 10,000 DM 13.50 PESETAS 625 D KR 59

# i-D

© i-DEAS, FASHION, CLUBS, MUSIC, PEOPLE

## FASHION'S FRESH VISION

quentin tarantino
luscious jackson
liza bruce
steve albini
billion dollar babewear
art terrorism
jungle chic
the new mods

# suede
## The Art Of Falling Apart

"Oasis and Suede? The singing electricians
versus the limp-wristed glamourpuss"

**Brett Anderson, musician, no133**

interview by **tony marcus**
photography by
**jean baptiste mondino**
styling by **zoe bedeaux**
hair by **guido** at tony & guy
using tigi linea products
hair by **pat mcgrath**
at streeters
shot at click studios
brett wears schoolboy suit
by agnès b

# Brett St

Last year, they were Britain's biggest and
best band. This year, so the rumours go,
Suede are falling apart. As they prepare to
release an astonishing second album,
singer Brett Anderson confounds his critics
in a confessional about sex, success and
rock'n'roll excess.

In the current mass celebration of fashion, with models as cultural icons and photographers as household names, the people really responsible for eye-catching images remain the industry's unsung heroes. Yet stylists today are more influential than ever. Nobody, it seems, can dress themselves"

**Edward Enninful, i-D Fashion Director, no134**

sound of the underground

interview by **tony marcus**
photography by **matthew r lewis**

i-D's Sound Of The Underground special starts with Mixmaster Morris. Musician, DJ and ambient evangelist: he is the man who came to the party but didn't want to dance. Pop's most unlikely warrior, his patience and persistance have issued a global wake-up call for a new generation of electronic innovators. Though unique, Mixmaster Morris' story is essentially the same as those of Richie Hawtin and Goldie, which appear on the following pages. All are men on a mission, in love with music, creating the sound of this century and the next. What started as a rave, as drug music for dark, strobe-lit rooms, has become a soundtrack for life beyond dance. Ambient, techno, jungle: all different, yet all music for the next decade and further....

Mixmaster Morris is probably the least chilled person on planet earth. Smoking spliff after spliff, he plays an endless succession of relaxing records but is unable to ease a sense of purpose that makes him tense, angry, even manic. Best known as a leading ambient DJ and as recording artist The Irresistible Force, he's spent most of his adult life fighting to produce and promote weird and beautiful electronic music. With a Napoleonic sense of strategy, he's utilised the media, DJ culture, computer networks, remixes and the record industry like a general fighting a war. "You can't have progress without conflict," sighs Morris. "I will certainly use all means necessary to bring radical music that's not getting any attention to a wider public. People are ready for new music, but it's not getting exposure because the music industry spends so much money trying to force crap down their throats. I don't mind using every means at my disposal to try and redress the balance."

He speaks like a fanatic, with a level of seriousness for which he's been derided, mocked and all but crucified. For many people, Morris is that weirdo in the holographic suit, the DJ spinning slogans like 'I Think Therefore I Ambient' while trying to get work in house and techno clubs playing records without beats. He's the man that came to the party but didn't want to dance. And we laughed, because the ambient gesture looked more like a contradiction of the house movement than an integral part of it. Even the so-called inventors of ambient house, The KLF and The Orb, refused to take it seriously. In 1989, to accompany their *Chill Out* LP, The KLF issued a press release made up of 18 contradictory statements: ►

## Greetings, Earthlings

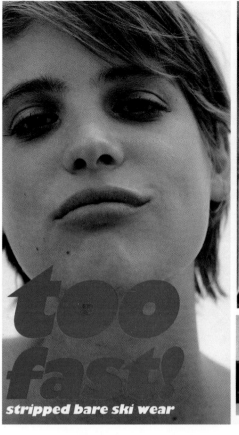

Sleeveless top by Dirk Bikkemberg from Jones Women, 13 Floral Street, London WC1; ski pants by Ellesse from sports shops nationwide.

photography by **mark borthwick**
assisted by **srenica**
styling by **jane how**
assisted by **sara humberstone**
and **fabienne**
hair and make-up by
**houda remita** for bridget hebant
model: **helene filliers** at select

## too fast!
### stripped bare ski wear

Red puffa jacket by Kly Bit from Ad Hoc, 33 Kensington High Street, London W8 and Hervia, Royal Exchange, Manchester; sports knickers from billywhites, 24-32 Regent Street, London.

The late Ray Petri produced this picture years before it was fashionable for men to wear skirts. A truly seminal stylist, his influence on the industry still lives on.

### MELANIE WARD, 30

describe your style. I don't work to a stock formula. I would say it's quintessentially character-orientated, individual and modern. what do you like about styling. Being paid to use my imagination and being able to work with my friends. background. Editorial for i-D, The Face, Interview, Vogue Hommes International, French Glamour and Italian Donna; advertising campaigns for Levi's, Calvin Klein, Barneys, Yohji Yamamoto and Helmut Lang; styling for over 30 artists including U2, Iggy Pop, David Bowie and The Rolling Stones. current work. Consultant and stylist for Helmut Lang, Jill Sander and Lira Bruce; Contributing Fashion Editor to French Glamour; editorial for i-D and The Face. ambition. I hope that my work affects a positive change in the industry, that it somehow makes a difference and, most of all, that I always keep my integrity and values.

# THE STYLE COUNSEL

Stylists are fashion's subversives. Creators in their own right, these visionary upstarts control the images we consume daily - yet you still won't know their names. This is a celebration of unsung heroes.

story by edward enninful

**12•94**

"I'm influenced by contemporary culture:
Scotland's not all wank about fiddles,
ceilidhs and whisky"

**Irvine Welsh, writer, no125**

best of british

interview by **susan corrigan**
photography by **donald milne**

London lads on the pull or just taking the
piss? Blur are this year's Brit pop sensations,
defining a bold New Englishness out of smart
jumpers, sharp haircuts and some serious
attitude. Welcome to their modern world...

# have a go if you 're hard enough

## THUNDER AND JOY

### Sundays at RAW, London

**Never was a night so well named. A junglist heaven where sweat, style and smiles rule and everyone looks like they stepped out of an R Kelly video. Just wild!**

Mark, 21, Keeley, 17, and Annette, 20.
Clothes: Moschino. Favourite DJs Randall.
Favourite record: *Inner City Life* by
Metalheads. Perfect night out: "A jungle do
like this one - it's wicked to see a dance in
full swing."

Photography by Mark Alesky,
assisted by Simon Condliffe

# 1994

"With the ozone layer gone, what is a summer frock?"

Judy Blame, i-D Contributing Fashion Editor, no133

# 1995

January. The Future Issue no136. Cover star: Kiara. Photography by Craig McDean, styling by Edward Enninful

February. The New Faces Issue no137. Creative direction by Terry Jones

March. The Pin Ups Issue no138. Cover star: Drew Barrymore. Photography by Ellen von Unwerth, styling by Joe McKenna

April. The Tough Issue no139. Cover star: Nicki Umberti. Photography by Terry Richardson, styling by Patti Wilson

May. The Sharp Issue no140. Cover star: Tank Girl. Illustration by Jamie Hewlett

June. The Subversive Issue no141. Cover star: Shalom. Photography by Craig McDean, styling by Edward Enninful

July. The Boy's Own Issue no142. Cover star: Nadja Auermann. Photography by Craig McDean, styling by Edward Enninful

August. The Most Wanted Issue no143. Cover star: Greta. Photography by Ellen von Unwerth, styling by Patti Wilson

September. The Fun & Games Issue no144. Cover star: PJ Harvey. Photography by Craig McDean, styling by Edward Enninful

October. The Fifteenth Birthday Issue no145. Creative direction by Terry Jones

November. The Real Issue no146. Cover star: Emma Balfour. Photography by Craig McDean, styling by Edward Enninful

December. The Performance Issue no147. Cover star: Stella Tennant. Photography by Craig McDean, styling by Edward Enninful

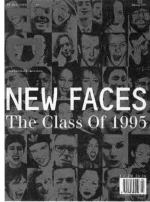

THE FUTURE ISSUE    NO.136    cover star kiara photographed by ... January 1995

*i-D*

© i-DEAS, FASHION, CLUBS, MUSIC

# THIS IS THE FUTURE!
## life in cyberspace

**the black dog • policing the internet**
**future shock fashion • cyborgfeminism**
**a guy called gerald • techno subversives**

£2.20  $5.50

9 770262 357020    01

FRANCS 38 LIRE 10,000 DM 13,50 PESETAS 625 D KR 59

"In the world of fashion, rock'n'roll is the new rock'n'roll. Just as well-dressed bands are turning Britpop on its head with their finely-tuned posturing, so too are modelling's new stars. Enter the indie boy brigade. Question is: can they sing?"

**Edward Enninful, i-D Fashion Director, no143**

**Moving Shadow** For their consistently brilliant series of singles released throughout 1994, Moving Shadow has to be label of the year. Some like Mo'Wax were more visibly hip, others like Basic Channel built a cult rep, but the Hertford-based jungle independent rolled out the hits, the remixes and the re-remixes one after another. There was Omni Trio's *Renegade Snares* (*Foul Play Remix*) with its chorus made out of fireworks and helium. And Deep Blue's duet for cyborgs and steel blades known as *The Helicopter Tune*. There was Blame's *Anthemia*, with its glitter-fusion satellites in orbit around the heaven of a woman's sigh. The interstellar jazz breaks of E-Z Rollers *Believe*. And still others: Dead Dred's *Dread Bass*, Renegade's *Something I Feel*, Foul Play's *Being With You* and Hyper On Experience's drumtrip into the art of darkness, *Lords Of The Null Lines* (*Foul Play Remix*).

Now midway between it's fourth and fifth year, the label started as a core of Rob Playford (Goldie's partner in the high-profile Metalheadz), Sean O'Keefe aka Deep Blue, and Simon Colebrooke - the three names behind 2 Bad Mice's '92 hardcore anthems *Warpmouse* and *Bombscare*. Today, producers such as E-Z Rollers and JMJ And Richie recombinate soft synths with shuddering bass and jazz-inflected breaks to produce nu-fusion genres with every other 12". In 1994 Playford relaunched Section 5, the label attached to the Kings Road shop of the same name, which releases singles by Hopa And Bones, Harmony And Extreme and Adam F. And MCs Flux, GQ and Five O ran things down at the fierce-yet-relaxed Voodoo Magic allnighters in Leicester Square. In 1995, new names to watch include Higher Sense (who made last year's *Cold Fresh Air*), DJ Nut Nut (responsible for the deep space ragga of *Pure Science*) and DJ Pulse.

Moving Shadow's expansion reflects the urge to make it new which ran through jungle last year. "We changed the format of music for the first time in a decade," declares Goldie, who remixed *The Helicopter Tune* as Rufige Kru and kicked off the label's guest artist *Two On One* series. "UK breakbeat has now created a culture that's unique. It's created an opening for people that would never be heard otherwise. 1994 has been about kicking down the doors. In 1995, Moving Shadow will be expanding in a more corporate direction." Playford elaborates: "Next year we'll see the music moving onto albums. We've got the Omni Trio album in January, Foul Play in March and then Hyper On Experience later on." Promises Foul Play's John Morrow: "We're writing up the score for live instruments on our album. The whole thing is going to work in a live setting." His collaborator Steve 'Brad' Bradshaw continues, "We're aiming at a visual thing. We'll have properly dressed musicians on one side and we'll be doing our own thing on the other." You could say that jungle is the last postmodernism of the last decade. But it's really the first artform for the 21st Century. And Moving Shadow is simply music for kids who want to dance in the fires of the new sun. Kodwo Eshun

# i-D's ESSENTIAL GUIDE TO FUTURE CLUBWEAR

photography by **jamie fry** styling and co-ordination by **voss & cornelius** hair and make-up by **claudia** and **keiko** at children of vision
models: **caroline** and **charlotte** at storm, **natasha**, **richard**, **jake**, **lisa**, **colin** and **spencer**

**grandmistress flash** Natasha wears silver wrist cuffs, £50; wrist cuffs, £13, and peak cap, £16, from Paradise, 41 Old Compton Street, London W1; patent jacket, £12, by Vicki from The Electric Ballroom, Camden High Street, London NW1; dinosaur jumper, £98, by Two Guys from Hyper Hyper, Kensington High Street, London W8; belt by Voss, £35, enquiries on 081 287 2385; cards by Lina's from branches of The Levi's Store nationwide; boots, £50-Ish, by Office from Office 60 Neal Street, London WC1

**bourgeois b-boy** Richard wears jacket, £112.50, and trousers, £80, by Good Enough from Bond, 10 Newburgh Street, London W1; shirt, £48, by The Duffer Of St George from The Duffer Of St George, 27 D'Arblay Street, London W1; belt by Stussy, £15, from American Classics 204-408 Kings Road, London SW10; shoes, £125, by Lawler Duffey from Junior, 12 Floral Street, London WC1

**rude boy** Jake wears T-shirt, £25, by Karen Savage from Sign Of The Times, 15 Shorts Gardens, London WC2; cashmere jumper from Cow Killer Clothing, £30, enquiries on (0181 435741); trousers, £23, by David Foyla Ltd from Portobello Market, London W11; boots £79.99, by Office as before.

**jungle** Lisa wears outfit by Tracey Corben, enquiries on 081 450 0585; shoes by Pornarina, enquiries on 010 397 5581 4962.

**bourgeois b-girl** Charlotte wears crochet skull cap, £20, by Nora Cie Pronto from Hyper Hyper as before; jacket, £230, by Jessica Ogden from Sign Of The Times as before; tights from branches of The Sock Shop nationwide; shoes, £225, by Jimmy Choo, available to order on 071 240 0862

**trip hop** Colin wears a jacket by Hang Ten, models own; T-shirt, £25, by Fat Boy, enquiries on 071 437 5673; trousers, £90, by Good Enough from Bond as before; shoes, £95, by Tracy from The Duffer Of St George as before.

**smoothie** Spencer wears jacket, £250, by Norton from Bond, 46 Godfrey Street, London SW2; jumper, £39.50, and trousers, £128, by Cecy from Cecy, enquiries on 071 439 1727; shoes, £95, from The Duffer Of St George as before.

**house music all night long** Caroline wears hat, £35, by Guard from Warehod Garage, 264 Kings Road, London SW3; top, £25, jeff skirt, £50, by Neil Whitten Warehod Garage as before; sports bag by Leotar, £59, from Warehod Garage as before; jacket own sports bag, £32, by Dollargrand from Warehod Garage as before; shoes, £219, by Jimmy Choo as before.

# 03•95
"Women make life worth living"

**Jarvis Cocker, musician, no145**

Lindsey, 26, plays guitar
with The Drags and
Jenny, 25, lead singer
with Spanky

Samoa, 28, lead guitarist
with Karen Black

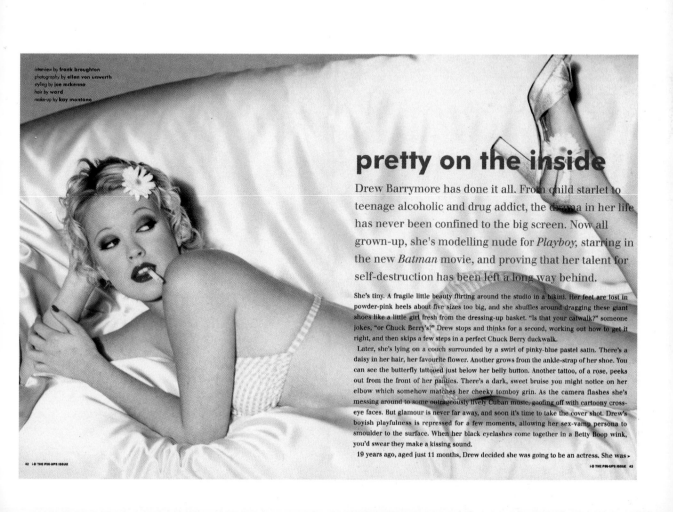

interview by frank broughton
photography by ellen von unwerth
styling by joe mckenna
hair by ward
make-up by kay montano

# pretty on the inside

Drew Barrymore has done it all. From child starlet to teenage alcoholic and drug addict, the drama in her life has never been confined to the big screen. Now all grown-up, she's modelling nude for *Playboy*, starring in the new *Batman* movie, and proving that her talent for self-destruction has been left a long way behind.

She's tiny. A fragile little beauty flirting around the studio in a bikini. Her feet are lost in powder-pink heels about five sizes too big, and she shuffles around dragging these giant shoes like a little girl fresh from the dressing-up basket. "Is that your catwalk?" someone jokes, "or Chuck Berry's?" Drew stops and thinks for a second, working out how to get it right, and then skips a few steps in a perfect Chuck Berry duckwalk.

Later, she's lying on a couch surrounded by a swirl of pinky-blue pastel satin. There's a daisy in her hair, her favourite flower. Another grows from the ankle-strap of her shoe. You can see the butterfly tattooed just below her belly button. Another tattoo, of a rose, peeks out from the front of her panties. There's a dark, sweet bruise you might notice on her elbow which somehow matches her cheeky tomboy grin. As the camera flashes she's messing around to some outrageously lively Cuban music, goofing off with cartoony cross-eye faces. But glamour is never far away, and soon it's time to take the cover shot. Drew's boyish playfulness is repressed for a few moments, allowing her sex-vamp persona to smoulder to the surface. When her black eyelashes come together in a Betty Boop wink, you'd swear they make a kissing sound.

19 years ago, aged just 11 months, Drew decided she was going to be an actress. She was ▸

interview by **kodwo eshun**
photography by **wolfgang tillmans**

**listen to the future
one of detroit's legendary
first generation, carl craig has
left behind the legacy he's
outgrown. ripping up techno's
rule-book, this 25-year-old is
making records for every
dancefloor. with three very
different albums due this
summer, could he change the
future sound of music?**

As a geographical scene and a vanguardist aesthetic, Detroit techno is no
longer at the cutting-edge; just as techno is no longer the definitive, single
direction for dance music. Detroit techno took music beyond the dance,
into the chaos of electronics, inventing a history and a future, a direction
and an ideal as successful as that other '80s neologism, cyberspace. ►

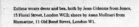

## treat her like a lady don't take it lying down: get tied up and play the bondage game

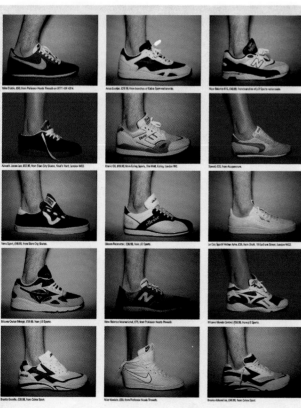

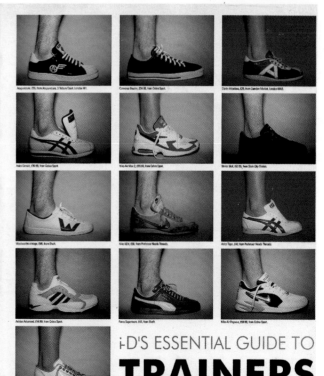

# i-D'S ESSENTIAL GUIDE TO
# TRAINERS

photography by **james fry** styling and co-ordination by **voss & cornelius**
assisted by **soraya** thanks to **andrew newman**

## access all areas

FORGET PARIS, LONDON, NEW YORK! THIS SEASON, MILAN TOOK THE STYLE WORLD BY STORM THANKS TO THREE LABELS: DOLCE E GABBANA, ANNA MOLINARI AND PRADA. BE BLOWN AWAY BY THIS BACKSTAGE REPORT, PHOTOGRAPHED EXCLUSIVELY BY JUERGEN TELLER.

# Anna Molinari

# 07•95

"I'll be dating young women when I'm sixty.
I'm scared to death of growing old"

**Puff Daddy, music mogul, no140**

**FRESH**
photography by annette aurell
styling by annett monheim
Karl Pace at MGM wears Jean Paul Gaultier
jeans from Galleria Gaultier, 171 Draycott
Avenue, London SW3 and Accent, 4 Queen
Victoria Street, Leeds; Nike trainers from
good sports shops nationwide.

jean genius: summer denim special
**the sun's out, the music's playing and all
you need to wear is a pair of jeans. Some
things simply never go out of fashion...**

**LOADED**
photography by jamil gs
styling by patti wilson
hair by johnnie sapong at
streeters using aveda
make-up by francisco valero
Maddon wears DKNY skirt from 29 Old Bond
Street, London W1; top by Kevin Robinson to
order on 051 718 369 4084; shoes by Miu
Miu from Pellicano, 63 South Molton Street,
London W1.

Esta wears top by Liza Bruce from Harvey Nichols, Knightsbridge, London SW3 and Room 7, 26 King Charles Street, Leeds; jeans by Wrangler from branches of Jeans West nationwide. Michaela wears sports shorts from Lillywhites, 24-32 Regent Street, London SW2; sweatshirt by APC from 126 Draycott Avenue, London SW1 and Hervia, Royal Exchange, Manchester; jacket by Juno Goh, to order on 0181 249 0434

Michaela wears bikini top by Liza Bruce from Harvey Nichols, Knightsbridge, London SW3 and Room 7, 26 King Charles Street, Leeds; hipsters by Junyo Watanabe from Comme des Garçons, 59 Brook Street, London W1.

# Arcadia
*England Dreaming By Dawn's Early Light*

"I enjoy looking like a tart and thinking like a politician"

**PJ Harvey, musician, no144**

Raina wears top by Helmut
Lang from Jones Women, 15
Floral Street, London WC2.

**prison camp honey, you gotta
get us out of here - the fashion
police got the wrong women...**

Bridget wears lace corset by La
Perla from Harrods, Knightsbridge,
London SW1; skirt by Blumarine
from Anna Molinari, 11 Old Bond
Street, London W1; shoes by Lisa
Bruce from Pellicano, 65 South
Molton Street, London W1. Nikki
wears suit from David's Outfitters,
NYC; shoes by Stephane Kelian
from 48 Sloane Street, London SW1.
Yalitzia wears top and skirt by Lisa
Bruce; shoes by Stephane Kelian.

THE FUN & GAMES ISSUE    NO.144

cover star **pj harvey** photographed by **craig mcdean**  september 1995

£2.20  $5.50

09
9 770262 357020

FRANCS 38 LIRE 9,000 DM 13,50 PESETAS 625 D KR 59

# i-D

i-DEAS, FASHION, CLUBS, MUSIC, P...

# WONDER WOMAN!

## POLLY PULLS IT OFF

### ARE DRUGS AND VIOLENCE KILLING FOOTBALL?

### KIDS IN AMERICA: FROM ROCKERS TO RAVERS

### BEHAVING BADLY: BRITAIN'S TEEN HACKERS

### JUNGLE HITS JAPAN • SERIOUSLY SEXY FASHION

interview by **bönz malone**
photography by **norman watson**
grooming by **jacqueline colligan**/ elizabeth watson inc

Wu-Tang Clan (clockwise from left):
Shallah Raekwon ("the Chef"),
Master Killer, Method Man,
Ghost Face Killer, Ol' Dirty
Bastard, Inspector Deck, U-God
(aka Golden Arms), RZA, GZA

# ENTER THE WU-TANG

Right now, Wu-Tang Clan are the biggest stars in the hip hop firmament. Since the release of 1993's album *Enter The 36 Chambers*, they've single-handedly regained the rap crown from the West Coast's young pretenders. What started as a self-sufficient entity now dominates an entire industry, with each member of the deep space nine working on solo projects: Method Man's album has gone platinum, Ol' Dirty Bastard is on his way, and this month comes Chef Raekwon. Welcome to the weird world of Wu-Tang. ➤

SIGNS OF THE TIMES... 1980 On the eve of a US tour, Joy Division frontman Ian Curtis hangs himself in his Macclesfield kitchen • Liverpool post-punk flourishes w
LPs from Echo And The Bunnymen and The Teardrop Explodes • The Blitz Club and the Goodge Place squat scene begin in London, the denizens of which (Spandau Ball
Strange, Jeremy Healy, Boy George) creep virus-like into the charts, clubs and shops of the 1980's and beyond • Fame is unleashed upon the nation's cinemas,
ing adolescent wardrobes with a plague of lavender leg-warmers and sawn-off sweatshirts • Sony's Walkman launches, much to the chagrin of parents, teachers and

juerger

**JOHN GALLIANO** Bias-cut dresses, puff sleeves, tailored tinfoil jackets, flamenco frills: Galliano's done it all. Since the mid-'80s, this enfant-terrible of British design has gone from strength to rock-bottom and then right back again, winning the last laugh with his prestigious appointment as head of the couture house of Givenchy. And Jeremy Healy still soundtracks his shows age **34** occupation **Couturier** favourite record *Tabloid Junkie* by **Michael Jackson** where do you get your clothes? **Wherever I find myself to be** what were you doing 15 years ago? **A student at St Martins School Of Art** what are you doing now? **Designing the John Galliano line of couture and pret-a porter and, for the house of Givenchy, there is haute couture and pret-a porter deluxe** what do you want to be doing in 15 years time? **I feel it's just the beginning** what makes life worth living? **Friends** biggest hope for the future? **To be happy**

# GENERATION TERRORISTS FIFTEEN YEARS OF MESSING WITH THE MAINSTREAM

d Bowie's last 'relevant' album, *Scary Monsters*, is released • Ska music and fashion dominate under the influence of The Specials, The Beat and Madness • *Sandinista* by The Clash
in as the first punk-rock treble LP • A generation mourns the 'assassination' of John Lennon, gunned down outside his flat by Mark David Chapman • The Buggles' *Video Killed*
dio Star is the first clip to be shown on MTV • Leigh Bowery arrives in London and lands himself a job in Burger King: greater things are yet to come • Five pretty boys
ng out at Birmingham's Rum Runner club form a band, taking their name from Roger Vadim's 1967 space-porn epic *Barbarella*. Ladies and gentlemen, we give you Duran Duran ➤

wolfgang tillmans

**BLUR** Who do they think they are? Outwardly-mobile scruffs with a penchant for missing aitches, last album *Parklife* went straight to the top of the charts through a combination of swottiness, snottiness and unabashed love for the eclectic beast known as English culture. New magnum opus *The Great Escape* proves there's a lot more going on in their heads than gahn dahn the dogs. Hands-down winners in the Battle Of Britain name Damon Albarn age 27 occupation Singer/songwriter favourite record *Shaved Fish* by John Lennon and *It's Great When You're Straight... Yeah!* by Black Grape where do you get your clothes? Bankrupt stock and odd shops what were you doing 15 years ago? Starting comprehensive school what are you doing now? Having my picture taken what do you want to be doing in 15 years time? Not talking about what happened 15 years ago what makes life worth living? Tomorrow biggest hope for the future? To invent an alcoholic drink that doesn't have any side-effects once you've drunk it

men who harass them. A nation of secret bum-pinchers shudder • Tonka, Mindscape and Sugarlump play techno at Glastonbury • Alexander Shulgin publishes *Pikhal*: of the book is his life-story, the rest is 200 pages of recipes for interesting chemicals • The Shamen's Will Sin drowns in Tenerife while filming the video for *Any Mountain*, the single that will finally propel them chartwards • Bored with the standard package, alternative tourism is a boom industry. Fancy a fortnight ing in the Kalahari desert or clubbing in Ibiza? Or Prague? Goa, even? No problem • Future Sound Of London release *Papua New Guinea*, one stage in the evolutic

matthew r lew

**SKIN TWO** This leather and rubber posse's gloss mag and glamorous parties proved that fetish can be fashionable. Thanks to them, there's no such thing as normal or abnormal shagging any more: just informed possibilities, safe but challenging fun, and PVC on sale in Miss Selfridge. Have the sex wars been won? name **Michelle Olley** age 2 and feeling fine occupation **Magazine editor/singer/club runner/semi-professional disco flake** favourite record *The Thrill Of It All* by Roxy **Music** where do you get your clothes? **Demented fetish gear from Murray & Vern and House Of Harlot, push-up bras from M&S, separate scavenged from my mum and my fabulous, glamourous gran, the Betty Grable of Lancashire** what were you doing 15 years ago? **Avoiding getting picked on for being a 'weirdo'** what are you doing now? **Editing** *Skin Two* **magazine, recording with my band Salon Kitty, and running a club, Street Life, which is Salon Kitty's irreverent take o what a fetish club should be like. At the last one we had Sheila Tequila and Donald from Beautiful Bend pissing on stage, and Pete Shelly from the Buzzcocks dressed as Andy Warhol, duetting on Homosapien with us dressed as The Velvet Underground** what do you want to be doing i 15 years time? **Either Salon Kitty's third season Caesar's Palace in Las Vegas, or running a male brothel** what makes life worth living? **Love, friends, Ricard on ice, Iggy Pop,** *The Simpsons,* hig **heels, a dirty mind wrapped in clean sheets** biggest hope for the future? **A cure for AIDS and that our generation does a better job of runnin things than the current shower**

no beyond the dancefloor • Richie Edwards of the Manic Street Preachers razorcuts '4 REAL' into his forearm in the middle of an interview. His behaviour is one
the first indicators of the widespread practice of self-mutilation amongst young adults • With women's magazines sold in sealed bags and sex education videos in
miths, porn comes out of its seedy brown wrapper and puts non-sexist erotica on the agenda. Most men now know that a vulva isn't something you park in a garage
e year of Balearic networking in clubs, with transnational gurning from London to Nottingham to Manchester to Birmingham • Ready for Ladchester? Poppers, ►

matt jones

**DAMIEN HIRST** The most famous pop artist of his generation came from humble beginnings in Leeds, setting the art world alight with unnerving cabinets full of surgical supplies and formaldehyde-preserved animals. His experiments with the living have been confined, so far, to Blur videos and procreation age **30** occupation **Artist** favourite record *Low Expectations* by Angus Fairhurst where do you get your clothes? **Thrift stores, John Pearce, Comme Des Garçons** what were you doing 15 years ago? **At school** what are you doing now? **Living in Devon** what do you want to be doing in 15 years time? **Living forever** what makes life worth living? **My baby Connor and my girlfriend Maia, and having the freedom to do whatever I want** biggest hope for the future? **Carrying on**

Matt Jones snaps a naked Damien Hirst. Hirst cites his favourite record as Low Expectation by Angus Fairhurst and claims to buy John Pearce, Comme de Garçons and shop in thrift stores.

THE FIFTEENTH BIRTHDAY ISSUE   65

No 145. The Birthday Issue. October 1995

Ben wears plastic-front jacket and trousers by Commes
Des Garçons Hommes Plus
from 59 Brook Street,
London W1 and Pollyanna,
16 Market Hill, Barnsley;
trainers by Nike from Cobra
Sports, branches nationwide.

photography by **donald christie**
styling by **karl plewka**
grooming by **neil moodie** for
Zoo using aveda products
models: **edward** and **ben**

Ben wears devoré top by
Owen Gaster from Pellicano,
63 South Molton Street,
London W1; nylon trousers
by Sabotage from
Autograph, 15 Ethel Street,
Birmingham.

**RUNNING MEN THE LONELINESS OF THE
LONG DISTANCE FASHION MODEL: IT'S
NOT ALL PRADA HANDBAGS, Y'KNOW...**

# 1995

Biggest hope for the future? "To invent
an alcoholic drink that doesn't have any
side effects once you've drunk it"

Damon Albarn, musician, no145

## We'll Take Manhattan!

Downtown in attitude and uptown
in aspiration, these are our
tips for the top from the cream
of New York's young fashion crop

havin' it with the shamen
somehow they've always
managed to shock. last time
round it was singing about
class A drugs on kids telly.
now, with this summer's new
album, the surprise might just
be the shamen's mastery of
perfect pop. or the fact that it
could be their final record...

## Spaced Out

ACCORDING TO RESEARCH, FIFTEEN
MILLION AMERICANS BELIEVE THEY
HAVE BEEN ABDUCTED BY ALIENS.
MASS HALLUCINATION, GOVERNMENT
DISINFORMATION... OR JUST A POP
CULT STAPLE? THE SPACE RACE IS ON.

Teenage Kicks

SKIP TO THE BEAT

# 1996

January. The Wonderland Issue no148. Cover star: Carolyn Murphy. Photography by Terry Richardson, styling by Edward Enninful

February. The Survival Issue no149. Cover star: Kate Moss. Photography by David Sims, styling by Anna Cockburn

March. The Alternative Issue no150. Cover star: Kristen McMenamy. Photography by Juergen Teller, styling by Edward Enninful

April. The Fresh Issue no151. Cover star: Lorraine Pascale. Photography by Craig McDean, styling by Edward Enninful

May. The Sound Issue no152. Cover star: Guinevere van Seenus. Photography by Mark Bothwick, styling by Jane How

June. The Supernova Issue no153. Cover star: Shirley Manson. Photography by Ellen von Unwerth, styling by Patti Wilson

July. The Love Life Issue no154. Cover stars: Björk and Goldie. Photography by Lorenzo Agius

August. The High Summer Issue no155. Cover star: Naomi Campbell. Photography by Paolo Roversi, styling by Paul Sinclaire

September. The Pioneer Issue no156. Cover star: Brett Anderson. Photography by Nick Knight

October. The Capital Issue no157. Cover star: Iris Palmer. Photography by Max Vadukul

November. The Energised Issue no158. Cover star: Angela Lindvall. Photography by Juergen Teller

December. The Undressed Issue no159. Cover star: Jamie Rishar. Photography by Matt Jones, styling by John Scher

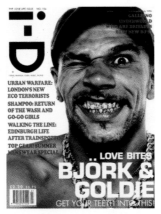

THE WONDERLAND ISSUE ISSUE    NO.148

cover star: **carolyn murphy** photographed by **terry richardson** january 1996

# i-D

**i-DEAS, FASHION, CLUBS, MUSIC, PEOPLE**

## STONED AND DETHRONED?
## ROSES ON THEIR THORNY YEAR

# HEY, BABY!

## SAY HELLO TO THE NEW SUPERMODEL SUPERNOVA

## COOLIO • NICOLETTE • GREEN DAY • RACHEL WILLIAMS

## SCREEN TEST: IS NEW BRIT CINEMA WORTH WATCHING?

£2.20  $5.50

## MAXIMUM ROCK'N'ROLL AMERICAN PUNK'S NOT DEAD

9 770262 357020

01

FRANCS 38 LIRE 9,000 DM 13,50 PESETAS 625 D KR 59

# 01•96

"The way the English deal with sexuality is quite awkward and I don't think it's very natural"

**Juergen Teller, photographer, no158**

MARTINE SITBON/**PARIS**

KATE MOSS AND TRISH GOFF

Craig McDean

CAROLYN MURPHY

**Private View** Usually only industry insiders, black shades glistening and egos bristling, get so close to the backstage fashion action. Craig McDean, Terry Richardson and Mark Borthwick present this seasons view from behind the catwalks of Paris, London and New York

MIU MIU/ NEW YORK

MILLA AND
NIKKI UMBERTTI

Terry Richardson

**02•96**

cover star: **kate moss**

i-D

IDEAS, FASHION, CLUBS, MUSIC, PEOPLE

KATE MOSS

JARVIS COCKER

PRINCE NASEEM

IRVINE WELSH

NICK CAVE

LOU REED

LL COOL J

LOUISE WENER

EWAN MCGREGOR

£2.20    $5.75

9 770262 357020

02

FRANCS 38 LIRE

**Alien**

make-up by **Kay Montano** at Smile
hair by **Ward** for Rumble & Bumble
photography by **Ellen Von Unwerth**
model: **Carolyn Murphy** at WomenNYC
Purple eyeshadow by Shu Uemura from
Liberty, Regent Street, London W1. Hair
gelled with Grip and Antimatter from
Rumble & Bumble, NYC

# LOOKS CAN KILL HAIR STYLISTS AND MAKE-UP ARTISTS TAKE CENTRE STAGE TO DEFINE A DANGEROUS NEW BEAUTY

**Three In One**

make-up by **Miranda Joyce** for Aveda
hair by **Guido** at Toni & Guy
photography by **David Sims**
styling by **Anna Cockburn**
model: **Kate Moss** at Storm
Foundation by Aveda from Harvey Nichols,
Knightsbridge, London SW1 and Frasers,
21-45 Buchanan Street, Glasgow. Hair
styled with Essential Spray And Shine and
Hold And Gloss by Toni & Guy from 28
Kensington Church Street, London W8 and
75 King Street, Manchester.

Leather dress by Alexander Molyneux
from Pellicano, 63 South Molton Street,
London W1; leather tights from Ad Hoc,
38 Kensington High Street, London W7;
boots by Robert Clergerie from 67
Wigmore Street, London W9

photography by **craig mcdean**
styling by **edward enninful**
assisted by **neil shuart** and **cyprien de coteau**
hair by **eugene souleman** for trevor sorbie
make-up by **pat mcgrath** at streeters

## WHO'S BAD GIRL

When Madonna graced our screens way back in *Desperately Seeking Susan*, Milla Jovovich was just ten years old. "She represents a whole era and we'll know we've passed into another when we're not into her anymore," says this smart, sassy 20-year-old, who's wearing a good approximation of Material Girl gear. "I love the fluorescent stuff - look, I've got that acid coloured nail varnish on." The years since then have been a blur for Milla, international fashion model and star of *Blue Lagoon II* while still a teenager; "I was totally driven by my mother (a Russian who worked as an actress in the '60s), but I rebelled against my life when I was 15. I'd got pretty big headed and that whole existence was stifling me." After her wild child break, Milla's made an impressive return - "I prayed to God every night to give me it all back" - and right now is doing just fine, thank you. She's the new Calvin Klein Escape girl; she catwalks for Katharine Hamnett and Blumarine; she's starring Luc Besson's new movie, *The Fifth Element*, currently filming in Prague, Africa and London. Although it's modelling that's paying her rent, the movie business is what really excites her. "Film shows how good you are because you've got to feel emotional for real every time." She coyly refuses to be drawn further, though: "Besson is very, very anal about his script and you don't screw around at this level - anyway, he'd get mad at me..." If you want to know more about Milla, there's nothing for it but wait. It's okay. You'll surely be hearing from her. **Christopher Rentrade**

Top by Ghost from Gloucester, Somerset
widerworld; Sneakers by Prada from 43/45
Sloane Street, London SW1

## FASHION edited by edward enninful and bomi odufunade

photography by sean ellis assisted by jd hair by eugene souleman for trevor sorbie grooming by alice ioanna at premier using aveda natural colour cosmetics models: james and guy defferay at storm, jesse at take two, quentin, jai-ci and polite dave

<u>Suits You</u> Spring, and a young man's fancy turns to... style, of course. If duffle coats and Hush Puppies aren't quite your thing (cheers, Oasis) then some might say a bit of smart suiting is in order. Just roll with it!

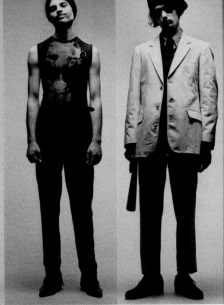

styling by Gianni Couji
Quentin wears suede jacket, sweater, trousers and shoes by John Rocha from Jaeash, 26 Sloane Street, London W1 and Gorgon, 36 St Mary's Street, Manchester.

styling by Bomi
James wears cotton jacket and matching waist trousers by Griffin from Space NK, 40 Northumberland Street, London WC2 and Aspecta, 85-87 Bridge Street, Manchester; boots by Red Wings from Shellys, branches nationwide.

styling by Cyprian De Coteau
Jesse wears suit by Brian Clarke from 2 Gerard Street, London W1; shirt by Dewhal Bachino from 9 Vimo Street, London W1; studded belt by Richard from Tucci, 100 High Street West, Sunderland, two-tone boots from Shellys.

styling by Neil Stuart
Guy wears taffeta trousers, devoré tigerprint vest and shoes by Alexander McQueen from Liberty, Regent Street, London W1.

styling by Pete Voss
Polite Dave wears cotton suit by Squire to order on 0171 404 1000, tie and smock by R Newbold from 7 Langley Court, London WC2; brogues by Paul Smith from 41-44 Floral Street, London WC2 and Smith & Westwood, Clayton Square Centre, Liverpool; beret by Kangol from department stores nationwide; sunglasses by Stussy from Doctor Jives, 113 Candleriggs, Glasgow.

styling by Soraya Dayani
Jai-Ci wears cotton jacket, shirt and trousers by Byrne from 31 Tower Street, London WC2; shoes by John Sweeper from The Duffer Of St George, 27 D'Arblay Street, London W1; tie by Soraya Dayani to order on 0171 729 1156.

14 i-D THE ALTERNATIVE ISSUE

i-D THE ALTERNATIVE ISSUE 15

---

Teresa wears lace body by Ann Summers from 70 Wardour Street, London W1 and 12-14 White Chapel, Liverpool.

photography by annette aurell
assisted by wade
styling by jane how
assisted by paula
make up by mary jane frost
hair by allan pichot for lora and guy
models ben jackson and teresa stewart

Teresa wears top by Helmut Lang from Jones, 13 Floral Street, London WC2; secondhand shirt from Camden Market, London NW1; shoes from Dancia, 187 Drury Lane, London WC2. Ben wears trousers by Helmut Lang from Browns, 23-27 South Molton Street, London W1; T-shirt from Rokkit, 225 Camden High Street, London NW1; vintage loafers from Black Out II, 51 Endell Street, London WC2.

# MORNING GLORY

## SO WHAT'S THE STORY?
## DON'T ASK, DON'T TELL

"What's the best way to dress to get sex?
You're asking the wrong boy! It's been so
long I'm obviously not doing it right"

**John Galliano, designer, no156**

Lace top by Helmut Lang from Shines, 13
Floral St, London WC2; jeans by Hysteric
Glamour from Hip, 14 Thomas Arcade, Leeds.

Halter top by Martin Margiela.

Sequin print dress by Martin
Margiela from Browns, 23-27
South Molton St, London W1.

photography by **mark borthwick**
assisted by **alex**
styling by **jane how**
hair by **ward** for bumble and bumble
make-up by **kevny campbell**

# SHOOTING
# STAR
Each and every season,
one particular model
captures fashion's zeit-
geist. Last time round it was androgyne aristo Stella
Tennant, before that perfectly poised Shalom Harlow,
and before her teutonic blonde bombshell Nadja
Auermann, who singlehandedly saw grunge off.
Guinevere Van Seenus is the new 'it' girl. This 18-year-
old Californian's kooky offbeat look is a world away
from the industry's Helenas and Lindas, yet designers
like Jil Sander, Miuccia Prada, Versace and Dolce e
Gabbanna are all queueing up to use her in their shows
and campaigns. "It feels really strange," she smiles. "I've
never thought of myself as pretty, but perhaps that's why
people remember my face. After you've seen a hundred
gorgeous models, when I appear it's kinda like 'who's
that girl?'" Who indeed? Just watch her star shine.

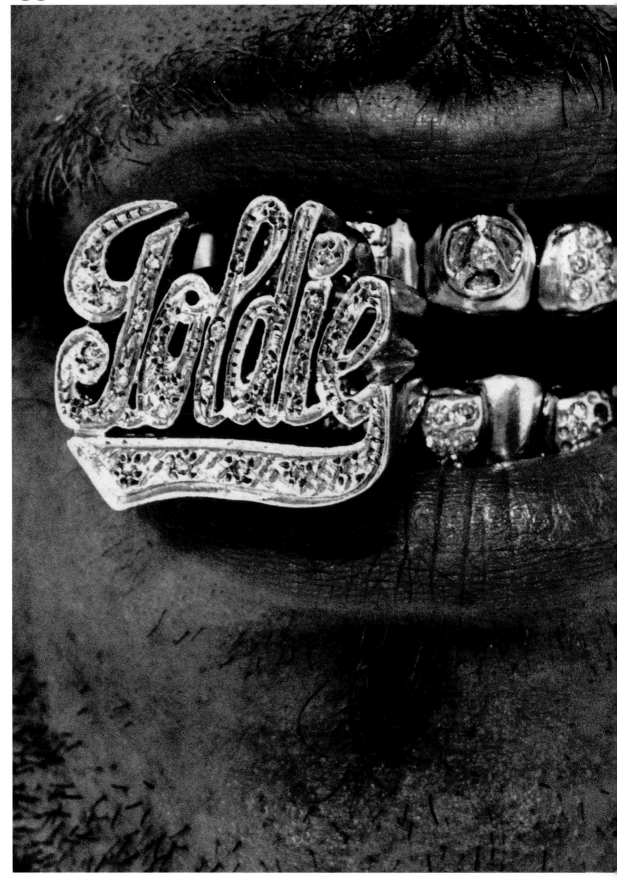

interview by **bethan cole**
photography by **lorenzo agius**

Goldie is jungle's first fully-fledged celebrity. You know this by now. He dates Björk. His debut album has sold quarter of a million copies. If his life before was intense, it was nothing like the last eighteen months. Now there's a new TV series, a film and another record. Can he continue to keep it real?

**G**old teeth flashing, glinting copper eyes fixed in concentration, compact muscular frame locked in perpetual kinetic activity; Goldie exudes an aura of energetic celebrity that seems like second nature. He paces around. He gesticulates emphatically. He morphs conversation into a vivid multidirectional segue of street philosophy, wild theory, anecdotal observation and incisive wisdom with a passion and charisma and wit that's hypnotic, intriguing and totally, utterly unique. When he nods sagely and says "I've always had a feeling ➤

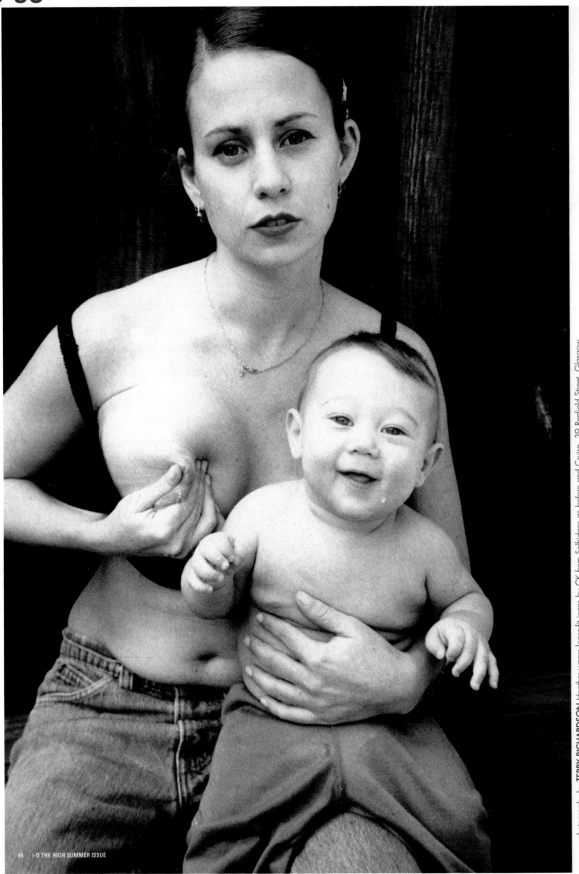

photography by **TERRY RICHARDSON** Heather wears loosefit jeans by CK from Selfridges as before and Cruise, 39 Renfield Street, Glasgow.

44   I-D THE HIGH SUMMER ISSUE

"It gets boring, the misconception of me
being so mean, moody, such a bitch. I'm not
a nasty person"

**Naomi Campbell, model, no155**

COME AGAIN
OH BOY,
WONDER WOMAN
EVA HERZIGOVA
IS BACK!

**London is ruling.** After a few grim years when all was quiet and glum, a bubble of energy burst in the capital, unleashing a wave of angry young talent. Out came Alexander McQueen, Copperwheat Blundell and Hussein Chalayan - the new rude school of design. Out came Suede, Elastica and Sleeper - the noise of Britpop. Damien Hirst, the Chapman Brothers and Mark Wallinger cut through the arty fart. The dirty realism of photographers Juergen Teller, David Simms, Corinne Day and Craig McDean ripped up the humourless artifice of high fashion. And everyone asked how long it could last?

Energy builds on energy. It is London-based photographers who are now at the helm of the international fashion industry. It is English models who are in the limelight - punky aristocrat Stella Tennant is the face of Chanel, Kate Moss is a household name. John Galliano is steering Givenchy, Vivienne Westwood is rumoured to be taking over the House Of Dior. Alexander McQueen, the foul-mouthed genius from the East End, is now being filling wardrobes for Sharon Stone and a post-natal Madonna. Danny Boyle's *Trainspotting* is a transatlantic box office smash. Ewan McGregor is Hollywood's new It man.

Everyone wants to buy what we've got. And back in London there are more in the making. Designers Antonio Berardi, Fabio Piras, Jessica Ogden and Brother Julian are cutting to the quick. Models Iris Palmer, Cali Rand, Honor Fraser and Jade Parfitt are striding through glossy magazines. London Fashion Week is round the corner and finally all eyes are on us. What we gave the world with a defiant two fingered salute is now being honoured worldwide. And as to its staying power? Well, after ten years of Thatcherism, the children who came of age in the '70s and '80s know the only thing to do is get on with it.

# CAPITAL
## WHY IS LONDON CALLING AGAIN?

TEXT BY HARRIET QUICK
PHOTOGRAPHY BY MAX VADUKUL
ASSISTED BY MARC BOYCE
CO-ORDINATED BY EDWARD ENNINFUL AND MATT JONES
MAKE-UP BY SHARON DOWSETT AT PREMIER USING ADEVA NATURAL COLOUR COSMETICS
HAIR BY LISA EASTWOOD AT PREMIER USING AVEDA PURE-FUME HAIRCARE
SHOT AT THE TOP FLOOR (CONTACT TONY ON 0973 650784)

**David Kappo**, 27, fashion designer for Dave & Joe. Wears army fatigues, shirt, shades and Nike trainers borrowed from boyfriend. **Favourite record?** *What Do I Have To Do?* by Kylie Minogue **Favourite place in London?** At home **Best thing about living in London?** Brilliant people

**Iris Palmer**, 19, model. Wears dress and shoes from Portobello Market, Sock Shop tights and Phillip Treacy hat. **Favourite Record?** *I Feel A Car Crash Coming On* by Sharkbait **Favourite place in London?** My flat **Best thing about living in London?** My friends

**11•96**

THE ENERGISED ISSUE    NO.158

cover star: **angela lindvall** photographed by **juergen teller november 1996**

## FASHION SPECIAL
# INTRODUCING NEW YORK'S NEW COOL

# i-D

©

i-DEAS, FASHION, CLUBS, MUSIC, PEOPLE

## OCEAN COLOUR SCENE IS DRUG TESTING TAKING THE PISS? HEAD RUSH: SPORT'S NEW HARD LINE THIS THUG'S LIFE: THE LEGACY OF TUPAC EVAN DANDO ON OASIS BOMBING THE BASS IN BOSNIA

# pure sexy!

**£2.20    $5.75**

## JUERGEN TELLER SHOOTS TO SCORE

FRANCS 38 LIRE 9,000 DM 13,50 PESETAS 625 D KR 59

"I created the Sound Factory. I should have probably not played ever again"

Junior Vasquez, DJ, no147

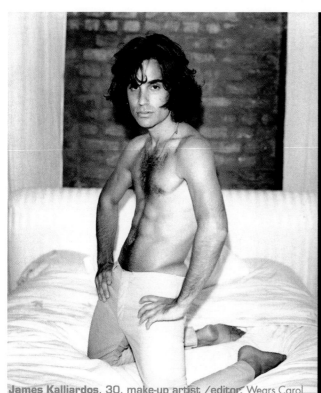

James Kalliardos, 30, make-up artist /editor. Wears Carol Christian Poell trousers and sheets by Sybilla. **What makes life worth living?** Sex **If you had one wish...** To be the next Jeff Stryker **Why are you in NYC?** There is no other place to be

Marina Faust, 24, artist. Wears secondhand dress and trousers and shoes from Florence. What makes life worth living? Sex and a square deal and one wish... Some I know and if you had one wish... to succeed in Why are you in NYC? Because where

Melissa Burns, actress, 18 (Ladies never tell). Wears cowboy rock'n'roll stripper outfit by Mojo and shoes by Vannessa Lundborg. **What makes life worth living?** A square deal and a firm handshake **If you had one wish...** To have a successful career in art and entertainment **Why are you in NYC?** Because I'm trying to build that career

THE UNDRESSED ISSUE    NO.159

cover star: **jamie rishar** photographed by **matt jones** december 199

# i-D

i-DEAS, FASHION, CLUBS, MUSIC, PEOPLE

unzip

THE UNDRESSED ISSUE

## DO WE HAVE TO SPELL IT OUT?

£2.20   US$5.75

9 770262 357020

CAN $6.95 FRANCE 28 LIRE 9,00, DM 12,50 PESETAS 635 9 KR 60

"I get paranoid. When I'm writing I have to make sure no-one can see. When I wrote *Kids* I had to do it in my grandma's basement"

**Harmony Korine, film-maker, no146**

PHOTOGRAPHY BY ELLEN VON UNWERTH HAIR BY WARD MAKE-UP BY KAY MONTANA BRANDI AND BIJOUX WEAR CLOTHES FROM PARIS FLEA MARKETS. **Brandi and Bijoux**, 18, models. **Fragrance?** Essential rose oil **Last thing you take off at night?** Underwear **First thing you put on in the morning?** Drink coffee, don't put anything on **Where are you happiest naked?** On the beach **Who would you most like to undress?** Nobody yet

Thought you had seen the back of Kylie?

40   I-D THE UNDRESSED ISSUE

# 1996

"The whole road protest movement is about people in Britain having a vision which counteracts the popular image that we're the blank generation, that we've got no beliefs and no energy"

**Kate, eco warrior, no150**

# 1997

January. The Escape Issue no160. Cover star: Kelli. Photography by Stephane Sednaoui, styling by William Baker and Neil Rodgers

February. The Next Generation Issue no161. Cover star: Annie Morton. Photography by Terry Richardson

March. The New Beauty Issue no162. Cover star: Sharleen Spiteri. Photography by Craig McDean, styling by Edward Enninful

April. The Outlook Issue no163. Cover star: Courtney Love. Photography by Ellen von Unwerth, styling by Wendy Schecter

May. The Desirable Issue no164. Cover star: Gaz Coombes. Photography by Lorenzo Agius, styling by Greg Faye and Justin Laurie

June. The Hot Issue no165. Cover star: Susan Carmen. Photography by Craig McDean, styling by Edward Enninful

July. The Clean & Fresh Issue no166. Cover star: Raina. Photography by Matt Jones, styling by Karl Plewka

August. The Obsession Issue no167. Cover star: Kate Moss. Photography by Terry Richardson

September. The Next Issue no168. Cover star: Kylie Minogue. Photography by Mark Mattock, styling by Fiona Dallenegra

October. The Killer Issue no169. Cover star: Audrey. Photography by Juergen Teller, styling by Venetia Scott

November. The Influential Issue no170. Cover star: Mel B. Photography by Terry Richardson, styling by Patti Wilson

December. The Outrage Issue no171. Cover star: Laura Foster. Photography by David Sims, styling by Edward Enninful

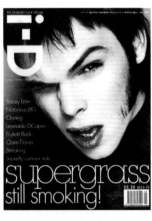

THE NEW BEAUTY ISSUE NO. 162

cover star: **sharleen from texas** photographed by **craig mcdean** march 1997

# SPECIAL BEAUTY ISSUE

i-DEAS, FASHION, CLUBS, MUSIC, PEOPLE

**UGLY BEAUTIFUL: WORKING FASHION'S LATEST LOOK**

**MIUCCIA PRADA AND REI KAWAKUBO UNZIPPED**

**FIGHTING FIT: CLASH OF THE TRAINER TITANS**

**ARE DRUGS DRIVING YOU MAD?**

**TEXAS • PRINCE NASEEM • LUSCIOUS JACKSON**

# you're gorgeous!

£2.20  US$ 5.75

## PUTTING ON FASHION'S FRESH NEW FACE

03

9 770262 357020

CAN $6.95 FRANCS 38 LIRE 9,000 DM 13,50 PESETAS 625 D KR 59

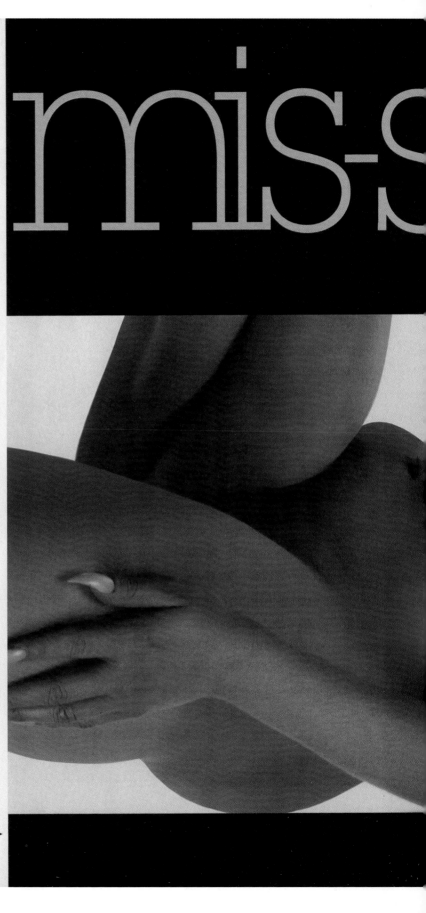

"Photographing Sophie Dahl felt like breaking fashion's last taboo. After all, there are no images of women who look like this - to be honest, there isn't even the vocabulary to describe women who look like this. But I'm sure that this size and shape of model is about to break through. I shot Sophie naked so you could see the flesh, without clothes getting in the way. It's something I'm going to push if it kills me. Not that I'm criticising skinniness, but it's disappointing that fashion only takes into account one body shape. Sophie is a gorgeous, powerful extreme; what we need is an acceptance of the whole range of sizes between that and thin, an acknowledgement that there's no need to conform to the so-called 'perfect shape' any more. I'm not sure how it'll happen: perhaps this kind of fashion revolution has to be designer led."
**NICK KNIGHT, PHOTOGRAPHER.**

"There's nothing sexual about models' typical androgynous skinniness. I look a bit pornographic and that scares people. It's a Freudian thing; breasts are confrontational. One of my first jobs was an Italian *Vogue* shoot with photographer Ellen Von Unwerth and the stylist was absolutely horrified by me. At first she thought I must be some kind of assistant and demanded I made the tea. When it was pointed out that I was actually one of the models, she shrieked, "Oh my God, what the hell am I supposed to do with *that*?" She put me in a gold lamé dress, the only thing she had that wasn't a size eight, and I just burst into tears because I looked like a Hollywood Boulevard whore. But Ellen was fantastic, she said "Ignore the bitch, we'll shoot you naked." I'm big and sexy and not ashamed of it. If people have a problem with that then it's very much *their* problem."
**SOPHIE DAHL, MODEL.**

**NOT SO LONG AGO YOU KNEW WHERE YOU WERE WITH BEAUTY. NOW THE MISTAKES AND MISFITS HAVE TAKEN OVER AND PIN-UPS AIN'T WHAT THEY USED TO BE. BUT WILL FASHION'S LATEST LOVE AFFAIR BE ANYTHING MORE THAN A FLEETING FLIRTATION?**

Funny old business, fashion. Not so long ago you knew where you were with it. Now the mistakes and misfits have taken over and pin-ups just▸

napes

photography by **nick knight** art direction by **alexander mcqueen** styling by **katy england** hair by **clovis** at aurelien make-up by **topolino** at topo management model: **sophie dahl** at storm computer artist: **steve seal** shot at metro studios, london

# Just enough to tease ya!

ANNIE

PHOTOGRAPHY BY
TERRY RICHARDSON.
STYLING BY
EDWARD ENNINFUL,
ASSISTED BY
NEIL STUART.
HAIR BY
JOHNNIE SAPONG
AT CUTS USING AVEDA.
MAKE-UP BY
FRANCELLE VALERY
AT STREETERS NY.
MODEL:
ANNIE MORTON
AT DNA NYC.
THANKS TO DAVID
RODGERS AND ALL AT
THE KATY BARKER
AGENCY.

Sequin dress by La
Perla from
Harvey Nichols,
Knightsbridge,
London SW2; knick-
ers by Calvin Klein,
from department
stores, nationwide.

Jennifer wears secondhand tube dress from Oxfam, branches nationwide; net top, stylist's own.

# SW16
## HARD LINES FOR TUFF TIMES IN THE DEEP SOUTH

PHOTOGRAPHY BY DONALD CHRISTIE STYLING BY
TARA ST HILL. MODELS: GEORGINA AT ELITE
PREMIER, JENNIFER AT STORM, KEVIN AND DANIEL.

Georgina wears print top by Flynow Chanman from Pellicano, 65 South Molton Street,
London W1; trousers by Joelynian from Koh Samui, 65 Monmouth Street, London WC2
and Geese, Barton Arcade, Deansgate, Manchester.

Kevin wears print T-shirt by People Corporation from Jones, 13 Floral Street, London
WC2, enquiries on 0171 251 9961; trousers by 6876 from Stoosrs, 22-27 South Molton
Street, London W1 and Aspecto, 95 Bridge Street, Manchester; vintage Nike Air Max
trainers from Hurne, 39 Beak Street, London W1.

cover star: **courtney love** photographed by **ellen von unwerth** april 1997

£2.20 US$5.75

9 770262 357020

i-D

DEAS, FASHION, CLUBS, MUSIC, PEOPLE

ex!

uccess!

ll-American

xcess!

OURTNEY

omes clean

ECSTASY

Is there

still

something

you don't

know?

86   i-D THE OUTLOOK ISSUE

HUSSEIN CHAYLAYAN IS AVAILABLE
FROM JONES, 15 FLORAL STREET,
LONDON WC2, INFO ON 0171 240 5224
PHOTOGRAPHY BY JULIE SLEAFORD
ASSISTED BY ALAN SCRYMGEOUR
HAIR BY LISA EASTWOOD AT
PREMIER USING AVEDA
MAKE-UP BY WENDY ROWE AT
DEBBIE WALTERS FOR SHU UEMURA
MODEL: ELLIE AT BOOKINGS

PHOTOGRAPHY BY
DONALD CHRISTIE
STYLING BY
JUDY BLAME
HAIR BY
NEIL MOODIE
FOR ZOO USING AVEDA
MAKE-UP BY
DEBBIE STONE
AT PREMIER
MODELS: MARTA
AT STORM
AND GUY AT TAKE 2

# SCARED STIFF
### sewing seeds on the crow road

Knit and silk scarf dress by Darryl Black from Regular Store, 16
Earlham Street, London WC2.

Coat and suit by Paul Smith from 40-44 Floral Street, London WC2 and Strand, 22
Queen Victoria Street, Leeds; fluorescent jacket by PS Paul Smith from Harvey
Nichols, Knightsbridge, London SW3 and Van Mildert, 21 Elvert Bridge, Durham.

"People expect art to be a surrogate religion, to show everything that's edifying, principled and wonderful. At the movies, gratuitous violence and sex are accepted as a condition of theatre but going to look at art means meaningless paintings. Why should that be?"

**Jake and Dinos Chapman, artists, no171**

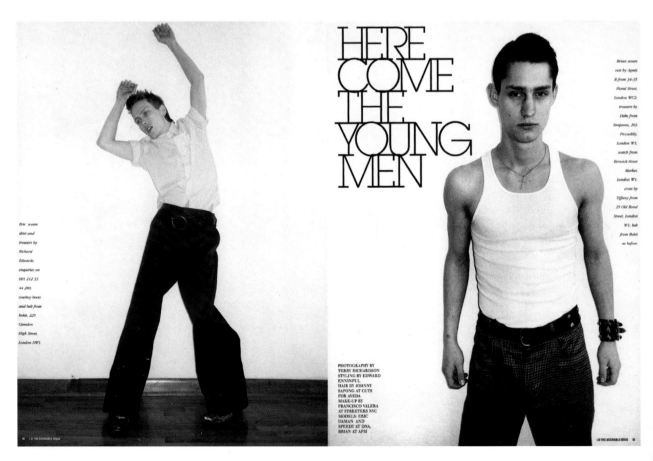

*Eric wears shirt and trousers by Richard Edwards, enquiries on 001 212 55 44 280; cowboy boots and belt from Bukit, 225 Camden High Street, London NW1.*

HERE
COME
THE
YOUNG
MEN

*Brian wears vest by Agnès B from 34-35 Floral Street, London WC2; trousers by Daks from Simpsons, 203 Piccadilly, London W1; watch from Berwick Street Market, London W1; cross by Tiffany from 25 Old Bond Street, London W1; belt from Bukit as before.*

PHOTOGRAPHY BY
TERRY RICHARDSON
STYLING BY EDWARD
ENNINFUL
HAIR BY JOHNNY
SAPONG AT CUTS
FOR AVEDA
MAKE-UP BY
FRANCESCO VALERA
AT STREETERS NYC
MODELS: ERIC
DAMAN AND
SPEEDY AT DNA,
BRIAN AT APM

# clarity

Photography by Steven Klein
Styling by Edward Enninful
Hair by Gavin for John Frieda Salon

Photography by Matt Jones
Styling by Vanina Sorrenti
Hair by Zaiya at Susan Price Inc
Make-up by Shally at Streeters
Model: Lola Schnabel

Lola wears dress by Ghost from
13-14 Hinde Street, London W1.

# purity

Jacks Lamp by Tom Dixon
Alek wears shirt by Comme des Garçons, as before; hot pants by Mark Whittaker from Liberty, Regent Street, London W1; shoes by Alexander McQueen from Pellicano, 63 South Molton Street, London W1 and Hervia, The Royal Exchange, Manchester.

Fantastic Plastic Elastic
Chair by Ron Arad

Alex wears boob tube by Mark Whittaker, as before;
shirt and shoes by Alexander McQueen, as before.

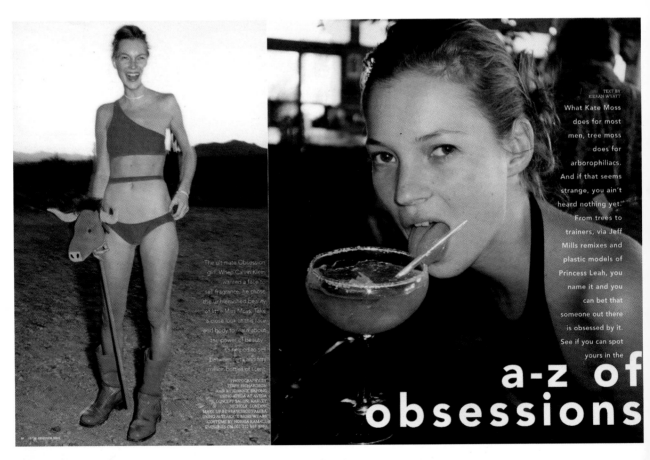

The ultimate Obsession girl. When Calvin Klein wanted a face to sell fragrance, he chose the unblemished beauty of little Miss Moss. Take a close look at this face and body to learn about the power of beauty. It's helped to sell between forty and fifty million bottles of scent.

PHOTOGRAPHY BY TERRY RICHARDSON. HAIR BY JOHNNIE SAPONG USING AVEDA AT AVEDA CONCEPT SALON, HARVEY NICHOLS, LONDON. MAKE-UP BY FRANCESCO VALERA USING AVEDA. KATE MOSS WEARS COSTUME BY NORMA KAMALI. ENQUIRIES ON 001 212 957 9797.

TEXT BY KIERAN WYATT

What Kate Moss does for most men, tree moss does for arborophiliacs. And if that seems strange, you ain't heard nothing yet. From trees to trainers, via Jeff Mills remixes and plastic models of Princess Leah, you name it and you can bet that someone out there is obsessed by it. See if you can spot yours in the

# a-z of obsessions

CONCEPT BY
PAT MCGRATH
PHOTOGRAPHY BY
CHAYO MATA
CO-ORDINATION BY
MICAELA TOLEDO

# angels of harlem

Jo-Ann Broomfield,
18, sales assistant
at PayLess

PHOTOGRAPHY BY MARK BORTH
ASSISTED BY CHRIS S
STYLING BY JANE
ASSISTED BY REBECCA
AND CAMERON
HAIR BY NEIL MOODIE FOR
MODELS: ZORA STAR A
AND CORDELIA AT S
THANKS TO ALL AT SALT FALLS
EQUINUNK, ENQUIRIES: 717 22

*modern nature*

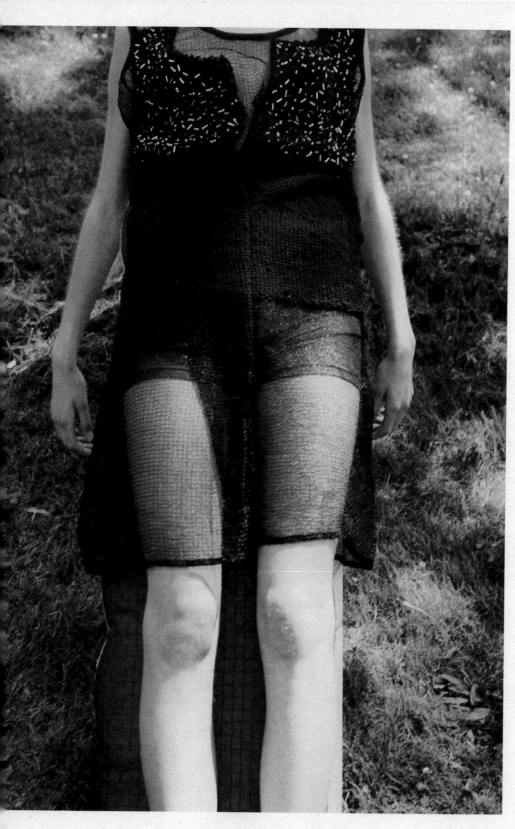

Far left: **Zora** wears dress

by Alexander McQueen

from Browns, 25-27 South

Molton Street, London W1

and Brown Thomas, 88-95

Grasgon Street, Dublin;

scarf from John Lewis,

branches nationwide.

Left: **Cordelia** wears shorts

and dress by Comme Des

Garçons, 59 Brook Street,

London W1, enquiries on

0171 493 1258.

"Apart from all the usual hopes for the
world and the future that everyone shares,
we hope that i-D continues with the
independent force and voice that it has
always used"

**Maison Martin Margiela, design house, no166**

Right: Sam wears jogging pants by Raf Simons, shirt and tie by Prada. Below: Shey wears shirt by Burberry's from 165 Regent Street, London W1 and Fenwick, Northumberland Street, Newcastle-Upon-Tyne, jumper and belt by YSL from 76 Long Acre, London WC2 and Limeys, 58 Bridlesmith Gate, Nottingham, pants by Raf Simons, shoes by Birkenstock from 37 Neal Street, London.

Left: Aaron wears T-shirt, trousers, coat, shoes, hat and belt by Paul Smith.  Above: Aaron wears wool check coat, trousers and shirt by Agnés B; brogues by Clarks; his own hat.

THE INFLUENTIAL ISSUE NO.170

cover star: **mel b** photographed by **terry richardson** november 199

# i-D

i-D ... CLUBS, MUSIC, PEOPLE

£2.20  US$5.75

the best!

"I always wear clothes for psychological reasons."

**isabella blow** photographed by mark mattock

"Lots of things inspire me. The unexpected, in obvious situations, never fails."

**jane how** photographed by carter smith

"My philosophy is basically to make people happy."

**joseph** photographed by jeremy murch

"I may be getting on a bit but I have a sense of danger and daring about what I do. I'm not afraid."

**judy blame** photographed by craig mcdean

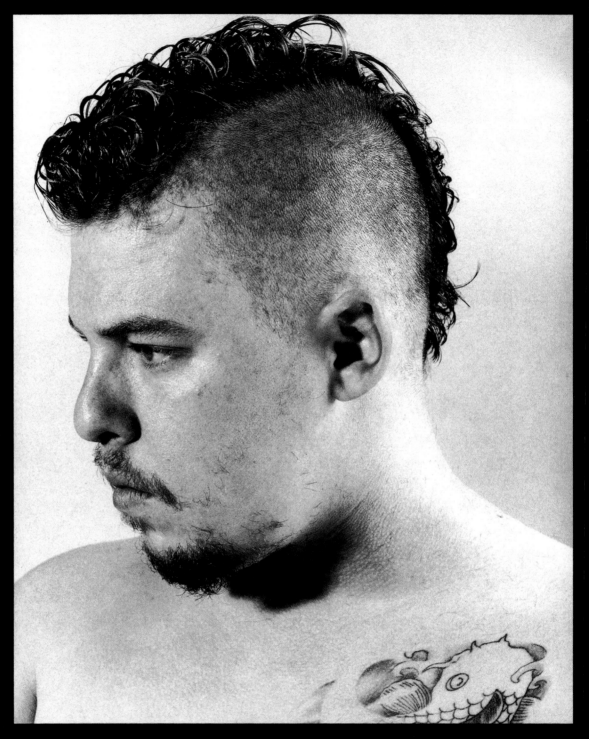

"If I've influenced fashion it's by pissing everyone off."

**alexander mcqueen** photographed by craig mcdean

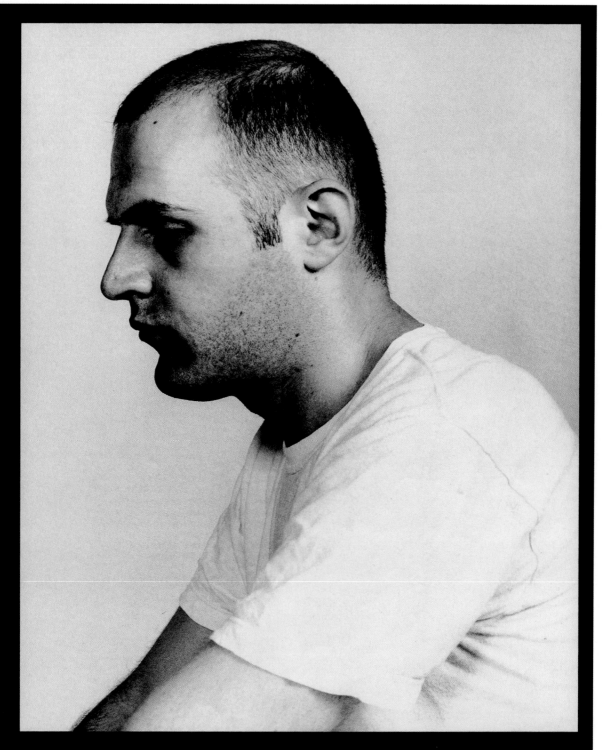

"People don't have to like what I do as long as they have some kind of opinion about it. I want my work to inspire in some way, like modern art."

**hussein chalayan** photographed by craig mcdean

THE OUTRAGE ISSUE NO.171

cover star: **laura fost**... ...tographed by **david sims** december 199...

£2.20 **US$5.75**

9 770262 357006

12

CAN $6.95 FRANCS 28 LIRE 9,700 DM 14.90 PESETA...

# i-D

...EAS... ...ION, CLUBS, MUSIC, PEOPLE

intrigue

# 1997

"I never ever set out to be famous. But to say it scares me also scares me, because it's as though I'm anticipating that happening when it may not at all"

**Kate Winslet, actress, no165**

# 1998

Jan/Feb. The Active Issue no172. Cover star: Naomi Campbell. Photography by Elfie Semotan, styling by Edward Enninful

March. The Ego Issue no173. Cover star: La Vera Chapel. Photography by Donald Graham

April. The World Class Issue no174. Cover star: Alec Wek. Photography by Mark Mattock

May. The Supernatural Issue no175. Cover star: Kirsten Owen. Photography by Paolo Roversi, styling by Edward Enninful

June. The Urban Issue no176. Cover star: Maggie Rizer. Photography by Craig McDean, styling by Edward Enninful

July. The Global Issue no177. Cover star: Naomi Campbell. Photography by Jamil GS, styling by Jason Farrer

August. The Very Blue Issue no178. Cover star: Erin O'Connor. Photography by Juergen Teller

September. The Adult Issue no179. Cover star: Devon Aoki. Photography by Ellen von Unwerth, styling by Edward Enninful

October. The Forward Issue no180. Cover star: Shalom. Photography by Carter Smith, styling by Jane How

November. The Extravagant Issue no181. Cover star: Alissa. Photography by Kayt Jones, styling by Merryn Leslie

December. The Cheeky Issue no182. Cover star: Gisele. Photography by David Sims, styling by Anna Cockburn

November. Family Future Positive. Cover by Terry Jones

cover star: **giselle** photographed by **david sims december 1998**

# i-D

front

£2.50 US$6.75

the
art
of
hip
pop

knackered

"Giselle is certainly gorgeous. I'd marry her"

**David Sims, photographer, no182**

Photography by Mario Sorrenti, styling by Jane How

**PERFORMANCE**
i act up therefore i am

04•98

THE WORLD CLASS ISSUE NO.174

cover star: **alek wek** photograph
by **mark mattock april 19**

# i-D

©

i-Deas,fashion,clubs,music,

up

2.50 US$6.75

04

440

Photography by Mark Borthwick

"A team comprising 19 members"
## MAISON MARTIN MARGIELA
(House Of Martin Margiela)
He's viewed as the most influential force in fashion, the designer who pioneered grunge and created deconstruction. So all we need say about Martin Margiela's Spring/Summer '98 collection is that it'll be bound to catch on. Photographed here on members of his maison team, designed round the grocery bag and produced as a 'flat-pack', it's another innovation from a master of the art. **What are you working on?** Continuing **Future plans?** Continuity **What inspires you?** Continuance **Advice?** Continue!

---

Photography by Elfie Semotan, Styling by Edward Enninful

HAIR BY MICHAEL BOADI FOR BUMBLE & BUMBLE
MAKE-UP BY ISABELLA ROSENKRANZ AND DALIHA
MODELS LAURA MCDANIEL AT COMPANY MANAGEMENT,
EDWARD FERGUSON AT TAKE 2, JAN WEINOLD AND CLEMENS REYER AT FLAIR
ALL CLOTHES BY HELMUT LANG
THANKS TO WALTER SCHUPFER MANAGEMENT
SPECIAL THANKS TO THE ACADEMY OF FINE ARTS/SEMPA DEPOT VIENNA

"Ask my family and friends"
## HELMUT LANG
When it comes to modern ideas, no designer compares with Helmut Lang. For his Spring/Summer '98 collection, photographed on the following pages, he created new silhouettes through changing women's proportions. Hips were enhanced, traditional waistlines dropped and the body elongated by using stiff undershirts, slashed chiffons and coated fabrics to dramatic effect. What else can we say? Here's to another ten years of unsurpassed creativity.
**What are you wearing?** Nothing **What do you do?** Keep work and life in balance **What are you working on?** Moving to New York and keeping work and life in balance **Future plans?** I don't think about that **What inspires you?** I am still finding out but what ever it is, it's working **Advice?** Hold on

**04•98**

Photography by Sophie Delaporte, Styling by Kanako B Koga

PHOTOGRAPHIC ASSISTANCE BY EMANUEL PINEAU
PROP STYLING BY LITZA GEORGOPOULOS
HAIR BY WATARU AT L'ATELIER NY
MAKE-UP BY WILLIAM FALKNER AT CALLISTE
SHOT AT LE PETIT OISEAU VA SORTIR

Ostrich skin dress by Fred Sathal

"Sharp, mystic, resolute, player, luminary"

**FRED SATHAL**

From the creative costuming of Perrier's 'Ice Queen' ads to the dressing of style muse Björk, Fred Sathal always takes an intelligent art perspective on fashion design. **What do you do?** Projection of the spirit upon the body, anticipate, avoid easiness and common places

**What are you working on?** A linear figure covered by a special cut enhancing movement, the anatomy's articulation seen with a mineral, vegetal, urban vision: a hybrid body **Future plans?** Creating a real laboratory cell inside my house, creating organic clothes that harmonise with the earth **What inspires you?** Life, in all its shapes, that keeps on surprising me **Advice?** Keep simple

124 i-D THE WORLD CLASS ISSUE

442

# 05•98

## "Beauty is obscene"

**Nobuyoshi Araki, photographer, no175**

Photography by Paolo Roversi, Styling by Edward Enninful

ASSISTED BY MERRYN LESLIE, HAIR BY EUGENE SOULEIMAN
USING TIGI HAIRCARE PRODUCTS FOR TONI & GUY,
MAKE-UP BY PAT McGRATH FOR AVEDA, MODELS: KIRSTEN OWEN AND LINDA BIRE
THANKS TO VINCENT AT MARYAN DE BEAUPRE PRODUCTIONS AND YVLTE EBERGUE

# white red

Alissa wears top by Yohji Yamamoto, leather gloves, as order, by La Croix.

Hadil wears vest by Daryl K, suede necklace by Eaclesse Bracciali, gloves by La Croix.

Sleeves and stockings by Ann Demeu

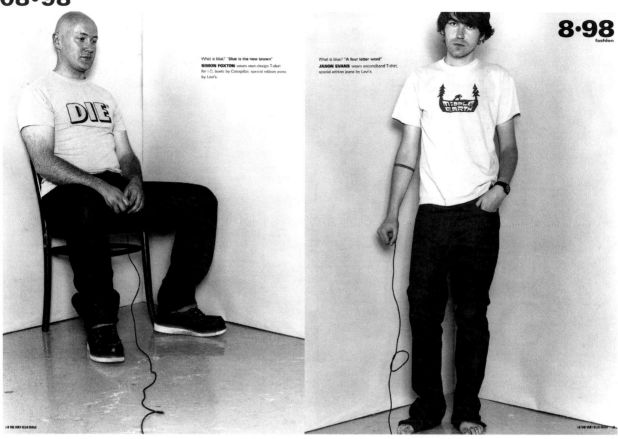

What is blue? "Blue is the new brown"
**SIMON FOXTON** wears own-design T-shirt
for i-D, boots by Caterpillar, special edition jeans
by Levi's.

What is blue? "A four letter word"
**JASON EVANS** wears secondhand T-shirt,
special edition jeans by Levi's.

What is blue? "Blue is my Little Walter tattoo"
**ARMANI EXCHANGE PHOTOGRAPHED BY COLIN LANE**
Thanks to Raja at Colour Edge, NYC. El Capitan wears denim hat, £24, by Armani Exchange.

What is blue? "Old ladies' hair rinses"
**DIESEL PHOTOGRAPHED BY JEREMY MURCH**
Styling by Fiona Dallanegra. Ulla at Models 1 wears denim skirt, £65, by D Diesel, 'bomba' jacket by Boudicca.

What is blue? "Roses are red, violets are blue, onions are smelly and so are you"

**MARTIN MARGIELA PHOTOGRAPHED BY MARIO SORRENTI**

Photographic assistance by Source. Styling by Jane How. Styling assistance by Christine Baker. Thanks to Richard Lore studios, NYC. Denim dress, £85, by Martin Margiela; Jack-in-a-box by Jane How.

What is blue? "Not my political tendencies"

**LEE PHOTOGRAPHED BY PETE DRINKELL**

Styling by Nell Stuart. Louise Hargreaves at Select wears slim-fit denim jacket, £59.99, and jeans, £54.99, by Lee; belt to order by Rifat Ozbek; crochet mules by Christian Louboutin for Julien MacDonald.

What is blue? "my favourite colour"

**TOMMY HILFIGER PHOTOGRAPHED BY CRAIG MCDEAN**

Joe Williams wears utility jeans, £70, by Tommy Hilfiger.

What is blue? "The sky"

**APC PHOTOGRAPHED BY MICHEL MOMY**

Lucien wears indigo jeans, £29, by APC; vest by Jellybaby.

Interview by Tony Marcus
Photography by Matt Jones

McQueen's not
dead - just being
born anew. Fear
and clothing are
still the passions
of fashion's
fresh prince

# I AM THE
# RESURRECTION

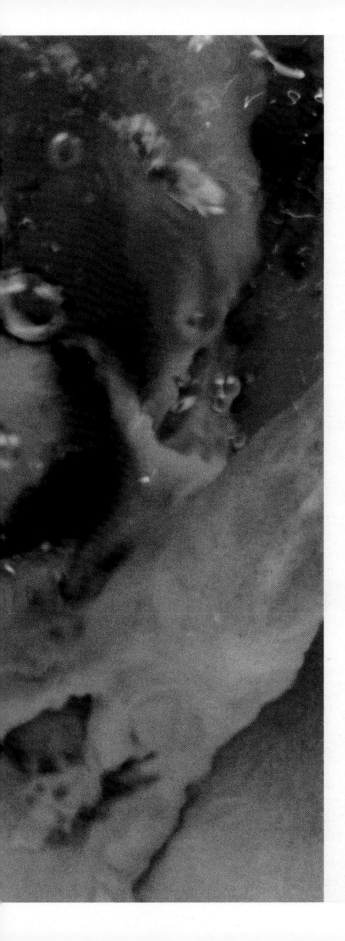

**"So you're not a fashion journalist,"** sniffs Alexander McQueen. His tone suggests this might make communication difficult. Not that it matters where I come from - the results, he insists, will be the same. "I don't think I've ever come across one journalist that actually writes what comes from their heart. It comes from what they think people want to hear. Most of the time I don't even read the shit any more."

So the next hour will be a challenge, then?

"Not at all," he says. "It's a challenge to yourself. To see if you can understand me and get me right. It's not a challenge for me."

Alexander McQueen's pre-interview chat suggests he more than senses his own importance. The fashion world rightly believes McQueen to be the most exciting designer on the planet, defining the way we'll dress in years to come. He's also the most celebrated. The very essence of 'cool' (and often cruel) Britannia, he combines provocative attitude with a precocious talent. And his rise has been meteoric: from St Martin's student to head designer at French couture house Givenchy in less than five years, this rocket has no brakes. So an hour with Alexander McQueen is rare and precious time - and he knows it.

To start, I ask about one of his designs. We're in his Hoxton studio (Lee, as he likes to be called, is finishing a lunch of jacket potato with shrimp-pink chilli-muck) and right up close is a man's frock-coat, seemingly priestly or historical. It's grey, white and sparkles with a showering of beads. Beneath and seemingly printed onto the beads (funky stuff, but McQueen is master of fabric and technique) is a Victorian photograph of two little girls. It's a very beautiful coat - it seems designed to be looked at, a museum piece or clothing for a world yet to exist.

"It's a kind of clerical-looking coat," muses Lee. "But then you have these young girls... I'm a really anti-church type person. You can say this juxtaposition refers to paedophilia by the church but it covers a wide range of things. I can't work on just one reference."

It sparkles most prettily, I hazard.

"There's a naievety to it," he replies. "The idea is to subvert authoritarianism. It goes with the church, teachers at schools, politicians. It comes with hierarchies. I always turn a negative into a positive. I don't sit there and moan about it. I show it the way it is."

Alexander McQueen is far out. Nobody else would dare cut a coat in such an image. But his clothes and his catwalks seem loaded with residual and personal meaning. In fact, his shows are expressive enough to suggest abstract, symbol-making forms like contemporary dance and physical theatre. His 1997 presentation, *Joan*, ended with a distinct visual metaphor - a model, in a red beaded dress, her face covered in a red beaded hood, dancing (or, more accurately,

➤

2001 (m

For the 1998 Florence Biennale, fashion and film fa

With the creative participation of Julien Macdonald, Daryl K, Comme des Garçons
Scott Crolla, Susan Cianciolo, Hussein Chalayan, Veronique Branquinho, Antonio Berardi,
Walter Van Beirendonck, John Bartlett, Alessandro Dell'Acqua, Tristan Webber, Junya
Watanabe, Ter et Bantine, Rossella Tarabini, Lawrence Steele, Raf Simons, Jeremy Scott,
Kostas Murkudis, Issey Miyake, Alexander McQueen, Martin Margiela

inus 3)

forward together to the future

**10•98**

mons PHOTOGRAPHED BY Kayt Jones STYLED BY Merryn Leslie GROOMING Jennie Roberts PHOTOGRAPHY ASSISTANT Teresa Cottrell PROPS Combis by

Wool cape, wool pleated skirt, leather boots and silver
mirror head mask, all by Hussein Chalayan.

# wild life

**"Horror is the** appropriate response," says photographer Nick Knight about *Ape*, his startling photograph of a skinned monkey. Fur and flesh stripped back to reveal the raw meat inside, teeth bared in a final defiant snarl, it shows a once wild animal reduced to nothing more than a sack of sinew and bone. "I shot it with reference to the fashion industry," says Knight, whose visionary images have helped to shape that set-up over the last two decades. "It wasn't supposed to be anti-fur but it was an attempt to bring home the truth - if you take the skin off an animal, this is how the animal looks." An appropriate message for a season where fur stalked the capitals' catwalks, where the theme of luxury got translated back into an age-old cliché of wealth and glamour. "I wanted to show the shock of the fur trade and what it really does to animals," Knight adds, explaining that the monkey died of natural causes and was borrowed from a taxidermist for this shoot. "People should be aware of what they wear and where it comes from. Then they can make a value decision." **AVRIL MAIR** *Ape, 1997* by **NICK KNIGHT**

## bodily functions

**I want Mario Testino** to take a picture of me. I want him to make me look beautiful, make my skin glow and capture my smile for posterity. I want him to record on film the definitive image of myself: spirit, soul, warts-and-all, because that is what he does - he captures the moment. His first book, *Any Objections?*, is full of them, his most amazing images being created from 'non-moments'. In black and white, and also in colour, he documents the farcical, the intimate, fat, thin, ugly, beautiful, the tacky and the chic. He has waved ➤

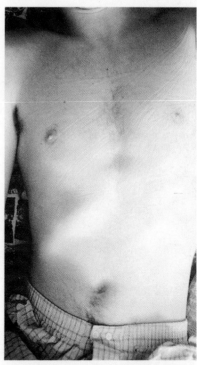

# IS THIS LUXURY?

a wide open space or a wardrobe wedged full of costly cuts? what would make your life more luxurious?

Photography by Marc Lebon
Styling and concept by Soraya Dayani

Photography assisted by Jake Gavin

Shot at Crunch Studios

Models: Nick Taylor, Omon Prunner, Carryl Phillips, Luther Emmiful, Darren Davey, Tom Hartley, Stephen Moray and Jake Gavin

## FACE IT

This page: Tom wears jacket by Paul Smith; wool shirt by Kenzo Homme; secondhand tie. Right, from top to bottom: Jake wears secondhand shirt; evening jacket by Alexander McQueen. Nick wears moleskin jacket by Byblos; secondhand Pan Am T-shirt; customised shirt by Muji. Karl wears polka dot jacket by Etro; shirt by Paul Smith; T-shirt by Michael Robinson.

You can tell why he's Madonna's favourite. At the age of 21, Theyskens is already dressing the Material Girl in his aggressively dramatic designs, favouring floor-sweeping ballgowns and S&M-inspired leather corsetry. And all this after just two collections. Cheekiest thing you've done? "Something to do with frogs... you couldn't try"

**OLIVIER THEYSKENS PHOTOGRAPHED BY DUC LIAO**

Maverick, modernist and thorn in the side of French fashion, Scott has graduated from frightening Rich White Women with his one-legged trousers to patronage by Björk and the prestigious Futur Grand Createur prize at the Venus de la Mode Awards. What's cheeky about this? "What's cheeky?"

**JEREMY SCOTT PHOTOGRAPHED BY DUC LIAO**

# a girl called gisele

Gisele, commercial girl, on the cover of i-D. Excuse me? Is this some heavy dose of super-irony, or a simple case of being blown-away by unquestionable beauty? Maybe it's both. With sexy covers for mainstream men's mags, not to mention campaigns for big-hitting clients like Ralph Lauren, D&G and Missoni, the global profile of this 18-year-old belle from Brazil is shooting sky high. And with that all-important Steven Meisel stamp of approval, Gisele can comfortably lay claim to the title of 'model of the moment'. But so what? Shouldn't we be using 'odd' models to create new boundaries of beauty, to redefine industry standards and then watch those self-same girls move into the mainstream to make a mint? Well, yes. But in a humorous twist of trends, this girl from the pages of American Vogue and Bazaar has now made her way leftfield towards us, propelled by the passion of photographer David Sims who just can't get enough of her hitherto undiscovered edge. "She's certainly gorgeous," says Sims. "I'd marry her". Yet by dressing Gisele in customised Champion T-shirts, and eschewing the clichéd body-defining oils which have characterised much of her previous work, Sims manages to show Gisele in a radically different and highly delectable light. Very funny - popular and ha ha.

**TOBIAS PEGGS**

Photography by DAVID SIMS
Assisted by LEE BROOMFIELD
Styling by ANNA COCKBURN
Hair by GUIDO at Nicky Clarke using Haircmotherapy Products
Make-up by LINDA CANTELLO for Jed Paris

Left: GISELE wears antique padded quilt jacket by Jessica Ogden.
Right: GISELE wears box-tie dress by Jessica Ogden and customised Champion T-Shirt by Noki (available at The Pineal Eye, Broadwick Street, London W1)

**Matt** wears long wax cotton

Karl wears multi-zip coat by Raf Simons.

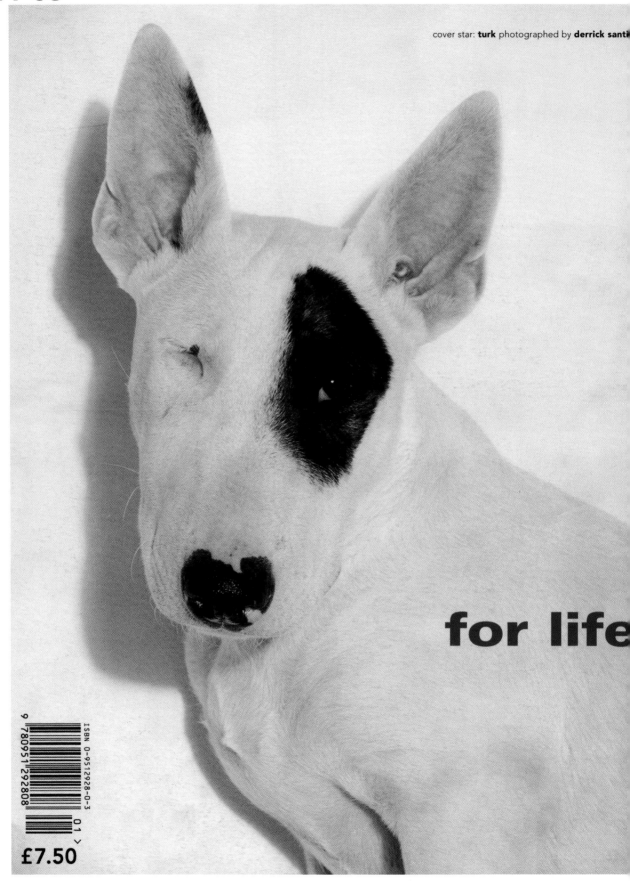

cover star: **turk** photographed by **derrick sant#**

for life

ISBN 0-9512928-0-3

£7.50

"Just because I'm a faggot, I can still give someone a whack if I want to"

**Alexander McQueen, designer, no179**

McQueen's Juicy Good Time Girl, aka Juice, and Alexander McQueen

England's Hope And Glory, aka Mouse, and Katy England

knight, nick

knight, nick

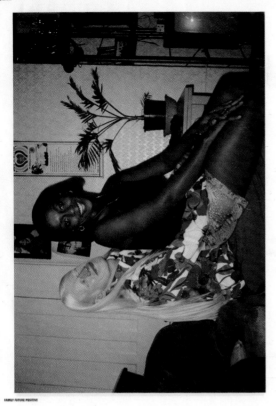

borthwick, mark and maria

borthwick, mark and maria

BORTHWICK, MARK AND MARIA Family means love and complete whole.

Mark, Maria, Bibi and Joe Borthwick - forever

Overdue, November 13, 1998

In memory of my brother Davide

Matt and Jicky's engagement day, 10 June 1998. This picture is dedicated to Amanda

**JONES, TRICIA** Wales - the view we've
shared with all the people we love.

# 1998

"Clear out your head. Ideas matter, the more austere the better. Intelligence is the new black"

Bethan Cole, writer, no180

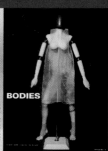

# 1999

Jan/Feb. The Emergency Issue no183. Cover star: Mel C. Photography by Donald Christie, styling by Merryn Leslie

March. The Kinetic Issue no184. Cover star: Amber Valetta. Photography by Richard Burbridge, styling by Edward Enninful

April. The Serious Fashion Issue no185. Cover star: Colette. Photography by Richard Burbridge, styling by Edward Enninful

May. The Skin & Soul Issue no186. Cover star: Heidi Klum. Photography by Max Vadukul, styling by Debbi Mason

June. The Intrepid Issue no187. Cover star: Lisa Ratcliffe. Photography by Paolo Roversi, styling by Edward Enninful

July. The Romance Issue no188. Cover star: Bridget Hall. Photography by David Sims, styling by Anna Cockburn

August. The Audible Issue no189. Cover star: Oluchi. Photography by Richard Burbridge, styling by Edward Enninful

September. The 1.9.99 Issue no190. Cover star: Christy Turlington. Photography by Richard Burbridge, styling by Edward Enninful

October. The Elevator Issue no191. Cover star: Guinevere. Photography by Craig McDean, styling by Edward Enninful

November. The Ideas Issue no192. Cover star: Naomi Campbell. Photography by David LaChapelle, styling by Patti Wilson

December. The Wisdom Issue no193. Cover star: Milla Jovovich. Photography by Matt Jones, styling by Cathy Dixon

"I hate people who say being famous is crap. I fucking love it"

Mel C, Spice Girl, no183

cover star: **amber valetta** photographed by **richard burbridge march 1999**

# i·D

*kinetic*

£2.80 US$7.25

03

LIRE 13.500 DM 18.00 PESETAS 890 D KR 78

9 770262 357044

Skirt by Yohji Yamamoto; clear mask and silver lips, both by Naomi Filmer.

SWINGING

Photography by David LaChapelle
Styling by Patti Wilson

Hair by Renato Campora for L'Atelier
Make-up by Sharon Gault for The Artist Group
Set design by Jason Hamilton
Models: Carolyn Park at Women,
Will Kemp of *Swan Lake* and De La Guarda

# N THE RAIN

THE SERIOUS FASHION ISSUE NO.185

cover star: **colette** photographed by **richard burbridge** april 199

# i·D

©

## seriously

£2.80 US$7.25

04

9 770262 357044

LIRE 13,500 DM 18.00 PESETAS 890 D KR 78

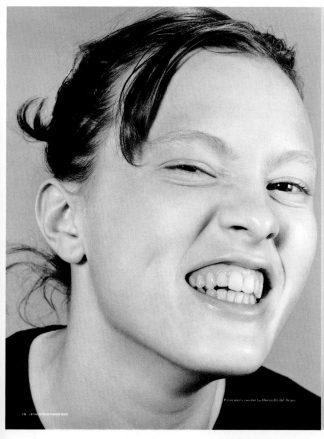

Karen wears sweater by Alessandro dell'Acqua

# DO WE LOOK SO STRANGE?

**Photography by Sophie Delaporte**
**Styling by Kanako Bouelle-Koga**

Photographic assistance by Emmanuel Pineau
Styling assistance by Ryoko
Hair by Terry Saxon at B Hebant
Make-up by Maria Olsson at C Heuze Vensemann
Model: Sian at Viva
Set design by Severine Baerel
Special thanks to Processus (01 4356 8787)
and 'Copy des Halles' (01 4233 2434)

Bracelet-sleeve T-shirt and jersey trousers, both by Dorothee Perret.

Trompe l'oeil print dress by Y's Yohji Yamamoto; leather shoes by Sartore.

05•99

THE SKIN & SOUL ISSUE NO.186

cover star. **heidi klum** photographed by **max vadukul** may 19

£2.80 US$7.25

05

9 770262 357044

LIRE 13,500 DM 18.00 PESETAS 890 D KR 7

i-D

bad sex

size does matte

what scares
men in bed

sex, scandal and
other wild things

obscene amounts
of sex

mountains c
molehills: the grea
big tit debate

wild life - kinky sex
among animals

constant stiffies

teach the wife t
bellydanc

why men are
scared of you

any woman
any time: pick u
tricks that never fa

sexy husband tricks

do you and h
equal great sex?

make your ow
sexy vide

get weird in bed

readers on th
rampag

tight little bums

twice as much sex
who's having i
how to get

hot new reasons
to have sex

478

Hell, look at that peach. I think I'm in love.

Max, please tell me it's not him again.

Photography by Max Vadukal
Styling by Debi Mason
at Art & Commerce

Photographic assistance by Luke Irons
Hair by Ric Pepino at Bryan Bantry
Make-up by Tracie Martyn at Artists
Models: Heidi Klum at Next, Diana Gartner
at Marilyn and Butch Hogan

ANY
WOMAN.
ANY
TIME

Left: Heidi wears sheer bikini by Alberta
Ferretti. Butch wears shorts by Diesel.
Above and following spread: Diana wears
bandeau bikini by Jean Paul Gaultier. Butch
wears T-shirt and shorts, both by Moschino.

Linen jacket by Polo
Ralph Lauren; stripe
T-shirt by Agnes B.

**VANINA SORRENTI**

Models: Susan Cianciolo, designer and
Lucia Pieroni, make-up artist

"Skin and soul. Balance and harmony."

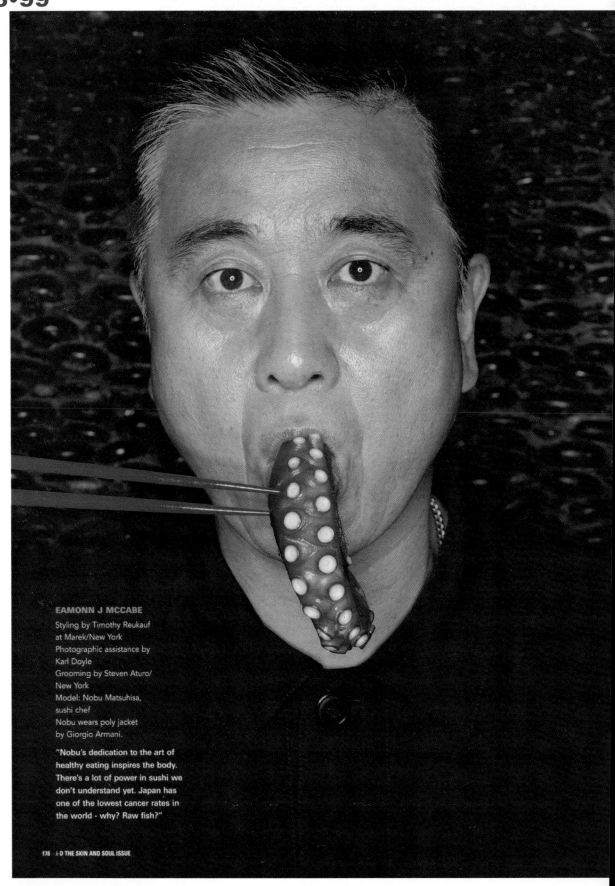

**EAMONN J MCCABE**

Styling by Timothy Reukauf
at Marek/New York
Photographic assistance by
Karl Doyle
Grooming by Steven Aturo/
New York
Model: Nobu Matsuhisa,
sushi chef
Nobu wears poly jacket
by Giorgio Armani.

"Nobu's dedication to the art of
healthy eating inspires the body.
There's a lot of power in sushi we
don't understand yet. Japan has
one of the lowest cancer rates in
the world - why? Raw fish?"

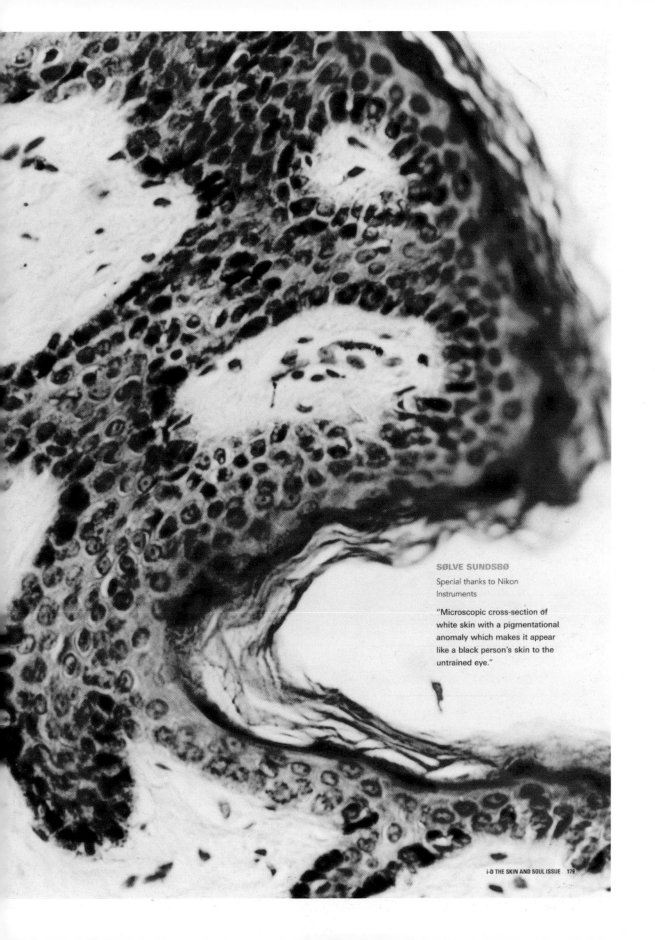

SØLVE SUNDSBØ

Special thanks to Nikon
Instruments

"Microscopic cross-section of
white skin with a pigmentational
anomaly which makes it appear
like a black person's skin to the
untrained eye."

## 06•99

"The thing I respect fashion for is its speed. Nobody's pressuring conventional artists to change every season. It's that weird thing fashion has, that unique love-me-hate-me thing. I know about you now so therefore I want to know about somebody else next season. I find that exhilarating"

**Nick Knight, photographer, no199**

Photography by Orion Best
Styling by James Sleaford

Colour artistic assistance by Daniel Garnett and Ros Rushton
Styling assistance by Charlotte Holdsworth and Lisa Horn
Make up by Liz Pugh at The Industry using Ruby & Millie
Hair by Robin Pawlok using Aveda
Model Zeke at Take 2

# FLY ME

Asymmetrical zip nylon jacket by Miu
Miu, shirt by Burro.

Leather scarf by Quentin Mackay; skirt by
Miu Miu; dog tags from Laurence Corner.

Jacket by AF Vandevorst.

Photography by Paolo Roversi
Fashion Editor Edward Enninful

Styling assistance by Lucy Allen
Hair by Eugene Soulieman
Make-up by Pat McGrath
Model: Emily at Next
Special thanks to John at Art and Commerce

Stole by Sonia Rykiel.

# WAITING FOR PETER

Dress from Rokit;
hand-held mirror from
Portobello Market.

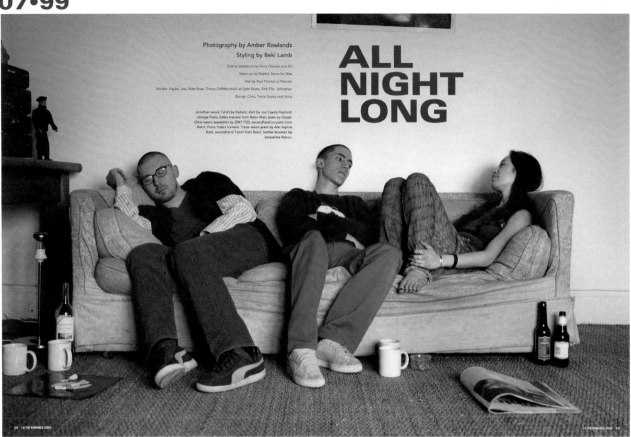

Photography by Amber Rowlands
Styling by Beki Lamb

Styling assistance by Anna Clausen and Kit
Make-up by Debbie Stone for Mac
Hair by Paul Percival at Premier
Models: Hayley, Joe, Matt Rose, Emma Griffiths-Malin at Little Boats, Rich File, Johnathan
Burnip, Chris, Tracie Storey and Skiny

Jonathan wears T-shirt by Kickers; shirt by Joe Casely-Hayford;
vintage Puma Dallas trainers from Retro Man; jeans by Diesel.
Chris wears sweatshirt by 20471120; secondhand trousers from
Rokit; Puma States trainers. Tracie wears jeans by Ann Sophie
Back; secondhand T-shirt from Rokit; leather bracelet by
Jacqueline Rabun.

# ALL NIGHT LONG

Heidi wears swimsuit from Domseys Warehouse,
NYC; kilt and leather boots by Wink, NYC.

# BADLANDS

Photography by Ellen Nolan
Styling by Malcolm Beckford

Photographic assistance by Rick Giles
Models: Matt, Nadia, Heidi and Jeff Von Schmidt
Special thanks to Rick Giles, Erica and Anne

cover star: **oluchi** photographed by **richard burbridge august 1999**

# i-D

soul

£2.80 US$7.50

08

LIRE 13.500 DM HFl 14.95 YEN 1500

9 770262 357044

# 08•99

"It's important for people to understand how shallow I am and stop reading things into my work. I just react to sound and see what kind of pictures it puts in my head"

**Chris Cunningham, video director, no188**

THE PARTY'S OVER

Photography by Carmen Freudenthal at Nel
Styling by Elle Hagen at Nel

"I don't want to make cool music. It's too much effort, I'm too old and it's too boring"

**Sharleen Spiteri, musician, no186**

# FAR AWAY EYES

Photography by Jan-Willem Dikkers
Styling by Soraya Dayani

Styling assistance by Ursula Gesaidmann
Thanks to Cynthia, Bobby G, Raymond, Dennis, Ron, Ken, Kris
and Bob, Grandad, Mac, Scott, Dan, Cool and Dom, Terri,
Barbara and Patti, Gin and Tonja, Pure and Terri
Thanks to The Hob Cafe and Saloon
Shot in Fairplay and Hartsel, Colorado

Ken, ecological architect, wears top by Gap; jeans by Levi's; glasses by Ray Ban.

Photography by Kayt Jones
Styling by Merryn Leslie

Hair by Kylie Crompton for
Aveda Concept Salon at Harvey Nichols
Make-up by Angela Chung using Ruby And Millie
Model: James Rousseau at Select

This page: Transparent sequin vest and silk taffeta
domino coat, both by YSL rive gauche homme.
Right: Silk taffeta casaque top and wool trouser,
both by YSL rive gauche homme.

"There are elements that are feminine, or from the couture vocabulary, that I use to get a different definition of masculinity."

# 09•99

"I try desperately to hide my first thought –
I am so much smaller than I look on TV..."

**Kylie Minogue, pop icon, interviews herself, no192**

DE BEAUVOIR N1

Photography by Duc Liao
Styling by Kanako B Koga

Photographic assistance by Stéphanie Reboux
Styling assistance by Ryoko
Hair by Manon Anne at Un Air
Make-up by Karim Rahman at Calliste
Models: Pauline at Modela and Hawa at Nathalie

Pauline wears shirt by Vivienne
Westwood Red Label, skirt by Yves
Saint Laurent, vest foot cover by
Christofle, leather bag and shoes,
both by Prada. Hawa wears sleeveless
top by indiv. by Masaru Tagama, skirt
by Ralis, Christian Lacroix, dress by
Colette Dinnigan, sandals with fake
fur by her. Pauline wears top by indiv.
by Masaru Tagama, culottes skirt by
Jean Paul Gaultier, stockings by
Zazzaz, watch by Seiko, shoes by
Michel Perry.

# LIFE IN THE ELEVENTH

cover star: **guinevere** photographed by **craig mcdean october 199**

# i·D

©

£2.80 US$7.50

uplift

**SKIN**
Photography by Kayt Jones
Styling by William Baker
Photographic assistance by Jermaine Francis
Shot at The Tricycle Theatre, London NW6

**What are you wearing?** Copperwheat Blundell boots and dress
**What do you do?** Songwriter/singer **Career high?** Singing in front of 60,000 black South Africans with Chaka Khan in Johannesburg for Nelson Mandela at his 80th birthday concert in July 1998 **What are you working on now?** Earning more than an acrylic disc in the United States of America **Influences?** Anglo-Japanese/French fashion, indie music, internet sites, travelling, good company **What makes life worth living?** Seeing the mountain once you've climbed the hill **Ideal elevator music?** ABBA **Who would you like to be stuck in an elevator with?** David Bowie and Imac. Intelligence, art and politics. Hideously brilliant combination

**VIVIENNE WESTWOOD**
Photography by Kayt Jones
Photographic assistance by Andy Eaton and Jermaine Francis
Shot at The National Portrait Gallery, London WC2

**What are you wearing?** A gown of black duchess and gold lamé named Carnival **What do you do?** Fashion designer **Career high?** It's always the next collection **What are you working on now?** An incredible shoe **Influences?** Ideas – what other people have said and done **What makes life worth living?** The cultivation of talented artists and thinkers which sometimes occurred in the past produced stunning works of art and ideas. One cannot imagine how they got there - how was it humanly possible? **Ideal elevator music?** Maybe bird song, especially if the names of the birds were announced, perhaps with encouraging information. 'Skylark, there are still four left' **Who would you like/hate to be stuck in an elevator with?** In either case there would be too many people to fit in the lift

**DAVID SIMS**
Photography by
Johnny Giunta
Shot at Northwick House,
London NW8

**What are you wearing?** Jacket, old T-shirt, Levi's jeans, trainers **What do you do?** Fashion photographer **Career high?** Every job is a high **What are you working on now?** A beard **Influences?** The usual stuff **What makes life worth living?** I'm scared of death **Ideal elevator music?** Bob Pollard **Who would you like to be stuck in an elevator with?** So many people because 'I'm a real people person'

**KIM GORDON**
Photography by Johnnie Giunta
Shot at the Sonic Youth studio, New York

# 10•99

"Women are everything for me. I hate them, I detest them, I love them and respect them. I started to work in fashion with the sense that I could help protect women from dangerous circumstances"

**Yohji Yamamoto, designer, no184**

**YOHJI YAMAMOTO**
Photography by Alexia Silvagni
Shot at the Yohji Yamamoto office, Tokyo

**What are you wearing?** Jersey jacket, pants and tank-top (all from Y's for men Red Label) **What do you do?** I make clothes **Career highs?** I enjoy this very moment, this period... Now is the time I think is the best (No!! You liar!) **What are you working on now?** Collection that is exactly the same as 20 years ago... and am also working on the next Spring/Summer collection **Influences?** Absolutely everything **What makes life worth living?** To have a hot shower and to drink a nice cup of coffee **Ideal elevator music?** Love Sick by Bob Dylan **Who would you hate to be stuck in an elevator with?** Young Japanese high school girls who do not have common sense, hardly ever go to school and can't even say thank you when they got off the elevator. They don't understand the language Japanese anymore. Also, huge/giant guys who can't even see where I am standing. They breathe heavily from their nose on my 'wide' forehead

**KATE MONCKTON**
Photography by Hamish Milne
Shot with Bunny at The Hempel, London W2

**What are you wearing?** APC shirt **What do you do?** Promote and advise designers through the minefield called 'the fashion industry' **Career high?** Watching young talent grow and get recognised as important influences within their industry **What are you working on now?** Three-day fashion and art event during London Fashion Week, supported by Mandarina Duck **Influences?** My intuition **What makes life worth living?** My partner, my dog, my family and friends, meeting and working with creative individuals and, of course, the thought of reaching a stage when I can retire **Ideal elevator music?** Frank Sinatra **Who would you like to be stuck in an elevator with?** Flat Eric, a bottle of Champagne and a couple of comfy sofas

**SARAH HARMARNEE**
Photography by David Slijper
Assisted by Lee Powers
Shot with Regal at City Park, London EC1
Pony courtesy of Trent Park Equestrian Centre (0181 363 8630)

**What are you wearing?** Levi's Sta-Prest shirt, Porsche sunglasses, hunting crop by Sarah Harmarnee for Givenchy Couture, jodphurs, riding boots and spurs **What do you do?** Design shiny things to wear, carry, use and look at **Career high?** Remuneration **What are you working on now?** Jumping higher **Influences?** Horses, cars, architecture, Princess Ann and The Royal Horse Guards (I'm obsessed by them) **What makes life worth living?** My favourite horse Merlin and the Hickstead showjumping derby: the ultimate embodiment of precision, elegance, grace, beauty, passion, power and sheer goddamn genius! **Ideal elevator music?** Sergio Mendes **Who would you like to be stuck in an elevator with?** Regal the pony

**ALEXANDER MCQUEEN**
Photography by David Slijper
Assisted by Richard Baskott
Shot at myhotel, London WC1 (0171 667 6000)

**What are you wearing?** Can't remember **What do you do?** Stitch bitch **Career high?** 55,000 feet on Concorde **What are you working on now?** New York, New York - so good they named it twice **Influences?** Uranus **What makes life worth living?** Uranus **Ideal elevator music?** David Cassidy **Who would you like to be stuck in an elevator with?** Brad Pitt and my anus

**KATY ENGLAND**
**What are you wearing?** Levi's 501 jeans, Ann Demeulemeester sequin top, secondhand studded belt **What do you do?** Stylist and whatever else that means **Career high?** Working on the 'Access-able' feature with Alexander, Nick Knight and Dazed & Confused last year **What are you working on now?** The next McQueen show **Influences?** Everything around me **What makes life worth living?** Personal moments of real happiness **Ideal elevator music?** Shaft **Who would you like to be stuck in an elevator with?** I'd rather be alone in an elevator

# 10•99

"It's time to leave this whole idea about street style behind. All that's gone – it's an old idea. There's nothing so powerful on the street now that would force the creative mind to take it over"

**Helmut Lang, designer, no191**

Photography by Kayt Jones
Styling by Merryn Leslie

Hair by Teku at Premier for Stephen Carey
Make-up by Debbie Stone at Premier for Ruby & Millie
Photographic assistance by
Jermaine Francis and Lee Powers
Models Laura McDaniel at
Models 1 and Nathalie C at Select

Nathalie wears jacket and skirt by John
Galliano; shoes by Manolo Blahnik for John
Galliano. Laura wears dress by Ter at
Bantine; belt by Dolce & Gabbana; boots
by D&G; arm band by Geraint Edwards.

## FLIGHT

**Photography by Mario Sorrenti**
**Styling by Jane How**

Photographic assistance by Lars Beaulieu
and David Schechter
Styling assistance by Anna Foster
and Esther Rodman
Hair by Bob Recine
Make-up by Frank B
Dolls made by Jack at Smash Box
Special thanks to Maria!

## THE DISCREET
## CHARM OF THE
## BOURGEOISIE

Plaid shorts, jacket with sequin bow and
shoes, all by Comme des Garçons.

Taffeta dress with dotted voile by Christian Lacroix.

gathered shirt by Marni.

120  i-D THE IDEAS ISSUE

Naomi wears jacket by Fendi; necklace by Elsa Peretti for Tiffany & Co; boots by Roberto Cavalli; panties by Agent Provocateur. All men's shorts by Tom Of Finland.

# 12•99

## What have you learnt with the passing of time? "Never work"

**Quentin Crisp, eccentric, no193**

Introduction by Tony Marcus

# THE AGE OF REASON

Meet the leaders of the old school: living proof that experience brings wisdom

### John Lee Hooker
blues brother

Age I'd rather not discuss my age What do you do? I play guitar and sing the blues for a living How long have you been doing it? I've been doing it since I was a teenager 'til I got to where I'm at now. I used to work in footpress and theatres until I got successful as a singer Are you wise? Very wise in my own style, in my own way. I don't got no education but I'm wise in my own ways about people Who do you consider to be wise? So many wise people that I know. Lots of ordinary people - they ain't rich but they're wise in they own ways Where does wisdom come from? That's a good question. From God, born with it, some people have it and some don't. I think mine was a given talent. Where does it come from - that's a good question - not everybody's wise but why I don't know What's the best piece of advice you've been given? I tell you, it may come as a surprise - love people, treat people like you want to be treated, love people like you want to be loved, care about people. I care about people, I don't care who you are - we all was created by God. Some people, no matter how you treat them they're gonna be backstabbers. Treat them real good and they think you're dumb and they walk on you. They lie to your face. But I say, what people What have you learnt with the passing of time? I have learned so much about the world, it's hard to explain. I learned the good, I learned the bad, I learned a lot. I learned a lot about the people in the world today. Every year it changes. It's hard to pinpoint but you learn more and more as the years go by.
PHOTOGRAPHY BY KATE GARNER

### Louise Bourgeois
psycho-sexual sculptor

Age 88 What do you do? Sculptor How long have you been doing it? 75 years Are you wise? I'm Who do you consider to be wise? I always had greet respect for my teachers Where does wisdom come from? Wisdom comes from experience What's the best piece of advice you've been given? Make yourself useful and indispensable What have you learnt with the passing of time? Hopefully to get better and better
PHOTOGRAPHY BY ????

Mr Duong Nam Lein Nguyên wears tweed jacket by Polo Ralph Lauren; shirt by Yohji Yamamoto; hat by Lacoste; scarf by Dunhill.

# THE WORDLESS TRUTH

Photography by Duc Liao
Styling by Giannie Couji

Photographic assistance by Bruno Yonae
Styling assistance by Salvatore Caputo
Make-up by Young
Hair by Marion Anée at On Air
Thanks to Mrs Liao, her family and friends, and Sush

Mrs Cheng wears coat by Blanc-Manteaux; twin set by Chanel; skirt by Hermès; shoes by Rodolphe Ménudier. Mr Cheng wears jacket and trousers by Francesco Smalto; shirt by Polo Ralph Lauren; jumper by Hermès; shoes by Yohji Yamamoto.

Mr Bächai Inghé wears T-shirt by Polo Ralph Lauren; jacket and jumper by Dunhill; trousers by Francesco Smalto.

Mrs Liao wears coat by Yohji Yamamoto; jumper by Cerruti; skirt by Isabel Marant; bag by Louis Vuitton.

"When you see strong things, they often tend to be quite ugly. This is the issue for beauty now: an idea, a concept, can be beautiful in itself"

**Eugene Soulieman, hair stylist, no185**

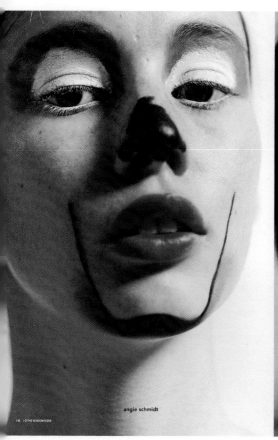

angie schmidt

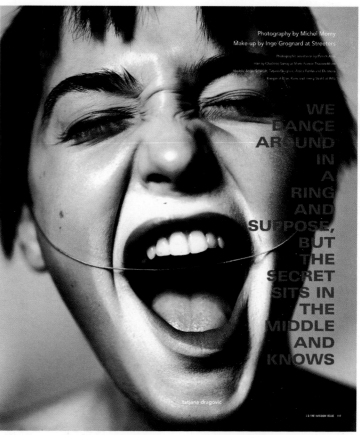

Photography by Michel Momy
Make-up by Inge Grognard at Streeters

WE
DANCE
AROUND
IN
A
RING
AND
SUPPOSE,
BUT
THE
SECRET
SITS IN
THE
MIDDLE
AND
KNOWS

tatjana dragovic

"I am interested in the vulnerability of man"

**Hedi Slimane, designer, no189**

**SHAFRAN, NIGEL**

Camping trip, Snowdonia 1999

Nelson Mandela's prison key for his cell

Visitors' waiting room

**VON UNWERTH, ELLEN**

Things money can't buy are love (I mean true love), trust, friendship, freedom.

Models: Rebecca and Christian Fourteau

### GIUNTA, JOHNNY

Patrick versus brain tumour. Patrick wins.

My friend Patrick was diagnosed this past December with a golf ball-sized tumour attached to the meninges surrounding his brain. The laceration and stitching is a result of a radically invasive surgical procedure called a craniotomy. Blindness and death were strong possibilities. Fortunately, the tumour was removed and aside from a large headache, Patrick's doing well. The photo was taken three days after the surgery. It's not until someone, either family or friend, becomes gravely ill that you realise how important they are to you and your life. That's something you can't put a price on. Life is beyond price.

### GARRETT, MALCOLM

For almost 20 years I have owned a (not particularly classic) American car from the late '60s. It was only the third car I ever purchased and I'll probably never part with it. Since you ask, it is a 1969 Plymouth Sport Fury. It is a two door 'coupe'. It was a metallic aquatic green when it left the factory, but now it is red. It has the obligatory black vinyl interior so prevalent in the '60s. It has a 318 cubic inch V8 engine (5.3 litres in Eurospeak), which is quite potent enough for London streets, although performance purists know that a 440ci would suit it better. There is, of course, no substitute for inches. Driving it has given me the most consistent level of pleasure throughout my adult life. It both fires me with enthusiasm and relieves all mental stress, as the worries of professional life simply fade away in its presence. Whether driving fast, or slow, or being parked, or even broken down by the roadside, I always love it. It is truly beyond price. You could say that it's only a car and money can certainly buy plenty of those, but what I'm trying to get at is how to express for you the feelings that are liberated when visiting this fount of automotive euphoria, feelings that encompass both a visual appreciation and an emotive state. Simply looking at it and admiring it, as I have from every conceivable angle, is great but driving it is... well, just better than that. Actually, if I'm being honest, it need not have been this particular car. There have been, and will continue to be, others that do almost the same thing for me, and I do currently own three more of similar vintage. However, in iconographic terms this one sums it up, especially as it has been a part of my life for so long. Those who know me, can't fail to know it too. In short: it's big, it's powerful, it's fast, it's beautiful, its styling says pure '60s, and culturally that's where I come from. You might say it's wilfully pretentious, or simply unnecessarily excessive in these days of conspicuous conservation, but when I'm at the wheel the world stands still, and that's all I need to know.

### GHERARDI, MANUELA

Things I believe in and that can be achieved without money: experience, tolerance, strong will, sense of morality. I can lose love or a job, but what I have gained in all these years is a wealth I'll always bring with me.

### WALKER, TIM

A happy childhood is beyond price.

**LACHAPELLE,
DAVID**

This is a picture of my
boyfriend, who could
not be bought

# 1999

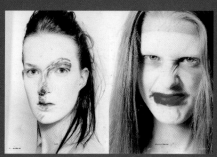

# 2000

"I shouldn't be an actress, I'm not cut out for this attention"

Chloé Sevigny, actress, no194

cover star: **chloe sevigny** photographed by **matt jones january/february 2000**

# i-D

## dynamite

2.80 US$7.50

770262 357044

13,500 DM 18.00 Hfl 14.95 YEN 1500

# 01•00

"You've got to be true to yourself in this industry. Part of me wants to prove myself. The other part says look, it ain't worth it. Just enjoy life while you're around"

**Stella McCartney, designer, no197**

Interview by Lena Corner
Photography by Matt Jones

# ONCE WE WERE KIDS

Chloë Sevigny and Harmony Korine were the epitome of edgy New York cool. Then they tired of the city and settled down in an upstate backwater. So why are their films still full of lesbians, schizophrenics and serial killers?

Jeans by Erhu.

Denim by Tommy Hilfiger; boots and belt from New York thrift store.

Photography by Kent Baker at ESP
Styling by Mark Anthony at ESP

Styling assistance by Felix
Thanks to Shari Simonson

# FOLK
# ROUND
# HERE

Portfolio by Craig McDean

## GAMES WITHOUT FRONTIERS

THE DRENCHED ISSUE NO.195

cover star: **gisele** photographed by **richard burbridge march 2000**

# i-D

chic

MADE IN THE UK

£3.10 US$9.99

LIRE 15.500 DM 20.00 FFO 15.95 YEN 1500

9 770262 357051

Photography by Donald Christie
Styling by Karl Plewka

Photographic assistance by Steven Fisher
Make-up by Inge Grognard at Streeters Paris
Props styling by Abbie 33 cm
Models: Jasmine Guinness at Models 1, Juliet and Rose Dowler at Select
Special thanks to Olivia Farrell and Rachel Tice at Z Photographic

**WET WEDNESDAYS**

Photography by Takay
Styling by Mark Anthony

Hair by Jonny Hallam at Blunt
Make-up by Liz Pugh for Nars
Models: Bill and Elizabeth at Storm,
Leigh at Select and Jody

Bill wears zip jacket by John Richmond; knit top by
YMC; jeans by Taishi Nobukuni. Leigh wears jacket by
Issey Miyake; print top from Blackout II; shirt by Issey
Miyake. Jody wears zip jumper by Taishi Nobukuni;
waterproof trousers by Issey Miyake.

**DAMP PROOF**

# 03•00

"I'm hyper. An addictive personality. I can't seem to balance anything, I'm into total extremes. I really am the last to leave the party kinda person"

**Marc Jacobs, designer, no201**

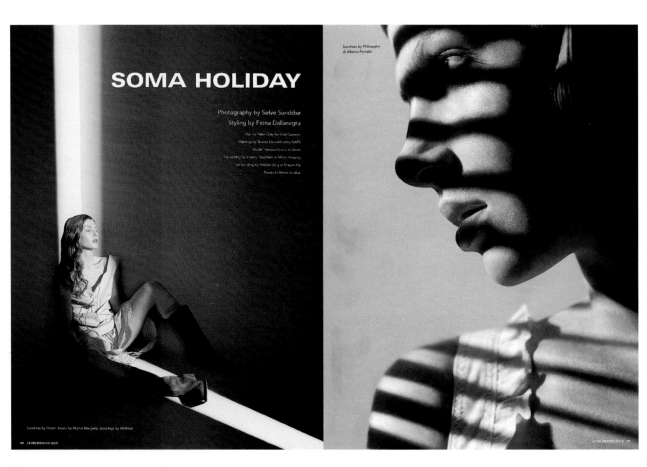

SOMA HOLIDAY

Photography by Sølve Sundsbø
Styling by Fiona Dallanegra

Hair by Peter Gray for Vidal Sassoon
Makeup by Sharon Dowsett using NARS
Model Vanessa Crecca at Storm
Retouching by Antony Crossfield at Metro Imaging
Set building by Robbie Doig at Dragon Fly
Thanks to Metro Studios

Sundress by Philosophy di Alberto Ferretti

Sundress by Ghost, boots by Martin Margiela, stockings by Wolford

"I'm surrounded by critical women.
If I stopped challenging myself, they'd
refuse to work with me. I like that"

**Junya Watanabe, designer, no195**

Photography by Thomas Schenk
Styling by Joanne Blades

Hair by Michael Boadi for Nicky Clarke Haromatherapy
Make-up by Troi Ollivierre for Tricose
Models: Stella at Woman, Malgosia at Next, Angela and
Shalom at IMG, Trish and Audrey at DNA

Malgosia wears silk chiffon dress and bikini top by Fendi;
ruffled rubber brief by Demask; fishnet tights by Wolford.

Angela wears treated cotton newspaper
dress by Miguel Adrover.

# SLIPPERY
# WHEN WET

**04•00**

THE HOTEL ISSUE NO.196

cover star: **l'il kim** photographed by **steven klein** april 2000

# i·D

**notorious**

MADE IN THE UK

£3.10 US$9.99

04>

LIRE 15,500 DM 20.00 AH 15.95 YEN 1500

9 770262 357051

"People in the hip hop industry are really starting to get more involved with the fashion world, which is great because we love to dress up. I spend tens of thousands of dollars a month on clothes. I mean, sometimes I can't even count"

L'il Kim, rapper, no196

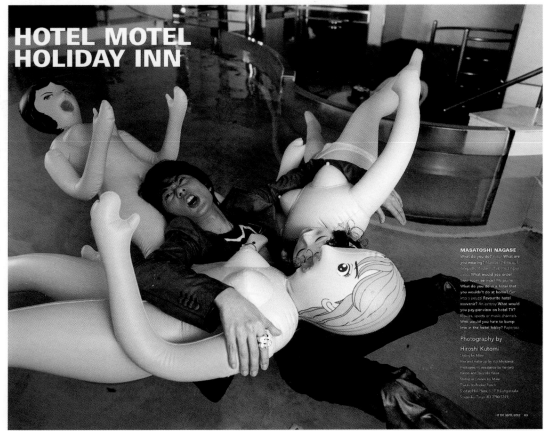

Each one stands alone as a simple word. The Ritz, The Intercontinental or even The Holiday Inn. But together they are one of the few universally understood phrases with the resonance of an international sign language. You don't need the lingo to know. These words are understood and translatable from anywhere across the globe. If you've never checked into a room, sampled the mini bar or even set foot in the lobby, it doesn't matter because you already know. Intrigue and personality reverberate long before the bricks and mortar: the Chelsea, the Met and the Mercer, the picture is intact, their reputation precedes them. So when we asked a collection of this season's hipsters to check into a hotel of their choice, they rose to the challenge. It didn't take much coaxing for Larry Clarke to install himself in a dirty joint on the Bowery, nor for Grace Coddington of American Vogue to welcome us into her suite of rooms at the Paris Ritz. Visionaire's creators opted appropriately for the Mercer, New York's fashion hotel of the moment, while Hollywood wildchild Bijou Philips checked into the Mondrian on Sunset Boulevard. Tossing aside every 'Do Not Disturb' sign we travelled the bedrooms, the jacuzzis, the pools and the bars before making a quick exit through the fire escape. The hotel is more than just a fixture on the global landscape and more than just a place to sleep: it's a home from home for the ever increasing flow of international traffic, a halfway house for an illicit moment or a twilight utopia with a bar that never shuts. Each one is a habitat for a tiny microcosm of society; a people in flux, caught in transit as their journey continues. Each one a perfect moment of time, captured neatly within four walls. Enjoy your visit.

HOTEL MOTEL
HOLIDAY INN

**MASATOSHI NAGASE**
What do you do? Actor. What are you wearing? Number Nine suit, Isetaeth, Route Shirt, Red Wing boots. What would you order from room service? Mushroom soup. What do you do in a hotel that you wouldn't do at home? Get into a jacuzzi. Favourite hotel souvenir? An ashtray. What would you pay-per-view on hotel TV? Movies, sports or music channels. Who would you hate to bump into in the hotel lobby? Paparazzi.

**Photography by Hiroshi Kutomi**
Styling by Maki
Hair and make up by Koji Miyazawa
Photographic assistance by Kentaro Kanise and Tsuyoshi Kasai
Styling assistance by Maki
Thanks to Booker French

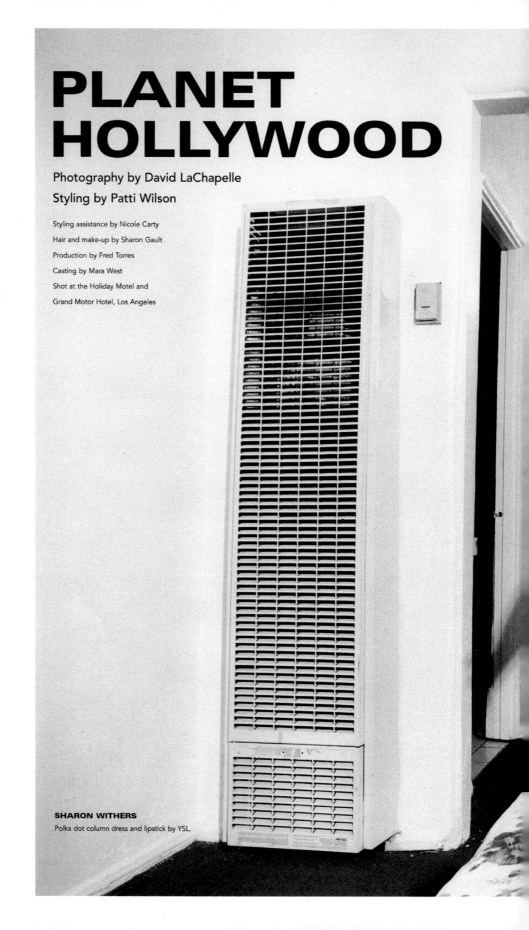

# PLANET HOLLYWOOD

### Photography by David LaChapelle
### Styling by Patti Wilson

Styling assistance by Nicole Carty

Hair and make-up by Sharon Gault

Production by Fred Torres

Casting by Mara West

Shot at the Holiday Motel and

Grand Motor Hotel, Los Angeles

**SHARON WITHERS**
Polka dot column dress and lipstick by YSL.

"If you're vivacious and a bit wild, they call you mad. That's the thing about being a woman and successful; if you were a bloke you would just be eccentric"

**Tracey Emin, artist, no202**

Rietje wears cotton skirt with silk scarves, jacket, leggings and shoes by Wendy & Jim.

**JUST WHAT IS IT THAT MAKES TODAY'S HOMES SO DIFFERENT, SO APPEALING?**

Images by Carmen Freudenthal and Elle Verhagen

"It's more difficult to be avant garde today.
You couldn't do something like punk now as
people have got used to everything"

**Vivienne Westwood, designer, no202**

Elie wears bikini bottoms by Benetton; denim high heels by Jean-Paul Gaultier; antique pendant by Dary's;
leather bracelet by DCP. Houssi wears printed shirt by Cimarron; trousers by Christophe Lemaire;
sandals by Maier Bruecher by Berkermann; silver ring by Trivet; watch, model's own.

Masanori wears printed shirt by Rusty; denim trousers by Rag Light; trainers by Kostas
Murkudis by Dexter USA; silvers rings and bracelet by Trivel; watch by Rolex.
Zhanna wears blouse by Zucca; mules by David Ackerman; antique pendant by Dary's;
leather bracelet by Dools; silver ring by DCP; earring by Flux.

# BIKINI
# ATOLL

**Photography by Duc Liao**
**Styling by Kanako B Koga**
Photographic assistance by Stephan Reboux
Hair by Marion Anée at On Air
Make-up by Karim Rahman at Callisto
Casting by Dominique Vinant and Brice Compagnon
Models: Elie, Houssi at Success, Yosuke, Shuko,
Zhanna and Shu at Karin, Sadaharu Ito, Masanori,
Angie at City, Anne Laure at Viva, Yoshiko, Sang Young,
Hee Song, Laurence
Special thanks to Caroline at Daylight Studio,
7 rue Morot, 75011 Paris

WHAT A LOVELY
ROOM, SAYS B AS
SHE SPRAWLS OUT
ON THE COUCH. I CAN
IMAGINE HOW MANY
LOVELY PARTIES YOU
AND YOUR HUSBAND
HAVE. REALLY, SAYS
M WITH A SMILE. AND
I WAS JUST ABOUT
TO COMPLIMENT
YOUR LIPSTICK. SUCH
A SMART SHADE.

Erin wears shirt by D&G.
Alek wears wrap dress by Celine.

THE HEARTBEAT ISSUE NO.199

cover star: **alek wek** photographed by **richard burbridge** jul

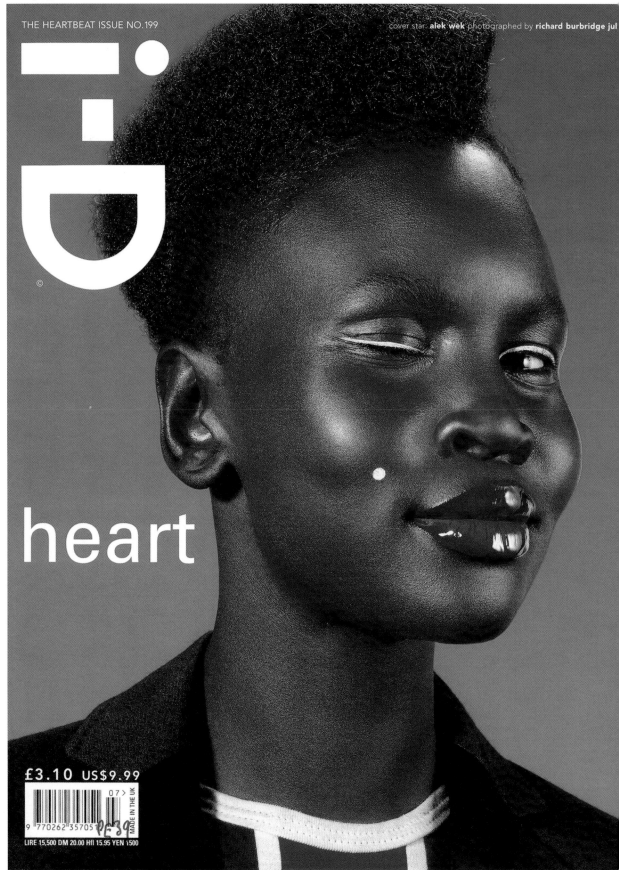

# i-D

©

## heart

**£3.10** US$9.99

07 >

MADE IN THE UK

9 770262 357051

LIRE 15,500 DM 20.00 Hfl 15.95 YEN 1500

"The worst kind of fashion disaster is banality and conformity. The biggest source of boredom is the obsession to be politically correct"

**Karl Lagerfeld, designer, no197**

# STREET FASHION

Photography by Jason Evans
Styling by Lawrence Green

Models: Terzan and Ben at Bookings
Thanks to Justin Smith

110 i-D THE HEARTBEAT ISSUE

536

Ben wears trousers, jacket and coat (under jacket) by Issey Miyake, trainers by Vans for Issey Miyake.

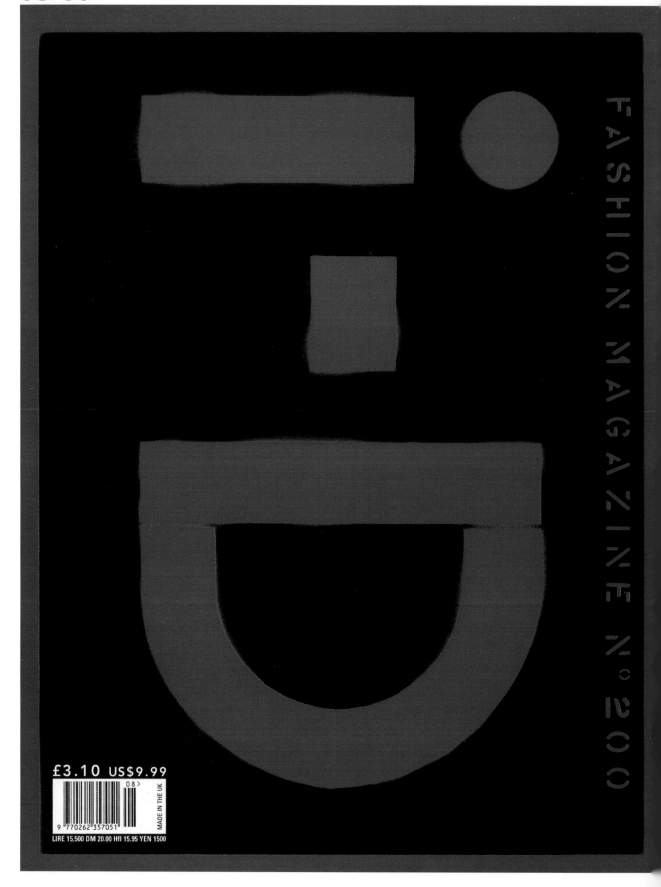

FASHION MAGAZINE Nº 200

£3.10 US$9.99

08>

MADE IN THE UK

9 770262 357051

LIRE 15,500 DM 20.00 Hfl 15.95 YEN 1500

# 08•00

Effie Semotan nominates

**DAVID ZWIRNER**

what are you wearing? Glad these questions are arranged in order of importance: New Balance 998's, Thomas Pink shirt, Helmut Lang sweater and pants (stylist's choice)
what do you do? Gallerist. I exhibit visual arts from around the world. I have two spaces in New York, one in SoHo and a partnership on the Upper East Side
what are you working on now? Exhibition of works by Jason Rhoades and a public commission by Franz West. Still getting used to being in two places at once
what gets you through the day? The ever-changing ideas of the artist
favourite record? Overall, probably in A Silent Way by Miles Davis
what were you doing 20 years ago? The usual: school, girls, drugs
what will you be doing in 20 years time? Hopefully playing with my grandchildren
what makes life worth living? Using one's brain. Learning, understanding things - processing knowledge to create something new
how would you like to be remembered? A gentleman!

photography by Effie Semotan
artwork by Thomas Ruff, nudes ana12

Dennis Schoenberg nominates

**MARCUS LUPFER**

what are you wearing? Martin Margiela jumper and one of my own scarves
what do you do? Fashion designer
what are you working on now? Preparing the next collection for Spring/Summer 2001 and organising the production for Autumn/Winter 2000
what gets you through the day? Coffee and cigarettes (unfortunately)
favourite record? Eureka by Jim O'Rourke
what were you doing 20 years ago? Being naughty and playing football with my friend
what will you be doing in 20 years time? Designing my 44th collection
what makes life worth living? Who knows? Is it sex?
how would you like to be remembered? Kind

photography by Dennis Schoenberg

Walter Schupfer nominates

**JESSICA CRAIG-MARTIN**

what are you wearing? Quiksilver hat, red fur collar
what do you do? I am a hunter
what are you working on now? Getting rich enough to stop working
what gets you through the day? Questionnaires
favourite record? Loaded by Velvet Underground
what were you doing 20 years ago? Sniffing glue in Kilburn
what will you be doing in 20 years time? It involves two oiled, brown-skinned boys in loincloths who speak no English and a bottle of tequila
what makes life worth living? It's the better option
how would you like to be remembered? As a good friend, lover, photographer, dresser, conversationalist, daughter...

photography by Reiner Hirsch

Vanina Sorrenti nominates

**ZAC POSEN**

what are you wearing? My father's underwear (French cotton)
what do you do? I search for the place where the outside culture meets the human skin to form a shell soothing that protects, transforms, enhances and obstructs the perception of the body
what are you working on now? Honing my craftsmanship, enhancing my intellect. I am attempting to achieve this feat at my university, Central St Martins in London
what gets you through the day? Using imagination within my environment and translating it into my work. Learning from history's array of artists, writers and creative minds
favourite record? Nino Rota, The Wonders soundtrack, Bessi Smith, Tina Turner, Marlene Deitrich, Prince, Madonna
what were you doing 20 years ago? I was a homunculus inside my mother (two months due!)
what will you be doing in 20 years time? Continuing to fulfil my aspirations and dreams
what makes life worth living? Family, friends, food (oh and fashion!)
how would you like to be remembered? Vividly

photography by Vanina Sorrenti

540

Fiona Dallanegra nominates

**MARCUS CONSTABLE**

what do you do? With sponsorship from Ben Sherman, I design clothes for a more refined woman who likes to remain prim and buttoned up to the neck but sexy underneath
what are you working on now? Production for Autumn/Winter orders and preparing Spring/Summer 2001 collection for catwalk show. Also trying to remain inspired throughout the turbulence of the fashion industry
what gets you through the day? A good night's sleep
favourite record? The Dream Machine by Suka
what were you doing 20 years ago? Straightening my hair to look like Limahl from Kajagoogoo and tye dyeing T-shirts in my mum's back garden
what will you be doing in 20 years time? Ruling my empire from my bed
what makes life worth living? My two sons
how would you like to be remembered? Prim but sexy underneath

photography by Jeremy Murch
styling by Sarah Richardson
model: Heather Stoller at Models 1

i-D 20/20/2000 115

Paul Hunwick nominates

**MARI-RUTH ODA**

what are you wearing? Gilly Langton jewellery. Next top. Benetton skirt
what do you do? I make ceramic sculptures, mainly wall-pieces that are inspired by natural forms, such as fruits, bones and the human figure
what are you working on now? I have started working on a larger scale sculpture for an exhibition that will be touring for about two years through Scotland, Germany and the USA
what gets you through the day? The enjoyment of what I do
favourite record? My music taste differs depending on my mood. I like anything from Placebo to Prismatica
what were you doing 20 years ago? At primary school in Japan
what will you be doing in 20 years time? Probably dealing with adolescent children while trying to make a significant impression with my work, possibly in Japan
what makes life worth living? The appreciation of all the things I already have in life
how would you like to be remembered? I would like to be remembered for my work, as well as for being a good partner, mum (hopefully) and friend

photography by Nicole Trevillian

Larry Dunstan nominates

**MIGMAR TSERING**

what are you wearing? Free Tibet shorts, Free Tibet bag, Helmut Lang T-shirt
what do you do? I'm the designer for Free Tibet clothing label. I climb mountains to raise funds to build schools in Tibet. I hang out in bars chatting up women
what are you working on now? Spring/Summer 2001 collection and my sun tan – working to bring freedom to Tibet. And my Elvis Presley look?
what gets you through the day? Hope, alcohol, food and women. Most of all, the blessings of His Holiness the Dalai Lama
favourite record? Don't Be Cruel by Elvis Presley
what were you doing 20 years ago? Shitting in my nappy and thinking about women
what will you be doing in 20 years time? I'll be living in Tibet because Tibet will be free – and shitting in my nappy and still thinking about women
what makes life worth living? My family, my beliefs and Elvis Presley's records
how would you like to be remembered? As a great freedom fighter, fantastic lover and the world's best Elvis Presley impersonator!

photography by Larry Dunstan
thanks to the Tibet Foundation

198 i-D 20/20/2000

134  i-D 20/200/2000

Kevin Davies nominates

## MARLENA

**what are you wearing?** Yellow John Galliano
**what do you do?** Musician and a singer/songwriter. I get to use my imagination all day
**what are you working on now?** Currently working on an album for V2, with my co-producer and partner Benny Di Massa
**what gets you through the day?** Triple bacon sandwiches, love and laughter
**favourite record?** My favourites promote good feeling and memories such as *Sooner Or Later* by The Beat, *I Want You Back* by The Jackson Five and *Bitter Sweet Symphony* by The Verve. Oh, and *Come On Eileen* by Dexy's Midnight Runners
**what were you doing 20 years ago?** Sucking my thumb
**what will you be doing in 20 years time?** Let me consult my tarot reader...
**what makes life worth living?** Apart from the obvious – family, friends – just knowing that I can never stop learning and feeding my inquisitive mind
**how would you like to be remembered?** Don't ask me that. It freaks me out

photography by Kevin Davies
styling by Jamie Huckbody
photographic assistance by Mark Pavey
styling assistance by Nicola Irving
make-up by HB using Alchemy
hair by Dino Pereira using Techni Art
Thanks to Miss Smith for the location (07879 632623)

Amanda Harlech nominates

## TALLULAH ORMSBY GORE

**what are you wearing?** A Sid Vicious T-shirt
**what do you do?** I have to go to school
**what are you working on now?** My exams
**what gets you through the day?** Laughing
**favourite record?** Chicane
**what were you doing 20 years ago?** I was the best thought in my parents' head
**what will you be doing in 20 years time?** On my tenth film
**what makes life worth living?** Love
**how would you like to be remembered?** The greatest actress of all time

photography by Amanda Harlech

THE ORIGINAL ISSUE NO.201

cover star: **björk** photographed by **mert alas and marcus piggott** september 2000

i-D

original

£3.10 US$9.99

# Untitled 5

Photography by Corinne Day
Styling by Panos Yiapanis

Models: Erika Wall and Laura McDaniel at Models 1, Tanya Court at Select, Andy Young at Storm and Orlando Mian)

Erika wears smocked silk tulle top by Sophia Kokosalaki; Sisters Of Mercy T-shirt, stylist's own; corduroy skirt from Camden Market.

Orlando wears jacket, stylist's own; shirt by Raf Simons; T-shirt from Oxfam; retailored trousers by Helmut Lang; lace garter from Ann Summers; Converse All Stars.

# Untitled 4

Photography by
Paolo Roversi
Fashion Director:
Edward Enninful

**Make-up by Lisa Butler at Streeters**
**Hair by Julien D'ys**
**Styling assistance by Lucy Allen**
**Models: Noot Seears at Aline**
**Souliers: Bianca at City**

All clothes by Comme des Garçons;
customised hosiery by Jonathan
Aston

## 009eye
edited by mark hooper

# straight up, guv'nor

**The idea of** simply photographing someone on the street, head-to-toe, may not seem particularly imaginative today. But when Terry Jones invented the 'straight-up' in 1980, it was a truly new idea. Back then, the notion of 'street fashion' was not one that people really understood. Proper 'fashion' was regarded as a discipline or craft that could never belong to youth, especially not English working class youth. However, conventional wisdom was already hanging on by its fingernails - a decade of mods, skins, casuals, punks and rude boys had already proved that style could originate on the street. London's King's Road had become a parade for the styles of the young thanks to boutiques such as Mr Freedom, Granny Takes A Trip and ultimately Westwood and McLaren's many guises at No 430. And in i-D, Issue 1, there it is... head-to-toe portraits, real people, whitewash wall – a simple, honest mirror to the world. Ever since then, the 'straight-up' has been reproduced everywhere from Sunday supplements to TV commercials, in every possible guise. So 20 years later, how does street casting fit into a modern i-D? The original images may have appeared more candid, more innocent, perhaps because that was the way people dressed then. When this magazine started, marketing and advertising strategies were more primitive and less aggressive than today, especially towards the youth market. Ironically, it was just the sort of reportage seen in i-D that initially alerted those marketeers. Today, they are so omnipresent that almost any new sub-culture will have its heart and soul ripped out, its ideas homogenised, repackaged and plastered across a billboard for the spendthrift masses. Fortunately, however homogenised the world becomes, there will always be a few who will choose to swim against the tide of mediocrity. The people chosen here may not initially appear leftfield or outlandish, yet they are all individual in the way they dress, and their unique identities are reflected in the honest, head-to-toe poses. Straight up, guv'nor.

PHOTOGRAPHY BY TESH
TEXT AND CASTING BY MARCUS ROSS
PHOTOGRAPHIC ASSISTANCE BY CHANTAL MURRAY

**shuyeb uddin**
what are you wearing? Kameez; tracksuit bottoms by Adidas; trainers by Nike; army gilet what do you do? Student favourite record? Recitation of Al-Qur'an by Abdur Rahman Sudais what makes life worth living? Recognising the creator and worshipping Allah who's original? Prophet Mohammed

**sasha toronyi-lalic**
what are you wearing? Vintage dress from Blackout 2, Endell Street, London WC2; hairband, worn around waist, from Spitalfields Market, London E1; jacket by Plein Sud; shoes from Camden Market, London NW1; ring by Kiki McDonough; vintage Gucci bag from Portobello Market, London W11 what do you do? Source art and design for internet company premierfind.com favourite record? Superfly by Curtis Mayfield what makes life worth living? Friends and colours and good music who's original? Marcel Duchamp

**yashi**

**what are you wearing?**
Headband from Glastonbury;
strap on polo neck from a sale
in Florence; a rubber-spine
mesh top from The Dispensary;
sailor trousers from Army &
Navy store; trainers by Nike
**what do you do?** I make art,
friends and influence people
**favourite record?** No! **what
makes life worth living?**
Solecism **who's original?** I am

**richard nicoll**

**what are you wearing?** T-shirt
by Hussein Chalayan; jeans by
Levi's; hiking boots from Snow
& Rock; secondhand shirt from
Red Cross shop **what do you
do?** As much as possible of
whatever keeps me smiling
**favourite record?** *Washing
Machine* by Sonic Youth **what
makes life worth living?** Fear
of death **who's original?** The
inventor of Coca-Cola and
Roman Signer

**mia c de solabarrieta**

**what are you wearing?** A long
skirt I made myself; stripey skirt
from Camden Market, London
NW1; stripy sleeveless top,
present from my friend; blanket
from Nepal; flip-flops by Reef;
jewellery, presents from various
friends; tooth in ear belonged
to a badger, but alas, after an
unfortunate death, now belongs
to me **what do you do?** Model
and actress of sorts. I also make
clothes, bind books and design
the insides, and I'm going back
to college to learn how to make
shoes **favourite record?** Today
I'm in favour of a band called
Celtica, a psychedelic Celtic
trance band, but normal days
I like folky acoustic guitar music
like Nick Drake, Jeff Buckley,
David Usher, Neil Young etc
**what makes life worth living?**
My friends, family, the thought of
another sunny day, the trees, the
birds, the countryside, the parties,
the music, my bus and lots of
adventures **who's original?**
Everybody and nobody

**koki kang**

**what are you wearing?** Vivienne
Westwood scarf given to me
by a friend; denim jacket by
Levi's; secondhand poloneck
from Oxfam; jeans by Diesel;
Gripfast boots given to me by
Zowie and Brian from Boudicca,
which I customised **what do you
do?** I try to find out who I am,
and I also study fashion at
the University of Westminster
**favourite record?** The man who
recorded the "mind the gap"
announcement on the underground **what makes life worth
living?** Meeting fucking
gorgeous people **who's original?**
Everybody except Jesus

Leather top by Yves Saint Laurent; goggles by Yohji Yamamoto

# Untitled 1

Photography by Mario Sorrenti
Styling by Jane How

Photographic assistance by Lars Beaulieu
Styling assistance by Anna Foster
and Esther Roitman
Model structures by Jack Flannigan
Model-makers: Mario Sorrenti,
Jane How, Frank B, Bob Recine,
Jack Flannigan, Anna Foster,
Esther Roitman, Lars Beaulieu,
Mary Frey, Meghan Glennon, Edward

frill top by Hussein Chalayan.

THE SELF ISSUE NO.202

cover star: **angela lindvall** photographed by **max vadukul october** 200

centred

MADE IN THE UK

£3.10 US$9.99

9 770262 357051

Halterneck dress by Azzedine Alaïa; bracelet by Karina Arabian.

Photography by Kayt Jones
Styling by Giannie Couji
Starring Dolores Chaplin

## THE PLAYER

Leather jacket by Azzedine Alaïa; choker by Scott Wilson.

## PARADISE GARAGE

Jenny, riding a Yamaha XT250 1980, wears jacket by Balenciaga; dress by Wendy & Jim; stockings by DD; boots by Bruno Frisoni; wristband by Chrome Hearts; earrings by Yoshiko.

Yohan and Regis working on a Yamaha 600 XTE 1997. Yohann wears Honda shirt by Shinichiro Arakawa.

# straight up yo'self

**Who needs fashion week** when you've got a sheet of cardboard and the streets of Milan for inspiration? As this is our Self issue, we thought we'd start by shying away from the self-indulgent, the self-centred and the self-important and concentrate on what really matters in fashion: the people on the street. Photographer Simon Flamigni went off the stiletto-worn track of the Galleria to find her own catwalk. Once she'd found some likely subjects, she gave them the cardboard as a backdrop/prop, a remote control shutter release, and let them get on with it. The results are these self-straight ups: an alternative snapshot of Milanese style, away from the in crowd and the air kisses and the faux sincerity. Straight up, no chaser. **PHOTOGRAPHY BY SIMON.**

### michiko unno

**what are you wearing?** Dress and cardigan by Betsey Johnson; high heels by Anna Sui **what do you do?** Fashion designer and illustrator **what makes life worth living?** Health, growth **favourite record?** Elliott Smith, Cake, Asian Dub Foundation **describe yourself in five words?** Wool, time, 21, Japan, tantrum

### elton botteon

**what are you wearing?** Trousers by Helmut Lang; secondhand T-shirt; trainers by Nike **what do you do?** Travel, skate, model **what makes life worth living?** Enjoying the world's beauties **favourite record?** Chemical Brothers, Korn, Skunk Anansie, electronica and popular Brazilian music **describe yourself in five words?** I'm a very happy person

Photography by Matt Jones
Styling by Rushka Bergman
Hair by Kevin Ryan for Willie Smart Salon, LA
Make-up by Denise Markey for Club Monaco Cosmetics
Production by Sven Kaufmann
Location Van supplied by Industry
Site location courtesy of Frank Glover Productions & Universal Display
Model: Nadja Auermann
Nadja Auermann, a photographic celebration, is published this month
by Schirmer/Mosel Verlag.

**SHE'S NO DUMMY**

Lizard shoes by Prada.

Silk chiffon top and leather boots by Helmut Lang.

THE WHITE ISSUE NO.203

cover star: **luciana curtis** photographed by **kayt jones** november 200

£3.10 US$9.9*

i-D

©

gloss

9 770262 357051

11 >

MADE IN THE UK

LIRE 16,000 DM 20.00 Hfl 15.95 YEN 150

"The idea of trying to make something out of nothing and creating your own identity without having to buy something to accomplish that, that was always something that touched me and filled me with energy and that was something I saw as the backbone of i-D"

**Wolfgang Tillmans, photographer, no203**

Elisabeth wears nylon cropped parka, ski pants and pearl necklace by Chanel; underwear set by Victoria's Secret.

Elmira wears hand-woven ribbon sleeveless turtleneck and nylon skirt by Chanel; knickers by La Perla; garter by Alice Underground.

# FEARED BY MEN ...

**Photography by Terry Richardson**
**Styling by Patti Wilson**

Hair by Rebeccah Forecast at Wall Group
Make-up by Charlotte Willer at Frame
Models: Carolyn Park and Kelly Sawyer at Karin,
Kelly Stuart and Elmira at Boss,
Katya and Taylor at Ford,
Hillary Small and Elisabeth Stone

# 11•00

"I've tried to find a new modernity, a new elegance. It's not easy because people seem to want to be shocked. They want explosive fashion. I try to avoid that because explosions don't last, they disappear immediately and leave nothing but ashes"

**Giorgio Armani, designer, no196**

Laura Caldow

Mrs Carol Guckle, widow of Sir Christopher Guckle, founder of the school

Helena Slee

These photographs are not about escape, they are about experiencing physical possibilities and limits in ways few of us will ever know

Maria Defise Sakemura

Emma Heatley

Mia Driver

Eriko Masazuka

# i-D

©

give

# 2000

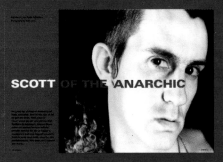

SCOTT OF THE ANARCHIC

OH, WE DO LIKE TO BE BESIDE THE SEASIDE

CARRY ON GALLIANO

ICED-T

ENFANT TERRIBLE

© 2001 TASCHEN GmbH
Hohenzollernring 53, D–50672 Köln
**www.taschen.com**

Creative director: Terry Jones, London
Text editor: Avril Mair, London
Creative co-ordinator: Matthew Hawker, London
Design assistants: Shay Lam and Ritz Yagi at Obviousu,
Oriana Reich, London

Special thanks to Jörg Koch, Berlin
Thanks also to Dylan Jones, Penny Martin, Eloise Alemany,
Jane Peverley, Sophie Carruthers, Hokuto Katsui, Kate Ellis
and all the many i-D contributors, without whom the
magazine would not exist.

Editorial co-ordination: Simone Philippi, Anja Lenze, Cologne
Production co-ordination: Ute Wachendorf, Cologne
German translation: Clara Drechsler, Cologne
French translation: Simone Manceau, Paris

Printed in Spain
ISBN 3-8228-5778-5

zubezahlen. Neben der Gestaltung weniger Seiten für Vogue half sie ihrer Freundin Vivienne Westwood, neue Ideen für Mode und Bondage zu entwickeln. Wir sprachen darüber, für sechs Monate in Streik zu treten und dann mit einer Art Manifest in die Welt der kommerziellen Modemagazine zurückzukehren.

1977 arbeitete ich meine Zeit bei Vogue ab, wo die Kündigungsfrist offiziell ein Jahr betrug. In diesem Juli blickte ich einer ungewissen Zukunft entgegen. Ich hatte mit Aurum Press ausgehandelt, dass sie ein gemeinsames Buchprojekt von mir und Steve Johnston veröffentlichen würden. Das Projekt hatte ursprünglich den Arbeitstitel *What The Fuck's Punk?*, eine Reaktion auf unzählige diesbezügliche Fragen, die einem bei Reisen zu den Druckereien nach Italien oder bei der Arbeit an dem Magazin *Sportswear* in Deutschland gestellt wurden. Es war vielleicht nicht sonderlich überraschend, dass Aurum Press bald die Lust an dem Projekt verlor. Sie hatten Schwierigkeiten, internationale Kooperationspartner zu finden, die sich an den Druckkosten für 10.000 pink-fluoreszierende Seidensiebdruck-Cover beteiligten. Mein Wunsch, Al McDowells Gemälde *Dumb Readers Eat Shit* auf den Titel zu drucken, ließ auch nicht gerade auf reißenden Absatz hoffen. Nachdem es eine Zeit lang nicht vor und nicht zurück ging, gab ich nach, und das Buch erschien 1978 unter dem Titel *Not Another Punk Book*, zwei Jahre vor der ersten Ausgabe von i-D.

Im Laufe eines Jahres reiste ich regelmäßig als Berater zur deutschen Vogue, zu Jesus Jeans in Paris, und als Europäischer Artdirector für Fiorucci. Darüber hinaus arbeitete ich in Italien an den ersten Ausgaben des Magazins *Donna*. Ich beauftragte Steve Johnston, für *Donna* auf der Kings Road Ganzkörperporträts zu schießen, weil ich überzeugt war, die Straße sei ein wesentlich kreativeres Umfeld als Modegeschäfte. Der Herausgeber Flavio Lucini konnte sich für „Streetstyle" allerdings nicht erwärmen und war überzeugt, so etwas könne kommerziell nie erfolgreich sein. Ich solle damit warten, bis er *Donna* und *Mondo U'Omo* so weit etabliert hätte, dass sie gegenüber der italienischen Vogue und L'Uomo Vogue konkurrenzfähig waren.

Nach sechs Monaten bei *Donna* lernte ich Jolly kennen, einen Freund von Caroline Baker, dessen Firma Better Badges Punkfanzines druckte, und wollte endlich meine Idee für ein Streetstyle-Magazin umsetzen. Das „i-D" als Logo hatte ich schon im Kopf; es war aus Kritzeleien für Informat Design entstanden, die Firma, die ich noch während Vogue-Zeit gegründet hatte. Jolly wollte eine Auflage von 2000 Stück auf eigene Kosten drucken, und ich kaufte ihm ab, was ich losschlagen konnte. Wegen seiner Einzelblatt-Druckmaschine kam nur das Format A4 in Frage. Ich wollte die Heftung auf der Schmalseite haben, damit sich die Doppelseite weit aufklappen ließ, um die Vielfalt der Streetfashion zu versinnbildlichen. Dieses Quer-Format erwies sich jedoch als problematisch, weil die Zeitschriftenhändler es nicht in ihr Sortiment nehmen wollten und auch die Heftung ablehnten. Während der Arbeit an *Not Another Punk Book* hatte ich mich mit Al McDowell angefreundet, der einer der wichtigsten Mitarbeiter der ersten Nummern wurde. Die frühe Produktion von i-D fand teils in meinem Haus, teils in seinem Studio in der Berwick Street statt, das „Rockin' Russian" hieß. Der Name war von einem Beschwerdebrief über das Vivienne-Westwood-T-Shirt inspiriert, der auf der Rückseite des Punk-Buchs abgedruckt gewesen war. Al selbst arbeitete in seinem Studio meistens für die Musikindustrie. Seine ersten Kunden waren die Rich Kids, die Band dreier Schlüsselfiguren der aufblühenden Londoner Clubkultur, Glen Mattlock, Midge Ure und Rusty Egan.

Perry Haines war der erste Chefredakteur von i-D. Al und ich verdienten unseren Lebensunterhalt durch kommerzielle Kunden und fanden, dass wir einen Mann „vor Ort" brauchten, um die zeitgenössische Szene zu beobachten. Perry kam zu i-D, als wir die erste Ausgabe zusammenstellten, und seine geschäftige Art machte ihn schnell zur Stimme des Blatts. Perry, ein ehemaliges Blitz-Kid aus Folkstone, studierte Mode-Journalismus am St Martins und hatte die Bezeichnung „New Romantics" geprägt, mit der später Bands wie Spandau Ballet oder Duran Duran charakterisiert wurden. Perry investierte 100 Prozent seiner Energie darein, i-D aus dem Kofferraum von Malcom Garretts Cadillac zu vertreiben, ganz zu schweigen davon, dass er nebenher Veranstalter der i-D-Nächte in der Meard Street in London war, Adam Ant ausstaffierte und sich mit seinem Clubveranstalter-Kollegen Chris Sullivan und Blitz-Club-Stammgästen wie Steve Strange, Rusty Egan und Boy George austauschte. Als die ersten Ausgaben erschienen, breitete sich das Geflecht britischer Stile, von Rocker bis Rockabilly, Psycho bis Psychobilly, Punk, Goth oder Hippy weltweit aus.

**So weit so gut** von Terry Jones

Das Jahr 2000, Heft Nr. 200 und 20 Jahre i-D. Ein Blick zurück und ein Blick in die Zukunft. Aus der Durchsicht von zwei Jahrzehnten i-D ist mehr als nur ein Geschichtsbuch entstanden. Als eine Mischung aus Speisekarte und Tagebuch zeichnet Smile i-D die Reise hinter die Fassade gängiger Mode nach. Bei der Zusammenstellung dieses Buches wollte ich so viele unserer Mitarbeiter wie möglich zumindest einmal vertreten sehen: so eine Art „Wer-war-was-und-was-machen-sie-heute". Alle, die wir aus den Augen verloren haben, melden sich hoffentlich wieder, wenn sie das lesen. Als ich die ersten 200 Ausgaben im Geist noch einmal durchging, erinnerte ich mich an meihe Antwort auf die Frage: „Warum i-D machen?" Ich erwiderte: „Weil es mich zwingt, die Augen offen zu halten." i-D war weder die erste Zeitschrift, bei der ich arbeitete, noch die erste, die ich konzipierte. Als die erste Nummer 1980 erschien, hatte ich bereits zehn Jahre für Modezeitschriften gearbeitet, am längsten, von 1972 bis 1977, als Artdirector bei der englischen *Vogue*. Obgleich ich gute Freunde in der Branche hatte, war ich um 1976 die immer gleichen Abläufe in der Modewelt leid und fand Musikclubs und Street Culture inspirierender als Modeschauen.

Um diese Zeit versuchte ich, Geld aufzutreiben, das offiziell für ein Zeitschriftenprojekt namens *Picture Wallpaper* gedacht sein sollte, und glaubte blauäugig, ich könne *Vogue* dafür interessieren. Der Fotograf Steve Johnston kam, gerade frisch von der Art School, in die *Vogue*-Redaktion, um mir sein Portfolio zu zeigen. Ich sagte ihm, er solle versuchen, das zu dokumentieren, was sich damals gerade auf der Kings Road abspielte, und drei Monate später rief er mich an und sagte, er habe einige Aufnahmen; aus Kostengründen in erster Linie ein Bild pro Person. Auf den von Irving Penn und August Sander inspirierten Porträts posierten seine Modelle vor einer weiß getünchten Wand. Nicht nur seine Aufnahmen standen unverkennbar im Zeichen des Punk, auch Steve selbst hatte sich verwandelt: Bei seinem zweiten Besuch in den *Vogue*-Räumen hatte er gefärbte Haare und trug ein zerrissenes, mit Sicherheitsnadeln zusammengehaltenes Jackett über einem mit Slogans bekrakelten Hemd. Beatrix Miller, die Herausgeberin von *Vogue*, kam in mein Büro, schaute einmal hin und hatte glatt vergessen, was sie mich eigentlich fragen wollte. Wir führten später eine hitzige Diskussion über die Bedeutung von Punk für die Mode, aber wir schrieben 1976, und Englands Vorstellung von Punk gründete sich ausschließlich auf die stumpfsinnigen Artikel in der *News Of The World*.

Aurum Press, der Verlag, in dem das Buch *Masters of Erotic Photography* erschienen war, für das ich das Layout gemacht hatte, suchte den Kontakt zu Oliviero Toscani, den ich von der gemeinsamen Arbeit bei *Vogue* kannte. Wir trafen uns im Portobello Hotel, wo seine Agentin Francis Grill zu uns stieß, und ich wurde überredet, ihr erstes Buch zusammenzustellen. Sie hatten die frühere *Nova*-Stylistin Caroline Baker gebeten, an einer neuen Anzeigenkampagne für Benetton zu arbeiten. Wir waren alle desillusioniert von der Welt der Modemagazine, und Caroline galt zwar als extrem, brauchte aber doch Aufträge, um ihre Hypotheken ab-

Terry n'aurait pas pu réussir tout seul et, outre les gens que j'ai déjà mentionnés, il en est d'autres – Tricia, sa belle et patiente épouse, leur fille Kayt et leur fils Matt, Tony Elliott (copropriétaire du magazine depuis 1984), Perry Haines, Al McDowell, Steve Dixon, Steve Johnston, Mark Lebon, Moira Bogue, Nick Knight, Edward Enninful, Avril Mair, John Godfrey, Matthew Collin, David Swindells, Craig McDean, Jane How, Pat McGrath, Stephen Male, Karl Plewka, Eugene Souleiman, Kevin Ellis, Suzanne Doyle, Rick Waterlow – dont je sais le rôle immense qu'ils ont joué dans le succès continu du magazine.

D'une certaine façon, ces gens ont tous contribué à faire de i-D une institution. Ces vingt dernières années ont vu l'industrie de la mode devenir aussi puissante, aussi dévorante, aussi omniprésente que n'importe quel autre secteur de la culture de la célébrité. Et pourtant, à travers tout cela, i-D a réussi, d'une manière ou d'une autre, à se maintenir à la distance d'un projecteur du devant de la scène. S'il ressemble aujourd'hui davantage à un répertoire téléphonique farfelu qu'à un fanzine de mode, il a résolument gardé sa place de provocateur caustique, de bastion d'individualité et de champion de l'avant-garde, du ridicule et du scandaleux. De Steve Strange à Craig David, cela a été un drôle de voyage.

Mon conseil, c'est de continuer à décocher des clins d'œil. On ne sait jamais où cela peut mener.

**Dylan Jones est l'éditeur de *GQ* magazine.**

derniers centimètres en bas des épreuves, et mon article se terminer, clic-clac, au milieu d'une phrase. Sentant mon appréhension, il s'est tourné vers moi et m'a souri : « Sans quoi, ça collera pas. »

Ce devait être le premier d'une longue liste d'affrontements, dont Terry sortit victorieux dans la plupart des cas. J'ai travaillé là de fin 1983 à fin 1987, quatre années au cours desquelles nous avons essayé – inlassablement, religieusement, et je dois dire avec quelque semblant de succès – de réinventer notre roue à nous. Utilisant des graphismes de guérillero, des photographies taillées au rasoir et des textes insolents (« Pourquoi Dieu a-t-il créé les homosexuels ? », demandait un rédacteur de mode gay, dans un article particulièrement irrévérencieux. « Pour emmener les grosses en boîte »). Sous la direction de Terry Jones, i-D s'est rapidement fait une réputation de brûlot situationniste et de bible de la mode de la rue. Non seulement Terry m'a offert une carrière, mais il a fait de même pour des centaines d'ados et de petits jeunots pleins d'aspirations. De Nick Knight et Juergen Teller à Caryn Franklin et Alix Sharkey, de Corinne Day et Robin Derrick à Simon Foxton et Ray Petri, de Judy Blame et Mark Lebon à Richard Burbridge et Donald Christie, de Craig McDean et Edward Enninful à Kathryn Flett, Beth Summers et Georgina Goodman. Pour n'en citer que quelques-uns.

Les vraies stars du magazine n'étaient pas les collaborateurs, mais plutôt les sujets présentés, que ce soit Leigh Bowery en délire dans les profondeurs de Taboo, un jeune cyclo japonais en blouson Eisenhower ou un DJ anglais, au fond d'un garage, et dont le nom est tombé aux oubliettes. Ou bien Sade, Madonna, Björk, Kate Moss ou L'il Kim, chacun clignant de l'œil comme s'il jouait là sa carrière (ce qui était souvent vrai). Chaque couturier, photographe, styliste, coiffeur, cinéaste, acteur, mannequin, journaliste de mode, visagiste, animateur de club, DJ ou pop-star qui a contribué d'une façon ou d'une autre à ce qu'on appelle ironiquement le zeitgeist de ces vingt dernières années est, à un moment ou à un autre, apparu dans i-D. « Combien est-ce que je dépense en vêtements ? », se demandait Paul Rutherford, de Frankie Goes To Hollywood, en 1984. « Jean Paul Gaultier est-il riche ? Est-ce que Yohji Yamamoto voyage en classe affaires ? » L'histoire de i-D, c'est l'histoire de la culture pop des vingt dernières années du vingtième siècle, un répertoire du grand, du bon et du peu recommandable, une litanie de comportements déplaisants et de diététiques malsaines. Si *The Face* pouvait se flatter d'une influence équivalente, aucun magazine n'a produit, comme i-D, une telle galerie de portraits criminels.

J'ai des douzaines de couvertures favorites de i-D – Kirsten Owen par Paolo Roversi en mai 1998, Leigh Bowery par Johnny Rozsa en mai 1987, Kate Moss par David Sims en février 1996 et Scary Spice par Terry Richardson en novembre 1997, pour commencer – bien que mes deux préférées se situent, ironiquement, au tout début et à l'extrême fin de ma collaboration au magazine. La première est la photo de Sade, prise par Nick Knight, publiée fin 1983, non pas uniquement parce que c'était le premier numéro auquel j'ai travaillé, mais aussi parce qu'avec un simple petit clin d'œil, elle en disait davantage sur les années 80 que mille éditoriaux. Dans une pose provocante, affirmant parfaitement ses intentions, Sade avait l'air prête à conquérir le monde. (Ce qu'elle a d'ailleurs fait, 18 mois plus tard). L'autre couverture que j'adore, c'est la dernière sur laquelle j'ai travaillé, la couverture « sourire » de décembre 1987, qui comportait le clin d'œil de i-D et annonçait l'arrivée de la musique acid house. C'est une des meilleures couvertures de magazine des années 80.

Depuis, Terry Jones a sorti plus de 150 numéros de i-D, et sa passion pour le magazine reste tout aussi dévorante. Il a toujours eu le sens infaillible de la « bonne matière » et se laisse rarement entraîner par le faux ou le frivole. Il a du mal à supporter les imbéciles, et se plaît à renvoyer aux gens un regard de poisson mort. Si l'on dit quelque chose de trop prévisible ou même d'un peu bêta (comme cela arrive parfois en présence d'un des meilleurs directeurs artistique du monde), il peut incliner légèrement la tête et vous décocher un regard en coin. Avec un peu de chance, il vous offrira un sourire. Sinon, il hochera lentement la tête et ne vous adressera sans doute plus jamais la parole.

Vingt ans après son lancement, il ne fait aucun doute que i-D est un des magazines les plus influents au monde. Naturellement il a toujours prétendu l'être (ah, l'arrogance de la jeunesse !). Mais aujourd'hui, c'est irréfutable.

figures politiques, et que les politiques s'identifiaient aux guignols. Chacun était un catalyseur, tout le monde était une star. Quand Andy Warhol a déclaré que, dans l'avenir, tout le monde serait célèbre pendant 15 minutes, il ne parlait pas de New York en 1973. Il décrivait, sans le savoir, le Londres de 1985. Vortex d'hédonisme et d'esprit d'entreprise, Londres n'avait pas autant bougé depuis 1966.

Et c'est i-D qui a donné le départ avant les autres, car il a été le premier à refléter ce qui se passait, à exploiter cette explosion de la jeunesse, à se montrer à la hauteur de la réputation naissante de Londres, creuset de talents jeunes et éphémères. D'une certaine manière, le magazine a fait une tentative réelle, sinon toujours cohérente, pour rendre le contrôle du monde de la mode à ceux qui le peuplaient.

Profitant de la liberté d'un magazine que ne liait aucune contrainte, Terry pouvait souvent se montrer pervers dans ses choix artistiques et rédactionnels. Contradictoire. Sanguinaire. Si une image avait l'air bien composée, bien cadrée, alors Terry la coupait en deux, l'imprimait à l'envers, la balafrait de cyan à 30 pour cent. La meilleure photo d'une série serait publiée en réduction, alors que la pire paraîtrait en double page. Quand on l'interrogeait sur ses choix, il rétorquait : « Pourquoi faire comme tout le monde ? » Et en général, il avait raison. Des extraits vidéo ou des arrêts sur image télé étaient utilisés pour produire un sens de vitesse et d'inattendu. Le corps du texte et les titres étaient impitoyablement tordus, tandis que les caractères de typographie informatique devenaient l'une des caractéristiques du magazine, dix ans avant d'autres publications telles que *Wired* et *Dazed & Confused*.

Terry aime à décrire sa méthode graphique comme du « design instantané », une « super-pâtée » de photos et de graphismes, de couleurs et de typographies. Mais bien que le résultat donne souvent l'impression d'avoir été atteint par pur hasard, il ne faudrait pas nier la rigueur de son exécution. « Je n'aime pas le concept de perfection », a dit un jour Terry, « à cause de la finalité qu'il implique. J'aime que le produit fini ait l'air facile, et cela demande beaucoup d'efforts. Le design instantané est [de fait] un mensonge : ça n'est jamais instantané. »

Si on laissait des choses traîner, assez longtemps dans le bureau, on avait de fortes chances de les retrouver dans le magazine. Passeports, carnets d'adresses, factures de taxi, Terry finissait toujours par leur trouver une autre utilisation. Une fois, j'ai commis l'erreur de montrer à Terry de vieilles photos de famille. Quand je suis revenu de vacances, je les ai vues dans le magazine. Et voilà. Si on ne parvenait pas à se procurer l'original d'une photographie, pourquoi se priver de photocopier, tout simplement, le livre dans lequel on l'avait trouvée ? Il y avait peu de chances que quelqu'un s'en aperçoive. C'était aussi un lieu de travail très démocratique, où l'on pouvait un jour virer une réceptionniste et le lendemain, la réengager comme journaliste. D'ailleurs, depuis, elle est critique de télévision à l'*Observer*. Et c'est tant mieux, car comme réceptionniste, elle était nulle.

Parce que i-D était autant une expression artistique que journalistique, le magazine s'en est trouvé aléatoire, irrationnel, et même férocement prétentieux. Les lecteurs l'ont bien compris et s'en sont, d'une certaine façon, accommodés. Du moins, certains. Dans le numéro du cinquième anniversaire – qui contenait aussi les portraits inoubliables faits par Nick Knight des cent personnalités les plus influentes à avoir paru dans i-D (un groupe assez éclectique, avec des noms aussi communs que Patsy Kensit, Morrissey ou John Peel, ainsi que certaines des personnalités les moins inhibées qui puissent exister), on demandait à plusieurs lecteurs comment ils définissaient le magazine. « On y découvre tous les talents cachés et tous les savants fous », a écrit Michael Odimitrakis, de Kostas, tandis que J Dominic, de Deptford, comparait le magazine au rayon confiserie de Marks & Spencer (un sacré compliment). Le commentaire que je préfère, et que j'avais oublié jusqu'à ce que je feuillette récemment ce numéro, venait d'un anonyme et était plus que succinct : « Bande de branleurs branchés débiles et ignares ! » Charmant, ma foi.

Pour un journaliste, l'indifférence totale de Terry au texte imprimé était, parfois, extrêmement pénible. Je me souviens de la première fois où j'ai été victime de ses réactions imprévisibles. Jeune débutant, je venais de rentrer de mission – sans doute l'interview en toute ingénuité partagée d'un créateur de mode, d'un animateur de club ou d'une pop star montante –, et j'ai trouvé Terry en train de préparer le numéro suivant. Comme je jetais un œil sur la mise en page prévue pour l'un de mes articles, j'ai vu Terry couper les trois

Il a toujours été de taille A4 (légèrement plus mince que la plupart des revues sur papier glacé), quoique, au début, on ait opté pour le format paysage plutôt que le portrait. Il s'ouvrait – de manière quelque peu agaçante – sur sa longueur. Le premier numéro comportait une quarantaine de pages maintenues par trois agrafes bancales, et coûtait 50 p. Une affaire. «Revue de mode n°1», proclamait la couverture, et tout était dit. A l'intérieur se trouvaient plusieurs douzaines de «prises sur le vif» de gens venus de tous les horizons ou en route vers eux: Cerith Wyn Evans, étudiant à St Martins, quelques gosses du Blitz, l'air pas très commode, un ou deux Rockabilly, un Goth et quelques loubards de Brighton. Pennie, une fille interrogée sur sa tenue vestimentaire, disait à propos de son pull-over: «Je l'ai trouvé dans une boutique d'Oxford Street. Je ne me souviens plus du nom. Je suis tellement hypnotisée par ce que je vois quand je fais du shopping dans Oxford Street, que je ne remarque jamais les noms.» (Pour les premiers numéros, Terry ne permit aux photographes que deux clichés par personne, les planches contact sont donc devenues des œuvres d'art en soi, une sorte de dossier de police vestimentaire. Il y avait aussi quelques pubs de mode pour Fiorucci, Robot et Swanky Modes. Il y a même eu une espèce de manifeste: «i-D est un Magazine Mode/Style. Le style, ce n'est pas ce que vous portez, mais votre façon de le porter. La mode, c'est la manière dont vous marchez, vous parlez, vous dansez et vous vous baladez. Avec i-D, les idées voyagent vite et loin des idées reçues! Venez donc vous joindre à nous là où ça bouge!»

Pour imprimer le magazine, Terry s'est adressé à Better Badges, de Londres, qui publiait la majorité des fanzines de la ville. Il a expliqué à l'équipe qu'il voulait produire le premier fanzine de mode jamais vu, et ils ont accepté d'imprimer 2 000 exemplaires à condition que Terry lui-même achète l'ensemble du tirage. Le lancement a été plutôt perturbé, car les vendeurs de kiosques se sont plaint des agrafes: les gens se piquaient les doigts et répandaient du sang sur d'autres magazines à l'étalage. Cela s'avéra un tel problème que deux kiosques seulement acceptèrent de prendre les numéros 2 et 3. C'est alors que Virgin est entré en scène, nous garantissant la distribution à l'échelon national, ce qui a permis une augmentation fantastique de notre tirage. «C'est de là que tout est parti», dit Terry.

Il tenait à montrer que le style de la rue était un processus démocratique et déstructuré. Et, à vrai dire, i-D est loin d'être un baromètre de la mode. Même si le magazine s'est d'abord présenté comme «le Manuel International du Style», il n'a jamais été un prescripteur de la mode, ou alors rarement. Avec raison, Terry a toujours cru à l'importance d'apprécier aussi les trucs moches. «J'ai voulu faire passer ce concept que nous n'avions pas à établir les règles sur ce qu'il convient de porter, cette idée de mode ‹éphémère›», répétait-il. Il n'a jamais été particulièrement attiré par le journalisme incitatif, ni aimé classer les gens dans des groupes sociaux arbitraires. Pour la quintessence du magazine de mode, c'est une ironie, sachant que les autres magazines «de style», de même que les rubriques «style de vie» des journaux venus s'inscrire dans son sillage, semblent se vouer à ce rôle réducteur. i-D a été beaucoup de choses – irritant, exaspérant, délibérément obscur, extravagant à l'extrême, et souvent impossible à lire –, mais il a rarement été sans substance.

Dans un monde à présent inondé de magazines de mode ciblés sur chaque groupe social, il est facile d'oublier qu'il y a vingt ans, il n'existait aucun magazine tel que i-D. Il a été la première revue de la rue, un méli-mélo de mode punk et de style DIY (faites-le vous-même), une éponge culturelle pop, absorbant tout ce qui passait par là avec rapidité et inélégance. Pendant une décennie, alors que les mailles du filet social se desserraient, i-D s'est fait le témoin d'une culture de survie individuelle, même s'il ne s'agissait parfois que de survie vestimentaire. Si, bien sûr, les années 80 ont été celles où «designer» est devenu non plus seulement un titre, mais aussi un adjectif qualificatif, elles ont été également celles de l'individualisme échevelé et souvent forcené.

Les années 80 n'ont pas manqué de rebondissements. Si les années 60 ont été des années de bonheur et de contestation, et si les années 70 post-punk ont été émaillées de changements sociaux, les années 80 se sont vu envahies par une génération consacrée à l'épanouissement personnel et à l'amélioration de soi. Ce fut une décennie qui vécut l'urgence d'aller de l'avant. Se ré-inventer était presque devenu un préalable au succès, alors que les vedettes de feuilletons télé devenaient des pop-stars, que les pop-stars devenaient des

**Un clin d'œil vaut bien un sourire** par Dylan Jones

Ça a commencé, assez naturellement, par un clin d'œil, comme c'est souvent le cas pour les amitiés, surtout celles qui durent. Un clin d'œil, un sourire et la promesse de lendemains qui chantent.

L'idée de départ était simple, quelque chose que Terry Jones, le majordome de i-D, avait couvé, quand il était encore directeur artistique du *Vogue* britannique. Terry a été chez *Vogue* de 1972 à 1977, et il n'en est parti qu'au moment où il est devenu évident que ses collègues ne partageaient pas son enthousiasme pour cette nouveauté passionnante, la culture de la rue, qui a fait explosion en tandem avec le mouvement Punk. Il a donc quitté le magazine, et a lancé i-D pendant l'été 1980. Au début très semblable à un fanzine punk, i-D était essentiellement un exercice de reportage de société, un catalogue de photos avec des gens « vrais » portant des vêtements « vrais ». Ceux que Terry aimait appeler « les normaux ». Dans la rue. Dans les bars. Dans les clubs. Chez eux. Tous comme à la parade. Et si au cours des vingt années suivantes, le magazine est devenu une revue de style à la renommée internationale, grâce à une multitude de photographes créatifs et de mannequins des plus fantaisistes, cet élément « normal » n'a jamais été gommé. Plus que tout, i-D s'est toujours intéressé aux gens.

Dès sa parution, il ne ressemblait à aucun autre magazine, et cela reste vrai à bien des égards. Tourné sur le côté, le logo de i-D évoque un clin d'œil mais aussi un sourire, et sur toutes ses couvertures, depuis son premier numéro, on a vu ce visage souriant, décochant un clin d'œil. Cela a doté le magazine d'un icone identitaire aussi fort que celui développé par *Playboy* dans les années 50 (avec toujours une silhouette de lapin quelque part sur sa couverture). Je me rappelle encore où je me trouvais quand j'ai vu le premier numéro, en septembre 1980. Il était sur le bureau d'un copain, au premier étage du département des arts graphiques, deuxième année, de St Martins School of Art, à Covent Garden, où j'étais étudiant. Depuis longtemps avide lecteur de magazines de décoration intérieure *(New Style, Viz, Midnight, Boulevard)*, et de leurs homologues américains *(Interview, Punk etc.)* – qui se polarisaient tous sur des mini-groupes de micro-célébrités –, j'ai trouvé rafraîchissant de découvrir quelque chose qui plongeait au fond de la contre-culture britannique, un journal de mode à l'infra-rouge, qui offrait une place au moindre culte de jeunes existant, aussi bien les Punks, les Soul Boys, et les New Romantics que les Psychobillies, les Rockers ou les tout premiers Trustafarians. Avec *The Face*, lancé juste quelques mois plus tôt, i-D s'est soudain imposé comme l'expression d'une génération : une génération sans nom.

Pour Terry Jones, le meilleur moyen de refléter la créativité qu'il admirait dans le style de la rue, c'était « l'immédiateté », le langage visuel plutôt que le texte écrit. Ainsi, le magazine a utilisé de simples caractères de machine à écrire, des titres du type téléscripteur et des graphismes erratiques, souvent pervers. Et bien que ce style soit né de la nécessité autant que de n'importe quelle idéologie, cela a conféré au magazine une identité qu'il a conservée jusqu'à ce jour.

Terry hätte das niemals allein geschafft, und neben den bereits Erwähnten gibt es weitere Menschen – Terrys reizende, unendlich geduldige Frau Tricia, ihre Tochter Kayt und ihr Sohn Matt, Tony Elliot (seit 1984 Mitbesitzer des Blattes), Perry Haines, Al McDowell, Steve Dixon, Steve Johnson, Mark Lebon, Moira Bogue, Nick Knight, Edward Enninful, Avril Mair, John Godfrey, Matthew Collin, David Swindells, Craig McDean, Jane How, Pat McGrath, Stephen Male, Karl Plewka, Eugene Souleiman, Kevin Ellis, Suzanne Doyle, Rick Waterlow –, die alle ihren unverzichtbaren Teil zum anhaltenden Erfolg des Heftes beigetragen haben. Jede/r von ihnen hat auf seine Weise mitgeholfen, i-D zu einer Institution zu machen. In den letzten 20 Jahren ist die Modebranche ebenso einflussreich, vereinnahmend und allgegenwärtig geworden wie die anderen Bereiche der Starindustrie, und dennoch hat es i-D irgendwie verstanden, bis heute einen Scheinwerfer weit Distanz zur großen Modebühne zu halten. Mittlerweile sieht i-D zwar eher wie ein Telefonbuch als wie eine Modezeitschrift aus, aber es behauptet sich immer noch beharrlich in vorderster Front, ist immer noch eine Bastion des Individualismus und ein Fürsprecher der Avantgarde, des Schrillen und des Empörenden. Von Steve Strange bis Craig David – es war eine lange, bizarre Reise.

Ich kann nur dazu raten, weiter zu zwinkern. Man weiß nie, wohin es einen bringt.

**Dylan Jones ist Herausgeber der Zeitschrift *GQ*.**

macher, Clubbesitzer oder zukünftigen Popstar, und traf Terry beim Layouten der nächsten Nummer an. Als ich einen Blick auf das Layout eines meiner Artikel warf, sah ich, wie Terry die letzten Zentimeter der Fahne abschnitt, wodurch mein Text, ratsch-patsch, mitten im Satz abgewürgt wurde. Terry, der spürte, dass ich damit nicht ganz einverstanden war, drehte sich um und grinste: „Tja, es passt einfach nicht."

Es folgte die erste von zahlreichen Auseinandersetzungen, von denen Terry die meisten gewonnen hat. Ich war von Ende 1983 bis Ende 1987 dabei, vier Jahre, in denen wir hartnäckig, mit religiösem Eifer und – so darf ich sagen – auch mit einem gewissen Erfolg versuchten, unsere persönliche Version des Rads neu zu erfinden. Durch radikales Layout, extremistische Modefotografie und ironische Artikel („Warum hat Gott Homosexuelle gemacht?", fragte ein schwuler Moderedakteur in einem besonders schnippischen Editorial: „Um fette Mädchen in die Disco zu begleiten.") machte sich Terry Jones' i-D schnell einen Namen als komplett situationistisches Blatt und Street-Fashion-Bibel. Terry ermöglichte nicht nur mir den beruflichen Einstieg, sondern auch Hunderten anderer hoffnungsvoller Talente. Von Nick Knight und Juergen Teller bis Caryn Franklin und Alix Sharkey, von Corinne Day und Robin Derrick zu Simon Foxton und Ray Petri, von Judy Blame und Mark Lebon zu Richard Burbridge und Donald Christie, von Craig McDean und Edward Enninful bis Kathryn Flett, Beth Summers und Georgia Goodman. Um nur einige zu nennen.

Die wahren Stars des Blatts aber waren nicht die Mitarbeiter, sondern die, über die sie berichteten, sei es der Performancekünstler Leigh Bowery, der in den Abgründen des Taboo sein Unwesen treibt, ein junger japanischer Motorradfahrer in Eisenhower-Blouson oder irgendein englischer Garage-DJ, dessen Namen längst vergessen ist. Oder Sade, Madonna, Björk, Kate Moss und L'il Kim, die alle zwinkerten, als hinge ihre Karriere davon ab (was oft sogar der Fall war). Jeder Modemacher, Fotograf, Stylist, Haarstylist, Filme-macher, Schauspieler, Modejournalist, Visagist, Clubbetreiber, DJ oder Popstar und jedes Model, die in den letzten 20 Jahren etwas zu dem beigetragen haben, was albernerweise „Zeitgeist" genannt wird, waren irgendwann einmal in i-D. „Ob ich viel Geld für Klamotten ausgebe?" fragte Paul Rutherford von Frankie Goes To Hollywood 1984 in i-D. „Ist Jean Paul Gaultier ein reicher Mann? Fliegt Yohji Yamamoto erster Klasse?" Die Geschichte von i-D ist die Geschichte der Popkultur in den letzten 20 Jahren des 20. Jahr-hunderts, ein Index der Genialen, Guten und Anstößigen, ein endloses Register schlechten Benehmens und ungesunder Ernährung. *The Face* kann zwar den Anspruch erheben, nicht weniger einflussreich zu sein, aber keine andere Zeitschrift hat so viele „Ersttäter" erkennungsdienstlich erfasst wie i-D.

Ich habe Dutzende von Lieblingstitelbildern – Kirsten Owen von Paolo Roversi im Mai 1998, Leigh Bowery von Johnny Rozsa im Mai 1987, Kate Moss von David Sims im Februar 1996 und Scary Spice von Terry Richardson aus dem November 1997 zum Beispiel – obgleich ironischerweise meine beiden absoluten Lieblingscover genau Anfang und Ende meiner Zeit bei dem Magazin markieren. Das erste ist Nick Knights Foto von Sade, das Ende 1983 gemacht wurde, nicht nur weil es das erste Heft war, bei dem ich mit-machte, sondern auch weil es mit einem kleinen Zwinkern mehr über die 80er aussagt, als es 1000 Edito-rials könnten. Sade, in herausfordernder Pose, ein lebendes Bild der Entschlossenheit, sieht aus, als sei sie im Begriff, die ganze Welt zu erobern. (Und 18 Monate später tat sie das auch.) Das andere Cover stammt vom letzten Heft, bei dem ich dabei war, das „Smiley"-Cover vom Dezember 1987, das das i-D-Zwinkern mit der Ankunft von Acid House verband. Eines der besten Titelbilder der 80er.

Seit damals hat Terry Jones mehr als 150 Nummern von i-D produziert, und das Heft ist noch immer seine ganze Leidenschaft. Terry hat ein unfehlbares Gespür, was gute „Inhalte" anbelangt, und lässt sich nicht oft vom Falschen und Flüchtigen blenden. Er hat nicht viel Geduld mit Idioten und ist ein Meister darin, jemanden eiskalt abfahren zu lassen. Wenn du etwas zu Vorhersehbares, vielleicht sogar ein wenig Dummes sagst (was Menschen in Gegenwart eines der besten Artdirectoren der Welt mitunter tun), neigt er den Kopf leicht zur Seite und sieht dich aus dem Augenwinkel an. Wenn du Glück hast, grinst er anschließend, wenn nicht, nickt er nur und redet wahrscheinlich nie wieder mit dir.

Zwei Jahrzehnte nach der Gründung wird kaum noch jemand daran zweifeln, dass i-D zu den einfluss-reichsten Magazinen der Welt zählt. Von sich behauptet hat es das schon immer (die Arroganz der Jugend!), aber mittlerweile ist es definitiv nicht mehr zu widerlegen.

Voraussetzung für Erfolg: Soap-Stars wurden Pop-Stars, Pop-Stars wurden Politiker, und Politiker waren nicht mehr von ihren Spitting-Image-Puppen zu unterscheiden. Jeder war der Mittelpunkt seiner eigenen Party, jeder war ein Star. Als Andy Warhol sagte, in der Zukunft könne jeder für 15 Minuten zum Star werden, sprach er nicht vom New York des Jahres 1973, sondern beschrieb, ohne es zu ahnen, London im Jahre 1985: ein Strudel von unternehmerischem Hedonismus, seit 1966 hatte London nicht mehr so geswingt.

Und i-D war als erstes Magazin hip genug, das widerzuspiegeln, was es sah, die boomende Jugendkultur und Londons zunehmenden Ruf als Schmelztiegel durchreisender junger Talente aufzugreifen. In gewisser Weise machte das Magazin den ganz ernsthaften, wenn auch nicht immer konsequenten Versuch, die Verfügungsgewalt über die Modewelt denen zurückzugeben, die tatsächlich in ihr lebten.

Terry genoss die Freiheit eines an keinerlei Einschränkungen gebundenen Blatts und konnte in seinen Layout- und Design-Ideen ausgesprochen unkonventionell sein. Widersprüchlich. Blutrünstig. Wenn ein Bild danach schrie, ganzseitig abgebildet zu werden, dann gefiel es Terry, es auf die Hälfte zu stutzen, es auf dem Kopf stehend abzubilden und 30 Prozent Zyanblau mitten durch das Motiv laufen zu lassen. Das beste Bild einer Fotoserie wurde winzig klein abgedruckt, das schlechteste zur Doppelseite aufgeblasen. Wenn er darauf angesprochen wurde, konterte Terry gewöhnlich: „Warum es so machen wie alle anderen?" Und meistens lag er damit richtig. Videofetzen und vom Fernseher abfotografierte Standbilder wurden benutzt, um ein Gefühl von Tempo und Unerwartetem zu erzeugen. Die eigentlichen Texte und die Headlines wurden gnadenlos vertauscht, und Computertypografie wurde charakteristisch für das Magazin, zehn Jahre bevor sie in Publikationen wie *Wired* und *Dazed & Confused* auftauchte. Terry beschreibt seine grafische Sparte gerne als „instant design", einen satten „Mischmasch" von Fotos und Grafik, von Farbe und Schrift. Wenn das Resultat oft einfach und zusammengeschustert wirkt, so täuscht das über die Sorgfalt bei der Ausführung hinweg. „Ich mag die Idee von Perfektion nicht", meinte Terry einmal, „weil sie Endgültigkeit bedeuten würde. Ich möchte, dass das Endergebnis ganz mühelos wirkt, und dazu ist ein ziemlicher Aufwand nötig. ‚Instant design' ist im Grunde eine Lüge: auf die Schnelle geht es nie."

Man musste etwas nur lange genug in der Redaktion liegen lassen, dann landete es mit hoher Wahrscheinlichkeit im Magazin. Reisepässe, Adressbücher, Taxiquittungen – Terry konnte alles brauchen. Einmal machte ich den Fehler, Terry ein paar alte Familienschnappschüsse zu zeigen, die ich dann im Heft wiederfand, als ich aus dem Urlaub zurückkam. Hoppla! Wenn man nicht an die Originalvorlage eines bestimmten Fotos kam, warum nicht einfach das Buch fotokopieren, in dem man es entdeckt hat? Wem würde das schon auffallen? Außerdem war es ein sehr demokratisches Arbeitsumfeld: Die Pförtnerin konnte heute gefeuert und schon morgen als Autorin wieder eingestellt werden. Besagte Empfangsdame ist heute Fernsehkritikerin des *Observer*. Ein Glück für alle, denn sie war eine miserable Empfangsdame.

Weil i-D nicht nur eine Plattform für grafische, sondern auch für journalistische Experimente war, geriet das Blatt oft willkürlich, irrational und gelegentlich ausgesprochen snobistisch. Die Leser begriffen das und spielten mit. Einige zumindest. In der Jubiläumsnummer zum fünfjährigen Bestehen – darin findet sich auch Nick Knights unvergessliche Studie über die 100 einflussreichsten Persönlichkeiten, die je in i-D auftauchten (eine reichliche bizarre Truppe, zu der neben so bekannten Namen wie Patsy Kensit, Morrissey und John Peel auch einige der am schlechtesten gekleideten Leute zählten, die man sich vorstellen kann) – wurden verschiedene Leser um eine Charakterisierung des Blattes gebeten. „Man entdeckt lauter verborgene Talente und verrückte Erfinder", schrieb Michael Odimitrakis aus Kostas, während J. Dominic aus Deptford das Magazin mit Marks & Spencers „Continental Biscuit Assortment" verglich (wahrlich eine seltene Auszeichnung). Mein Lieblingskommentar, den ich ganz vergessen hatte und erst neulich wiederentdeckte, als ich die Ausgabe durchblätterte, wurde anonym eingeschickt und war wirklich kurz und bündig: „Ihr seid ein bescheuerter Haufen ignoranter Trendwichser." Offensichtlich ein entzückter Fan.

Für einen Journalisten war Terrys völlige Missachtung des gedruckten Wortes gelegentlich extrem schmerzlich. Ich weiß noch, wie ich das erste Mal Opfer seiner Launen wurde. Als junger Reporter kam ich gerade von einem Auftrag zurück – wahrscheinlich ein Interview mit einem ebenso blauäugigen Mode-

Das Heft erschien von Anfang an im A4-Format und war etwas dünner als die meisten anderen Illustrierten. Allerdings wurde es in den frühen Tagen im Quer- statt im Hochformat gedruckt und ließ sich – etwas unhandlich – längs aufklappen. Die erste Nummer hatte nur 40 Seiten, war mit drei mickrigen Klammern geheftet und kostete 50 Pence. Nachgeschmissen. „Fashion magazine No.1" stand auf dem Cover, und mehr brauchte man nicht zu wissen. Drinnen gab es mehrere Dutzend „Straight-ups" von sozial auf- oder abwärts mobilen Exhibitionisten: Cerith Wyn Evans, ein Student vom St Martins, ein paar ziemlich durchtrieben aussehende Blitz-Kids, ein oder zwei Rockabillys, ein Goth und einige Teddy Boys aus Brighton. Eine gewisse Pennie sagte auf die Frage nach der Kleidung, die sie trug, über ihren Pullover: „Ich hab ihn aus einem Laden in der Oxford Street. Den Namen weiß ich nicht mehr. Wenn ich auf der Oxford Street shoppen gehe, bin ich immer so hin und weg, dass ich auf die Namen gar nicht achte." (Da Terry die Fotografen bei den ersten Nummern nur zwei Bilder von jeder Person machen ließ, wurden die Kontaktabzüge selbst zu Kunstwerken – eine Art Fashion-Vorstrafenregister, sozusagen.) Dazu kamen ein paar Modeanzeigen von Fiorucci, Robot und Swanky Modes. Außerdem fand sich im Heft sogar eine Art Manifest: „i-D ist ein Fashion/Style-Magazin. Style hat nichts zu tun mit dem, was man trägt, sondern wie man es trägt. Fashion ist die Art, wie du gehst, stehst und redest. Dank i-D verbreiten sich Ideen schnell und unabhängig vom Mainstream – so join us on the run!"

Drucken ließ Terry das Heft bei Better Badges, einer Londoner Firma, bei der die meisten in der Hauptstadt erscheinenden Fanzines hergestellt wurden. Er sagte ihnen, er wolle das erste Fashion-Fanzine der Welt produzieren, und sie erklärten sich bereit, die erste 2000er-Auflage zu drucken – unter der Bedingung, dass Terry die komplette Druckauflage selbst abnahm. Die Markteinführung verlief etwas unglücklich, weil sich Zeitschriftenhändler über die Heftung beschwerten: die Leute verletzten sich daran die Finger, und das Blut tropfte auf andere Zeitschriften an den Ständen. Das wurde so problematisch, dass überhaupt nur zwei Händler bereit waren, die zweite und dritte Auflage ins Angebot zu nehmen. Dann schaltete sich Virgin ein, garantierte den landesweiten Vertrieb und ermöglichte damit, die Auflage des Magazins beträchtlich zu erhöhen. „Von da an lief es wie von selbst", erinnert sich Terry.

Terry wollte „Streetstyle" als demokratischen, amorphen Prozess abbilden. Und i-D ist, ehrlich gesagt, keineswegs ein Modebarometer. Auch wenn sich das Magazin ursprünglich „The Worldwide Manual of Style" nannte, wurden darin nie – oder nur selten – Regeln aufgestellt. Terry war klugerweise immer davon überzeugt, dass es wichtig sei, auch die hässlichen Dinge zu mögen. „Ich wollte die Botschaft rüberbringen, dass wir den Leuten nicht vorschreiben, was sie anziehen müssen, nicht diese ganze Idee von In und Out in der Mode", sagte er damals. Er hielt nicht viel vom Drive-by-Journalismus und war nicht daran interessiert, Menschen in willkürliche soziale Kategorien einzuordnen. Fast eine Ironie bei dem prototypischen Style-Magazin, wenn man sieht, dass die Style-Magazine und Lifestyle-Kolumnen, die in seinem Kielwasser aufkamen, auf Verallgemeinerungen und Pauschalurteile spezialisiert zu sein schienen. i-D war alles Mögliche – irritierend, ärgerlich, bewusst schwer verständlich, übertrieben extravagant und oft völlig unleserlich –, aber nur selten beliebig.

In einer Welt, die in Modemagazinen ertrinkt, die sich an jede erdenkliche Zielgruppe richten, vergisst man schnell, dass es vor 20 Jahren Zeitschriften wie i-D einfach nicht gab. i-D war das erste Magazin für Street Fashion, ein Sammelsurium aus Punk-Mode und DIY-Stil, ein popkultureller Schwamm, der alles um sich herum mit uneleganter Hast aufsog. In einer Zeit, in der das soziale Netz immer durchlässiger wurde, dokumentierte i-D eine autarke Kultur, auch wenn diese Kultur bisweilen einzig und allein durch die Wahl der Kleider bestimmt war. Sicher, die 80er waren ein Jahrzehnt, in dem „Designer" nicht mehr nur Präfix war, sondern zum Adjektiv wurde, aber sie waren auch das Jahrzehnt eines erzkonservativen und häufig rabiaten Individualismus.

An die 80er wurden große Erwartungen geknüpft: Waren die 60er das Jahrzehnt konfliktfreudiger Glückseligkeit und die Post-Punk-70er das der Gesellschaftsverbesserer, erlebten die 80er den Ansturm einer Generation, die nach Selbstverwirklichung und Selbstveredlung strebte. Es war ein Jahrzehnt, das gar nicht schnell genug über sich hinaus wachsen konnte. Sich ständig neu zu erfinden, wurde beinahe zur

## Ein Zwinkern sagt mehr als tausend Worte von Dylan Jones

Es begann ganz unschuldig mit einem Zwinkern, wie Beziehungen oft anfangen, besonders solche, die lange halten. Ein Zwinkern, ein Lächeln und das Versprechen auf eine aufregende neue Zukunft.

Die Grundidee war simpel – Terry Jones, der Creative Director von i-D, hatte sie bereits im Kopf, als er noch Artdirector der englischen *Vogue* war. Terry war von 1972 bis 1977 bei *Vogue* und hörte dort auf, als er einsehen musste, dass die Kollegen seine Begeisterung für die neuen, aufregenden Trends im „Streetstyle", die sich mit dem Punk explosionsartig verbreiteten, nicht nachvollziehen konnten. Also verließ er *Vogue* und startete im Sommer 1980 schließlich mit i-D. i-D, das auf den ersten Blick eher wie ein Punk-Fanzine aussah, war im Grunde eine Bestandsaufnahme der gesellschaftlichen Alltagskultur; eine Sammlung von Fotografien „richtiger" Menschen, die „richtige" Sachen trugen – „Straight-ups", wie Terry sie zu nennen pflegte. Menschen auf der Straße, in Kneipen, in Nachtclubs, zu Hause. Einer nach dem anderen exerzierte vorbei. Und obwohl das Heft in den vergangenen 20 Jahren zu einem Modemagazin von internationalem Renommee geworden ist, in dem die fantastischsten Fotografen und noch fantastischere Models zu finden sind, hat es sich dieses „Straight-up"-Element erhalten. In i-D ging es immer in erster Linie um Menschen.

Als i-D auf den Markt kam, sah es vollkommen anders aus als andere Zeitschriften. Das hochkant gesetzte i-D-Logo erinnert an ein Augenzwinkern und einen lächelnden Mund. Und seit der Startausgabe war auf dem Titel immer ein zwinkerndes, lächelndes Gesicht zu sehen. Mit diesem Motiv hatte die Zeitschrift eine ebenso unverwechselbare Identität wie der *Playboy* in den 50er Jahren (auf dessen Cover war immer irgendwo eine Bunny-Silhouette zu finden). Ich weiß heute noch, wo ich im September 1980 die erste Ausgabe zu Gesicht bekam: Ich entdeckte sie auf dem Pult eines Freundes in der Grafik-Klasse im ersten Stock der St Martins School of Art in Covent Garden, wo ich eingeschrieben war. Da ich schon länger ein begeisterter Leser britischer Style-Magazine *(New Style, Viz, Midnight, Boulevard)* und ihrer amerikanischen Pendants *(Interview, Punk etc.)* war, die sich alle auf eng vernetzte Zirkel von Micro Celebrities konzentrierten, war es erfrischend, auf eines zu stoßen, das einen direkten Draht zur englischen Subkultur hatte, ein Blatt, das da war, wo etwas passierte, in dem jede aufkeimende Jugend-Subkultur des Landes Platz fand – von Punks, Soul Boys und New Romantics bis zu Psychobillies, Rockern und Cyber-Haschrebellen. Zusammen mit *The Face*, das einige Monate früher am Markt gestartet war, war i-D plötzlich Sprachrohr einer ganzen Generation, einer Generation ohne eigenen Namen.

Terry Jones fand, die Kreativität, die er am „Streetstyle" so bewunderte, ließe sich am besten durch Unmittelbarkeit, durch Visuelles eher als durch reinen Text wiedergeben, daher kamen im Magazin Schreibmaschinen-Typografie, Telexstreifen-Headlines und ein wüstes, bisweilen bizarr anmutendes Layout zum Einsatz. Obwohl dieser Stil zu gleichen Teilen von reiner Notwendigkeit und von Ideologie diktiert war, prägte er die Identität, die sich das Magazin bis heute bewahrt hat.

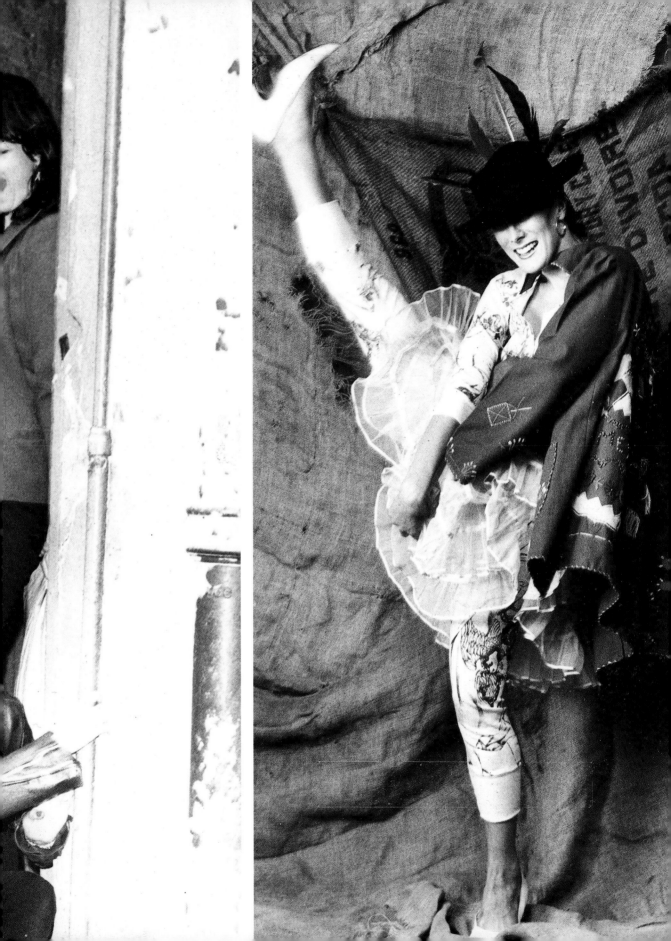